World
History
A Christian Interpretation

World
History
A Christian Interpretation

Albert Hyma

Sovereign Grace Publishers, Inc.
P.O. Box 4998
Lafayette, IN 47903

Printed In the United States of America
By Lightning Source, Inc.

PREFACE

This book is intended as a textbook in world history in junior high and high schools. The author is trying to fill the urgent demand on the part of devout Christian parents who feel that their children need not any longer be exposed to a pagan or at least a materialized conception of world history. Although no proof has been found for the evolutionary account of early man and his environment, practically all the textbooks now in use take for granted that the Biblical narrative is entirely false and that the Christian religion is based upon legends. It has been a source of great disappointment to many Christian educators to observe how our public schools have gradually adopted paganized versions of world history. Not only has the guiding hand of God in all human affairs been totally disregarded, and not only is the hand of the Creator ignored, but throughout all the centuries of history the events are unfolded as being simply the outcome of material forces.

When parents take their children to church and hear the pastor expound the nature of sin and human folly, they get an entirely different view of history from that now taught in the public schools. Is it any wonder that even in the Christian schools the pupils are wondering why the books used in their Sunday schools tell them one thing and those in the other schools something very different? Either their pastor must be in the wrong or else their textbook in world history. What they hear on Sunday is often the exact opposite of what they read on Monday. Such a ridiculous situation must be corrected sooner or later, and the sooner the better. The world is now showing plainly the result of paganized teachings promulgated in our textbooks. If our schools may not any longer have Christian books, parents of Christian and orthodox Hebrew children may certainly insist that their children in school shall have access to a story of the human race that supports rather than seeks to destroy the basic elements of the Hebrew-Christian faith. Moreover, the pupils in the Christian schools should have an opportunity to become convinced that their teachers know what they are talking about when they condemn certain sections in the textbooks they have used thus far. As the editor of an influential periodical wrote recently, the teachers had to "fight their textbooks almost every day in their classrooms." The pupils did not know what to believe, the words of their teachers or those of their textbooks. It is because of this unbearable situation that a new type of world history now appears upon the scene, in order that pupils can at last read a story that is fully supported by their own teachers, or their own parents, or both.

Four chapters in the early part of the present work bear a close resemblance to several chapters in another book by the same author, entitled, AN OUTLINE OF ANCIENT HISTORY, and published in New York by the firm of Barnes & Noble. The reason for this is that both versions are an outgrowth of the original manuscript copy written in the year 1939. Those readers who should feel an urge to consult this outline (which gives a more extensive survey of ancient history than is given here), will understand why the outline has strongly appealed to orthodox Christians in various great denominations.

The exercises for student activities at the end of each chapter were prepared by J. F. Stach, principal of Nazareth Lutheran School, Detroit, Mich.

Appreciation is due F. S. Crofts & Co., New York, publishers of Boak, Hyma, and Slosson's *The Growth of European Civilization,* for their kind assistance in helping make possible the illustrations in this edition; also Concordia Publishing House of St. Louis, Mo., and The National Union of Christian Schools, Grand Rapids, Mich., for the use of maps.

TABLE OF CONTENTS

Contents—Continued

List of Illustrations

World History

A Christian Interpretation

CHAPTER 1

The Beginnings of Civilized Life

THE CREATION OF MAN. In the first chapter of the Bible we are told that God in the beginning created the heaven and the earth, together with plant and animal life. First came the earth, then followed the plants and next the animals, while man was the last to appear. All great scholars today accept this viewpoint, but we do not yet know when the first human beings were created. For hundreds of years nearly all Christians believed that God created Adam and Eve about 4000 years before the birth of Christ. In recent times, however, even some of the most pious Christians have come to believe that the human race is much older than a mere six thousand years. But one thing remains certain in the mind of every good Christian, namely that the human race began with two persons, as the Bible has so clearly stated. These were Adam and Eve.

DIFFERENCE BETWEEN HUMAN BEINGS AND ANIMALS. Many writers say that man is a social animal, or that animals and human beings are very closely related. In their opinion the first human beings developed out of so-called ape-men. Gradually the finest of the apes became human. This must have taken them perhaps millions of years to do. As long as we allow these ape-men plenty of time in which to perform their task, they can in their own power turn themselves into human beings. One scholar in a book published in the year 1951 said that time is better able than God to change ape-men into men. His exact words were: "Time moves in a deliberate way its wonders to perform." He was making fun of the statement in the Bible so dear to all good Christians: "God moves in a mysterious way His wonders to perform."[1] What he did not wish to know was that God created man in His image, with a soul or spirit, or both. Animals do not have the same spiritual gifts that man has received from God. But unfortunately there are many millions of so-called Christians today who believe that the human race did not start with two persons but with thousands upon thousands of creatures

---

1. W. K. Gregory, *Evolution Emerging*, 2 vols., New York, 1951. See Vol. I, p. 494.

that were partly human and partly animal. It is too bad for them that they have never been able to find a skeleton of such a strange being.

Errors Made in the Past. Until the middle of the nineteenth century very few scholars understood the early history of the human race. Nearly everybody in Europe and America thought that the first two chapters in the Bible as we now have them must be explained to mean that God in six days created everything in heaven and on earth. Moreover, when Adam and Eve were in Paradise and ate the forbidden fruit on the tree God had planted in a garden, this tree must have been a real tree with apples or pears or other fruit hanging on it. The fall of man was simply the eating of something like an apple or a pear or a fig. But today our best scholars, even in the Christian schools, believe that the Bible must not be explained always in the absolutely literal sense. After many years of bitter quarrels among friends and foes of the Christian religion the church leaders and the most learned professors in all universities and colleges agree that there was both creation and evolution at work when God made the first human beings.

The Biblical Account. In the first two chapters in the Bible both creation and evolution are indicated. Plants appeared before the arrival of animals, while among the animals the lowest orders came before the highest. At the very end of the process of creation God made man, exactly as all scientists now believe. In Chapter I of Genesis six days of creation are mentioned, but in Chapter II the whole work is said to have happened in only one day. For this reason many Christian scholars have reasoned that there was first a spiritual creation and then a material one. We read in Chapter II that God created plants before they grew in the ground. For this reason many Christian scholars at various times have said that God first made things in His mind or on a spiritual plane. These scholars were sometimes called realists, because they reasoned that the only reality in things was that called by them the substance or invisible shape. The Latin word for thing is *res*. From this the word "realist" was first derived. The three most famous realists in philosophy were Plato, St. Augustine, and Thomas Aquinas. In some of the following chapters you will read more about these three great thinkers.

Other Literary Sources. In ancient Mesopotamia and Egypt narratives were written long before the Book of Genesis in the Bible was composed. They tell of the creation of man by either one God or several gods. One Egyptian story said that God laid the foundation in his heart "of all the multitudes of things that came into being." More important is the Babylonian account written on seven tablets.[1] It is somewhat similar to the Biblical narrative, though more vague and more crude than the latter. In India, China and Greece various theories appeared in the literary sources, telling about a creation of plants, animals, and human beings. But these were also much less trustworthy than that which was attributed to the Hebrew leader Moses in the Bible.

THE TWO CHRONOLOGIES OF THE OLD TESTAMENT. During the first three centuries of our era the Christians used a version of the Old Testament known as the Septuagint. This name was derived from the belief that about the year 200 B. C. seventy Hebrew scholars had translated the Old Testament into Greek. According to this version and also according to the testimony of the first Christian leaders, Adam and Eve had been created some 1540 years earlier than the date indicated in the Bibles used generally after 400 A. D. The oldest copies of the Bible favor the chronology of the Septuagint Version, dating the creation of Adam and Eve in 5540 B.C. rather than about 4000 B.C. Recent excavations in Mesopotamia and adjoining regions have proved that the human race originated earlier than 4000 B.C.

RECENT CHANGES IN THE DATING OF PERIODS. Illuminating is the report in a book written by a British scholar on prehistoric civilizations and published in 1951.[2] The author correctly states that the experts used to err greatly in dividing the period before 5000 B.C. into "clear-cut ages — the Palaeolithic or Old Stone Age, the Neolithic or New Stone Age, the Chalcolithic or Copper Age, and the Bronze or Iron Ages." It would be better to employ the name "cultures" instead. In other words, it is no longer believed by the leading authorities that there was first the Old Stone Age, next the New Stone Age, then the Copper Age, and last the Iron Age. About the year 2000 B.C. there existed side by side the Old Stone Culture, the New Stone Culture, the Copper Culture, and the Iron Culture. The same was true one thousand years earlier.

THE EARLIEST CENTERS OF CIVILIZATION. The latest researches of archeologists and historians seem to indicate that Mesopotamia and Egypt witnessed the rise of the world's first cities. But excavations on the site of ancient Jericho in Syria point to the founding of a town there as early as 5000 B.C. Equally ancient

---

1. A. Hyma, *The Christian Interpretation of History* (Grand Rapids, Mich., 1954), Appendix A.

2. Dorothy Davison, *The Story of Prehistoric Civilizations,* London, 1951.

is perhaps the city of Hassuna, near the former capital of Assyria known as Nineveh. In the lower valley of the Tigris and Euphrates Rivers cities grew before 4000 B.C. For a short time the authorities concluded that the waters deposited by the two rivers mentioned formed deposits of silt so huge that the Persian Gulf gradually changed its coastline, as happened in the Gulf of Mexico near the mouth of the Mississippi. But since the year 1952 another view has gained much credence: The water and silt were not deposited into the Persian Gulf so much as into huge holes formed beneath the bottoms of these streams. That being the case, all the maps of ancient Mesopotamia that seemed to be the most reliable must now be greatly altered. The northern shore of the Persian Gulf in 5000 B.C. was not much farther north than it was in 1000 B.C. Once more, then, it seems likely that the oldest cities were constructed in the famous Plain of Shinar, where the Garden of Eden was thought to have been located. Here stood the very ancient town known as Edinu, and here was fabulous Babel with its well-known tower.

THE LATEST GEOLOGICAL DISCOVERIES. In the year 1952 two distinguished British geologists published the following statement in *The Geographical Journal:* "The Tigris, Euphrates and Karun rivers are not building forward a normal delta; they are discharging their load of sediment into a tectonic basin which is the successor to a geosyncline in which many thousands of feet of sediment have been accumulated in the past, over a period to be measured in hundreds of millions of years." These scholars mention one local area where during the past 6000 years about eight feet of surface level has been accumulated. Their discovery has forced many archeologists to revise their views about the location of the oldest cities in the world. Ancient though Jericho and Hassuna were, it is apparent today that in southern Mesopotamia, near the shore of the Persian Gulf, cities were constructed that were still older.

LIFE AND APPEARANCE OF THE FIRST HUMAN BEINGS. At the present time the most distinguished anthropologists believe that the first human beings were not the type of creatures depicted formerly by a host of writers, including many prominent historians and sociologists. On the contrary, *"homo sapiens* (our own race as it now appears), instead of being the descendant of pygmy ancestors, is really a diminished derivative of such supergiants as Gigantopithecus and Megathropus." Thus reads one of the most comprehensive studies devoted to the development of evolution: W. K. Gregory, *Evolution Emerging,* 2 vols., New

York 1951. Actually, as the title-page states, it is "a collaborative work of the American Museum of Natural History and Columbia University." In this manner have the world's leading anthropologists confirmed the words of the Bible: "There were giants on the earth in those days." It is likely that these giants did not only have magnificent bodies but also stupendous minds.

VIEWS OF THE EARLY CHRISTIANS. The Apostle Peter was at first the chief leader of the group of Christians in Jerusalem in the period from 31 to 45 A.D. At that time Paul was being trained in Arabia and elsewhere, and Peter led the little flock after the departure of the Master. He was the main speaker at the great meetings which caused some five thousand converts to be added to the first Christian congregation. In one of his sermons he remarked that originally man was a powerful person, so highly endowed with physical and mental energies that a life of a thousand years did not seem remarkable. But gradually his energies and talents declined, as evil living took its toll.[1] In short, the story told by Moses in the Book of Genesis was not refuted by recent scientists, but actually confirmed.

ANTIQUITY OF MAN. In the Septuagint Version of the Old Testament a chronology is presented that is fairly close to the actual facts. It is not yet known how many names of Adam's first descendants were omitted in the copies we now have. Perhaps many names were lost in the process of copying and preserving the most ancient records. No doubt the human race began its existence somewhere between 12,000 and 10,000 B.C. The result of the latest excavations in Mesopotamia and adjoining regions show that we can no longer accept the old views about the times in which Adam and Eve lived.

THE SO-CALLED JAVA MAN AND THE PILTDOWN MAN. In the year 1891 a Dutch scholar found a few bones in Java about fifty feet apart and fixed up a skeleton of a creature which was called the Java Man. But he himself has recently admitted that he had found only a high-class monkey. Just the same, many textbooks still take this Java Man seriously. Furthermore, an English attorney put together the skull of a human being and the jaw of a monkey, calling this the Piltdown Man. In many books, even in the *Encyclopedia Britannica*, this Piltdown Man was said to be proof of evolution from monkeys to human beings. But in November 1953 some really great scholars in England showed that

---

1. A. Hyma, *Op. cit.*, Ch. IV.

the Piltdown Man was a fake. Thousands of pictures of this so-called man had been shown in history textbooks, magazines, and newspapers. Those Christians who did not want to accept such nonsense were laughed at, but today everybody laughs at the stupid English lawyer who deceived millions of young people in their history classes whenever his "man" was shown in pictures. It would have been better for these young students if they had gone to schools where their teacher would have refused to honor the Piltdown Man. The same may be said for other "missing links" between apes and human beings.

LACK OF EVOLUTION IN HISTORY. The human race does not rise higher and higher every century, but occasionally there is a time of setback and decline. You must not believe the story that so many boys and girls have been taught in the past, namely, that the first human beings were utter barbarians. On the contrary, they were civilized from the beginning.

THE LAW OF GROWTH AND DECAY. It would seem that among human beings certain laws operate as they do among plants and animals. One of these is that which governs the rise and fall of nations. Just as individuals come and go, so do the nations arrive on and depart from the scene of history. Some last a long time, like the majectic redwood trees in California, while others flourish for but a short time, as is always the case with even the large sunflowers. There is a season of growth and then one of decline and decay.

EXAMPLES IN HISTORY. The latest researches in Egypt and Mesopotamia clearly reveal that a period of high degree of civilization would be followed by one of much less culture. In some instances from twelve to fifteen different layers of culture were exhibited, indicating that upon various urban levels a high degree of civilization had been reached, while some later cities were much less highly civilized. After the destruction of such cities it may have taken centuries to restore the level of prosperity and culture that had once existed upon that site. We all know, for example, that Rome, the greatest city of the ancient world, was invaded many times, so that during the sixth century of our era the records refer to a total loss in population. With the return of peaceful conditions several thousand citizens would come back to their former homes, but after the sixth century Rome was never again a huge metropolis until the nineteenth century. Other cities, like Nineveh and Babylon, simply disappeared forever. The site of Nineveh was unknown until the year 1920, while Ur in southern Mesopotamia was for centuries mentioned only in the Bible.

EXAMPLES OF RETROGRESSION IN HISTORY. During the past two centuries it has been commonly assumed by certain educators that the human race continually reaches higher and higher levels of culture and progress. First came the Old Stone Age, then the New Stone Age, etc. The first human beings were thought to have been very similar to monkeys or apes, while after some 500,000 years a vast amount of change had been accomplished for the better. It took a long time to learn to make fire, and metals were not used for many thousands of years. But all scholars know that during the period from 250 to 500 A.D. nearly the whole area around the Mediterranean Sea underwent a terrible decline. An economic depression, lasting about two hundred years, witnessed the partial ruin of the ancient world from Mesopotamia to the shores of the Atlantic Ocean. Is it then surprising to learn of the same fate experienced by some of the cities in the ancient Near East? Moreover, when the highly cultured inhabitants of certain regions ventured forth to establish homes in areas hitherto uninhabited by human beings, they occasionally lost many characteristics of an earlier and more highly civilized age. In this manner certain peoples retrogressed from a metal age to a stone age culture. Europe was probably peopled by persons from the ancient Near East, who were not able at first to maintain the high level of agriculture, commerce, and industry to which their ancestors had been accustomed. At the end of the Middle Ages the cities of Europe possessed very few broad and beautiful streets, whereas Alexandria in Egypt had had a network of such as early as 200 B.C. In the year 1492 Columbus crossed the Atlantic Ocean with ships measuring only 100 tons each, while 1500 years earlier ships of 3,000 tons were common in the Mediterranean Sea.

ANCIENT HISTORY. This period begins with the appearance of the first human beings upon our planet. It may be divided into the following two parts: (1) preliterary, which covers the period in which human beings were not interested in writing or unable to make use of it; and (2) literary, or the time when writing was in use, that is, after about 3000 B.C. The end of the ancient world must be considered to fall in the fifth century of our era, since the great majority of historians have assigned the fall of the Roman Empire in the West (476 A.D.) as the final event in ancient history.

MEDIEVAL HISTORY. The Middle Ages have been so named

because they were placed between ancient and modern history. The word "modern" was frequently used by scholars during the fifteenth century, and it must have seemed to them as if a new world was being shaped in their own lifetime, which was true. They also talked about the ancient world, but the thought did not occur to them that they were living in a medieval period. This idea could not gain much adherence until some three centuries had passed after the year 1453, when Constantinople, or the New Rome, had fallen into the hands of the Turks. Another important date which often has been considered as the end of the medieval period, is the year 1492, when Columbus discovered America and the Mohammedans lost their last state (Granada) in Spain.

MODERN HISTORY. Needless to explain, the modern period begins at exactly the same date which marks the end of the Middle Ages. As a rule no specific year is indicated, but it is generally assumed in European and American schools that the beginning of the sixteenth century is the most suitable line of demarcation.

Student Activities

1. With the aid of a dictionary write out definitions for the following words: *confirmed, descendants, induced, intellect.*
2. Which chapters of the Bible tell the story related in the first chapter of your book?
3. Copy the following from your Bible, giving chapter and verse citations: a. That God made the world and everything in it perfect, b. The command not to eat of the forbidden fruit, c. The creation of woman, d. The sin of Adam and Eve, e. The shame of Adam and Eve after their sin, f. The first promise of the Saviour, g. The expulsion from Paradise.
4. What is the source of ALL evil in this world?
5. Make a list of some of the miseries which molest you as an individual and the world in general at the present time.
6. How may we at the present time talk to God?
7. Can you find a text in your Catechism which proves that the sin of our first parents brought death to ALL people?
8. Show how the first sin of Adam and Eve led to other sins.
9. Adam and Eve preferred to believe the falsehood of Satan rather than the truth of God concerning the TREE of the KNOWLEDGE of GOOD and EVIL; how do people still act when confronted with the TRUTH on the one hand and a LIE on the other hand? (P. T. Barnum, the great Circus and Showman, said that the people WANT to be FOOLED).
10. Why is the Biblical account of the Story of Creation the only reliable account? In your school library find books which try to explain the Creation by means of the Theory of Evolution. How long did it take for the world to come into existence on the basis of the "Evolutionary" Theory? Do the accounts agree on the number of years?

CHAPTER 2

From Eden to the Flood

WHERE WAS THE GARDEN OF EDEN? The Garden of Eden was located in the region called Mesopotamia. This word means the land between the two rivers, which are known as the Euphrates to the west and the Tigris to the east. The Bible story says that there were four rivers flowing out of Eden, including the Tigris and the Euphrates, but the Tigris is mentioned by its older name (Hiddekel).[1] The other two rivers must have been shorter and of lesser importance. Perhaps they disappeared after the great flood which destroyed all human life in Mesopotamia. At any rate, we know where the Tigris and the Euphrates were. You can find these two rivers on any good map of western Asia.

THE EARLIEST INHABITANTS OF SOUTHERN MESOPOTAMIA. When Adam and Eve left the Garden of Eden in southern Mesopotamia, they undoubtedly moved only a short distance from their first home. They spent their lives in southern Mesopotamia. The story of their first temptation and fall became known not only to the man who wrote the first book in the Bible (Moses) but also to many persons who lived even before the time of Moses. For example, there is in the British Museum in London a valuable round stone upon which was engraved the account of the temptation. The picture shows a tree with a man on one side and a woman on

---

1. The book of Ecclesiasticus (which is accepted by the Roman Catholic Church as a part of the Bible) in Ch. XXIV, 25-26, mentions the Tigris together with the Euphrates and the third river, the Pison. Consequently, we may conclude that the Pison must have been located near the Tigris, and no doubt in Mesopotamia. The fourth river mentioned in the Bible story is the Gihon, which ran through the land of Cush. Near Cush was situated the country named Havilah, which produced gold and precious stones. We gather from reliable sources that southern Mesopotamia in ancient times did produce gold and precious stones. It appears, then, that both the Pison and the Gihon were canals in southern Mesopotamia before the Flood. They ran parallel with the Euphrates near the head of the Persian Gulf. One canal was called the Khoaspes, which was the continuation of the river which is still called the Kerkhah today. It took its rise among the mountains of the land inhabited by the Kassites, and thus named Kas. This word closely resembles the name "Cush." No doubt the Bible story can be trusted again rather than the opinions of skeptics. Moreover, "Edinu" was the ancient Sumerian name for Babylon. In other words, Eden was not far from the later city of Babylon in southern Mesopotamia.

the other side, while the serpent stands behind them. This stone came from ancient Mesopotamia and is about five thousand years old in its present appearance. Similar picture stories were also made in other countries, even as far away as Egypt. They prove that the ancient peoples of Mesopotamia and Egypt knew something about the temptation and the fall of Adam and Eve. But unfortunately these crude stories cannot be compared with the splendid narrative which Moses wrote down in the book of Genesis under the influence of the Holy Spirit.

WHY THE FIRST HUMAN BEINGS LIVED So LONG. Adam's first son was called Cain, and the second son was Abel. When Adam was 230 years old he became the father of Seth.[1] Seven hundred years later Adam died, long after having seen his own grandchildren and great-grandchildren grow up to be big men. Many persons today laugh at those figures about the age of Adam and Eve, thinking that human beings at first were no better than they are now. But this was not the case among the disciples of Jesus Christ and their followers. For example, as we have seen, the Apostle Peter said in one of his sermons that the first human beings were very strong physically, for the work of sin had not as yet made so much progress in corrupting their bodies. It was not remarkable in Peter's opinion that some persons lived to be almost a thousand years old.[2]

METHUSELAH AND ENOCH. However, no one attained the age of one thousand years. The person who came closest to that figure was called Methuselah, who died at the age of 969 years. He must have owed much of his strength to his good father, Enoch, who was so different from other people, even Adam and Eve after their fall, that God did not let him die at all but took him up to heaven when he was 365 years old.

THE FIRST CITIES. About 5500 B.C. the first large city was constructed somewhere in Mesopotamia, a fact confirmed by all recent excavations in that region. We also read in the fourth chapter of Genesis that among the descendants of Cain there was a man called Jabal, who was a builder of tents and the owner of herds of cattle,

---

1. In the Bible used in modern times the figure 130 appears, but we can tell from the writings of the early Christians that their Bible was closer to the version we call the Septuagint, which was the Greek translation of the Old Testament used by them. Here the figure is 230 years. According to the Septuagint version, and also according to the early Christian writers, God created Adam about the year 5600 B.C. This date is in agreement with the latest archeological discoveries in Mesopotamia.

2. See, for example, the work entitled *Recognitions of Clement of Rome*, Book IV, Ch. IX. This work was written during the first century after the birth of Christ. Although it must not be treated as being inspired as was the Bible, these early Christians did know much that is valuable for us to learn about.

while his brother, Jubal, was a musician. These two men in turn had a half-brother, Tubalcain (Tubal Cain), who wrought implements out of brass and iron. Again we find that archeologists have supported the truths of the Bible, for below the desert lands of Mesopotamia of today there have been found a multitude of objects that prove the skill of the ancient inhabitants of southern Babylonia.

MANKIND WAS ALREADY CIVILIZED AT THE BEGINNING. What actually happened was this. Mankind was civilized from the very beginning, as may be seen in certain regions between the Tigris and the Euphrates, where layer upon layer of cultures have been unearthed upon the sites of the earliest cities. Some layers showed a higher culture than those immediately above them or below them, and in some instances the lowest level carried unmistakable evidence of a high degree of civilization. From ancient Mesopotamia a certain number of inhabitants removed to other regions, where their descendants sometimes lost the traces of earlier culture and became savages, just as in several cities in Mesopotamia the natives occasionally grew less civilized than their ancestors had been. A similar process may be observed in other countries later on, as we shall see.

SIN INCREASES. Men and women multiplied rapidly after the fall of Adam and Eve in Eden. Among the descendants of the wicked Cain there were many who were noted for a sinful nature. One man, for example, committed murder, while before that deed he had married two women, thus being guilty of *bigamy*. Perhaps it might be argued that afterward many of the Hebrew leaders also had more than one wife. But it is remarkable that the custom was apparently begun by a man who afterward became a murderer.

THE DESCENDANTS OF CAIN AND SETH INTERMARRY. The descendants of Cain were skillful in the arts and sciences. Their daughters were beautiful, and they attracted the attention of the descendants of Seth, who are called in the Bible the sons of God. These men were endowed with great physical and spiritual power, owing to the righteous lives of their ancestors. When they married the daughters of the unrighteous men, they committed a sin, but that sin did not prevent their children from inheriting from them a large amount of physical and spiritual strength. Consequently, the Bible story tells us that "there were giants on the earth in those days." Some of their skeletons have been found in recent years.

God Decides to Punish Sinful Mankind. As wickedness increased, God was not merely content with the shortening of human lives and the lessening of power with which He endowed men and women, but He determined to destroy nearly every human being. Only Noah and his wife, and Noah's three sons with their wives were permitted to escape the great annihilation of human and animal life. They were instructed to build the ark, which would house them and a large number of animals.

Ancient Stories of the Flood. It is a remarkable fact that not only in Babylonia and Egypt but also in Rome and Greece traditions of the Flood have been found by historians. Moreover, even in China, India, and South America such traditions were preserved. Especially significant is the Babylonian account engraved upon a clay tablet now to be found in the British Museum. This version of the Babylonian record agrees with the Biblical story in that both speak of a flood caused by divine power (but the Bible refers to one God and the Babylonian tablet to several gods), that both mention one man and his family who were saved from destruction, that birds were sent out by the man who was the head of the family, that the ship in which the family was preserved rested upon the slope of a mountain, and that the family offered a sacrifice for having been spared from the disaster.

Important Discoveries Show That a Great Flood Did Occur. Equally interesting is the result of an expedition by the British Museum and the University of Pennsylvania, which excavated certain areas in Mesopotamia from 1922 to 1929. It was discovered that a race of people called the Sumerians had settled in the valley of the Tigris and the Euphrates. Level after level was unearthed which contained their pottery and numerous household utensils. Presently the excavators reached an entirely different layer of soil, which was plain clay without pottery and rubbish. This clay soil had a depth of eight feet and had obviously been deposited by water. And beneath this layer of clay soil there appeared once more another kind of earth which contained pottery and implements.

Date and End of the Flood. The date of the Flood has never been exactly proved by historians and archeologists.[1] The place where the ark came to rest was a hill in the country called Ararat, which was a part of Armenia, to the northwest of Mesopotamia.

---

1. In the opinion of the present writer the date was 3538 B.C., as is shown in the Septuagint version of the Old Testament.

From this region Noah and his family must have moved southward back into Mesopotamia, where the four rivers mentioned in the paradise story probably had changed their respective courses considerably, so that it is no longer possible to trace their original location.

WHAT HAPPENED WHEN THE TOWER OF BABEL WAS BUILT. You have learned before in our Bible story books that not long after the Flood the descendants of Noah, who were then still in southern Mesopotamia, decided to build a great tower. They were living in a city called Babel, which may well have been the place where later the great city of Babylon stood. They were very proud of their ability to build beautiful buildings, just as they were proud of their fine clothes, their elegant furniture, and their statues. God saw all this and determined that a punishment was needed to make these conceited persons understand that they were dependent on Him for all their needs. So He came upon them with His great power and made them speak a number of different languages. Those who could not understand the language of the people in Babel, had to leave. Some went eastward into what we now call China; others to India; still others to Africa. The Semites were the descendants of Shem, the son of Noah who would not take an advantage of his old father. The other members of the white race, including many in northern Africa, were descendants of Japhet. But Ham, the wicked son of Noah, was the ancestor of the black race, the people who did become the servants of the white race, as God had decreed.

Student Activities

1. With the aid of a dictionary write out definitions for the following words: *archeologists, traditions, versions.*
2. How do we know that the ancient peoples of Mesopotamia knew something about the fall of Adam and Eve?
3. Why did human beings live so long when the world was young?
4. The sentence of God after the Fall of man was that all men must die; what notable exception did God make? Why?
5. Which history books dealing with ancient times are more reliable, those published recently or those published earlier? Why? What is therefore very important to note in any history book? Look over the histories in your school library and note the date when they were published.
6. How did intermarriage between the descendants of Cain and Seth lead to increased wickedness?
7. Which chapter in the Bible gives the Story of the Deluge? What other accounts of the Deluge are mentioned in your book?

8. What other proof have we that a great flood did occur?
9. Look up in a geography the location of Mount Ararat.
10. How did the various races and states originate? Read the account of the Tower of Babel in your Bible. What is the meaning of the word BABEL?

CHAPTER 3

The Story of Ancient Babylonia

GEOGRAPHY. Mesopotamia, as we saw in the preceding chapter, was the home of the first human beings. The word "Mesopotamia" is derived from the Greek; it means the land between the Euphrates and the Tigris. Today this region is called Iraq. Both the Euphrates and the Tigris have their sources in Armenia, which is a part of Asia Minor. For a distance of about 800 miles the two streams run parallel, flowing southeastward into the Persian Gulf. During he past five thousand years the rivers have not changed their courses. Long ago the land near the Persian Gulf was traversed by canals, which were rediscovered early in the year 1954.

THE SUMERIANS. It was in the south that Mesopotamian civilization originated. About 4000 B.C. the lower valley was invaded by a tribe called the Sumerians. These people constructed buildings, created a wonderful literature, and pursued agriculture, commerce, industry, and the arts. In other words, these industrious and intelligent people worked farms very much in the same way as was done for three thousand years after their time in both Asia and Europe. They raised fine crops and kept cattle; this kind of work we call *agriculture,* which word is derived from the Latin for "field." When we say that the Sumerians were engaged in *commerce,* we mean that they bought and sold goods, that they traded with each other. The Sumerians also had some forms of *industry,* meaning that they made goods in fairly large quantities. In this way many people could make a living, for the farmer would sell his products and buy in exchange clothes, furniture, and groceries in the stores. The storekeepers made a profit in selling their goods, and those who made them also had a profit. There were also many persons engaged in certain *trades,* such as carpenters, plumbers, shoemakers, etc. When people live together that way we say that they are *civilized,* while we speak of *barbarians* when we have in mind persons who do not know how to live together in an orderly community with stores, farms, and places where goods are made (now called *factories*).

THE CITY OF UR. One of the cities built by the Sumerians was Ur, where, according to the Bible story, was the first home of Abraham. For several hundred years Ur was the most important city in the land of Sumer, or southern Babylonia. It had a king of its own, who also served as a city god. As early as 3000 B.C. the inhabitants of Ur constructed beautiful buildings for themselves; the lower floor of each was made of baked brick, while the upper floors were built of sun-dried bricks. Some of their houses had as many as thirteen or fourteen rooms, which were built around a central court. Commerce and industry flourished in the city of Ur, and agriculture was developed in Sumer to a high degree.

THE COMING OF A SEMITIC PEOPLE. About the year 2500 B.C. the southern half of Mesopotamia was conquered by a Semitic tribe which established a great state in the region. These people were Semites, like the Hebrews. Their state was later called Babylonia, and for that reason we shall hereafter refer to southern Mesopotamia under the name of Babylonia. But you should note that the civilization of ancient Babylonia was not much higher than that of the Sumerians, who had developed it to a great height, never surpassed except in a few particulars by the Babylonians themselves.

AGRICULTURE. The Sumerians and the Babylonians learned to drain the swamps and to control and regulate the flood waters of the rivers by means of ditches and dikes. They retained the fertility of the soil by letting one-third of the fields lie idle (fallow). The domestic animals employed in the fields were the oxen and the donkeys. The plow was a clumsy wooden implement, drawn by oxen, though sometimes the peasants would pull it whenever the soil was fairly well broken up. Sheep and goats were kept in fairly large numbers; and chickens, geese, ducks, swans, and doves were prized. The donkey was used for carrying burdens, but later the camel was preferred. Only a part of the land belonged to the king or the state, and a large proportion was the property of private individuals.

COMMERCE AND INDUSTRY. Commerce and industry developed rapidly, owing to the favorable location of Babylonia. The country was easily reached from Egypt to the west and from India to the east, while there was also a great deal of contact made with

Syria in the west and the people of Asia Minor to the northwest. As yet no currency or coinage was used, but it was the custom for the merchants to employ copper, silver, and afterwards a small amount of gold in the form of bars or in other shapes. Barter continued to be employed for hundreds of years. The Priests in the temples often operated banks and loaned money at high rates of interest.

CUNEIFORM WRITING. The Sumerians invented the system of writing that was imitated by all the peoples of ancient Mesopotamia. They made use of about 350 signs, not pictures, but wedge-shaped strokes made with a so-called *stylus*, which was a pointed stick of wood or a reed. The strokes were engraved upon soft clay tablets, and because of the wedge-shaped strokes, this form of writing was called *cuneiform*. Each sign represented a whole syllable. The clay tablets were baked in ovens, and in this way they became so hard and durable that they have retained their form until the present day.

THE BABYLONIAN CODE OF LAW UNDER HAMMURABI. We are very fortunate to have the elaborate code of laws drawn up for one of the greatest of Babylonian kings, whose name was Hammurabi. He reigned about the year 1700 B.C., and had his code engraved upon a huge cylinder which was eight feet in height. Neither Hammurabi himself nor any of his scribes was the author, but he and his scribes merely assembled the ancient laws of the Sumerians and *codified* them. In other words, they carefully put them together in an orderly way, so as to make a collection of laws which we call a *code*.

DESCRIPTION OF THE CODE. Hammurabi's code was made up of 282 laws which were carefully organized, and grouped into various divisions. By this code property rights were well protected, and business relations were also clearly defined and regulated. A great many personal relationships were described. Punishment was meted out according to the nature of the crime, and the manner in which the criminal committed it. You will read below a few of the laws.

6. If a man has stolen the goods of the temple or the palace, that man shall be killed, and he who has received the stolen thing from his hand shall be put to death.

8. If a man has stolen ox or sheep or ass, or pig, or ship, whether from the temple or the palace, he shall render tenfold. If the thief has nought to pay, he shall be put to death.

14. If a man has stolen the son of a freeman, he shall be put to death.

> 196.   If a man has caused the loss of a gentleman's eye, his eye one shall cause to be lost.
> 198.   If he has caused a poor man to lose his eye or shattered a poor man's limb, he shall pay one mina of silver.
> 218.   If a doctor has treated a gentleman for a severe wound with a lancet of bronze and has caused the gentleman to die, or has opened an abscess of the eye for a gentleman with the bronze lancet and has caused the loss of the gentleman's eye, one shall cut off his hands.

BABYLONIAN SOCIETY. From this code we learn that in ancient Babylonia a clear distinction was drawn between the kings and the nobles on the one hand and the middle class and the lower class on the other hand. The priests and the soldiers formed a class of their own. The priests functioned as bankers, scribes, and scholars. The merchants enjoyed a relatively high place in society. But the free workmen and the slaves were treated rather harshly. The slaves were the property of their masters, just as the master owned his cattle. However, there were various grades of slaves in Babylonia, and some were treated comparatively well.

MARRIAGE AND PROPERTY LAWS. Marriage by contract was legally recognized. Both husband and wife might start proceedings for divorce, which was granted in case they could not get along with each other. Women had the right to own property in their name, and single women of the upper class were even permitted to conduct business establishments of their own.

BABYLONIAN LITERATURE. In addition to the code of Hammurabi, we possess thousands of tablets upon which were inscribed various kinds of public records, while many of them also contained poetry and history in various forms. Especially noteworthy are the stories about the flood, the creation, and of a shepherd who tried to fly to heaven on the back of an eagle.

PROGRESS IN MATHEMATICS AND ASTRONOMY. In the whole history of Mesopotamian civilization the Sumerians are noted for having made the greatest progress in mathematics. They divided the circle into 360 degrees and the day into 12 hours. Each of these hours was sub-divided into 30 minutes, so that each of the minutes was equivalent to four of our minutes. The Sumerians and the Babylonians also made great progress in the field of geometry. They drew excellent maps, and in one case they attempted to make a map of the whole world. They were, however, not able to get beyond the year of 354 days divided into 12 months and based upon the changes of the moon. In Chapter IV you will learn more about this ancient moon (lunar) calendar.

ARCHITECTURE, THE TOWER OF BABEL. The Sumerians and Babylonians were noted for their huge palaces and temple towers. The temple tower was constructed on a square platform of stone. It comprised several levels of stories, the higher one slightly smaller than the one beneath, until it tapered off to a narrow point at the top where the temple itself was situated. The tower of Babel was no doubt one of the earliest temple towers built in southern Mesopotamia.

FALL OF ANCIENT BABYLONIA. Shortly after the year 1600 B.C. the kingdom of Babylonia was invaded by various peoples from the north, and during the next 600 years it suffered a steady decline. In the twelfth century B.C. Babylonia was conquered by the Assyrians, who had established a kingdom in northern Mesopotamia.

WHO THE ASSYRIANS WERE. The Assyrians belonged to the numerous Semitic tribes that had originally inhabited northern Arabia, from where in three successive waves of migrations they spread over the whole of Mesopotamia. We have already seen that the Babylonians were also a Semitic tribe, but that the Sumerians had lived in Mesopotamia before the Semites did. Among the Semitic peoples may be noted the Hebrews, the Phoenicians, the Aramaeans, and the Chaldeans — whose history we shall study in a following chapter.

Student Activities

1. With the aid of a dictionary, if necessary, write out the definitions for the following words: *parallel, flourished, code* (law), *functioned, contract, migrations.*
2. Look up Mesopotamia in a geography text book and draw a sketch of that region.
3. Why was the Tigro-Euphrates River Valley a wonderful place for development of nations?
4. Why do people generally settle in river valleys? Where were the first settlements in America as a rule located?
5. Look up Genesis, chapter 11, in the Bible, and note in what connection the city of Ur is mentioned.
6. Explain the CUNEIFORM writing. Make drawings of it.
7. Write a brief account of Hammurabi.
8. What contributions did the Sumerians make to mathematics and the calendar?
9. Name the peoples who belonged to the Semitic race. Select and prepare a topic for a report to the class by additional readings in encyclopedias and other books in your library.
   Suggested topics: World's important deltas, Picture writing, The warlike Assyrians and their methods of warfare and conquest.

CHAPTER 4

The Story of Ancient Egypt

WHAT KIND OF A LAND EGYPT WAS. Egypt was and still is a land of mystery and romance where for thousands of years civilized people have lived, undisturbed by invasion and conquest until about 1750 B.C. A noted Greek historian[1] once said that "Egypt is the gift of the Nile." He meant that Egypt owed its prosperity almost entirely to the annual floods of the Nile. Without the waters and the silt sent by this stream through annual flooding of the lowlands, there could have been no Egypt such as history has described it for us. Ancient Egypt was little more than the valley of the Nile, which might be called a huge oasis in the midst of desert land. The length of the valley was about 650 miles, that is, the distance between the so-called First Cataract (waterfall) in the south and the Mediterranean coast in the north. In the north the valley becomes wider and spreads out like a fan, through which several arms of the Nile flow to the sea. This region is called the Delta.

THE ANNUAL FLOODS. As a result of the abundant spring rains in the higher regions to the south and the melting of the snows on the mountains of Abyssinia (also called Ethiopia), where the Nile has its sources, the river rises rapidly in the month of May and continues to rise until October, when it reaches its greatest height—from twenty to forty feet above the normal level. The flood level remains almost stationary till the first week in November, when the waters recede, so that in January the river is once more confined to its narrow bed.

RESULTS OF THE FLOODS. In ancient times the annual flood exerted much influence on the Egyptians. They were compelled to organize themselves into a community with a definite form of government, in order that they could guide the silt-laden waters of the Nile along numerous ditches, and thus fertilize the fields. They

1. This was Herodotus.

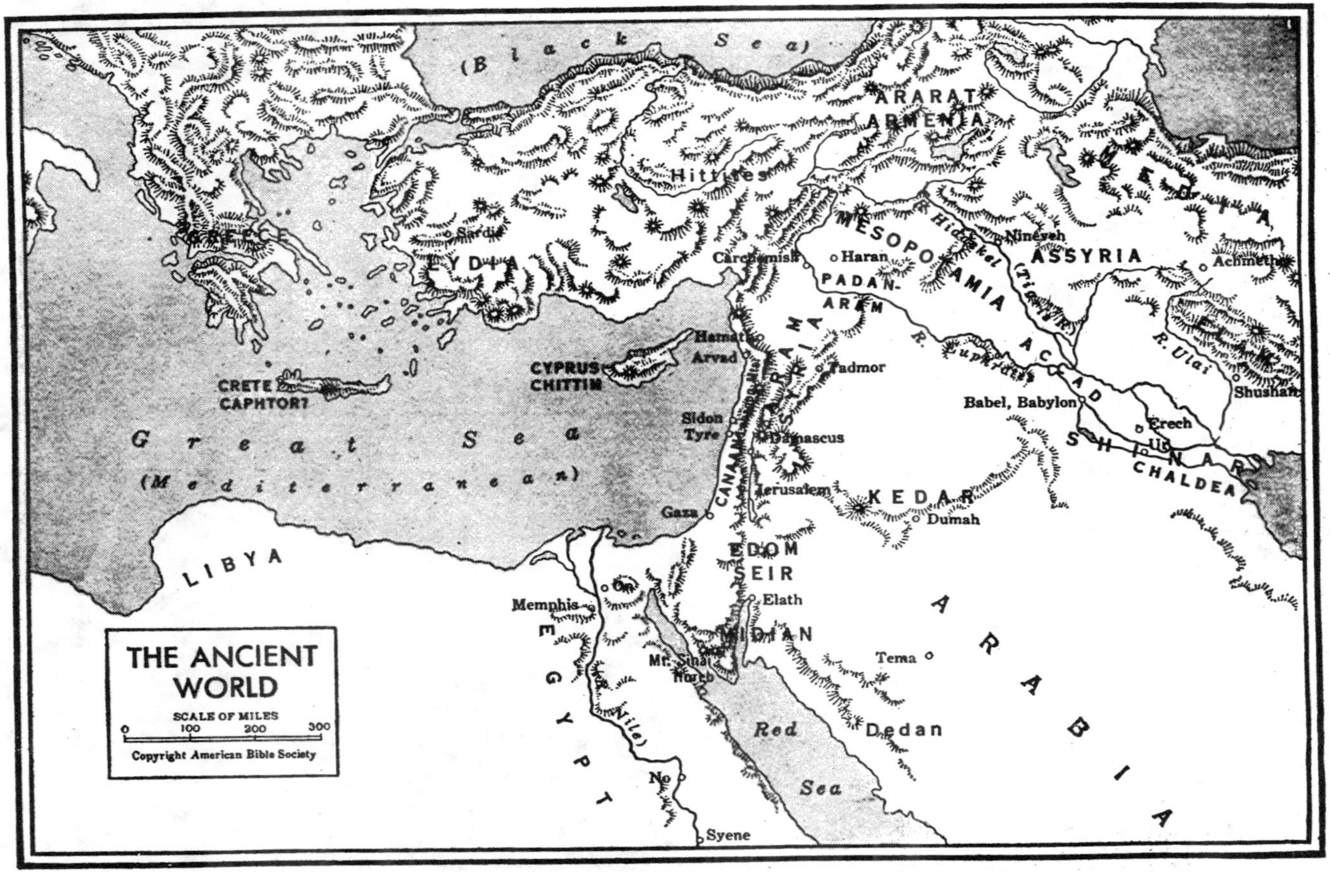

THE ANCIENT WORLD

THE PYRAMIDS AT GIZA AS SEEN
FROM THE NILE VALLEY

RAISING WATER BY MEANS OF THE
SHADUF

Egyptian farmers used irrigation.

HIERATIC AND HIEROGLYPHIC
WRITING

The hieratic is at left. the hieroglyphic at
right. Writing was done on papyrus, from
right to left.

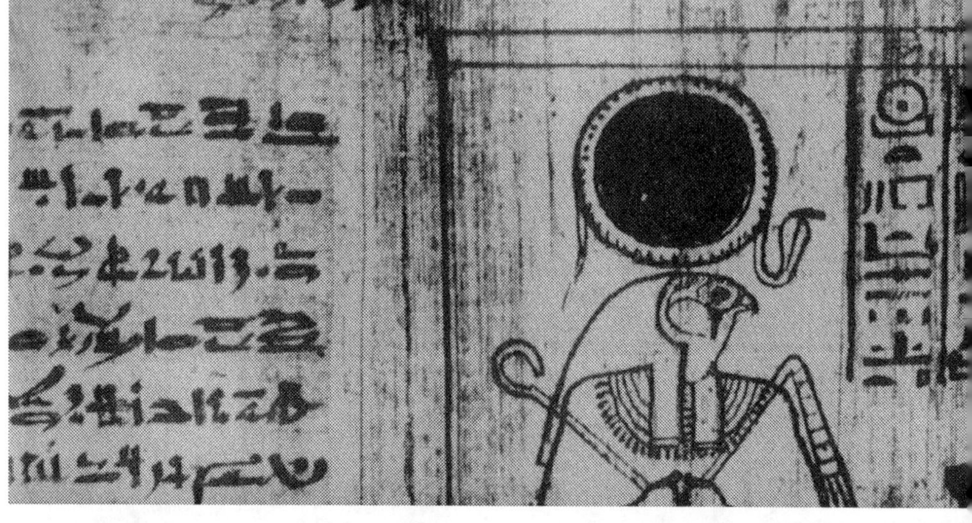

also wanted to retain the precious moisture as long as possible. As a result the black soil of the valley was *famous* for its *fertility*.

THE PEOPLE. The inhabitants of ancient Egypt were so closely related to the peoples of northern Arabia, Syria, and Mesopotamia that in the opinion of some scholars the first books of the Bible were either written in the Egyptian language or based upon sources that had been composed in Egypt. We know that Moses, the actual author of Genesis, had spent many years in Egypt before writing this book. From the numerous paintings and statues which show the features of prominent men and women in ancient Egypt we gather that they had rather deep-set eyes, fairly thick lips, large cheek bones, a comparatively short nose, and black and straight hair. Their skin was white, though tinged with tan from being exposed to the hot rays of the sun.

POLITICAL HISTORY. Upper Egypt and Lower Egypt (meaning southern and northern Egypt) at first were separate kingdoms, but they united about the year 3000 B.C. The period after 3000 B.C. may be divided as follows: First came the Old Kingdom, from about 3000 to 2270 B.C.; then the Middle Kingdom, from 2060 to 1788 B.C.; and finally the New Kingdom, or the Empire, from 1580 to 1100 B.C. Those eras not covered by the dates just given are periods of transition, or change, while that from 1100 to 525 B.C. is the period of decline, ending with the conquest of Egypt by the Persians in 525 B.C. From about 1780 to 1580 B.C. Egypt was partly under the domination of an Asiatic people called the Hyksos, and from about 1550 to 1250 B.C. the Egyptians reversed the tide of conquest and ruled over Syria and northern Arabia.

THE GOVERNMENT. During all these years Egypt was governed by a king whose official title was Pharaoh. He was considered a descendant of the gods and consequently thought to have divine powers and qualities. All the land in Egypt belonged to him, and he charged rentals for the use of the fields by his subjects, usually payable in the form of a portion of the crops raised by the tillers of the soil. He appointed all civil officers, and, being considered a god upon earth, he was the head of the priesthood and could appoint or discharge whom he pleased. Furthermore, he required personal services of the lowly inhabitants, either in the army or in the civil functions of the government, which included irrigation works.

How the King (Pharaoh) Was Worshipped After His Death. The king was even greater in death than in life, for the utmost care was taken by his people to provide his corpse with suitable surroundings. It was so carefully embalmed that many such *mummies* are in existence today, clearly showing the features of the pharaohs who died more than three thousand years ago. The mummy was placed in a wooden casket, beautifully decorated. Beside the body there were laid treasures for the supposed benefit of the spirit of the dead monarch. Not content with that, the pharaoh compelled many thousands of his subjects to erect for him a monument in keeping with his important position in life. For example, the Great Pyramid of Gizeh is made up of about two and a half million limestone blocks, each of which weighed about five thousand pounds.

The King's Officials. The king could not possibly supervise all the details of the government and merely appointed the chief officials himself, while the latter in turn appointed inferior officials. The king was a real *autocrat,* for he ruled in his own power. He was a *monarch,* because he alone ruled and all officials were responsible to him. He was an *absolute monarch* for that reason: his power was not limited by an assembly elected or appointed by the people. He was also a *despot,* since he did what seemed best to him; he did not have to listen to advice from anyone. His officials comprised a *bureaucracy,* which is the body of officials appointed by a ruler and responsible only to him.

The Aristocracy. Gradually, however, an *aristocracy* arose which began to share supreme power with the king. An aristocracy is a class of persons who form the upper section of society — the men with extensive property, or social prestige, or political or religious power. In case these persons gain control of the government, that form of government is called aristocratic, or an aristocracy, that is, "the rule by the best."

Ministers, Governors, and Priests. In Egypt such a development was made possible for the simple reason that the king had to have important officials (*Ministers*). Moreover, since the country had to be divided into districts or provinces, each of these units was ruled by a *governor* for the king. The office of governor became hereditary, which means that a class of *nobles* originated whose sons inherited from them both their position and their title. Among the priests a similar process took place, so that many of the powerful priests held important civil offices and thus threatened to seize the powers formerly controlled entirely by the king. For a time high priests reigned in the south (Upper Egypt) as real pharaohs.

THE ARMY. The Egyptians as a rule were not a warlike people, and only in one period, as we saw, did they attempt to rule over other peoples. Only after they had borrowed from the inhabitants in Mesopotamia the custom of employing chariots drawn by horses did they become powerful upon the battlefield. The Egyptian army was made up for the most part of militia levies serving as infantry and armed with axes, bows, arrows, spears, and daggers, while using for defensive purposes the shield. During the period of empire building the Egyptian government also employed soldiers who fought for money or its equivalent, hence called *mercenaries*.

SOCIAL CLASSES. As in all ages, rich and poor, strong and weak were living side by side. On the one hand certain families were becoming ever more powerful, while the masses of the people were reduced to a position bordering upon actual slavery. Those men and women who were no longer obliged to work for a living, devoted themselves as a rule to the cause of learning and art. It was they who created the marvelous civilization that formed the glory of ancient Egypt. But the downtrodden folk beneath them in the social order provided the manual labor needed to maintain the state and the people. Between the two classes just mentioned, however, you can distinguish a group of persons that might be called the middle class. They were able to lease their own land and employ hired labor in their fields. Many others in their class were government officials, scribes, soldiers, merchants, or craftsmen.

THE WOMEN WERE TREATED WITH GREAT RESPECT. Egypt was remarkable in that its women were treated in many respects as the equals of men. A large number of queens ruled the country in their own right, though they were outnumbered by kings. Not only did women have the right to own property, but property was inherited through the mother.

AGRICULTURE. Throughout its history, Egypt was primarily an *agrarian* country, that is, most of the people were employed in agriculture, and it was agriculture that formed the chief basis of prosperity. During the season from November to May the fields were cultivated, the crops grew to maturity, and then the harvest followed. Wheat and barley were the principal grain crops. Among the vegetables grown may be mentioned the pea, bean, radish, cu-

cumber, lettuce, and leek. Vineyards and olive trees were plentiful, while date palms were also abundant. Flax was grown for the production of linen, and cotton was also produced. The domestic animals used in the fields were the oxen and the donkeys, just as in Mesopotamia.

INDUSTRY AND COMMERCE. Industry was favored in ancient Egypt by the fact that the fertile soil produced a surplus of food supplies, so that the natives could exchange grain and oil for copper (mined in Cyprus and northern Arabia), wood (from Syria and other regions to the north of Egypt), spices, and incense (from India and adjoining countries). Large numbers of skilled workers were employed in making bricks, quarrying stones, perfecting linen cloths, and building stone structures. Wooden boats were constructed in large numbers, for the Egyptians early began to extend their shipping from the Nile River to the southern coast of the Mediterranean, the shores of the Red Sea, and the southern shore of Arabia, reaching into the Indian Ocean. Great progress was likewise made in metalwork. From about 2000 to 1200 B.C. the Egyptians practically controlled the trade of the eastern Mediterranean. They ventured as far as the island of Cyprus and the Aegean Sea, exchanging their grain and manufactured products for wood and copper.

SCULPTURE AND ARCHITECTURE. In the fields of sculpture and architecture the Egyptians were exceptionally successful. They carved statues of kings and sacred animals out of both wood and stone, while bronze figures were also produced in large quantities. We would like to know how they were able to make stone figures of such colossal proportions that they weighed up to more than two million pounds. Among the wonders of the ancient world may certainly be reckoned their sphinxes and pyramids. Noteworthy also are the magnificent temples, especially that at Karnak, which contains huge stone blocks in one hall, each weighing about eleven thousand pounds. Carefully carved and beautifully shaped in the form of round cylinders, they were piled on top of each other to form pillars.

THE PYRAMIDS. The chief wonder of ancient Egypt was the Great Pyramid at Gizeh (Giza), mentioned above. It was constructed under the pharaoh named Khufu, or Cheops, about the year 2500 B.C. Although each side at the bottom was as much as 755 feet long and the height of the monument was 481 feet, the whole structure of two and a half million blocks of stone was so skilfully built that absolute perfection in measurements was reached within one ten-thousandth part of the length of one side. The joints between the big blocks had a width of only one-thousand part of an inch. You can scarcely imagine how the engineers of ancient Egypt in 2500 B.C. could shape blocks weighing five thousand pounds each and have their sides cut with such minute care as to "equal the opticians' work of today," as one scholar has recently remarked. These stones had to be perfectly straight and they had to be placed in their proper positions so that two and a half million of them would form one structure that would endure for thousands of years.

THE EGYTIAN SYSTEM OF WRITING. The Egyptians devised a system of writing that is known partly as *hieroglyphics* (inscribed on stone, hence this word), and partly as *hieratic* (written with a pen made of reed on a piece of papyrus). In this connection you must note that the Egyptians perfected paper which they made out of the pith of a plant called papyrus. They made ink out of vegetable gum and soot, or carbon. They did not write letters such as we now employ, but used pictures which had a definite meaning and also represented sounds, though only consonant sounds, not those of vowels. For example, the picture of two arms raised up stood for a soul or spirit and also for the sound *ka*.

DEVELOPMENT OF THE ALPHABET. The Egyptians did much to prepare the way for the making of the alphabet. First they developed picture writing, in which drawings represented ideas, not words. Then they took the second step which was the *phonetic* stage. Each object developed a fixed form and stood for a special word, and finally a syllable. Thus they could make compound words and word combinations, and eliminate pictures. Finally, they took still a third step and created an alphabet, in which a sign represented an elemental sound, like *ka*.

DECIPHERMENT OF ANCIENT EGYPTIAN WRITINGS. Until the end of the eighteenth century European scholars were unable to decipher the hieroglyphics of ancient Egypt. In Egypt itself the ability to read those hieroglyphics was no longer possible after 300 B.C. But it seems that a number of priests who possessed many secrets concerning mummification, the art of healing, and the mysteries of the spirit world, still knew how to read this script of their ancestors. The public at large no longer understood the symbols of old.

THE ROSETTA STONE. When in the year 1799 Napoleon came from France to attack the British Empire by way of Egypt, he took with him not only soldiers but scholars. Among the latter was one to whom was shown a stone that had been discovered by one of the soldiers. It became known as the Rosetta Stone, named after the town of Rosetta in Egypt. The stone is now in the British Museum in London. It was made of basalt and was black in color. On this stone there had been inscribed in three different languages the decree of a ruler, dated 196 B.C. The languages were Greek, hieroglyphic, and hieratic. Thus scholars were able to decipher and translate the ancient symbols of Egyptian writing.

THE WORK OF CHAMPOLLION. Unfortunately, however, the scholars that Napoleon had taken to Egypt with him were not able to do this work, since most of them were interested chiefly in the natural sciences. But in 1822 a French historian named Champollion made a careful study of an obelisk upon which were inscribed royal names in both Greek and Egyptian letters. He saw that the Egyptians had made use of a real alphabet, and of the twenty-four consonant sounds he learned twelve. Thus, with the use of the Rosetta Stone other scholars began to decipher the writings upon the walls of the temples and upon obelisks.

THE EGYPTIAN CALENDAR. Very valuable for the western world was the development of the Egyptian calendar. In contrast to the widely used calendar based on the phases of the moon, which established a year of 354 days, the Egyptian calendar followed the course of the earth around the sun, though the Egyptians themselves did not yet realize that it was the earth that moved, rather than the sun. The solar year consisted of twelve months of thirty days each and five days at the end of the year added in the nature of holidays. You will note in a later chapter what changes were later made in this calendar.

EGYPT TEACHES US A VALUABLE LESSON. Strange though it may seem, the Egyptians were most successful in the period of the Old Kingdom, that is, before 2300 B.C. In that period the greatest of pyramids was constructed, mummification invented, the calendar devised, the irrigation system perfected, medical science founded, the alphabet begun, and a great literature established. In the two thousand years that followed, very little was done for the growth of western civilization. You would think that Egypt ought to have done better than remain on the same level so long and decline for such a long time. But the Bible clearly explains what was wrong with the Egyptians in the time of Moses, that is, about 1500 B.C. They refused to worship the God of the Hebrews and no longer followed the advice of their religious leaders who had lived in an age of great wisdom. Thus Egypt as a nation decayed after a time of great glory and power, just as plants and animals grow and wither, to make room for others. The great nations of the past have come and gone, as it pleased God to show us how human beings must live in order to continue in His grace.

Student Activities

1. With the aid of a dictionary, if necessary, write definitions for the following words: *transition, autocracy, aristocracy, bureaucracy, hereditary, phonetic, decipher.*
2. Draw a map of Egypt with the aid of a standard geography text.
3. Write an essay of 100 words showing that Egypt is the "Gift of the Nile."
4. Describe an Egyptian pyramid. Why did the Egyptians take such great care in preserving the bodies of the dead? Did they believe in the resurrection of the dead?
5. What is meant by the following statement: "The Pharaoh was in theory an absolute monarch but in practice Egypt was ruled by the priests and bureaucrats."
6. Read Exodus, chapter I, in the Bible. What is meant by the statement, "Now there arose up a new king over Egypt, WHICH KNEW NOT JOSEPH?"
7. To what present day instruments of war could the horse drawn chariots be compared?
8. What is meant by the term, "Middle Class?"
9. How did men learn to read the Egyptian writing?
10. Why was the "religion" of the ancient Egyptians a false religion?
11. Why did Egypt decay and pass away after a certain time?
12. Write a summary of this chapter of about one hundred words. Be sure you mention those things which you consider important.
13. Perhaps you have been in a paper factory, if you have, describe how paper is made now and report to the class. The Chinese, before the invention of paper, used bamboo strips to write on. These strips were about twelve inches long. What other material has been used for writing purposes?

CHAPTER 5

The Hebrews and the Phoenicians

IMPORTANCE OF THE HEBREWS. In the ancient world the Hebrews did not seem at all important, for they formed only a very small nation. They built few great cities with huge temples and palaces, such as might be seen in Egypt or Babylonia, and later in Assyria, Persia, Greece, and Rome. Only for a short time, under David and Solomon, did they enlarge the boundaries of their little kingdom, but not so very long after that the Assyrians and Persians came to Palestine and destroyed the Hebrew nation. The Hebrews were led away into captivity time after time. They were despised by the haughty Greeks and Romans. And yet they surpassed all the peoples of the ancient world in the fields of religion, law, prophecy, and certain forms of poetry.

THE CAREER OF ABRAHAM. We read in the Bible that Abraham was the ancestor of the Hebrew race and that he lived at one time in the great city of Ur. But from about 1750 to 1920 many scholars used to make fun of the Bible account, thinking that there was never such a city and that Abraham probably was a person of no great importance in history. Imagine the surprise of some of these doubters when in 1924 many ancient buildings of Ur were uncovered by industrious men who learned from the old clay tablets written five thousand years ago that here was once the city of Ur. Moreover, a person like Abraham, owning large flocks of cattle, used to be honored as a real prince. When in 2150 B.C. he left Ur to go to Palestine, he was indeed a great man.

THE GEOGRAPHY OF CANAAN. Canaan was the name of the country which Abraham visited. Later it was called Palestine, after the Philistines, who are mentioned so often in the Bible. In Abraham's time Canaan was but thinly populated, and, as in the time of Jacob, it was not always able to provide its inhabitants with sufficient food. Abraham was obliged at one time to go to Egypt to buy food. There is no doubt that Canaan was in touch with both Mesopotamia and Egypt. But the country differed considerably from the lowlands of Egypt and Babylonia. The climate was not so hot and dry. Unfortunately, much of the soil was mountainous and rocky, and only in the spring and late summer were the rains abundant. However, valleys were to be found in various parts, and pasture lands were upon the whole excellent.

THE ANCIENT HEBREWS. Here Abraham and his descendants lived with their flocks. They learned to cultivate the soil besides. As the population increased, some of Abraham's descendants became actively interested in commerce and industry, but it may be said that throughout the long history of the Hebrew nation only a small proportion of the people lived in the towns. As long as the Hebrews remained in their native land, they were noted as a *pastoral* people. Many of them, however, cultivated the fields and grew olive and fig trees, and produced abundant grain crops.

THEIR GOVERNMENT. Until about the year 1025 B.C. the government of the Hebrews may be described as a *theocracy,* that is, a rule of a people by the church or a priesthood. God communicated with the people through their priests and prophets. First under Moses, then under the judges, and finally under the prophets, the Israelites or Hebrews were firmly held together, though they were divided into twelve tribes. Under King Saul, who ruled about the year 1020 B.C., the Hebrews became a united nation. Saul, however, was barely able to defend the country against the Philistines to the southwest.

DAVID AND SOLOMON. But it was Saul's successor, King David, who enlarged the nation far beyond its earlier borders, so that it now included a fairly large district east of the Jordan River, and the region stretching to the north of the Sea of Galilee. David conquered the city of Jerusalem and made it the national capital. Under David's son, Solomon, the country reached its greatest prosperity, but, owing to the heavy taxation and other burdens levied upon the people by their ambitious king, many of his subjects became disappointed with his rule, and there were leaders who wished that they had never asked for a monarch but had remained under the rule of God and His priesthood. On the death of Solomon about the year 940 B.C., the kingdom was divided into two parts: the north was called hereafter Israel, and the south Judah.

FALL OF THE KINGDOMS OF ISRAEL AND JUDAH. These two kingdoms were ruled by separate monarchs, until in 722 B.C. the Assyrians conquered the northern kingdom with its capital, Samaria, and carried off a large proportion of the inhabitants to Mesopotamia. The Bible tells us a great deal about the sinful lives of the kings who ruled Israel, so that both king and people finally lost their independence. We also understand the wretched fate of the southern kingdom, which, after having been ruled by several wicked kings, fell in 586 B.C. before the army of Nebuchadnezzar, the king of Babylonia. Once more a large number of Hebrews were deported to Mesopotamia, but fifty years later, in 536 B.C., when a Persian king ruled over Babylonia, the Hebrews living there were permitted to return to Palestine. Many did so at once, but a large number chose to remain, and their descendants spread over various lands of the ancient world, including Egypt. After the destruction of the two Hebrew kingdoms just mentioned the Hebrews were generally called the Jews.

THE LOST TRIBES OF ISRAEL. Since so many of them remained outside of Palestine, the sources in several countries speak of the "lost tribes of Israel." And one day when Jesus of Nazareth had preached a powerful sermon and had talked about taking His departure, some people wondered whether He was going to preach to the lost tribes of Israel.

MANY JEWS BECOME BUSINESS MEN. Not all the Jews remained herdsmen or farmers. Many of them became successful business men, bankers, or scholars. Since their laws did not permit them to loan money at interest to their own people but allowed them to charge interest to Gentiles, they were encouraged to transact business with foreigners and to loan their money freely to them. Furthermore, the Christian nations of the Middle Ages did not favor the loaning of money at interest by Christians, because of the law of the Hebrews, which they had accepted as binding upon themselves. This was one of the reasons why it became customary for Christians to borrow money from the Jews, and so it happened naturally that the Jews became the leading bankers in some European countries.

PERSECUTION OF THE JEWS. Since they were often persecuted, they tended to band together and support each other. This will explain why the Jews in Germany have been so harshly treated in recent times. Many Germans claimed that it was impossible for anybody to receive attention in certain hospitals, especially in Berlin, unless one were a Jew. The proportion of Jewish physicians in Berlin was so high and the number of Jewish professors in some German universities so great that the others became alarmed. Moreover, there seemed to be too many wealthy Jewish bankers.

THE HEBREWS WHO REMAINED IN PALESTINE. The Hebrews who continued to live in Palestine never acquired great material wealth. For one thing, the country was very small, only about ten thousand square miles in area. And, as we saw, much of the soil was very poor. During the long summers there was seldom enough rain. Minerals and forests were also lacking. When King Solomon desired to build a great temple in honor of Jehovah, he was obliged to fetch the lumber from regions to the north of Palestine and metal from countries to the south. He even had to employ foreign architects and workmen, and when he had finished the structure, it was but a small and simple building compared with the huge temples of Mesopotamia and the vast structures of Egypt.

LITERARY CONTRIBUTIONS. Nevertheless, the Hebrews made up for this lack of wealth by giving to the western world their great literature, their just code of laws, and their wonderful religion. The Old Testament contains the oldest and the most reliable history of the human race up to the time of Abraham. Moreover, the prophetic and the poetical books show an overwhelming superiority over all similar productions of the ancient world, including India and China. There is certainly nothing in the literature of Egypt and Babylonia that can at all be compared with the book of Psalms.

THE CODE OF MOSES. Even the famous code of Hammurabi is but a simple and crude document when studied side by side with the much more extensive code of Moses to be found in the first five books of the Old Testament. Although Hammurabi's code is about two hundred years older than that of Moses, there is no need of drawing the conclusion that for this reason Moses must have copied the older code. Both codes appear to have had a common Semitic source, for they repeat certain older laws and theories, such as that of "an eye for an eye and a tooth for a tooth." If a person knocked out a tooth in the mouth of another person, he would have to lose one of his teeth, as we have already seen. But the peculiarity of Hammurabi's code is that this was only required if an important or wealthy person had lost his tooth. In case he had knocked out several teeth in the head of a poorer person, he merely paid a small fine.

MOSES AND HAMMURABI. Moses, who lived in the fifteenth century, B.C., had been instructed at the court of an Egyptian princess and was thoroughly familiar with the most advanced legal thought in Egypt. Furthermore, on the peninsula of Sinai in northern Arabia, where the Israelites lingered on their way from

Egypt to Palestine, Moses received instruction directly from God. When these facts are borne in mind, we can understand readily that Moses had not the slightest desire to copy the inferior code of Hammurabi, which has nothing to do with the quality of sin and spiritual values or powers. There are also no Babylonian expressions to be found in the code of Moses. Moreover, the spirit of the two codes and the modes of expression are entirely different. The laws of Moses were complete at the very beginning.

HEBREW LAWS ARE SUPERIOR TO ALL OTHERS. The code of Moses places a high value on human life and requires kind treatment of slaves. It demands proper care of the poor and of strangers, something neglected by the Babylonians. The code of Moses requires that witchcraft and idolatrous sacrifices are punishable by death, but the Babylonian lawgivers thought such practices were not wrong. The reason for the difference is simple. The Hebrews were expected to trust in God and His prophets, who would tell them all they had to know. There was no need to go to mediums and ask questions of spirits of departed persons. Thus we read in the first book of Samuel that when King Saul refused to listen to Samuel any longer and God would not tell him anything worth while in dreams, and when he went to see a "witch," that is, in this case a medium, he committed a serious crime.

THE HEBREW RELIGION. The Hebrews had a remarkable religion in that they as a whole nation were obliged to worship only one God. There were other peoples in antiquity among whom *monotheism* was practiced by a few individuals, and in Egypt a certain monarch had tried to enforce monotheism in the country, but such cases were exceptional. The Hebrews alone had a God who was not like human beings but a spiritual force. True, Moses was once asked by God to view His glory in a physical form, but we are not informed that God had a body like that of human beings. The Hebrews alone were prohibited from considering their kings as more than purely mortal beings in their capacity as rulers, and as descendants of the gods. Even the Romans, as we shall see, had to worship their emperors at one time. It was only at the beginning, before the Flood, that monotheism was widely practiced in the ancient world.

THE INFLUENCE OF THIS RELIGION. Through the influence of the Christian religion the thoughts of the Hebrew prophets, judges, and singers were made known to all the western nations of modern times. The literature of England, Germany, France, Spain, and Italy cannot possibly be understood without a thorough knowledge of the Old Testament. Nay, more than that, the whole history of the western world bears the stamp of the Hebrew mind. Every Sunday our great department stores pay tribute to it by remaining closed all day. No great university would require its students and professors to attend classes on the Christian Sunday.

THE HEBREW ALPHABET. Still another gift left by the ancient Hebrews remains for our consideration. We have in mind the origin of our alphabet, for which until very recently the credit was given to the Phoenicians, a Semitic people living immediately to the north of Palestine. Recent excavations upon the site of Lachish, the chief walled city of Judah, have revealed that the Hebrews used an alphabet and passed on their knowledge to the Phoenicians, while the latter instructed the Greeks. From the Greeks in turn the Romans derived their alphabet, but the common source of all is that made by the Hebrews about the fourteenth century B.C. During the wanderings of the Hebrews on the Sinai Peninsula they had learned to develop the beginnings of their alphabet, which was completed by the middle of the fourteenth century B.C.

THE PHOENICIANS WERE MERELY TRADERS. The Phoenicians were chiefly interested in commerce and industry, and from their two famous ports, first Sidon, then Tyre, they sent out their many ships to trade in all parts of the Mediterranean Sea. Much attention used to be given to their supposed invention of the alphabet. It had not yet occurred to many scholars to ask how a people like the Phoenicians, so lacking in literary talents and so little interested in philosophy and religion, could really have originated the alphabet.

WHAT MOSES DID FOR THE HEBREWS. The Hebrews were vastly superior to the Phoenicians and the Babylonians in the field of literature. For had not Moses in Deuteronomy VI, 4-9, instructed the Israelites to write the commandments of God upon the doorposts of their houses and upon their gates? How could he have asked them to do that unless they had known how to write? And they could not have done these things if they had been obliged to copy the clumsy writing of the Egyptians or the complicated script of the Babylonians. We read also in the Bible (Deut. XXVII, 2-8) that Moses instructed Joshua to "write upon the stones all the words of this Law very plainly."

OUR DEBT TO THE HEBREW AND PHOENICIAN ALPHABETS. But it was the good fortune of the Phoenicians to transform the Hebrew letters into a more convenient script which closely resembles Greek letters. This process took place about the ninth century

B.C. It was the last chapter in a long development, in which the Hebrews played by far the largest role. The latter wrote their documents upon pieces of papyrus and used ink in very nearly the same fashion as we do now. Perhaps this knowledge may impel us sometimes when we put our pen to a piece of paper to remember how much we owe to the people of Israel.

Student Activities

1. With the aid of a dictionary, if necessary, write out the definitions for the following words: *excavators, pastoral, extensive, monotheism.*
2. In your Bible History you will find a map of Palestine. Draw it.
3. Which chapters in the Book of Genesis tell the story of Abraham?
4. What was the most important promise that God made to Abraham?
5. Why were the people disappointed with the rule of King Solomon?
6. Why did the Jews become money lenders?
7. Where did Moses receive the laws for his people?
8. How did the Hebrews consider their kings? How did the Egyptians, Assyrians, and Babylonians consider their kings? In which commandment does God forbid idolatry?
9. Who were the Phoenicians?
10. Did the Hebrews at the time of Moses have an alphabet?
11. What is the most important thing that we have received through the people of Israel?
12. The people of Israel were chosen by God as HIS PEOPLE. What does that statement mean?
13. Who are the chosen people of God?
14. Write out ten important statements from this chapter.

CHAPTER 6

The Rise and Fall of the Assyrian Empire

THE ANCIENT STATE OF ASSUR. About the year 3000 B.C., that is, long before Babylonia was overthrown, a Semitic tribe settled in the northern valley of the Tigris River and founded there a state of its own. We may call it a city-state, for it was governed and controlled by the city of Assur, from whose name the word "Assyria" has been derived, as you may have guessed already. For a period of about eight centuries the people in this state retained their independence, until Babylonia extended northward and finally conquered it.

THE CIVILIZATION OF ANCIENT ASSYRIA. The Assyrians in this early age were very ambitious. They carried on a flourishing trade with the peoples of Syria and Asia Minor. Like the Babylonians, they employed a cuneiform type of writing, leaving behind them a wealth of literature in the form of clay tablets. From these we learn how they conducted their trade and agriculture, and how they made use of small silver bars carrying on them a stamp, so as to resemble money. They even had letters of credit, which are like checks in that they take the place of cash. Naturally, the Assyrians also were clever enough to loan money to the peoples of Asia Minor with whom they traded, charging about 20 to 30 percent interest a year.

THE KASSITES CONQUER AND RULE NORTHERN MESOPOTAMIA. You will remember that about 1785 B.C. the Kassites conquered Babylonia from the north and afterwards extended their rule over other sections of Mesopotamia. Under Babylonian domination the Assyrians had continued their trade with districts to the north and northwest, but it seems that the Kassites did not appreciate a high degree of civilized life. For several hundred years after 1785 B.C. Assyria declined together with Babylonia.

THE HITTITES. One of the most mysterious and at the same time one of the most powerful peoples of the ancient world were the Hittites, who inhabited Asia Minor and northern Syria. They are mentioned several times in the Bible. About the year 2000 B.C. they were the leading people in eastern Asia Minor, and in 1750 B.C. they even invaded southern Mesopotamia and sacked the city of Babylon. Although during the sixteenth century B.C. they for a time lost their political power, shortly after 1500 B.C. they created an empire in Asia Minor and extended their sway over the regions to the southeast. Thus they were able to hold in check the Assyrians, who were bent upon conquest again. These Hittites were not Semites, nor do they seem to have been closely related to such peoples as the Sumerians or Egyptians. Their language was Indo-European (Aryan), which is also true of the Persian language. Originally they seem to have inhabited the plains to the north of the Black and Caspian seas. They resembled the Kassites. They were ruled by a king, whose power was not nearly so great as that of the Babylonian or Sumerian kings. Their military organization was highly developed, for which reason they were able to hold the Assyrians so long in check. From the peoples of Mesopotamia they borrowed the cuneiform script. Some of their records show that they used to make treaties with the rulers of Egypt. They seem to have been the first people in the ancient world to have developed the iron industry, and it was from them that the Assyrians learned to use iron in the manufacture of weapons.

What the Assyrians Learned From the Hittites. Before 1500 B.C. the Assyrians had been dependent upon copper supply, but copper was not nearly so hard and durable as was iron. The Assyrians also learned from the Hittites an interesting style of architecture used in the construction of royal palaces. These palaces were built of brick and stone, and had a porch provided with numerous columns flanked by two square towers. On both sides of the entrance there was to be seen a huge stone figure of a lion, while the porch was also decorated with sculptures in relief.

Political History to 650 B.C. From 1785 to 1169 B.C. Mesopotamia was largely dominated by the Kassites. But during the twelfth century B.C. the Assyrians were favored by a number of circumstances which enabled them not only to secure complete independence, but to build an empire of their own. At that time the Hittites and the Egyptians were declining, and the Kassites were easily overthrown. Now the Assyrians with their improved arms and renewed ambitions conquered the whole of Mesopotamia and northern Syria. During the next four centuries they also extended their rule over the region directly to the north of

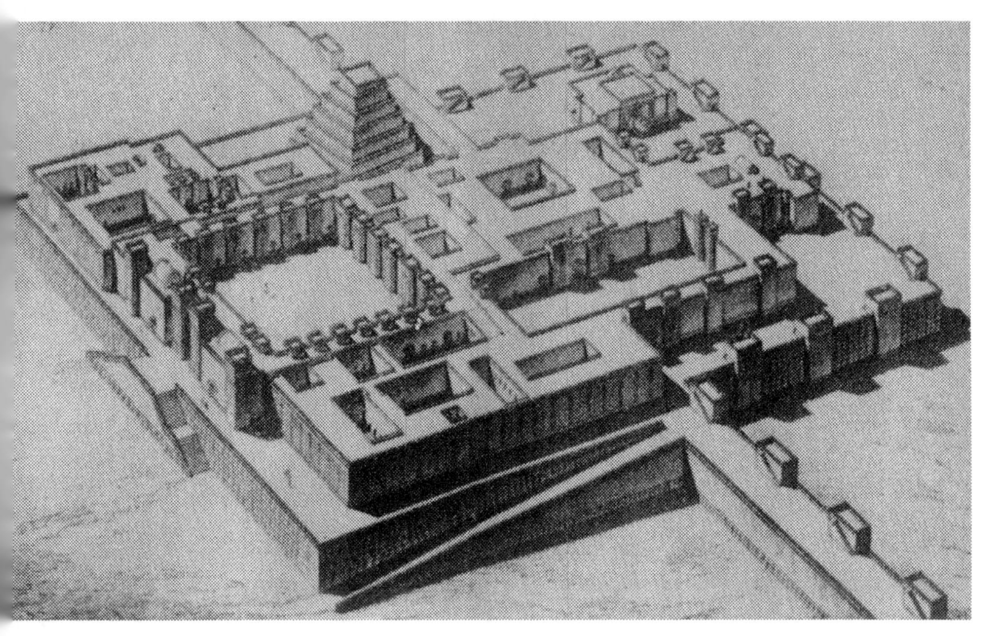

RECONSTRUCTION OF AN ASSYRIAN PALACE AT NINEVEH

AN AERIAL VIEW OF THE PERSEPOLIS TERRACE

Mesopotamia, while during the seventh century B.C. they even ruled Egypt for a short time. From about 750 B.C. to 650 B.C. Assyria was the greatest power in the ancient Near East. In 722 B.C. the Assyrians conquered the kingdom of Israel, as we saw, and in the reign of Sargon II (722-705 B.C.) about 200,000 persons were deported from conquered countries to Mesopotamia, including many Hebrews.

DECLINE AND FALL OF ASSYRIA. During the second half of the seventh century B.C. the Assyrians suddenly underwent a swift decline, ending with the fall of their great capital Nineveh in 612 B.C. and the total destruction of the state in 606 B.C.

THE GOVERNMENT OF THE ASSYRIAN EMPIRE. Unlike the ancient Babylonians and Egyptians, the Assyrians were able to establish a highly efficient government of the conquered lands. The administration of the provinces was excellent. The king established a royal postal service, and was kept in constant touch with the conquered territories through the official letters and reports. The king of Assyria established an absolute form of government. His officials were responsible to him alone, while he as civil ruler and as head of the priesthood was not responsible to the people at large but only to the national god who was called Ashur. Although many of the cities enjoyed a large amount of local independence (*autonomy*), they were nevertheless firmly ruled by the national administration.

ECONOMIC DEVELOPMENTS. Since Assyria was a large state in which a relatively small amount of land could be cultivated, most of the wealth of Assyria was owned in and near the city of Nineveh, the great capital. Commerce was extensive, but was carried on for the most part by foreigners. The Assyrians preferred to attend to agricultural duties. Like the Spaniards of a later age, they preferred to have commerce and industry administered by despised industrial workers. The Aramaeans, most of whom lived in Syria and were related to the Jews, were the traders of the empire. Much of the land was held by the king who donated a part of it to his officers and the temples, as well as to some of the city-states, where a large number of free farmers or peasants also held land of their own. Moreover, there were serfs, as in Egypt, who received the use of lands partly in return for labor and partly in the form of one-third of the crops they produced on these lands.

ASSYRIAN ART OF WARFARE. One reason why the Assyrians paid so little attention to commerce was that as a rule they were very busy with the arts of warfare. They employed both infantry and cavalry, but no longer used the old unwieldly chariot. Their soldiers were armed with lances, swords, bows and arrows, breast plates, helmets and shields. They developed great skill in attacking fortified cities. Since such cities as a rule were surrounded by walls made of brick, they were easily torn down. Unspeakable cruelties attended the seizure of cities and rural districts. The Assyrian Empire was truly built on military rule.

LEARNING AND ART. In keeping with the huge size of the Assyrian Empire, the rulers saw fit to have enormous palaces and temples constructed. These were built upon a stone foundation, but the structure itself was made of brick, although the columns were of stone. From the Babylonians they learned the use of the arch in the art in building, but used it much more extensively than the Babylonians themselves had done. The palaces contained a number of courts, each of which was surrounded by a large number of rooms. Within the central enclosure there was built a great tower temple. The building as a whole was fortified with heavy walls and the customary towers and gates. Assyrian sculpture is not very good, for the figures of human beings seem stiff and clumsy. On the other hand, great skill was displayed in depicting animals, particularly lions. Even so, this work was no more than an imitation of what had been done in Babylonia two thousand years before. Their writing was also an imitation of the Babylonian, while afterwards the Assyrians imitated the Aramaeans. But they surpassed the Babylonians in the size of their libraries that their kings built. From the library of King Assur-bani-pal 22,000 tablets have been recovered.

ASSYRIAN RELIGION. In the field of religion also the Assyrians failed to make progress. They adopted the Babylonian god Marduk, but retained their own god Ashur, and they worshiped fewer gods than the Babylonians. The priests in Assyria had much less power than those in Babylonia, because the king concentrated religious functions in his own hands for the most part. Like the Babylonians and the Egyptians, the Assyrians believed that the spirits of the dead remained for a long time near the corpses. Nevertheless, they made use of *cremation,* that is, they burned many of the dead bodies. It would not be hard for you to prove why their religious beliefs were so foolish and why God destroyed their empire so soon.

Student Activities

1. What is a city-state? Do we still have independent cities?
2. What is a *letter of credit?* Why do people have checking accounts at the banks?
3. Read 2 Samuel, Ch. 11,6. Who was Uriah? Why are the Hittites called a *mysterious* people? Note: The Hittites are mentioned in the Bible, but since no remnants of them were available for a long time, some people were inclined to believe that they had never existed. However, in the last twenty years much has been discovered concerning these people. This shows again that the Bible is always right.
4. Why were the Assyrians successful in establishing a powerful state?
5. Where in the Bible is the city of Nineveh mentioned in connection with a disobedient prophet?
6. Make a list of the peoples mentioned in this chapter.
7. What was the chief fault in Assyrian sculpture?
8. What did the Assyrians use for writing material?
9. Why do you suppose the Assyrians took the lion as a favorite subiect in their art?
10. Would you call the religion of the Assyrians *idolatry?* Why?
11. Why did God destroy the Assyrian Empire?

CHAPTER 7

The Story of New Babylonia and the Persian Empire

POLITICAL HISTORY OF BABYLONIA AFTER ITS REVIVAL IN 625 B.C. At one time, as you learned, Babylonia was a powerful state, but it had been ruled by several other countries after its decline about 1800 B.C. The last country to govern it had been Assyria, but in 625 B.C. Babylonia became independent again. The Babylonians were led by the father of the famous king Nebuchadnezzar, who became king in his turn in 604 B.C. It was Nebuchadnezzar who in 587 B.C. appeared with a huge army before Jerusalem and after a siege of eight months took the city. He captured thousands of Jews who were led away into Babylonia. But his state did not long survive his death, for in 538 B.C. it fell before the army of the Persians. You will remember the Bible story of the great festival the Babylonians were having one day when suddenly a hand wrote strange words upon a wall which were interpreted by the prophet Daniel to mean that the city had been condemned by God because of the many sins of the people. Thus another nation was swept off the face of the earth to prove that God will not tolerate for more than a certain time the wickedness of a sinful people.

THE CITY OF BABYLON IN THE REIGN OF NEBUCHADNEZZAR. At this time (604-561 B.C.) the city had a population of half a million and its walls had a circumference of thirteen miles. The outer wall, built of brick, was eighty-five feet thick; no wonder that the Babylonians could not understand how their city was doomed just because they were wicked! Like the great American cities of our day, the streets crossed each other at right angles. Imposing in particular was the huge palace of Nebuchadnezzar, the courtyard of which alone measured 193 by 180 feet, and one of the rooms 171 by 56 feet. The building was constructed of glazed (enameled) brick, but even more wonderful in the eyes of visitors from foreign lands were the so-called Hanging Gardens, which were roof gardens in the form of terraces. Here were grown magnificent plants and tropical flowers. Another great structure was the Temple of Marduk near which was constructed a temple tower upon a platform three hundred feet square.

BABYLONIAN CIVILIZATION ABOUT 550 B.C. Babylon was again the largest and most prosperous city in the world. Commerce reached a height never seen in Mesopotamia before. All the luxuries of the ancient Near East were brought together in this one city. Side by side with the thousands upon thousands of slaves and down-trodden free laborers, there existed a class of society which was bitterly criticized by some of the Hebrew prophets. The latter claimed that the city was doomed because of their luxurious and wicked mode of living.

POLITICAL HISTORY OF PERSIA. The Persians originally lived on the plateau east of Mesopotamia called Iran. About the year 550 B.C. they were led by a great ruler called Cyrus the Great. But they were still allied with and dominated by the Medes. In 549 B.C. Cyrus overthrew the Median government and seized its capital. Now the Persians became the masters of the Medes. In 539 B.C. Cyrus attacked Babylon, which fell in the next year. Upon his death in 529 B.C. his son Cambyses succeeded him. The latter made a conquest of Egypt in 525 B.C., something which the Assyrians had never been able to do. Cambyses was succeeded in turn by Darius (521-485 B.C.), who is chiefly known for his attempted conquest of the Greek city-states.

THE RISE AND FALL OF LYDIA. When in 546 B.C. King Cyrus conquered the kingdom of Lydia in Asia Minor, he found there one of the most remarkable states of the ancient world. Here lived a king of great wealth called Croesus, whose name is still used when reference is made to persons of exceedingly great wealth. It was the first country to establish the use of a coinage. The Lydians, like the Persians, belonged to an Indo-European race, and not to the Semitic race. They had succeeded the Hittites as the dominating power in Asia Minor. It was during the eighth century B.C. that the Lydians invented the use of metalic coinage, which differed from the gold and silver bars used by Assyrians and other merchants in that they were stamped with a statement saying that the government guaranteed the correct weight and purity of the metal used in making the coins. The first coins seem to have been made from gold and silver melted with some alloy. The standard gold coin of Lydia was called the *stater*. Being so busy with the making of money and the extension of commerce, the Lydians had failed to make a strong defense against the coming Persians, and so it naturally happened that their kingdom was quickly destroyed by King Cyrus.

THE GOVERNMENT OF THE PERSIAN EMPIRE. Establishing peace and order in an unwieldly state stretching from the borders of India to the waters of the Aegean Sea and the lands beyond the river Nile, was a difficult task. But the Assyrians had led the way in empire building and in the excellent administration of conquered provinces. The Persians improved on the system of the Assyrians, with the result that for more than two hundred years all the dominions were firmly held together by the Persian ruler in his capital called Susa, or Persepolis. One reason for the success of the Persian administration was that the conquered peoples enjoyed religious toleration. Moreover, taxes were carefully levied and commerce and industry were promoted by the central government. The king was a monarch, who said that he was responsible only to the chief god, which in the case of the Persians was Ahura-Mazda. This was not unusual, for an oriental king; even Hammurabi had followed this course. But the king was careful to consult his chief ministers, and he paid attention to local customs everywhere. The administration of justice and the collection of taxes was humane and just. This can not be said of the Assyrian rulers, for which reason no doubt their rule did not last so long as that of the Persians. The empire was divided into 21 provinces, called satrapies, each of which was ruled by a governor or satrap. This governor had military powers only in case of war, for it was held that the civil administration could not be combined in the hands of one governor with the military administration. The central administration sent regular inspectors to the different provinces, and it also maintained a secretary in each of them.

THE PERSIAN ARMY. The success of the Persian administration lay more in its efficient administration than in the strength of its army. The armed forces were collected from the various subject races throughout the empire, and formed units of ten thousand each, which in turn were divided into units of one thousand each. The officers naturally were Persians and Medes, so that they would be able to prevent rebellion of the soldiers.

THE PERSIAN NAVY AND MERCHANT MARINE. After the conquest of the western shores of Asia Minor and Syria, and a part of the eastern shores of the Balkan Peninsula, the Persians developed a huge navy, made up of 1000 Greek and Phoenician ships. A merchant marine was also developed, and explorers were induced to venture forth along the coasts of India. In Egypt navigation was restored between the Nile and the city at the head of the Red Sea called Suez. The military and naval strength of the empire was considerably enlarged by a fine system of roads and bridges. Along the roads were constructed relay stations and inns for the use of the garrisons that had to be stationed at various important points.

PERSIAN CIVILIZATION. The Persians resembled the Assyrians in that they were too intent on imperial administration to foster the fine arts and sciences. Their architecture and sculpture were merely an imitation of Babylonian and Assyrian patterns. From the Egyptians the Persians learned the use of *colonnades,* that is, a row of columns, or pillars. They also received from Egypt the solar calendar. Perhaps their greatest palace was that constructed in the city of Persepolis, which was built on a platform introduced by a huge stairway. This stairway, three hundred feet in length, was the most imposing one in the ancient Orient of which we have any knowledge. Impressive also was the beautiful gateway and the fine colonnade.

THE PERSIAN RELIGION. The Persians exhibited great originality in the development of their religion. Although at first they worshiped many gods (*polytheism*), in the seventh or sixth century B.C. a great religious reformer appeared in their midst, who was known as Zoroaster or Zarathustra. He explained to his followers in Persia that the worship of the sun, which had been common among them, was just as bad as the worship of the moon, which had been prevalent in such cities as Ur, as we saw. Zoroaster accepted the widely accepted belief in the existence of evil and good spirits, which had been supported not only in Egypt but also in Babylonia. According to Zoroaster, God had created the world for the purpose of providing for human beings a stage upon which powers of good and evil would oppose each other. In other words, human beings would be put through a school of training upon this earth, and they would be free to listen to either the good or the evil spirits. The latter in turn were guided by a high power, which in the case of the good spirits was the god called Ahura-Mazda.

THE PROMISE OF ETERNAL LIFE. It is interesting to observe that human beings who decided to be good upon this earth, were expected to be rewarded with eternal life, while, on the other hand, the others would be subject to darkness and misery in the realm beyond the gates of death. Some day in the remote future, good would triumph over evil, and the evil god with his evil spirits would be defeated and destroyed. After this contest was over, the earth would vanish, since it had completed its task. Many scholars have thought that this Persian belief was original and exerted much influence upon the Hebrew and Christian religions. But they have overlooked the important passages in the Old Testament concerning the conflict between God and Satan. We know very well that the religious literature left by the Persians can not be compared with the various books that make up the Old Testament. For that reason we must conclude that the influence exerted by the Hebrews upon the Persians was much greater than the influence exerted by the Persians upon the Hebrews.

Student Activities

1. With the aid of a dictionary, if necessary, write out the definitions of *vogue, toleration.*
2. Read Daniel 5. That chapter tells the story of the destruction of Babylonia by the Medes and Persians.
3. What were the "Hanging Gardens" of Babylon?
4. Draw a map of Persia. It is called Iran now.
5. Write a fifty word summary on Lydia.
6. How was the government carried on under the Persian kings?
7. What are "strategic points"?
8. Who was Zoroaster or Zarathustra? What is a "Mazda" lamp?
9. Where did the Persians probably get their idea of the struggle between good and evil?
10. God brought the Hebrews in contact with many peoples. Why?
11. Make a list of the empires of the Mesopotamia which you have studied thus far. Note that the Persian Empire exceeded all the previous empires of Mesopotamia in size and influence. In your study you will soon go over to Europe, and the center of gravity will shift from Egypt and Mesopotamia to Europe.
12. Write out ten important statements on the seven chapters that you have studied so far. What are the great empires of the world at the present time?

CHAPTER 8

Civilization Reaches Europe

EUROPE AND ASIA. The land-mass which we call Europe is the western extension of the vast continent called Eurasia. On a map of the world, Europe does not seem to be a separate continent at all and speaking as geographers might, we would look upon Europe as a mere peninsula of Asia, for Asia is five times as large as Europe. There is no doubt that the inhabitants of ancient Mesopotamia thought of Europe as a region of little importance. They saw no evidence of future greatness for any of the peoples inhabiting this uninviting appendix of Asia.

WHAT THE WORDS "EUROPE" AND "ASIA" MEAN. But about 1000 B.C., when the Phoenicians were sailing the seas far from their native land, they founded colonies along the coasts of the Mediterranean and traded with various peoples. They began to call Europe by a word which means sunset (*Ereb*), because it lay to the west, where the sun always did set. Asia was the land where the sun rose each day, hence it was named by them *Acu*, for sunrise. The Greeks borrowed these words from the Phoenicians, and applied them respectively to the lands west and east of the Aegean Sea. Gradually the meaning of the word Europe (*Europa*) was extended to all of what is now called Europe.

THE EARLIEST SETTLERS OF CRETE. It appears that the first fruits of civilization were brought to Europe from the south, that is, from Egypt. For reasons still unknown to us some Egyptians removed from their native land to the island of Crete, which is located about 400 miles to the northwest of Egypt. Before 2500 B.C. the earliest settlers built their homes in the southern valleys of Crete, where they transplanted Egyptian civilization. They learned to cultivate the soil and to grow the olive tree. Soon a relatively small number of people arrived from Asia Minor, as is indicated by the presence of broad skulls buried in Cretan soil, very similar to those of the earliest inhabitants of western Asia Minor.

CRETAN METALWORK AND POTTERY. As early as 2500 B.C. the Cretans were using tools made out of bronze, the earliest of which they may have imported from Egypt. But they soon discovered rich deposits of bronze on their own island, and they also found good clay for the making of pottery, which, unlike Egyptian and Sumerian pottery of the period between 3000 and 2000 B.C., was not made with the use of the potter's wheel.

WRITING. A graceful form of script was used by the earliest inhabitants, who undoubtedly took with them from Egypt the knowledge of hieroglyphic writing. Afterward the use of pictures in their script was replaced by a form of script which clearly was an imitation of Babylonian writing, for clay tablets were now employed and characters inscribed upon them which resemble the cuneiform writing of Babylonia. Unfortunately the two forms of script have not yet been deciphered by modern scholars.

CRETE'S GOLDEN AGE. The golden age of Cretan civilization lasted from about 1700 to 1400 B.C., when huge palaces were constructed for the kings and when Cretan ships extended the sway of Cretan political power over the islands of the Aegean Sea and the west coast of Asia Minor. In some respects the Cretans surpassed both the Egyptians and the Babylonians, for they invented an excellent system of water supply and drainage.

TROY AND MYCENAE. Among other centers of Cretan civilization may be mentioned the celebrated city of Troy in the northwestern corner of Asia Minor, and Mycenae in southern Greece. Excavations have shown a marked similarity between the culture of the original center, Crete, and those that were dependent on it. They flourished between 1500 and 1200 B.C. Being situated on the mainland, they required heavy fortifications, which are not to be found in Crete. Troy owed much of its prosperity to its position near the present site of Constantinople (Istanbul), where the straits lead from the Black Sea to the Aegean and where the land route connects Europe with Asia. The tolls levied upon commerce must have led to friction with the Greeks, who seem to have carried on a war with Troy, according to the first great Greek writer, Homer.

THE COMING OF THE GREEKS. Unfortunately, the Greeks did more than merely carry on a war with one of the centers of Cretan civilization. They swooped down from the north and practically destroyed the whole of this marvelous culture. But before they completed their destruction, they were able to learn much from their victims. In this manner Greek civilization was born.

The Geography of Greece. The mainland of Greece and the area along the eastern shores of the Aegean Sea, including the Aegean Islands, are noted for their lovely scenery. There are no great plains and valleys, and no large rivers. Many small mountain chains or separate mountains alternate with lovely lowland scenery. While on the slopes of hills and mountains cattle graze, the valleys are fairly fertile and produce fruits and vegetables. Grain was grown in the early periods, but it was soon found that it paid better to plant olive and fig trees, and to raise grapes and currants. Metals were not abundant, but stone for building was plentiful and of the finest quality. The result was that the Greeks, who arrived from northern countries as barbarians, became builders of beautiful temples and palaces, carved perfect statues out of stone and marble, and wrote very fine pieces of literature.

Greek Migrations. The Greeks arrived in successive waves of migrations between 1200 and 900 B.C. They soon were divided into two groups, the Ionians, who occupied most of the islands in the Aegean Sea and the major portion of the west coast of Asia Minor; and the Dorians, who settled the mainland to the west, the southern islands in the Aegean Sea, and the southwest corner of Asia Minor.

Greek Civilization Versus Christianity. From late medieval times until the beginning of the twentieth century (1350 to 1900) it was customary for leading scholars in the western world to assume that the Greeks created a world civilization of their own, in almost complete independence of Egypt and ancient Mesopotamia. Even in the United States there was a time when children in the public schools no longer were brought up on Bible stories and no longer learned to read from the Bible but received as their daily fare the mythology of the Greeks. The sources of Greek civilization were almost completely ignored and the Christian religion was reduced to a position of little importance.

Recent Excavations Have Revealed the Sources of Greek Civilization. How fortunate we are to be living in an age when excavations have revealed the true story of Greek civilization, which, as we shall see, was the continuation of older cultures, modified by a new race of people.

The Kingdoms. Between 1000 and 800 B.C. the Greeks founded a large number of independent city-states, each ruled by a king. These little states consisted as a rule of a number of small settlements, or villages which had united for a common purpose of defense and orderly government. Very often a fortified spot or a strong position on a hill was chosen as the center of the state, which the Greeks called the *polis*. From this word we have derived our word "politics." Most of these little states, ranging in size from about twenty to five hundred square miles, had at the head a king, though in parts of the mainland of Greece tribal states continued to exist for centuries after 1000 B.C. Altogether there were several hundred city-states by 700 B.C.

THE ARISTOCRACIES.   Between 800 and 700 B.C. a class of nobles grew to power in many of the city-states, overthrew the rule of the king, and set up an aristocratic form of government.

COLONIZATION.   At the same time the rapid increase in population resulted in migration of discontented inhabitants to lands beyond the sea or along the coasts not so far away. In this manner numerous colonies were founded to the north as far as the coasts of the Black Sea, to the south in northern Africa, and to the west in southern Italy, eastern Sicily, and the southern coast of what is now France. This colonizing movement continued until the opening of the fifth century B.C. It did not result in the building of a colonial empire, but each colony became a new city-state, allied with the mother-state at home in Hellas, as the Greeks called their native country.

ECONOMIC PROGRESS.   This colonization movement led to the establishment of a merchant marine and the rapid development of commerce and industry. The Greeks now became independent in commerce, while formerly they had been served by the Phoenicians. From the Lydians in Asia minor they acquired their coinage, of which the largest unit was called the *talent,* which was equal to 6000 *drachmas.*

THE MIDDLE CLASS AND SLAVERY.   The rapid growth of commerce and industry was accompanied by the establishment of prosperous classes of people whom we would call the middle class. They were responsible for the introduction of slavery, for they needed more workmen than the native population could supply, and so they imported slaves from Asia Minor, and later from other regions as well. This middle class asked for a share in the government, which was now in the control of the aristocracy.

TYRANTS, OR DICTATORS, RULE THE GREEKS.   A contest followed between these two classes which caused revolutions and disorders, so that dictators appeared who restored order. These dictators were called *tyrants* and their rule *tyrannies.* They often ruled ably and assisted in the rise of art and learning, for they had the means with which to employ artists and scholars. But their unjust rule did not appeal to the average Greek citizen, and so after 550 B.C. the dictatorship rapidly disappeared, having lasted but a century and a half (about 650 to 500 B.C.). It was the third form of government we have noted thus far, the first having been the monarchy from 1000 to 800 B.C., the second the aristocracy, from 800 to 650 B.C., the third the dictatorship. Among the greatest of dictators may be mentioned Solon, the lawgiver of Athens, who about 590 B.C. formed an excellent system of government for this state. He was one of the leading scholars who provided codes of law for their city-states.

GREEKS AND "BARBARIANS." The period from 1000 to 550 B.C. may be termed the age of Greek infancy, an age in which the beginnings were made of a great civilization, when the Greeks, taught by their more highly cultured neighbors to the east and south, adopted new habits and thoughts. Slowly coming out of a state of semi-barbarism, they afterwards came to look upon all other races as "barbarians," which was the term they applied to these peoples of the ancient world. Little did they realize then how much they owed to the Egyptians, the Sumerians, the Hebrews, and the Phoenicians. And it took the modern world several hundred years to discover how it had been deceived by these conceited Greeks!

Student Activities

1. Explain the origin of the words: *Europe* and *Asia.*
2. Locate the Island of Crete on a map of Europe and draw it.
3. Have you ever read the story of King Minos and his Minotaur? Who was the hero of that story?
4. Who was Homer? Ask your teacher to tell you about the Trojan War. Some of the mythical heroes of the Trojan War are: Ulysses, the clever, Nestor, the old, Argus, the many eyed. What was the Trojan Horse?
5. What are the outstanding features of the geography of Greece?
6. What is Greek mythology?
7. Explain what a Greek *Tyrant* was?
8. What is the origin of the term, *Barbarian?* What does that word mean at the present time?
9. Who was Solon?
10. You will perhaps have noted that occasionally the newspapers call our law-makers at Washington or at the state capitols *Solons.* Why?
11. What peoples were the teachers of the Greeks? Sometimes nations feel that they are superior to all their neighbors. While there are differences between nations as well as individuals, in many respects, yet before God they are all alike. They have all been redeemed by the precious blood of the Son of God.

CHAPTER 9

The Golden Age of Greece (500-150 B.C.)

THE RISE OF ATHENS AND SPARTA. Shortly after 500 B.C. two city-states in Greece rose to a position of great power and wealth. They were Sparta, the largest of all the states, with an area of about 3300 square miles, and Athens, which was about 1000 square miles in size. The total population of that part of Greece, which included the city of Athens, was about 280,000. Among these were about 80,000 slaves. The number of free citizens was about 40,000. Sparta had a free popultaion of only 15,000, but a total population of about 300,000, of whom about 180,000 were slaves, called *helots,* and about 100,000 allied subjects.

THE COMING OF THE PERSIAN INVADERS. The fifth century B.C. opened with a dangerous period for the Greeks. Across the valleys and along the shores of Asia Minor there approached a huge army sent by the king of the Persians. With the aid of about six hundred vessels, the Persians were able to cross the straits and enter European territory. They marched successfully southward until they reached the place called Marathon, about twenty-four miles to the northeast of Athens. Here they were defeated by a force of Athenian soldiers, about ten thousand men in number. Now followed ten years of peace, which passed all too soon.

THE PERSIANS ARE FINALLY DEFEATED. In the spring of 480 B.C. the largest army that the ancient world had ever seen, assembled on the northern shores of the Balkan Peninsula. In this hour of danger Athens and Sparta united to ward off the attack of the Persians. But at first it seemed as if complete victory awaited the great Persian host, which according to some Greek historians numbered more than one million men. As the Persians drew closer to Athens, the population fled. Now the Persian soldiers invaded the doomed city, and promptly destroyed it. But this was not the end, for in the same year, 480 B.C., the Greeks fought the naval battle of Salamis, in which the fleet of the Persians suffered complete disaster. In the next year followed the defeat of the Persian army at Plataea. This defeat for the Persians ended the conflict between Persia and Greece for the time being.

RIVALRY BETWEEN ATHENS AND SPARTA. No sooner had the Persian danger been overcome than a rivalry broke out between Athens and Sparta. In the war which they fought from 431 to 404 B.C., Athens was completely defeated by the Spartans and was forced to join Sparta. Within the next fifty years Sparta itself was defeated by a rival city-state in Greece, called Thebes.

OTHER WARS FOLLOW. Even that was not enough for the foolish Greeks. They kept on fighting among themselves and so became very weak. About 350 B.C. there arrived from the north an army led by Phillip II, the king of Macedonia. Taking advantage of the civil wars fought by the Greek city-states, the Macedonian king in a short time was able to conquer the whole of the peninsula to the south of his own country. Before Philip II died in the year of 336 B.C., he was pleased to see that Macedonia had taken the place of Sparta and Athens as a leading state.

THE CONQUESTS OF ALEXANDER THE GREAT. Now followed the reign of Philip's son, Alexander the Great, who was the greatest general in the history of the ancient world. Beginning with the conquest of Asia Minor in 334 B.C., Alexander and his army of about 35,000 soldiers won victory after victory, until they overthrew the whole of the Persian Empire. They even occupied Egypt, which fell in 332 B. C. Here, on one of the western arms of the Nile, Alexander founded the city of Alexandria, which was to become one of the greatest cities of the civilized world. In 331 B.C. Alexander won a decisive victory at Arbela, and now he had conquered an area of about two million square miles, almost equal to the whole United States of today. With an army of 50,000 men he had defeated a Persian host of more than a million soldiers. Thus he showed his military skill.

HIS ABILITY AND CHARACTER. With great ability he was always able to foresee events long before they occurred. He maintained an iron discipline, and he possessed a great power with which to govern other men by the tens of thousands. If only he were able now to master his own will power and his disorderly mind, he might live to attain old age and to rule all the civilized world for half a century more. But in June of the year 323 B.C., after a night of feasting and drinking, he contracted a serious illness and died at the age of thirty-three. His sudden death left his huge empire without a capable successor, and before long it began to decline.

THE SPREAD OF GREEK CUSTOMS AND LANGUAGE.   In spite of the short duration of Alexander's empire, he and his soldiers spread wherever they went the seeds of Greek culture and the use of the Greek language.   Along the roads and valleys that he followed, he built Greek cities and peopled them with Greek colonists The Greek language became the literary language of the whole Near East, including Asia Minor, Syria, and Egypt.

DIVISION AND FALL OF THE EMPIRE.   Alexander's empire was divided shortly after his death into three large states, the kingdom of Macedonia in Europe, the Empire of the Seleucids in western Asia, and the Empire of the Ptolemies in Egypt.   In addition to these three large states, an independent state was founded in northwestern Asia Minor and was called Pergamon.   But within a century after the death of Alexander the Great a new power arose to the west of Macedonia.   On the Italian Peninsula was built the Roman Republic, which, after having united Italy by the year 265 B.C., turned its attention to the east and in 196 B.C. conquered Macedonia.   Not content with this victory, the Romans went still farther eastward and in 189 B.C. overthrew the Seleucid Empire.   Although the Romans were slow to annex the conquered states in the East, they did finally in 148 B.C. turn the former state of Macedonia, including Greece itself, into a Roman province. In the year 133 B.C. the king of Pergamon deeded his country to the rulers of the Roman Republic.   Finally, in 30 B. C. Egypt was annexed by Rome, and thus the last remnant of the great empire of Alexander the Great became the possesion of the new Empire founded by the Romans.

GREEK GOVERNMENT.   Now that we have finished our story of the political history of the Greeks, we are prepared to study their political institutions.   You will remember that during the course of the fifth century B. C. the rule established by the tyrants was followed by a limited form of democracy.   Athens was the leader in this development.   Inspired by the brilliant mind of Pericles, the 40,000 free citizens of Athens developed a remarkable form of government, which may be described as a direct democracy.   Everyone of the 40,000 free citizens was permitted to cast his vote in the popular assembly, which used to meet ten times a year, but afterwards the number of meetings was increased to forty a year. Athens did not have a representative government, for every citizen represented himself in the national assembly.   This assembly possessed not only legislative power but also judicial and administrative. It elected nine civil officials, called archons, as well as the ten generals.

A VIEW OF THE ACROPOLIS AT ATHENS

RUINS OF A GREEK THEATER AT SYRACUSE, IN SICILY

THE JURY SYSTEM. Since there were no lawyers and judges in the proper sense of the word, cases were tried by juries. These juries were made up of the free citizens and as a rule were very large, the average number being 501 members. The jurymen voted by secret ballot.

THE ASSEMBLIES AND VOTING. In addition to the large assembly, there also existed a smaller body, which was the Council of Five Hundred. The members of this council, the jurymen, and all state-officials were chosen by lot, the only exception being in the case of the generals, who were appointed for their particular bravery, honesty, and efficiency. A peculiar custom in Athens was the so-called *ostracism,* which enabled the free citizens to dispose of undesirable officials. If a minimum number of 6,000 citizens voted for the exile of an unwanted official, he lost his position. They marked his name on a piece of pottery called *ostrakon,* hence the word *ostracism.*

COMPARISON BETWEEN GREEK DEMOCRACY AND MODERN DEMOCRACY. The form of government which was developed during the sixth century B.C. in the city-state of Athens was by no means a democracy such as the modern world has known. Only 40,000 citizens out of a total population of nearly 300,000 were permitted to vote. Furthermore, the choice by lot and the custom called ostracism were peculiarities which do not resemble anything known in our modern democratic countries today.

THE GOVERNMENT OF SPARTA. Remarkable though the government of Athens was, even more remarkable was that established in the city-state of Sparta. Here, as we saw, there were only about 15,000 free citizens. They were ruled by two kings, who were assisted by five officials, called *ephors,* and elected by the popular assembly. This assembly was made up only of adult Spartans who actually performed military service for the state.

HOW THE PEOPLE LIVED AND WORKED. We might well term the Spartan government a form of state socialism, for the free Spartan, although he had a family and owned a house, could not provide a living for his own family nor live in his own home for any length of time. The state gave him a piece of land upon which slaves, called *helots,* worked. These slaves supported the warrior's family with their labor, since he himself was obliged to spend nearly all his time in military training or active service. His training really began at his birth, for all male babies were carefully examined shortly after their birth by a board of government officials. Those who were not deemed fit for military service were left to die somewhere in a glen or other deserted spot in the country. The healthy male babies were permitted to remain with their mothers at home and sometimes in the care of nurses appointed by the state until the boys reached the age of seven. Then they were removed to a military camp where they were trained for a period of twelve years. At the end of this period they joined some military club and received further training. When they reached the age of thirty they were permitted to vote.

How the Girls Were Treated. Even girl babies were born into the service of the state. It was considered of the utmost importance that women be as healthy as possible, so girls were constantly assisted by government officials. Since women were necessary and served the state in a useful capacity, they were treated as the equals of the men, except that they were not permitted to vote nor regarded fit for military service. Their function was to take care of their families, and so it followed naturally that they also were not required to serve in the capacity of rulers.

Military Power of Sparta. As a result the Spartan armies could not be defeated for more than two hundred years (600 to 400 B.C.), and the Spartans were admired by all the Greeks for their valor and strength, though no other Greek state desired to imitate them. Besides, Sparta failed to produce a great culture such as that which made Athens immortal.

How Women Were Treated in Athens. On the other hand, in Athens, the center of an astonishing culture, women were treated as far inferior to the men. They were not permitted to move about freely in society, and even in their homes they were regarded as mere servants of the men. What is perhaps still worse, in both Athens and Sparta the slaves were often given cruel treatment. Greek civilization at its very height of glory was spoiled by injustice.

Taxation. The expenses incurred by the governments of the Greek city-states were met by revenues which were regularly and efficiently collected for the government by private companies. The latter paid a fixed sum to the government in return for the rentals on lands owned by the state and harbor dues collected at the ports from shipping. The government did not levy taxes on income or on real estate, and whenever lack of money appeared to endanger the efficiency of the state, members of the more wealthy classes were often expected to render services free of charge.

SLAVERY. None of the Greek city-states was what we would consider wealthy. Agriculture was always an important source of wealth, but it never could supply the population with enough capital, such as was the case in ancient Egypt or Babylonia. Furthermore, commerce and industry did not give rise to such huge cities as Babylon or Nineveh. The average business establishment in Athens employed but ten slaves; at the height of its prosperity, the city witnessed certain establishments growing to such proportions as to engage up to forty slaves. One firm is known to have employed 120 men in the making of shields. The slaves took the place of our modern machinery. Some had been bought by the merchant class in foreign lands, others had been captured in wars, and still others had in primitive times lost their personal liberty as a result of debts incurred. It was the custom of the master to work side by side with his slaves or free help.

HOW BUSINESS WAS CONDUCTED. Merchants often cooperated in chartering (renting) vessels for their business ventures. They were sometimes in need of capital and occasionally would borrow money from bankers at fixed rates of interest ranging from ten to twenty percent. But checks and drafts were not used. Since manufactured goods were usually sold at or in front of the shops, the merchant class was engaged largely in the export and import trade. They exported marble, olive oil, figs, furniture, pottery, woven goods, and articles made of bronze or iron. Among the products they imported were grain, cheese, dried fish, meat, wine, perfumes, spices, carpets, and tiles. They also brought to the Greek towns such raw materials as iron, lumber, ivory, hides, flax, and wool.

SHIPPING. The trade on land was handicapped by the lack of good roads, showing that it was not the policy of the governments to encourage commerce. Consequently, the foreign trade was carried on mostly by way of the sea, for which purpose two types of vessels were employed, the small boats for coastwise shipping, measuring about fifteen tons, and the larger vessels which could carry burdens of 350 tons. The vessels were propelled by oarsmen seated in rows and these were aided by sails in favorable weather. The trip from Athens to Crete, a distance of 170 miles, required about two days and a half. Seldom did the captain of the ship venture far enough from the shore to be out of sight from the land. Primitive sea maps were available, but no compass; also no lighthouses until about 250 B.C. The most famous of these was the lighthouse constructed at Alexandria in Egypt, which was built of stone, three stories in height with an altitude of 370 feet. A fire of wood was kept burning at night, visible perhaps as far as 30 miles. After 300 B.C. vessels became rather large, the largest being the famous ship called the *Syracuse,* with the astonishing capacity of 3900 tons for cargo space alone, and rooms for passengers and a crew of 600 men. Its total size was 5000 tons, as compared with a tonnage of 125 for the ship that led Columbus' tiny fleet in 1492.

THE CITY OF ALEXANDRIA. Another fact worth noting is that no city in early modern times could equal in size and wealth the port of Alexandria from 200 to 30 B.C. It had a population of about one million, and saw at its harbor ships from all parts of the Mediterranean Sea, and even from countries as far to the west as the British Isles, and as far to the east as India. Its streets, unlike those of Paris or London before the nineteenth century, were laid out with great care as to the needs of traffic and the beauty of the entire city. The streets intersected each other at right angles, and were crossed here and there by boulevards. Very different was ancient Athens or Sparta, both in size or in the appearance of the streets. The first city in Greece to have been laid out in a fashion like that followed in Alexandria was Piraeus, the harbor of Athens, when it was rebuilt. It was never more than a small town when compared with Alexandria, though not seldom it has received more attention in history courses than Egypt's mighty port.

CLOTHING WORN BY THE GREEKS. In examining for a moment the clothes worn by the Greeks in classical times (500 to 300 B.C.), we again remember the age in which the Greeks as a people lived. Their men and women were dressed very much as were other civilized persons in the Near East. Each wore a garment without sleeves called *tunic,* that was fastened about the shoulders with a clasp or a button. It hung loosely and gracefully upon one's body, permitting freedom of action. It might be made of wool or linen, in accordance with the change in the seasons.

Student Activities

1. With the aid of a dictionary, if necessary, write out the definitions for the following words: *invincible, capital, intersected.*
2. Write a short essay on how the Greeks defeated the Persians.
3. Who was Alexander the Great?
4. Explain the jury system of ancient Greece. How many people are on a jury at the present time?

5. The Greeks permitted babies to die because they were not physically perfect. Which commandment forbids that practice? Why did the Greeks do that? Why is that not done at the present time?
6. Which Greek state treated the women the worst?
7. How long were the small Spartan armies unbeatable? Why?
8. What did the Greeks use in place of our modern machinery?
9. Thomas Jefferson in our Declaration of Independence used the phrase, "All men are created free and equal." Did the Greeks believe that? Prove your answer.
10. What is meant by "Export" and "Import" trade? Name a number of products which the United States imports.
11. How did the Greeks propel their boats?
12. Which was the most famous port from 200 to 30 B.C.?
13. Describe the clothing of the Greeks.
14. Why is this chapter entitled, "The Golden Age of Greece?"
15. Why was it easy for Phillip II of Macedonia to conquer the Greeks?

CHAPTER 10

Greek Art, Literature, Science, Philosophy, and Religion

Art. The Greek arts were developed partly as an imitation of Egyptian and Babylonian masters and models, but they showed signs of independence on the part of the Greeks. Since stone and marble were to be found in abundance, the Greeks freely used them, though private dwellings continued in many cases to be built of sun-dried brick, as was also the case in ancient Mesopotamia. The Greek temples were very beautiful, though they were not so large as some of the buildings constructed by the Assyrians or the Persians. The use of the column was also not new. The typical Greek temple was made up of a rectangular hall, at the ends of which were placed one or two rows of columns, while sometimes columns also stood along the sides of the building. Occasionally porches were provided as well. The hall and porches were covered with a roof made of wooden beams and protected from the elements with tiles.

Architecture. The earliest style is the Dorian, and the most famous example the Parthenon built on the hill at Athens called the Acropolis. A little later the Ionic structure was developed, marked by a more slender column, which was adorned with a spiral roll near the top (the capital). A superb example is the temple of Diana (Artemis) at Ephesus, which was considered one of the Seven Wonders of the world.[1] The third style is the Corinthian; it grew out of the Ionic and is more complex than the two earlier kinds.[2]

Sculpture. Greek sculpture, even more than the architecture, shows the high qualities of the arts developed by the Greeks. They

---

1. The other six were: (1) the pyramids in Egypt, (2) the Hanging Gardens in Babylon, (3) the lighthouse at Alexandria on the island of Pharos, mentioned above, (4) the statue of Zeus by Phidias, (5) the Colossus at Rhodes, a bronze statue of the sun god, 100 feet high, (6) the Mausoleum at Halicarnassus, built for King Mausolus (died 353 B.C.) by his widow.
2. The best example of this type is the Choragic Monument of Lysicrates at Athens.

66

were one of the few peoples in the anicent world who were not dominated by religion, but applied themselves whole-heartedly to the things of "this world." Consequently, they freely portrayed the nude human body, depicted with ardor the beauties of nature, and used their active imagination. Taught by the country in which they found themselves, they developed the motto of "Nothing in excess, and everything in proportion." They combined simple lines with proper proportions. They also were true to nature, patient, and full of joy, free from restraint and superstition. For these reasons their statues and other figures carved out of stone and marble, as well as those made out of bronze, gold, and silver, are superior to nearly all similar productions of other peoples in the ancient or medieval world. Their greatest sculptor, Phidias, perfected the huge statue of the goddess Athena which was placed before the Parthenon. Since most of the Greek paintings were destroyed, we can only say that they probably resembled the sculpture in the admirable qualities just mentioned.

LITERATURE. Very remarkable were the contributions made by the Greeks in the field of literature. They used every form now known to us, including the satire,[1] but began with epic poetry through the pen of Homer, whom we may consider as the author of the *Iliad* and the *Odyssey*. However, it seems that he was not the only author of these epic works, but was assisted by others. The two chief writers of lyric poetry were the poet Pindar (about 450 B.C.) and the poetess Sappho (about 600 B.C.).

DRAMA. The Greek drama, both tragedy and comedy, reached its greatest height in the period from 525 to 400 B.C., when the three famous writers, Aeschylus, Sophocles, and Euripides, flourished. Aeschylus was noted for his description of scenes in the Persian Wars, in which he had fought. He was a serious-minded, philosophical person, given over to a sense of duty and patriotism, as may be seen in his masterpiece, *Prometheus Bound*. Perhaps even better known is his *Agamemnon*, in which he tells of the return of a hero from Troy and his murder by his rival, the lover of his own wife. Sophocles was more interested in ordinary human activities and relations than in heroic deeds. His finest work is the *Oedipus Tyrannus*, but it is probable that, since only seven out of perhaps over a hundred of his plays are still extant, some of his lost works even surpass that just mentioned. Euripides wrote plays about the masses of the people, of which we may note his

---

1. This does not mean, however, that we have derived every form of literature from the Greeks, as many admirers of the Greeks in their blind adulation would have us believe.

beautiful work, *Iphigenia Among the Taurians.* Aristophanes composed satires and comedies, including the *Frogs,* in which he satirized Euripides.

ORATORS AND HISTORIANS. The most famous composer of orations was Demosthenes (385-322 B.C.), whose best work was entitled, *On the Crown.* The two greatest of Greek historians were Herodotus and Thucydides, who both lived in the fifth century B.C. Herodotus has left a painstaking work dealing with the Persian Wars, and excellent descriptions of society in the many countries he visited, such as Egypt, Babylonia, and Italy. Thucydides wrote about the civil war between Athens and Sparta. He was much more accurate than his predecessor, Herodotus.

QUALITY OF GREEK LITERATURE. The classical literature of Greece is noted especially for simplicity of expression, realism (a truthful description of things as they really are), and appreciation of beauty and grace, both in the theme and the style. There has never been a people that was able to surpass the Greeks in these respects.

SCIENCE AND MATHEMATICS. But in turning to the fields of science, mathematics, philosophy, and religion, we must be on our guard, for fear that we shall repeat the exaggerated praise that has often in the past been bestowed upon the Greeks. The leading authorities on the history of mathematics are of the opinion that in arithmetic, geometry, and algebra the Greeks of classical times (550-330 B.C.) made very little advance over the Egyptians and the Babylonians, while they did still less with trigonometry. We owe to them, however, the terminology now used in geometry, the methods of proof, and the fundamental principles as expressed so ably in the textbook by Euclid, the *Elements.* A truly great mathematician was Archimedes of Syracuse, who died in 212 B.C. He invented many mechanical devices.

ASTRONOMY. The first of the important Greek astronomers was Thales. In his time (about 585 B.C.) it was known to scholars that the earth has the shape of a sphere, while before 300 B.C. it was understood that the earth revolves on its axis once every twenty-four hours. But this information probably was first known to the scholars to the south and east of Greece. It is not surprising that the first Greek philosopher and astronomer of importance, Thales, lived near the west coast of Asia Minor. In the third century B.C. lived Aristarchus, who developed the theory that the earth moves around the sun, but Euclid later reasoned against it, and so it was dropped as false on his authority.

Scientific Studies in Alexandria. The first of the Egyptian rulers after Alexander the Great founded at Alexandria the celebrated Museum, an institute for the promotion of research. He and his successors also established a great library, which contained more than 500,000 papyrus rolls. Two other libraries were founded at Antioch and Pergamon. In the period between 330 and 30 B.C., which is commonly referred to as the Hellenistic Age, Alexandria surpassed Athens as a center of learning, and Athens continued merely to be a great center of philosophical studies. So we must conclude that the scholarly work done at Alexandria was not entirely the result of Greek civilization, or that it was only a part of Greek culture, though the language of the scholars was Greek and their names Greek.

Medicine, Zoology, and Botany. In medicine and the natural sciences the Greeks were exceptionally successful. Ever since 500 B.C. the nature and the symptoms of diseases were carefully studied. Schools of medicine were established, among them that of the famous expert, Hippocrates, who insisted that medicine should be regarded as a serious occupation. His high ideals are repeated in the "Oath of Hippocrates," accepted even today by our physicians. The science of biology was practically non-existent until it was founded by Aristotle, whose works on the natural sciences were used as textbooks in the medieval universities. The same is true of his treatises on rhetoric and political science.

Philosophy. Aristotle's name leads us to the field of philosophy, in which the Greeks also were ahead of other peoples. He was a follower of Socrates (469-399 B.C.), who taught that there is but one God and that the soul is immortal. Socrates argued that one must learn to "know himself," meaning that a person should not waste so much of his time thinking and talking about things that are of no great importance, such as sports, the making of money, amusements, heavy eating and drinking, etc. He taught by means of the dialogue (the Socratic method), but left no writings of his own.

The Career of Plato. Plato (427-347 B.C.) was his most famous pupil and the greatest philosopher of antiquity. He was also the author of works on political science, such as his *Republic,* in which he described an ideal state of society. But he is known chiefly as a philosopher; even in his *Republic* he speaks more as a philosopher than as an expert in political science, as was his pupil, Aristotle. According to Plato, God is the creator of the universe, the supreme Spirit, who is present everywhere. The only things that are real and eternal are spiritual forces, or ideas. Man was originally perfect and good, but somehow fell from his privileged position. He must learn to return to this original position of righteousness and goodness.

THE WORK OF ARISTOTLE. Aristotle (384-322 B.C.), though a pupil of Plato, differed considerably from his master in that he was immensely interested in the world of material objects, in plants, animals, physics, political institutions, rhetoric, and grammar. He surpassed Plato as a scientist, but was inferior to Plato as a philosopher.

THE STOICS AND THE EPICUREANS. Shortly after the death of Aristotle, two new schools of thought made their appearance in Greece. One was called that of the Stoics, a name derived from the porch (*stoa*) where their founder, Zeno, taught. They emphasized the need of reason and virtue, the obligation to perform duties to the state and the family. The other school was that of the Epicureans, founded by and named after Epicurus. It was their belief that man's happiness is a worthy object of study and application, and that one need not wait until the life after death to find it; probably there is no such thing as life after death, they argued. The universe was made as a result of a remarkable course taken by atoms, which, flying through the universe, happened to have made mankind and the planets. In their opinion belief in gods was therefore a foolish fancy.

EDUCATION. In the period after Plato and Aristotle much progress was made in education. Formerly the state had provided only physical and military instruction or training, but now the children of free parents, sometimes girls as well as boys, received instruction in reading, writing, literature, and music. The pupils made use of wax tablets, corresponding to the clay tablets utilized in former days by Babylonian children. In many cases public endowments provided the means of support for these schools. There were also institutions of higher learning, financed as a rule by private capital, as was the case with Plato's Academy, for which Plato had left funds of his own. The *gymnasium* was a school to which only the children of purely Greek descent were admitted; they received physical training here, as well as instruction in reading, writing, and music. Those who graduated from it were more highly respected than college graduates have been in this country. In some modern countries, notably Germany, the word *gymnasium* has been applied to high schools which prepare the pupils for work in the universities.

DISAPPOINTING NATURE OF GREEK RELIGION. After having studied the various aspects of Greek culture which have revealed to us the greatness of the Greek mind, and particularly after having learned of the remarkable views of Plato, we shall be disappointed to find that Greek religion did not keep pace with Greek art and science. Plato was an exceptional person, and undoubtedly he had been in touch with some of the Jewish scholars who were to be found in many parts of the ancient Near East. Very few of his countrymen understood or followed him, not even his own pupil Aristotle. Consequently, we shall not be surprised to find that the Greeks developed religious views that were decidedly inferior to those of the Hebrews. Worse than that, they turned against the true religion.

GODS AND GODDESSES. In the period before Plato, that is, before 380 B.C., the Greeks had worshiped or believed in many gods. They considered their gods as having bodies and passions very much like those of human beings. As a matter of fact, even the greatest of the gods were supposed to be unspeakably bad; that idea clearly shows the spiritual blindness of the Greeks when they were at the height of their power, that is, in the fifth century B.C. They thought that the twelve principal gods lived on Mount Olympus, the highest mountain in Greece. Zeus was the chief of all the gods, and his wife was called Hera. Other important deities were Athena, goddess of wisdom; Apollo, the god of music and prophecy; Aphrodite, the goddess of love and beauty; and Artemis, the goddess of hunting and game. Hesiod, who wrote a book about the gods, believed that man originally had been much stronger, wiser, and better than he was after the Flood, having descended from the first age (of gold) to the fifth age (of iron). The story of the Flood also was one of the features of early Greek religion. But whatever may have been the sources of the Greek religion, it became a jumble and a confused mixture of myth, legend, and tradition.

DIVINATION AND ORACLES. The Greeks were of the belief that every state, social group, even the family, had some patron god for whom they had to do much in order to satisfy and please him. In each city the priests were appointed for public duties just as were the civil officials. The priests performed many functions, including *divination,* or the art of examining animals sacrificed to see what could be learned from their actions or the appearance of their internal organs. This practice was widely followed in the ancient world and is severely condemned in the Old Testament.

More important were the signs and omens presented at temples or shrines of the *oracles,* particularly that of Apollo at Delphi. Both private individuals and state governments consulted with the priests in these "sacred" places. The thought does not seem to have occurred to the leading Greek scholars between 700 and 400 B.C., that human beings might establish a spiritual relation with the gods or with God.

THE FUTURE LIFE. The notion of a future life was almost totally neglected by the Greeks. They could only think of a dull existence in the realm of the dead, controlled by the god called Hades. The demand for a more satisfactory religion led to the growth of the so-called "mystery" religions, which promised a life of future happiness after death to those who would cleanse their souls of impurity and sin, and would pass through certain secret ceremonies.

RELIGIOUS FESTIVALS. Very interesting were the great religious festivals held in various states, and intended to please the deities of the respective states. One of these was of a national character, that is, it made an appeal to the inhabitants of all the Greek states, and it was naturally held in honor of Zeus, chief of all the gods. The place selected for the festival was Olympia. Here were played the Olympic games, such as racing with horses and chariots, wrestling, running, jumping, and so forth. The players arrived from many Greek states and colonies. In 1896 the Olympic games were renewed, the first being held at Athens, the next in Paris (1900), the next in St. Louis, Mo. It will be seen that now, as formerly, they are held once in four years. That this would be the outcome of a religious festival among the Greeks was only natural, and proves the peculiar nature of Greek religion. Those who claim that Christianity is largely based upon Greek religion, have not yet become acquainted with either religion.

THE DECLINE OF GREECE. The age of Pericles was followed by a long period of decline. There was much skepticism and little true religion. Oriental luxury took the place of the old and homely virtues which had helped to make Greece the leader among all nations. Civil war, greed, selfishness, and envy spread among all classes of people, so that the legions of Rome experienced slight difficulty in annexing the whole Greek world. But even they could not restore the lost genius and enlightenment of the Greek masters. Never more would Greece or Asia Minor produce statesmen, literary men, mathematicians, scientists, artists, and philosophers as famous and beneficial as Pericles, Homer, Sophocles, Demosthenes, Thales, Hipparchus, Aristotle, Phidias, Herodotus, Hippocrates, Socrates, and Plato. Nor could Greece be expected to prepare the way for Christianity. Her religion had been killed by materialism, by falsehood, and by the vices that have always disgraced mankind when on the way to ruin.

Student Activities

1. With the aid of a dictionary write out the definition for the following words: *typical, portrayed, philosophical, exaggerated, fundamental, expert, biology, treatises, surpassed, legend, oracles, realm, virtues.*
2. Name the Seven Wonders of the ancient world.
3. What does the statement, "Nothing in excess, and everything in proportion," mean?
4. Have you ever attended "plays"? Who were the famous Greek playwriters?
5. Why was the city of Alexandria such an important center?
6. Who were the three great Greek philosophers? *Philosopher* means "Lover of Wisdom" or "Thinker."
7. What was Plato's idea about God?
8. The thinkers or philosophers consisted of groups called "schools". One group which had the same ideas was one "school." What two "schools" of Greek philosophers are mentioned in this chapter?
9. What is the present meaning of the word, *gymnasium?*
10. What was wrong with the religion of the ancient Greeks?
    Man by nature cannot learn to know the TRUE GOD, unless it is revealed to him by the Holy Spirit through the Gospel. Find texts in your catechism which proves that we are by nature spiritually blind, ignorant, dead and enemies of God.
11. In Acts 17, 15-23, we read that Paul visited the city of Athens; what did he find in that famous city of the Greeks?
12. Why was it easy for the Romans to conquer the Greeks?

CHAPTER 11

The Story of the Roman Republic

THE RISE OF A NEW NATION. While Greece was rapidly declining, a new power arose on the peninsula to the west (Italy) which was destined to build an empire surpassing even that of Alexander the Great. The center of civilization now moved once more to the west, deserting Greece, just as in former centuries it had forsaken in turn Egypt, Babylonia, Assyria, and Persia.

LOCATION AND CLIMATE OF ITALY. Italy had at least one advantage over Greece. It was centrally located in the Mediterranean Sea, and, besides, it was larger than Greece. Its temperate climate and the abundant rains in winter combined to make possible the production of grain, olives, grapes, vegetables, and semi-tropical fruits. Today one may see orange trees growing in the city of Rome, and especially in the island of Sicily oranges can be produced with ease. On the other hand, certain fruit trees like the apple tree, which does not flourish in the southern half of the peninsula, do very well in the northern section.

IMPORTANCE OF CATTLE RAISING. Two-thirds of the peninsula is mountainous, so that the area left for cultivation is not very large. But even the mountains used to add to the wealth of Italy. On the lower slopes excellent pastures were to be found, which explains why Italy used to be called "Vetulia" (Calfland). Moreover, the Latin name for money was *pecunia*, which originally signified cattle.

RESOURCES OF ANCIENT ITALY. The mainland and Sardinia contained good deposits of copper, and Elba was rich in iron. The sea also was a source of wealth, for it provided employment for numerous fishermen, and gave Italy an inexpensive means of transportation in a time when roads on land were still very poor. Among the numerous rivers of Italy you can easily remember the Po, which waters the largest valley in the peninsula; the Tiber, a stream of only 190 miles in length, but famous because Rome was

74

built upon its banks; and the Arno, which flows through a very beautiful and fertile valley — the heart of modern Tuscany.

THE EARLIEST INHABITANTS. Little is known about the earliest inhabitants of Italy except that about 3000 B.C. they are said to have arrived from northern Africa, and belonged to the Mediterranean white race. They made use of polished stone weapons, as well as the bow and arrow. They raised crops in a rather primitive fashion, and they kept tamed animals. The clothes worn by them were made of woven material, thus indicating some knowledge of primitive industry; their pottery is further proof of their comparatively good skill in making a suitable living.

CONTACTS WITH CRETAN MERCHANTS. About 2000 B.C. merchants from Crete and perhaps also from some of the islands of the Aegean Sea appear to have carried with them to Italy some elements of Cretan customs, as for example, the use of bronze. In this way the people in Italy changed from the Stone Age culture to the Bronze Age way of living.

THE COMING OF NORTHERN SETTLERS. About 1800 B.C. settlers arrived from the north, and in northern Italy they built lake villages with houses raised on wooden piles; later they constructed homes on piles even on dry land. They had already learned to use bronze in the lands north of the Alps, and seem to have introduced the horse into Italy.

MIGRATION TO THE SOUTH. Shortly before 1000 B.C. these peoples migrated farther south into central and southern Italy. Here they conquered the earlier inhabitants and learned much from them. They now passed from the Bronze Age to the Iron Age type of culture. They were later called Italians. One important tribe were the Latins living in Latium, along the west coast just south of the Tiber River.

THE ETRUSCANS. In the ninth century B.C. the Etruscans arrived from the Aegean area and before long conquered much of central Italy, reaching their greatest power in the sixth century B.C. After that century they were pushed back into what was later named after them Tuscany. Their language disappeared completely so that their inscriptions cannot be understood any more.

THE GREEK COLONIES IN THE SOUTH. In the extreme south of the peninsula and in eastern Sicily Greek colonies were founded, as we have seen. Although these were later annexed by the Latins, they retained their native language for centuries. You shall see soon that the Romans in the period before 100 A.D. were so impressed by the superiority of the Greeks that they decreed Greek to be one of the two official literary languages of their empire.

THE FOUNDING OF ROME. The city of Rome was founded about the year 1000 B.C., but the settlements on its seven hills were not united until the seventh century B.C. Rome was at first only one out of many cities in the Latin plain, which is usually called Latium. From about 600 to 509 B.C. Rome was ruled by the Etruscans. The city soon began to grow because it was well located on the banks of the Tiber at the spot where the best crossing of the river was to be found.

ROME BECOMES INDEPENDENT. After about a century of control by the Etruscans, some of the Roman nobles decided in 509 B.C. that the time had come for their city to assume its independence. They succeeded in their attempt and set up a new form of government, republican in character. Rome was now a city-state, ruled by two consuls who were each elected for one year. The consuls needed constant assistance from the popular assembly and the body called the Senate. They were upon the whole patriotic and devoted to the best interests of the new republic.

BEGINNINGS OF ROMAN EXPANSION. Shortly after 509 B.C. Rome entered an alliance with several cities in Latium, in order to keep the Etruscans and other hostile peoples at bay. The alliance lasted for 150 years, whereupon Rome fought a brief war with its former friends and subjugated them. This was the beginning of Roman expansion, which continued until the second century of our era. For a short time around 390 B.C. progress was halted by the advance of a Celtic tribe called Gauls from the northwest which seems to have captured Rome, but the city revived immediately and continued on its road to empire building. During half a century of almost constant war (325 to 275 B.C.) the Romans bent all their energies on the task of making the whole peninsula safe from rebellion and civil war. First the Etruscans and the Greek colonies in the south had to bow to Roman dominion; then others followed until by 265 B.C. all the different peoples were cemented together in an alliance of which Rome was the official head and in control of the foreign policies.

THE ROMANS FACE THE COMPETITION OF CARTHAGE. Hardly had this process been completed when Rome embarked upon a contest with the empire built up by the former Phoenician colony, the city of Carthage. At this time Carthage was the largest city in the Mediterranean world, with a population of about 750,000.

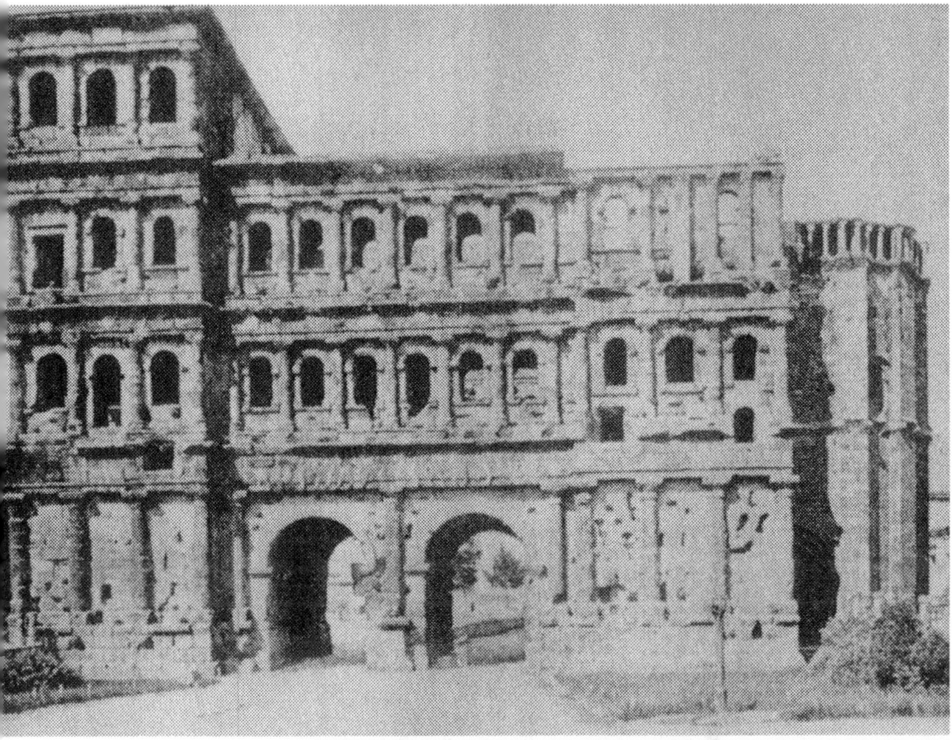

THE PORTA NIGRA
Ruins of a Roman gateway at Trier, in Western Germany.

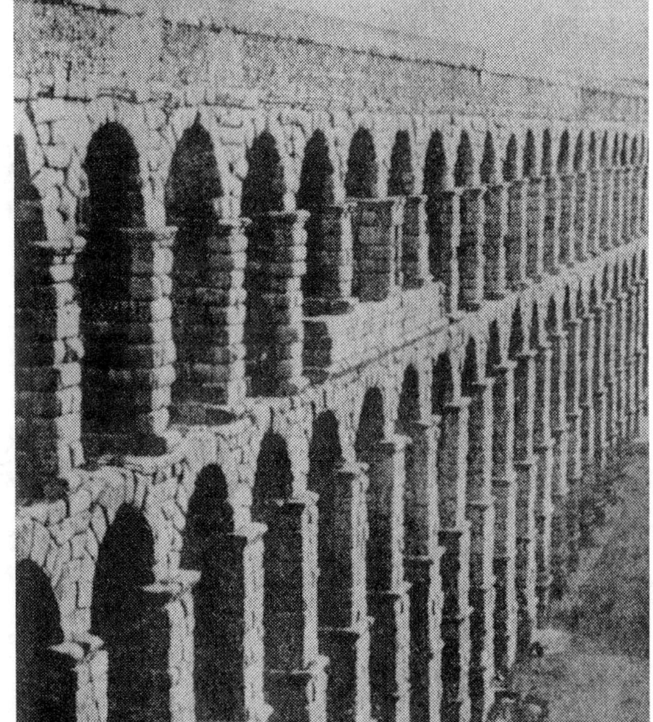

RUINS OF A ROMAN AQUEDUCT AT SEGOVIA, SPAIN

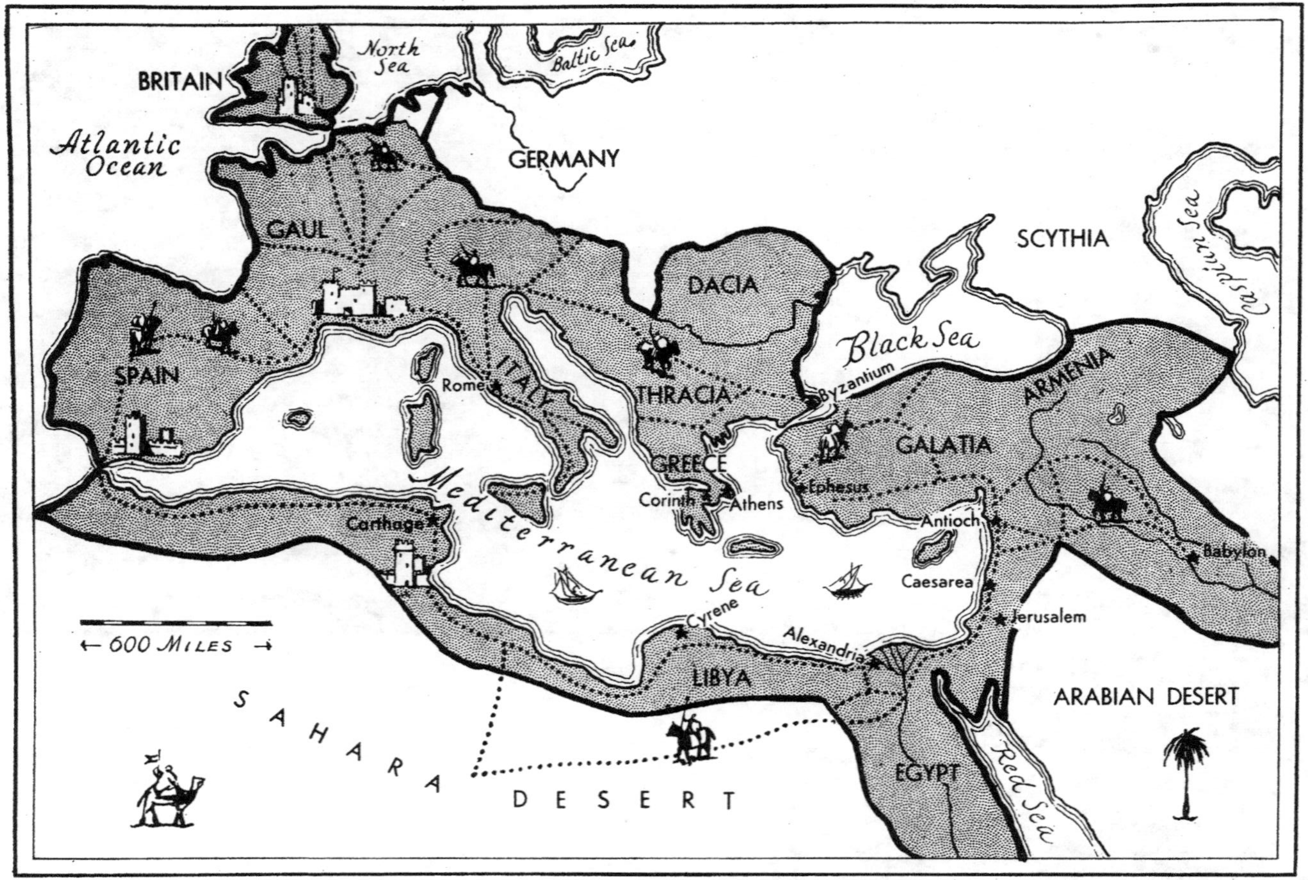

Adapted from *The Church Through the Ages*, Courtesy Concordia Publishing House

THE ROMAN EMPIRE

It controlled the commerce in the western Mediterranean and possessed valuable colonies in western Sicily and southeastern Spain. Its merchants carried home from Britain ample supplies of tin, from the Baltic countries the highly prized amber and furs, from Spain precious metals, notably silver. The merchant marine and navy established for Carthage a strong position. But the government of this far-flung empire was a *plutocracy*, that is, the rule of certain few wealthy business men who neglected the welfare of the people. Naval power was not supplemented by an adequate military force nor by a firm and efficient government at home.

THE THREE WARS WITH CARTHAGE. Rome and Carthage fought three wars which are sometimes called the Punic Wars. The first lasted from 264 to 241 B.C. and was chiefly fought over the possession of Sicily. The Romans were able to wrest from Carthage the western portion of the island (the region around Syracuse had been held by the Greeks), and a short time afterward they also annexed Sardinia and Corsica. The second war (219-202 B.C.) was fought in Italy, Sicily, Spain, and northern Africa. The great hero in this war was the Carthaginian general Hannibal, who marched from Spain along the south coast of Gaul (France), into northern Italy. If he had received proper support from the Carthaginian government, he would undoubtedly have reduced Rome to the position of a Carthaginian province. As he was being drawn ever farther into Italy and could get no fresh troops, he became discouraged. Finally he left Italy, and then with a weakened force, fought a disastrous battle at Zama, near Carthage (202 B.C.), where for the first time he suffered defeat. Now Carthage had to sue for peace, but received very harsh terms, paying a heavy indemnity to Rome, promising to destroy all her ships except ten small boats, and agreeing to fight no more wars outside of Africa, unless with the consent of Rome. She also lost her colony in Spain to Rome. Not satisfied with this victory over Carthage, the Romans in 146 B.C. wished to make certain of no more threats from their former rival, and completely destroyed the city.

CONQUEST OF THE EASTERN MEDITERRANEAN. In the meantime Rome had also taken steps to increase its power in the eastern half of the Mediterranean world. First the Romans fought a war with Macedonia, for their king had been allied with Hannibal. Next they attacked the ruler of Syria. They defeated him between 200 and 190 B.C., but they did not yet annex Syria. When the Romans saw that they were obliged to fight two more wars with the Macedonians, they finally, at the end of these wars, annexed Macedonia and Greece (148 B.C.). Moreover, Rome acquired Asia Minor in 133 B.C. and Egypt in 30 B.C. It was about the year 55 B.C. that Julius Caesar annexed Gaul and made it a Roman province. Thus Rome became the center of a huge empire before it had an emperor to rule over it.

CAUSES OF THE ROMAN VICTORIES. We might well ask at this point how the Romans had been able to win so many decisive victories and what were the arms they had employed? They were ably served by military leaders, such as Scipio, who had been largely responsible for the downfall of Hannibal. Caesar, just mentioned, is another example of an expert in the field of military tactics. What would the Roman legions have been able to do without such fine leadership? In later days, when it was no longer forthcoming, the army lost its strength, though all the knowledge left by Scipio and Caesar was still preserved and had been increased as well.

THE ROMAN ARMY. The legion was the principal unit in the army, and was made up of thirty "centuries," that is, groups of 100 men each. This was the infantry; it used to function in a formation called *phalanx*, in imitation of the famous units formerly employed by the Macedonians. But the Romans had learned that when they were fighting against armies which were fortified with elephants, the phalanx could not cope with the new situation. So the phalanx was dropped for the more flexible units of infantry in the legion. Gradually cavalry forces were added to the infantry and thirty centuries of cavalry and light-armed troops, or *auxiliaries*. The soldiers were taught to fight in three lines, with the third in the rear held as the reserves.

ROMAN WEAPONS. The Romans borrowed from the Samnites in the central Apennines the use of the javelin, and from the Gauls the *convex* shield, which was rounded on the outer side. They learned from the peoples in Spain the use of the two-edged sword. While the front ranks were engaged in fighting with the sword, the troops in the rear would throw the javelins at the enemy over the heads of the front line. For protection the infantry wore armor made of metal or leather, or parts of each; they used the helmet and shields besides. Their camps were always fortified in case the men had to stay in them over night. For siege operations the Romans constructed the customary covered terraces which enabled the men to approach the city without being in danger of attack from above. Battering-rams were also employed with much success.

How the Republic Was Ruled. The government of the republic was so managed as to keep control of the territory and the peoples that were conquered by the Romans. Governors were appointed to rule over the provinces. Their term of office was but one year, and they received no salary, as was also the case with the other officials employed in the republican government. Each governor in his province enjoyed complete authority over public and military affairs. He took care that taxes were collected from the inhabitants and that their own language and religion were respected. In many cases the taxes were paid by the subjects to so-called *publicans*, that is, professional tax collectors ("farmers"), who paid a fixed sum to the government and gathered all they could for themselves. Since the governors received no salary, they also were often guilty of graft, particularly if they had spent large sums of money in obtaining their position. You will remember that among the Jews in Palestine in the time of Jesus the publicans were not well liked by the people.

Patricians and Plebeians. Originally the republic had been controlled by certain members of the nobility whom we might style aristocrats, or patricians, and the government had been an aristocracy. But the masses of the people rapidly increased in number and influence, since their services were much needed in the wars. Led by officials who represented them, called tribunes of the *plebs* (the plebeians, or proletariat), they gradually compelled the patricians to make a number of concessions to them. By 287 B.C. the plebeians were considered the equals of the patricians before the law and in operating the government. Now they could have seats in the Senate and were eligible to positions in the national government. They were also permitted to vote in the general, or popular, assembly. Unlike the aristocracy of many a Greek city-state, the Roman nobles had always yielded on nearly every point rather than start a civil war. In this manner the Romans had acquired great political power and stability so badly needed in their many difficult wars.

The Senate. But, as is often the case, the leaders of the masses of the people, after having acquired for the people certain advantages, began to form an aristocracy of their own and to foster friendship and marriage alliances with the members of the original aristocracy. Once more the plebeians asserted themselves. They argued correctly that the Senate was a closed body, not a council which represented the people at all. It was made up of about 300 men who remained members for life. During the wars with Carthage the Senate had greatly increased its powers at the expense of the popular assembly, which was too unwieldly to arrive at decisions when such decisions had to be made quickly.

CIVIL WAR FINALLY BREAKS OUT. The new nobility also was reluctant to give up its hold on the landed estates throughout the peninsula. This time the patricians did not yield, and so civil war followed. During the course of these wars dictators rose to power and both the nobles and the plebeians began to use the army. Among the dictators in the first century B.C. we may note Sulla, Pompey, and Caesar. Order was finally restored by Octavian, who was the adopted son of Caesar, but is better known as Augustus. He overthrew the republican form of government and set up an imperial government.

ROMAN CITIZENSHIP IS EXTENDED TO ALL PEOPLES IN ITALY. While the leading citizens were fighting each other, the subject peoples in Italy rebelled against the Senate and demanded full citizenship. This was granted to every male inhabitant in Italy as a result of the wars, and all the laws and languages of the former subject peoples were merged into Roman law and the Latin language, so that Italy became a united nation.

WHAT KIND OF A CONSTITUTION THE ROMANS HAD. The Roman constitution was made up of the laws and political institutions existing at any given time. Only when the whole body of free citizens assembled and wished to change the constitution, could it be modified. The Romans were very successful in the management of local government by establishing municipal units. This work was brilliantly done.

THE NATURE OF THEIR LAW. Roman law was based upon a code of civil and criminal law perfected about 450 B.C. and written upon twelve painted wooden tablets, called the Twelve Tables. It was rather primitive, being intended for a small state of some four hundred square miles, in which agriculture was the principal mode of making a living. But capable judicial officers called *praetors* were employed by the national government in order to enlarge and liberalize the code. There were also other experts and lawyers who explained the law from time to time, so that Roman law always was adequate for the needs of the people.

FAMILY LIFE. Perhaps the greatest single cause of the power of Rome was the way in which family life was conducted. The father was the head of the whole unit, including the various members who were dependent upon it, both slaves and freemen. He had all power in his little domain and expected to be obeyed by all members. It was a definite part of Roman "piety" to render such obedience to an authority or superior. The Greeks, on the other hand, were too much interested in individual rights to foster such a spirit, and so their states quickly collapsed as soon as they faced the might of Rome. Another important point of difference was the manner in which the Greeks and the Romans regarded their women. The Romans were like the Spartans, and treated the women with proper respect, while the Athenians did the opposite.

SLAVERY. It cannot be said, however, that the Romans showed a kinder feeling for slaves than did the Greeks. By 30 B.C. there were about 400,000 slaves in and near Rome, and about 1,500,000 in Italy. Slaves were regarded as no better than cattle, having no rights, no permission even to get married as a rule. What a pity it was to see how highly educated men and beautiful women from oriental countries were treated by barbarous and ignorant masters! They were branded with a hot iron, and herded like cattle. These wretched creatures often passed the nights in damp cellars and were driven into the fields where once free citizens labored on their own land. Most of those free farmers and their descendants had lost their lands to wealthy neighbors, as they could no longer compete with the latter. They had gone to Rome in many cases, where now they were on relief. By 50 B.C. about 300,000 persons, or more than one-third of Rome's population, were dependent on government support.

BUSINESS EXPANSION. Business naturally expanded with the continual extension of the Roman frontiers. Nevertheless, it never reached proportions such as you might have expected to find in the center of the greatest empire that the world has ever seen. The Romans under their republican government remained essentially a simple-minded people, attached to their own homes and families, and always happy to find a retreat somewhere in the country from the uproar of the city crowds.

ROMAN ARCHITECTURE. The Romans made little progress in the arts and the sciences. Their earliest temples were constructed on a stone foundation, with a porch placed in front. The building was as a rule made of soft porous stone, covered with stucco. The roof was constructed of wood and decorated with sculpture. As the Romans became more familiar with the grand structures to be seen in the Greek cities, they were moved to rival the Greeks.

About the year 150 B.C. they invented cement, which enabled them to construct huge buildings out of brick, and to shape rounded arches in the building of bridges and triumphal monuments. Among their typical buildings we may mention amphitheaters, aqueducts, and *basilicas*—the latter were in the nature of public halls used for the administration of justice, while sometimes they were also built for private individuals as business offices.

STREETS AND ROADS. The Romans were in the habit of laying out their streets in rectangular fashion, in imitation of the plans followed by the Greeks in building Alexandria. Originally, as did the Greeks, the Romans had followed no definite plans, but it was obvious that straight and wide streets were much to be preferred to the narrow and crooked streets of old Rome. But in the matter of road building, the Romans required no instruction from other peoples. Even their first great road, the *Via Appia,* or the Appian Way, built before 300 B.C. from Rome southward to the sea, was so durably constructed that today, more than two thousand years later, it can still be used for heavy traffic. This road is mentioned in the Bible by the Apostle Paul.

THE HOMES OF THE ROMAN PEOPLE. The rich naturally owned beautiful stone structures of their own, while the others had to live in apartment buildings or small houses built of flimsy wood and stucco. In the country the difference in homes was not so great. In many cases a house was constructed around an enclosed garden, in imitation of the homes that had been built in Oriental countries.

SCULPTURE. The Romans never developed great skill in the field of sculpture, which was largely controlled by Greek artists. As a rule the sculpture that was produced in Italy, was practically nothing else than a copy of Greek models. Roman painting was similarly affected by the Greek artists and patterns. It is interesting to note that the Romans had the habit of carrying large wax images of their ancestors in funeral processions, which created a brisk demand for such examples of sculpture. Moreover, bronze statues of heroes in Roman history were often placed in prominent spots in the leading cities.

EDUCATION. In the Roman Republic public schools were not maintained, but instruction was given in private schools, under the influence of Greek teachers. Here the liberal arts (literature, arithmetic, geometry, astronomy, music, and logic) were taught as a rule by Greeks. The Roman alphabet was derived from the Greek alphabet; it consisted of 23 letters, everyone of which we

are using today. We have merely added the following three letters:
J, U, and W.

LITERATURE. The Romans were very slow in developing a
literature of their own, and we have occasion to mention only
Catullus, who wrote passionate lyric verse; Lucretius, the author
of *On the Nature of Things;* Cicero, the famous orator and writer
of orations; and Caesar, who left an excellent history of his cam-
paigns in Gaul. Sallust was a capable historian. The only important scientific work of this early period still in existence is that
called *On Medicine,* and was composed by Celsus.

THE NEW CALENDAR. About the year 50 B.C. the Romans
got a new calendar, called Julian Calendar, after Julius Caesar. It
was made by an Alexandrian astronomer, who established the
length of the year as 365¼ days, with one extra day added at the
end of February once in four years. It remained in use for more
than 1600 years before it was reformed by Spanish scholars for
Pope Gregory XIII. For that reason the new calendar has ever
since been called the Gregorian Calendar. It was established in
the year 1582, when eleven days were eliminated from the calendar
because in those 1600 years since the perfection of the Julian
Calendar eleven days had been wrongly added to the solar calendar.
The new calendar made the following change: Centennial years,
that is, every last year of a century, such as 1800 or 1900, were
regarded as leap years only when they could be divided by the
number 400. Consequently, the year 2000 A.D. is a leap year, but
the year 1900 is not a leap year. Russia and Greece did not adopt
the new calendar until after the World War, while England did
not change her calendar until 1752. Other nations were less conservative and changed theirs much earlier.

PHILOSOPHY. In the field of philosophy and religion the Romans
were not great leaders. Both Stoicism and Epicureanism were
widely followed, but Epicureanism often became a system of
thought which placed undue emphasis upon the pursuit of physical
pleasures. However, there were Roman philosophers who remained true to the best principles of the Epicurean philosophy.
Most notable among these was Lucretius.

RELIGION. Early Roman religion is often called *animism,* which
is the belief that spiritual powers reside in natural forces or objects.
It was thought that these powers may affect a human being either
for good or for ill. For example, there was Janus, the spirit of the
doorway, who according to the Romans could benefit anyone

entering through the door. Then there were the spirit of the hearth fire, the spirit of the storeroom, and the spirit of the landed property. These spiritual powers were worshiped in every home, the father taking the place of the priest. As in some of the Oriental countries we have been studying, so in the Roman Republic, it was widely believed that the spirit of a deceased person remained near his dead body, and if he had not been properly buried, his spirit would cause a great deal of trouble to those who were responsible for the error made. Good and evil spirits were thought to be present everywhere, and it was considered advisable to please the good ones as well as the bad ones.

ROMAN GODS AND GODDESSES. As the Roman state expanded, new gods were added to the list of the deities that people were expected to worship. Among these gods may be mentioned Jupiter, who was considered the sky god and was somewhat similar to Zeus of the Greeks; and Mars, who was the god of war. From the Greeks and the Etruscans the Romans borrowed the idea of omens and signs. As soon as they became acquainted with Greek mythology, they also took that over. Since they had developed no important religious dogmas of their own, they were upon the whole a tolerant people. They had no definite notions about the salvation of the soul or the immortality of the soul, but were of the opinion that somehow one could improve one's future by seeking the favor of the gods. You can easily understand why the Romans so freely tolerated the worship of many different gods. When Christianity first made its appearance in the city of Rome, many thousands of citizens gladly listened to the preaching of the missionaries. And what is more important still, it was the Roman peace that made it possible for the Christian religion in a short time to spread over the whole Mediterranean world.

Student Activities

1. With the aid of a dictionary write out the definition for the following words: *flourish, inscriptions, subjugated, annexed, tactics, infantry, extortion, municipal, tolerant.*
2. Draw a map of Italy.
3. Make a list of the various countries which the Romans conquered.
4. What were the Punic Wars?
5. Write a statement about Hannibal.
6. Why were the Romans able to win so many victories?
7. Note that in the days that you are now studying, the war elephant took the place of the modern "tank." What weapon did the Romans use which was a forerunner of present day artillery?

8. Who were the "publicans?" Why were they hated by the people? Note that Matthew, who wrote the first gospel in the New Testament, was a publican when Jesus called him as a disciple. Read Matthew, 9,9.
9. Show how wisely the Roman nobles dealt with the plebeians
10. Name three dictators of the Roman Republic.
11. List some of the evils of slavery in ancient Rome.
12. Who was Cicero?
13. What ideas did the Romans have about religion?
14. What is meant by the "Roman Peace" (Pax Romana).
Rome was at first a republic, then dictators arose and ruled. They in turn were replaced by emperors.

CHAPTER 12

The Roman World From Augustus to Augustulus

THE REIGN OF AUGUSTUS. As we have seen, Octavian in 27 B.C. overthrew the republican government of Rome and set up an imperial government in its place. He gave himself the title of Augustus, and he is remembered chiefly by that title, although his successors also held it after him. He and the other emperors until 235 A.D. were also called *Princeps,* meaning the *First.* Augustus was the head of the army as well as head of the whole government. Moreover, he was the *Pontifex Maximus,* or High Priest; in other words, he was the head of all religious worship. In the language of our day we would consider him the head of the Church. Such was the power of the man in whose reign Jesus of Nazareth was born. He ruled the Roman world for 41 years. Among the many provinces in his empire was Palestine, where many Jews hoped for the coming of the Messiah, *in order to obtain liberty from Roman rule.* Even the disciples of Christ were at first of the opinion that He would overthrow the Roman government. As the Gospel of John says, "He came unto His own, and they did not understand Him."

THE GOVERNMENT OF THE EMPIRE. At first both the Assembly and the Senate continued their work. They were like our Congress in this respect that they formed a kind of legislature. But gradually the Assembly lost so much power that it just disappeared, and the Senate also was greatly weakened. The governors were kept in the provinces, where they now received salaries and ruled for a longer term than one year. This was a great improvement over the time of the Republic, when the governors had to find an income for themselves at the expense of the people whom they ruled. Moreover, taxes were now collected more and more by government officials rather than the hated *publicans.* Beginning with the year 212, all free male members of regular cities were granted the Roman citizenship. You will remember that the apostle Paul was born a Roman citizen. For that reason he could appeal

86

to the emperor for justice; so he went to Rome to see Caesar, meaning the emperor.

THE ROMAN ARMY AND NAVY. There was little difference between the army in the time of Augustus and his successors, and that in the days of the Republic. Cavalry forces were being used more, and archers, who fought with bows and arrows, became more numerous. There were about 350,000 soldiers, half of whom were from the provinces, and the other half from Italy itself. The Roman legions remained invincible for a long time. During the first century some of them were defeated by Germanic tribes in the region just east of what we now call the Netherlands. Augustus was emperor then, and he is said to have wept when he heard the news. But very soon the Romans were victorious again. A little later there was a revolt in the island called Britain (now Great Britain); this was also put down in short order. The rebellion of the Jews we shall mention below.

SIZE AND POPULATION OF THE EMPIRE. The Roman Empire during the first two centuries had an area of about three and a half million square miles. It stretched from the British Isles to eastern Syria, and from southern Germany to the Sahara Desert in Africa. The emperors wisely made use of natural frontiers, including the Atlantic Ocean and the North Sea in the West, the Rhine and Danube rivers in the North, the Black Sea in the Northeast, the Syrian Desert in the East, and the Sahara in the South. They did have a fortified line between what we now call England and Scotland, and another one from the Rhine near Cologne to the Danube in southern Germany. It is difficult to estimate the figure for the total population; it seems to have ranged from sixty to eighty million.

THE REIGN OF TIBERIUS. When Augustus died in the year 14 A.D., he was succeeded by Tiberius (14-37 A.D.). This emperor ruled wisely, but was not well liked by the army, because he wanted to maintain peace. Besides, the nobles disliked him because he refused to pension them, and the poorer classes in Rome were dissatisfied because he would not give them enough free grain. It was in his reign that Herod was king of a part of Palestine, and Pontius Pilate was governor. For that reason Jesus appeared before both of them when the Jews wanted Him to be crucified.

NERO, VESPASIAN, AND TITUS. Tiberius was followed by two insignificant emperors, and then came the reign of Nero (54-68). This emperor is remembered for having persecuted the Christians and for having burned the city of Rome. He was a cruel tyrant, as well as a coward. When he finally faced a serious revolt, he killed himself. After a brief period of chaos in the imperial government, the soldiers chose Vespasian as emperor. He ruled the empire very successfully for nine years (70-79), but he was partly responsible for the terrible punishment which his son Titus inflicted upon the Jews when they rebelled in the year 70. Titus was the instrument in the hands of God, whose Son had told the Jews that they should not weep because of His sufferings but rather because of what was in store for themselves. One day, when the disciples had sat with Jesus upon a hill overlooking the city of Jerusalem, they pointed out to Him the imposing buildings that lay before them. The sight was a source of joy and pride to the disciples, for they were looking for an earthly kingdom in which they were to rule. Jesus quickly corrected them by saying that not one stone would be left upon another. Within forty years the prophecy was fulfilled.

THE "GOOD EMPERORS." From 96 to 180 five emperors ruled Rome and its provinces who because of their relatively excellent government were called the "five good emperors." It was in their time that the Roman Empire reached its greatest extent, including Arabia. The last was Marcus Aurelius, who is known for his famous book called *Meditations*. In this work he said some things that seemed very close to Christianity, and yet he persecuted the Christians.

A CENTURY OF DECLINE. From 180 to 284 the empire declined rapidly in wealth and population. In this period there were no good emperors, and the army was not well managed. As a result, people lost respect for the rulers and the soldiers. In the year 193, for example, the title and power of emperor was sold at public auction. On many occasions the soldiers interfered with the proper election of emperors, whose titles and offices could not be inherited. In only ninety years there were eighty emperors succeeding each other. A large number of them were killed. Terrible plagues swept over the empire; one of them killed several million persons. It seemed for a time as if the whole empire was doomed.

THE REIGN OF DIOCLETIAN. However, in 284 a capable emperor brought about many reforms and strengthened the armed forces of the empire. This was Diocletian, who ruled to 305. He gave himself the new title of *Dominus*, meaning Lord, and dropped that of *Princeps*. He also divided the empire into an eastern and a western half, each of which was ruled by an official called Augustus.

CONSTANTINE. Another important emperor was Constantine (307-337). Unlike Diocletian, who persecuted the Christians, he recognized their faith as the state religion. He is also well known for his act in removing the capital of the empire from Rome to Byzantium. That city was then named after him, Constantinople, and it retained that name for more than two thousand years. However, in recent years it has received a new name from the Turks, who have called it Istanbul.

THE END OF THE ROMAN EMPIRE IN THE WEST. For a short time under Emperor Theodosius (379-395) the empire was ably held together, but in 395 it was definitely broken up into two separate empires. Although the eastern half of the old empire was to have a brilliant future, the western half continued to decline until in the year 476 the last of the emperors in the West was deprived of his title. His name was Romulus Augustulus, meaning the "little Augustus." This event marked the end of the Roman Empire in the West. In this part of the world the next three or four centuries are called the "Dark Ages," because people were no longer well governed, and they no longer enjoyed prosperous times nor good schools and libraries.

LIFE IN THE COUNTRY IN THE TIME OF THE ROMAN EMPIRE. Since most people were still living in the country, we might as well start our study of Roman civilization with conditions in the rural districts. At first the slaves were still very numerous there, and they continued to do much of the farming. But gradually it was found that slavery did not pay very well any more, and the owners of the land preferred to employ help that worked for wages or a share of the crops. Besides, they liked the new custom of having the land worked by persons who were called *coloni*. These were neither slaves nor freemen, for they could not leave the land upon which they worked, but they were not the property of their masters. They were like the *serfs* of later times, whom we shall mention again.

FARMING. The average farm was not more than 25 acres in size, for such a piece could easily support a good-sized family. Stock ranches were of course much larger, and there were also estates of more than 500 acres each, just as is the case in many countries today. The Romans, like the Americans, understood the value of manure and lime as fertilizers. But instead of raising different crops on the same piece of land from time to time, which practice we call the rotation of crops, or crop rotation, the Roman farmers preferred to let some pieces lie idle (*fallow*). Upon the whole they grew about the same crops that are raised in European countries today, as well in various parts of the United States.

BUSINESS. The long period of peace maintained by the Romans helped to expand business. Low import and export duties also were a great help. Very valuable to the traders were the very fine roads built by the Romans. Finally, the government made a wise step in having all the different coins of the conquered peoples replaced by a *uniform* coinage. Both copper and silver coins were used. The Romans imported from India such goods as cotton, silk, linen, as well as spices and ivory; from China they bought raw silk, which was not grown in Europe until the year 550 A.D. In thousands of little shops cloths were woven or spun. Pottery, glassware, gold and silver statuettes, furniture, and all sorts of toys were made, very much as the Greeks had done before. The government naturally did all in its power to assist the ready flow of trade. One of its most useful acts was the institution of the postal service, providing relays of horses for the swift delivery of mail.

TRADE CORPORATIONS. It was customary for persons working in the same trade to have their shops and stores in the same street. For example, the masons lived and worked in the street of the masons, or Mason Street. The men who made pottery would all live in Potters Street; here each of them would have his shop on the first floor, probably in the rear; and he would sell his pottery in the front room or in some stand in the front of his home. For many centuries, way into modern times, this practice was continued in a number of European countries. It also happened frequently that the skilled workers became organized into groups called colleges. These were not like our modern trade unions, for the members usually owned their little shops. They kept their trade secrets this way, and they took steps to obtain political advantages in their towns. They also would often come together in some hall and enjoy social entertainment.

WHAT HAPPENED TO THE FREEDMEN. From time to time slaves were set free by their masters, and they were then called freedmen. Although they were not given the citizenship, they were allowed to obtain unimportant positions in the government. They could also seek and find employment in whatever jobs suited them best.

THE COMING OF INFLATION. After the bad times of the period from 180 to 284, the imperial government was no longer able to find funds for its expenditures. The regular revenues were not sufficient any more, because the people could not pay the taxes that were required, and there was a great deal of graft among the rulers. As a result the government had to find new sources of income. Instead of borrowing money by issuing government bonds, as governments in our time have often done, the officials reduced the amount of silver in the coins. Thus they *debased* the currency. The actual value of the coins decreased just as fast as the amount of silver in them became smaller. We call this *inflation,* for the less the coins were worth, the higher prices of goods went. Prices became "bigger," like a balloon that you blow bigger, and which you thus *inflate.* Before very long people would pass around money in sacks that were tied and were not opened any more to see how many coins there were in them. Such a condition could not last, and so the government was obliged to issue once more a sound coin which was called *solidus.* It was worth as much as one seventy-second part of a pound of gold.

ROMAN BUILDINGS. The Romans, after conquering many countries, felt inclined to celebrate their triumphs. The government had beautiful triumphal arches erected, mostly in the city of Rome. This was often done at the order of a certain emperor who wanted everybody to remember how he had won his battles; so his sculptors would decorate the arches with figures of warriors in battle. Some of these arches are still standing in Rome today. One of the finest of the old Roman buildings that has lasted through the centuries is the Pantheon. It is a temple with a dome for a roof, which the Greek temples did not have. Besides, it was not rectangular but round. Another famous building is the Colosseum, which was an open air theatre, with rows of seats in circular form rising above each other, like many a stadium in our universities, where football is played. It seated some 50,000 spectators. Much larger was the Circus Maximus, meaning the largest stadium or theatre. Unfortunately, it is no longer in existence. It was rectangular in form and seated about 150,000 persons. The center of activities in Rome was the market place called *Forum.* Here thousands of persons would meet and buy and sell, attend lectures, or hold meetings of various kinds. Most of the buildings are gone now, but some ruins are still left.

PAINTING. Vast numbers of Roman paintings have disappeared, which is also true of Greek paintings, but we do have those that are left among the ruins of the town called Pompeii. This place was located close to Mount Vesuvius, which suddenly in the year 79 A.D. became an active volcano and hurled thousands of tons of lava upon the inhabitants, killing them instantly. Nothing could be removed by the people. The sculpture and paintings were thus buried and preserved. They show how the citizens were dressed, and how they lived and worked. This type of art proves the great skill of the sculptors and painters, who were still under the influence of the Greeks and repeated what the masters of old had produced so well.

LITERATURE. Since the government now maintained public schools and fine libraries, large numbers of people could read, and so it naturally followed that the demand for books increased. Many read Greek as well as Latin books. Among the Roman writers we may mention Vergil, or Virgil, who wrote the *Aeneid*. He spoke of the great hero Aeneas, who was thought to be the Trojan ancestor of Julius Caesar. Horace and Ovid, on the other hand, were more given to lyric poetry. Livy and Tacitus were learned historians. Plutarch wrote in Greek. He composed the well-known work called *Parallel Lives,* which is a group of famous biographies of leading persons in the ancient world. Another important writer was the emperor Marcus Aurelius, whom we have mentioned above.

SCIENCE. The Romans did not do so well in the field of science as the Greeks had done. But among the great scientists of all time we may include Ptolemy, who wrote the *Geographical Outline;* and also Pliny the Elder, the author of a *Natural History.* Galen, though he was a Greek, came to Rome and composed important works on medicine. The governments of many cities did much for the cause of public health. Fine hospitals were built, and numerous physicians were employed by the government to take care of the sick at the expense of the state. This practice is called socialized medical care, and in the United States today there are many persons who think that it is an excellent thing for the poor, because they cannot pay for the services of good doctors, and yet they need good care just as much as others. Still better, however, is the work of the Church, which can also help the poor.

ROMAN LAW. The Romans surpassed the Greeks in the building of political institutions and the shaping of law. Even many Greeks, especially the famous Papinian, learned much from the Roman jurists, and spread among the peoples in the Orient the knowledge of Roman law. In the reign of Emperor Theodosius II, in 438, an excellent code of law was drawn up, called the Theodosian Code. In another chapter you will learn about a still more famous code of Roman law, namely, the Justinian Code. That was drawn up in the sixth century.

The Decline and Fall of the Roman Empire. In the eastern half, the Roman Empire lasted more than 1400 years, but in the West it fell to pieces about a thousand years earlier. We can easily tell what was wrong with Rome and with Italy. In the second century, when Rome had about a million inhabitants, the causes of the coming decline and ruin were already at work. The government went bankrupt and began to force numerous fine citizens to surrender their property whenever more money was needed. Frequently the soldiers refused to obey the orders of their superiors. Most of the people hated the tax collectors and also the soldiers. Many wealthy persons spent their time in gay feasting, while the poor could not get enough to eat. Robbers threatened travelers on the roads and the pirates made the seas unsafe. Very few citizens were willing to serve their government or their neighbors. The emperor had to be worshiped as a real god, although it was well known as a rule that he was not even a decent human being. Moreover, the idols and gods which the people worshiped showed how their minds worked. What they all needed and what few possessed was true religion, such as that preached by the Christians. In the next chapter we shall study the rise and spread of this religion.

Student Activities

1. With the aid of a dictionary write out definitions for the following words: *successors, pension, persecuted, expenditures, jurists.*
2. Who was Octavian?
3. Name the Roman emperors which are mentioned in this chapter.
4. Write three sentences about Vespasian.
5. What changes did the Emperor Diocletian make in the Roman Empire?
6. Why is the Emperor Constantine an important character?
7. Who was the last Roman emperor? What was he called? Why?
8. Who were the *coloni?*
9. Explain rotation of crops.
10. What is a *uniform coinage?* Do we have uniform coinage in the United States?
11. Who were the *freedmen?*
12. How did the Romans celebrate their victories?
13. What happened to the town of Pompeii?
14. Name some of the Roman writers.
15. Why did the huge Roman Empire finally go to pieces? Give about five reasons.
16. What is a *True* religion?
17. What were the *Dark Ages?* Why are they called *dark?*

CHAPTER 13

How the Christian Church Was Founded

THE IMPORTANCE OF THE CHRISTIAN CHURCH. Thus far you have read twelve chapters in this book which deal with the history of the ancient world. You have studied about famous empires of the past which rose and fell, and which deserve an important place in world history. But all these nations together have done less for us in making life useful and pleasant than did the Christians in the Roman Empire. Long after the empires of the Greeks and the Romans disappeared, the Christians still kept on building their own empire. Their kingdom was not made with human hands, and it will survive all the nations of the present and of the future. In the period from 500 to 1700 the vast majority of the people in all Europe were born into the Christian Church. Today, in the United States, at least half of the inhabitants are connected in some way with the Christian Church, even though many of them are not faithful believers in Christ. In South America and Central America there are also millions of Christians, and altogether there are said to be some seven hundred million Christians in the world. You can easily understand that the Christian Church has had a tremendous influence even upon those persons who refused to become Christians. The men and women who founded our own nation and drafted our wonderful constitution were nearly all Christians.

THE JEWS BEFORE THE REIGN OF EMPEROR AUGUSTUS. Palestine after the death of Alexander the Great in 323 B.C. formed a part of the Seleucid Empire. Although the Romans in 190 B.C. had overthrown this empire, they had been unwilling to annex Syria and Palestine. The Jews, however, remained under foreign rule with headquarters in Antioch. But in 168 B.C. they started a war for independence which lasted 25 years, and at the end of it they received their independence (143 B.C.). They enjoyed eighty years of freedom, until in the year 63 B.C. the dictator Pompey entered the city of Jerusalem with his victorious army. Hereafter

Palestine was a Roman province. The southern section was called Judea, the west central part Samaria, and the northern portion Galilee. For a short time Julius Caesar was in Palestine (48-44 B.C.), and after that another dictator called Cassius held the country (44-42 B.C.). It was during the reign of Caesar that Herod became governor of Galilee. During the next seven years Herod extended his power, and in 37 B.C. he occupied Samaria, and then took Jerusalem. He ruled as king of Palestine from 37 to 4 B.C.

The Taking of the Census in the Roman Empire. Early in his reign, Augustus issued a decree stating that henceforth every fourteen years a census was to be taken of the population in the empire. We are not certain when the first census was taken. In the Gospel of Luke we read that this occurred when Quirinius was governor of Syria, which included Palestine. We are also informed that Herod was still king, for it was he to whom the Wise Men came to ask where the king of the Jews had been born. The date of Christ's birth has very often been given as 4 B.C., meaning the year 4 Before the birth of Christ. Luke tells us that Joseph and Mary, like all other Jews, had to go to the place of their ancestor David in order to register for the Roman census. So they went to the city of Bethlehem in the country of Judea, where Jesus was born in a manger. In those days and for centuries to come the peoples of Europe and western Asia reckoned their dates from the founding of the city of Rome. After the fall of the Roman Empire in the West the custom gradually was established to change this manner of arriving at dates. By that time nobody was sure in which year Jesus was born, so a date was fixed, which did not happen to be correct. The Bible does not say how old Jesus was when He was crucified, but a great deal of work has lately been done by scholars in finding out when the crucifixion occurred. The most likely date is 31 A.D., meaning 31 *Anno Domini*, or, the year 31 in the life of our Lord Jesus Christ. So important has Jesus become in world history that everybody in our country and in many others besides pays respect to Him whenever he or she puts a date on the top of a letter. We begin our era with the date of the birth of Christ, even though we do not know just when that was.

The Life of Christ. Some day you will read other history books, and you will probably wonder why in these books so little attention has been paid to the life and work of Christ. There will be a discussion of the "Age of Napoleon," or the "Age of Louis

XIV," or the "Age of Metternich." You might well ask yourself why a whole age has been named after such men, although our world of today would not be very different if none of these men had ever lived. Practically no history textbook speaks of the "Age of Christ," even though the most bitter enemy of the Christian Church knows very well that Christ is a greater figure in world history than any European or Asiatic ruler. You would think that, since seven hundred million persons in the world today, that is, one-third of the whole population, are named after Christ, He would be mentioned in great detail by all writers of world history. Those who have not done so merely express their own ignorance of what is really important in history. How far do you have to go from your home to reach the nearest Christian Church? If you live in a town, you will probably see the influence of Christ in looking at a number of churches in which He is worshiped every Sunday, or Saturday. But where would you see the concrete proof of how important Alexander the Great is in the world today? And how important do you think some of the dictators in Europe that we so often used to hear about will be 1900 years from now?

THE PURPOSE OF CHRIST'S COMING. Human beings are born and live and die as they have done for ages. When Christ came into the world on the first Christmas day, He seemed to be just another baby. But His so-called father, Joseph, and His mother knew better. They had been told by God through the archangel Gabriel that this little boy would become the Savior of the world. He was the only begotten Son of God, and He was indeed unlike all human beings in that respect. His business was to save mankind from sin, to overcome the power of Satan (the devil), and to make it possible for His followers to inherit eternal life in heaven. If seen from a merely worldly standpoint Christ appears to be the most important person in world history, how great is His place in world history, do you think, in the eyes of a real Christian? Some day the whole world will understand Him, and then all human beings will at last pay Him the respect that He has deserved from the very beginning. He became a human being Himself in so far as His mortal body was concerned, except of course that He did not have a human father and was not in the power of a sinful human nature. But in taking upon Himself a human body, Christ fulfilled the demand of God that atonement must be made for the sins of the world from the time that Eve first fell from God's grace.

The Work Done By Christ Before His Betrayal and Crucifixion. The gospels tell us that Christ devoted much of His time to preaching and teaching. Very important indeed is His Sermon on the Mount, of which the first part is made up of a number of verses beginning with the words: "Blessed are." For this reason we often refer to these verses as the *Beatitudes,* the Latin for "blessed" being *beati,* in the masculine plural. Christ advised His hearers to love God above all things and their neighbors as much as their own selves. They should even love their enemies and do good to them, and thus He showed the world how war, murder, divorce, theft, and practically all other forms of crime could most easily be avoided. Christ is the greatest reformer of all time. He explained how kings and presidents should rule their subjects by remembering that people must "render unto Caesar that which is Caesar's," while at the same time reserving their worship for God only. He also healed the sick and often reprimanded those whom He had cured for having committed the sin that had caused their disease. But He did not imply that all disease is directly caused by a certain person's sin. He upheld the Ten Commandments of Moses in which we read that the sins of parents are having evil effect upon their descendants unto the third and fourth generation. He also knew that there are many causes of illness, including contagion. Most important of all, He spoke of His mission in the world, of His duty to suffer and die for sinful humanity.

The Crucifixion Is Important. There is one thing about the gospels that many people often overlook. They like to tell us how they enjoy reading the wonderful sayings of Jesus, and they receive inspiration from the accounts that describe the cures performed by Him. They are ready, so they say, to follow Him and become Christians. But when they are told that there was also a period of suffering in the life of Christ, they do not like to discuss that subject. One day the author of this chapter heard a certain Protestant pastor say that the account of Christ's suffering was a "slaughter-house theory." That is the part in Christ's career that many folks do not enjoy hearing about. But have you ever noticed how much attention the few days of suffering and the resurrection in Christ's life have received in the gospels? Christ lived at least 33 years before He was crucified. And yet those few days at the end were considered so important by the writers of our four gospels that Matthew devoted eight chapters to them, Mark six, Luke five and a half, and John nine. You understand why that was, don't you?

WHO PONTIUS PILATE AND HEROD WERE. You already know that Christ was crucified in the time of Pontius Pilate, the Roman governor, and you have read about the meeting between Christ and Herod. Perhaps you may have thought that this Herod was the same person as King Herod who was so jealous of the baby Jesus that he ordered all the little boys in Bethlehem to be killed. But the later Herod was not the same person after all. He was the son of Herod the Great. He had recently married Herodias, the wife of his brother Philip, for which reason he had been denounced by John the Baptist. Christ referred to him as "that fox." Pontius Pilate was procurator, or governor, of Judea from 26 to 36 A.D. In yielding to the clamoring of the Jews who hated Jesus, he showed himself a politician of no great courage. Even his own wife had warned him that in a dream the innocence of Jesus had been revealed to her. Little did Pilate know who this "King of the Jews" was.

PENTECOST. Christ had often told His followers that He would send a "Comforter." That was the Holy Spirit, Whose mission it was to comfort the sorrowful disciples, and to give them spiritual power. The first great outpouring of the Holy Spirit, and no doubt the only one of this nature thus far in the world was on the day of Pentecost, ten days after Christ's ascension. The disciples were assembled together with Mary, the mother of Jesus, and a little over one hundred others. They were all moved by the power of the Holy Spirit in such a way that cloven tongues of fire appeared above their heads. A little later they went out of doors and began to address a crowd of people in Jerusalem. They were telling their audience about the work of Christ, when suddenly the power of the Holy Spirit was upon them. They could now perform what we call miracles. Peter explained to some doubters that he and his friends were not drunk but sober; they were speaking many different languages through the power of the Holy Spirit. The account of this event in the Acts of the Apostles does not make it clear just how this was done. At any rate, the people heard the words in their own languages.

WHAT THE RESURRECTION MEANS. In dying for us sinners, Christ atoned for our sins, and made it possible for us to be forgiven by a just and merciful God. But imagine what would have happened if Christ had not risen from the dead? The Apostle Paul answers that question in the fifteenth chapter of I Corinthians: "And if Christ be not risen, then is our preaching vain, and your faith is also vain." You will remember that Christ had promised His followers everlasting life, but that He could base on His own Resurrection, not merely on His Crucifixion. He prepared the way for us in returning to the earth with a body that was visible and could be touched whenever He wanted it to appear in such a form. He said that He was not merely a spirit, for a spirit cannot be seen nor can it be touched by human beings. Christ promised the resurrection of the human body, though in a new form. Let us follow the story as it was told in the Gospels.

THE GOSPEL STORIES OF CHRIST'S RESURRECTION. The Gospel of Matthew informs us that near the end of the sabbath there was a great earthquake, while an angel appeared at the opening of the sepulchre and removed the stone that had been placed at the entrance. The soldiers who had been sent there to watch the grave and see that nobody would steal the dead body of Jesus became frightened and ran away. All of the four gospels together make it clear that Christ arose from the grave before sunrise on what we call Easter Day now. He was first seen by two separate parties of women and then by the disciples. At the same time other graves were opened and many bodies of the believers in Christ came forth to show the world how important Christ's resurrection was.

HOW THE FIRST CHRISTIAN CHURCH GREW. The church in Jerusalem began on the day of Pentecost with 120 members, including the twelve disciples, who were henceforth called the apostles, for the word "Disciple" means a person who is learning something, and an "apostle" brings news to others. While Christ was still with them, the twelve intimate followers were instructed by Him, and so were disciples. After the Ascension, which occurred 40 days after the Resurrection, the disciples became apostles. The 120 original members won some 3,000 others on the day of Pentecost, and these were all baptized by them. Furthermore, a few days later another 2,000 converts were added to the first church. This was largely the result of the cure of a lame man by the apostles Peter and John. Peter, remembering how he had forsaken his Master in the hour of crisis and humiliation, and how he had even denied being His disciple, remembered likewise the talk he had had with Jesus shortly after the Resurrection. At that time the Savior had told him that he would feed the sheep and the lambs of Christ. In other words, he would be a pastor in the Church. He boldly spoke whenever he could as a witness for the cause of Christ. He was the leading speaker in the nrst meeting recorded. He was also the chief speaker at Pentecost. And now, for the third time, he held forth, and he told the crowd that this lame man had been cured through the power of Jesus Christ. Peter was not one of these lukewarm Christians who admit that there are many ways leading to salvation. He said: "Jesus Christ is the stone which was set at nought by you builders, which is become the head of the corner. Neither is there salvation in any other."

THE APOSTLES REFUSE TO BE SILENCED. When the leading priests among the Jews heard about this cure, they sent for Peter and John, and asked them who had given them authority to speak so boldly to the people. Were not the members of the Sanhedrin the leaders of the people? What right did Peter and John have to ignore them? But the apostles replied that they would in this case obey God rather than man. They had been instructed by Christ to obey the government in all purely civil matters, but when they were required to do things contrary to the commands of God, they would refuse to obey the government. They would gladly pay taxes, and they would be ready to render various services to the government, except in so far as they would be asked to break the commandments of God. The high priest had to let them go this time, for he feared to offend the people in Jerusalem.

STEPHEN AND SAUL OF TARSUS. Thus far no one had been put to death for following Christ. Peter and John had been imprisoned, but an angel of God had set them free. But in the seventh chapter of the Acts of the Apostles we read about the fate of Stephen, the first martyr to die for the Christian faith. He spoke eloquently about the gospel of Christ. Shortly before he was stoned to death by the enemies of the Christians, he saw the heavens opened and Christ standing on the right hand of God. When he mentioned this to his persecutors, they became more furious than before, and they hurriedly laid some of their clothes at the feet of Saul of Tarsus, who was one of their assistants. He used to report to them the names of those who were worshiping the hated Jesus of Nazareth. He may have gloated over the sufferings of Stephen as he died for his Master. But it was not long before Saul also became a Christian. We shall see in the following chapter how this man Saul was re-named Paul, and served as the greatest of Christian missionaries.

Student Activities

1. With the aid of a dictionary write out the definitions for the following words: *reckoned, missionaries.*
2. What is the chief difference between the Christian Church and other kingdoms, empires, and republics of this world?
3. Why is there so little mentioned in other history books about Christ?
4. What was the purpose of Christ's coming into the world?
5. What is the birthday of the Christian Church? Why?
6. Which Herod was king at the time when Christ was crucified?
7. Tell how the first 3000 converts for Christ were made. See Acts 2.
8. Who was the first man to be put to death on account of his faith in Christ after the First Pentecost?
9. Who were the "important" characters during the crucifixion of Christ? World figures are people whom almost everybody knows. Name some world figures of the present time.
10. You have been taught by your teacher that we must constantly be on guard against three powerful enemies, the Flesh, the World, and the Devil. These three powers constantly attempt to get us away from Christ. The *World* are all those people who are not believers in Jesus Christ as the Saviour. These Unbelievers want all the followers of Christ to be like they are. They do not want anybody to be different. They use all kinds of methods to bring the believers away from Christ. What are some of the methods that were used against the first Christian Congregation at Jerusalem?

CHAPTER 14

The Christian Church Expands

REASONS WHY THE CHRISTIAN CHURCH EXPANDED SO RAPIDLY. In the first place, the Christians had a book in which they felt sure God had told them that their religion was the only true one. The Old Testament had been left to them by the Jews, and the New Testament was added by the Christians themselves. Because of the great value of the New Testament, we shall presently discuss all of its books. In the second place, no other religion could claim to have a founder like Jesus Christ, the only begotten Son of God. He was not a mere hero in a sort of fairy story that was believed in by persons because they wanted to do so. He had been seen by thousands of Jews. The miracles He had performed were known to vast numbers of people. In the third place, where else could one find a religious leader who had risen from the dead and had been seen by His followers? Had He not said to the doubting Thomas that he might touch Him? Had He not eaten food before the eyes of the disciples? In the fourth place, He had not only promised eternal life to His followers, as others had done before Him, but He had shown them His own body to prove that they would also some day possess a similar body, rather than a mere spirit. In the fifth place, He had preached the highest code of ethics that the world has ever known; this code, as we saw in the preceding chapter, can abolish all wars and all crime. Think how much our government could save if it would take to heart more seriously the advice of Jesus. The prisons would become unnecessary, and many institutions for mentally diseased persons could be used for better purposes. There would be no more strikes in our factories, and employers would be happy to help all ablebodied persons to find suitable employment. In the sixth place, Christ taught that women, who were despised among the Greeks and other peoples, were worthy of respect, and that the poor and the young likewise were entitled to proper consideration. Thus He favored the principle of democracy, and thus the fathers of our Re-

102

public followed in His footsteps when they wrote into our constitution the democratic system of government. Finally, He pointed out that God is not far away and is interested in human beings. He is our Father, who hears all our prayers. His angels have charge to watch over us, and the Holy Spirit, their commander, comes to pious Christians to give them spiritual power.

THE GOSPEL OF MATTHEW. This was written by the apostle Matthew. Being also one of the original twelve disciples, he wrote down some of Christ's sermons, especially the wonderful Sermon on the Mount, which he alone has fully recorded. According to the earliest Christian writers known to us, he wrote his gospel in the Aramaic language, so that his own people could most easily understand it. You must bear in mind that the Aramaeans had spread over Syria and their language had partly taken the place of Hebrew, even in Palestine. Matthew wrote for the Jews, and he took for granted that they were familiar with the Old Testament. His gospel is the oldest, dating from about the year 45. We are reasonably sure of this date, because the oldest records say that he wrote it at the time of the persecutions of the apostles by Herod Agrippa, the grandson of King Herod, which occurred in the year 42.

THE GOSPEL OF MARK. The writer of this second gospel was a pupil of the apostle Peter, and composed it about the year 55. He wrote principally for the Christians in the city of Rome, and used very few Aramaic terms. His language was Greek. He explained several important Jewish customs, showing that his readers were not expected to be only Jews. He was, however, a Jew himself. His style is very much like that of his teacher, the emotional Peter. Since he was not present at the time that the events in Christ's life occurred, he did not try to write down many exact quotations, but was content with a simple and fairly brief narrative.

THE GOSPEL OF LUKE. This gospel shows the Greek atmosphere in which the author was brought up. He was the companion of the apostle Paul when he wrote this gospel, which happened about the year 60. He used no Aramaic words at all, although Jesus Himself had preached in that language. He was probably a physician; in the introduction he tells us why he wrote this gospel, in order to make it known exactly what was the nature of the events that had happened in Palestine. Luke was also the author of the Acts of the Apostles, in which he carries the story up to the year 62 or 63.

THE GOSPEL OF JOHN. Like the third gospel, this was also written in Greek. The first chapter begins with the explanation of the Greek word and idea of the *logos,* or the *word.* It was written about the year 75 by John, the beloved disciple, who attained a great age. He was thoroughly familiar with Jewish customs and could tell exactly when certain events had happened. The rhythm in his style is Semitic, and his Greek reveals the Hebrew background very clearly. His aim was largely to explain the nature of Christ's mission upon the earth. He showed that he was intimately acquainted with the apostle Peter.

THE ACTS OF THE APOSTLES. As we saw, this work was written by Luke, the companion of Paul, and suddenly stops with Paul's first imprisonment in Rome in the years 61-63. It is highly valuble for us, since it contains for the most part the only reliable source of the story of the early Christian Church. Luke tells us about Christ's death and ascension, the work of Peter in Jerusalem, the day of Pentecost, the martyrdom of Stephen, the conversion of Paul, and then in great detail the missionary work of Paul. It also gives a very interesting description of the way the Christians in Jerusalem at first divided their property among themselves. But you must be careful not to confuse this practice with socialism or communism, for the Christians gave up their goods voluntarily, out of love for their neighbors, whereas the socialists and communists are very seldom interested in loving anybody except themselves. They want the state to help the poor while the Christians are glad to suffer hardship out of Christian love.

THE EPISTLES OF PAUL. These are also valuable, since they express many remarkable doctrines. Some of them, as Peter said, are hard to understand. They are beautifully written in Greek and show that the author was a real scholar. The earliest was I Thessalonians, written about the year 52, and the last is II Timothy. Altogether there are fourteen, addressed for the most part to individual churches, such as that in Rome, Corinth, Ephesus, Philippi, Colosse, which were cities; and Thessaly, which was a district in northern Greece. In Galatia, so says Paul himself, there were several churches. This district was located in central Asia Minor, the peninsula which is usually referred to as Anatolia today. Paul throws much light upon conditions in those churches, and he gives excellent advice to those persons whom he had converted to the Christian religion. The same is true of his epistles to his personal friends, Timothy, Titus, and Philemon. Excellent also is the Epistle to the Hebrews. In the eleventh chapter of this epistle is to be found his marvelous discussion of faith, and equally inspiring is his analysis of Christian love in I Corinthians XIII.

THE OTHER EPISTLES. Whereas Paul emphasized the importance of faith, especially in his famous Epistle to the Romans, James in his epistle speaks eloquently about the need of doing good works. In this way the second apostle balanced the views of the first. James was the first bishop, or pastor, of the church in Jerusalem, and died in the year 63. He was perhaps the son of Alpheus, but he is often referred to in the older writings as the brother of Jesus. The other disciple called James was the son of Zebedee, who was killed in the year 42 by Herod Agrippa, king of Judea and Samaria, and grandson of Herod the Great. Peter wrote his two valuable epistles about the year 64, shortly before his death. The Epistle of Jude was written by Jude Thaddeus about the year 63. Finally, the three epistles of John were composed by John the beloved disciple. They are very similar in content to some of the chapters in his gospel. He spoke much of love. The date of his epistles is about the year 75.

THE REVELATION OF JOHN, OR THE APOCALYPSE. Much of this work is of a visionary nature and difficult to understand. John was the author of this also. It contains important prophecies, most of which remain unfulfilled.

PERSECUTION UNDER HEROD AGRIPPA. As we have seen, Herod Agrippa, the grandson of Herod the Great, suddenly began to persecute the Christians in Jerusalem in the course of the year 42. James, the son of Zebedee and brother of John the disciple, was killed, and now most of the apostles left Jerusalem in order to spread the gospel of Jesus abroad. They seem to have left only James, the son of Alpheus, behind. This James, however, may have been a brother of Jesus, since some important sources say so. It is difficult for us to tell which James it was. At any rate, he was a saintly man and highly revered by the Christians. Between 60 and 70 he was martyred.

ADMISSION OF GENTILES INTO THE CHURCH. At first only Jews joined the ranks of the Christians. But after Peter saw the vision at Joppa of a sort of sheet let down from heaven with many kinds of animals in it, he understood from this that God did not want to exclude the heathen nations from His church. The Jews were not permitted to eat all kinds of animals, but the gentiles were free to do so. When Peter in the vision was told to kill all the animals and eat them he saw that henceforth the gospel of Christ was to be preached to both Jews and gentiles. Later on some of his friends objected to his viewpoint, but he held fast to the truth.

THE CHURCH IN ANTIOCH. In the city of Antioch, capital of all Syria, the Christians soon founded a flourishing congregation. Here they were first called Christians. Very likely in the year 42 some of the persecuted Christians in Jerusalem had fled from this city to Antioch. The church here was led by Barnabas, a Levite. He asked Paul the apostle to join him, and both remained here a year, and instructed many in the new faith. Afterwards they were to preach there again.

THE MISSIONARY WORK OF PAUL. Saul was brought up in the city of Tarsus in Asia Minor, where he had learned much. He became thoroughly familiar with Greek civilization, but it must not be overlooked that he also learned much from Gamaliel in the city of Jerusalem, who had taught him the doctrines of the sect called the Pharisees. Since these people insisted so strongly on ceremonies, and since many of them had been against Christ and His followers, Paul, after his conversion, felt obliged to preach against such unnecessary emphasis upon "good works." For about three years he was a Pharisee himself, but in the year 36 or thereabouts he was suddenly stopped on his way to Damascus by a bright light in the sky and a vision of Christ. He became blind for a short time, and then he was cured by one of the Christians in Damascus (Ananias). You may note that Jesus had called him Saul, for this was his original name. We know him better as Paul, which was his Latin name. It is customary to follow this same arrangement, calling him first Saul and then Paul. He immediately began to preach the gospel of Christ in Damascus, which was the old capital of the Arameans, and was located to the northeast of Palestine, while the great port of Antioch was situated to the north and near the Mediterranean Sea. Paul was soon recognized by some of the Christians and he felt that he should go away for a time in order to prepare himself for his great task. He was in Arabia for some time, and returned to Damascus. Three years later he was in Jerusalem, where he spoke to James, whom he called the brother of our Lord, meaning Christ. So there can be no doubt that there was an apostle in Jerusalem at that time who was called James and was a brother of Jesus.[1] Paul and Barnabus first preached in Antioch about the year 40-41. From there they went on their first missionary trip, namely to the island of Cyprus and southern Asia Minor. They were gone about three years (41-44). In the year

---

1. See Galatians I, 17-24.

49 Paul and Barnabas went to Jerusalem to attend the first Church Council,[1] in order to discuss with the apostles Peter, James, and John the question as to what customs (such as circumcision and the ritual laws of the ancient Hebrews) the gentiles had to follow in order to join the Christian Church. The apostles decided that the gentiles were not obliged to perform the old laws, and Paul in particular was eager to assist the gentiles in joining the ranks of the Christians.

PAUL'S SECOND MISSIONARY TRIP. From 50 to 52 Paul, accompanied at first only by Silas, and later also by Timothy and Luke, undertook his second great missionary trip, namely, in central and western Asia Minor, Macedonia, and Greece. He was ridiculed by some of the Greek philosophers when he preached on the famous hill called the Acropolis in Athens. Nevertheless, he started in Athens a small congregation, led by the famous Christian, Dionysius the Areopagite. In Corinth he had much greater success, for which we are very thankful, since he wrote to this congregation his two matchless Letters to the Corinthians.

PAUL'S THIRD MISSIONARY TRIP AND HIS ARREST. His third missionary trip lasted from 53 to 58. He started from Antioch and went to Galatia and Phrygia in Asia Minor, where he had been on his second trip, and also returned to Corinth. He spent two and a half years in Ephesus, on the west coast of Asia Minor. When in the year 58 he visited Jerusalem for the fifth time as preacher or Christian convert, some enemies of his caused an uprising against him, but he was rescued by a Roman guard. He was sent by a Roman tribune to Caesarea, where he talked with the procurator, Felix, and later with his successor, Festus. Finally, Paul appealed to the emperor in Rome, which happened in the year 60, in the reign of Nero. After suffering shipwreck in the Mediterranean Sea, he reached Rome early in the year 61. For two years he was a prisoner in a private home (61-63), and freely preached there. It used to be believed that in the year 64 he was martyred in Rome under Nero, but many scholars now believe correctly that he was set free again, and undertook a fourth missionary trip from 63 to 66, and visited Spain. Then he was imprisoned again, and was killed with the sword in the year 67.

THE CAREER OF THE APOSTLE PETER. This apostle was a stirring character. He was dramatic and emotional, but after Christ's resurrection he steadfastly preached the gospel of Christ and per-

---

1. See the Acts of the Apostles, Ch. XV.

formed remarkable miracles. Christ had once said to him that He would found His church on Peter's confession that Jesus was the Messiah. Later, as we saw, Christ told him that he would feed His sheep and His lambs. He was indeed the leader in the years from 33 to about 40, and perhaps later. In the Acts of the Apostles we read of "Peter and the eleven," and about "Peter and the apostles,"[1] so that it is not surprising that the Roman Catholics regard him as the first head of their church. All Christians agree that he was a very important preacher. But at one time he had to be corrected by Paul,[2] and he himself admitted in his letters that there was much in Paul's epistles that was difficult to understand. He was never a scholar, like Paul, and it seems that after the year 40 the leadership in the Church fell more and more into the hands of Paul. He preached in Antioch, and undoubtedly also in Rome. When he referred in his first epistle[3] to the church in which he was working and called it the "church in Babylon," he must have had in mind that in Rome, for at that time Rome was often compared with the ancient city of Babylon. Both were great world capitals and both had a bad name because of the immense amount of wickedness that prevailed in them. Peter probably died in Rome as a Christian martyr about the year 64.

THE APOSTLE JOHN. The beloved disciple of Jesus was not so active in preaching and traveling as were Paul and Peter, but he was nevertheless a man of great importance in the early Church. Christ, when hanging upon the cross, had asked His mother to act as John's mother in the future. He is said to have remained with her until her death. In the year 49 he was present at the first Church Council in Jerusalem. For many years he was the bishop of the church in Ephesus, but from 95 to 96 he had to live on the island of Patmos, because the Christians were being persecuted by the emperor in Rome. It was on this island that he wrote his Apocalypse.

THE CHRISTIANS IN ROME. Paul, in his Epistle to the Romans, spoke very highly of the Christians in the great capital. The Bible says little about this church, but since Rome was so huge, it was only natural that many Jews and Christians lived there. Nero, the cruel emperor, started the first great persecution of the Christians. Many of them were thrown before the wild beasts in the colosseum. Others were burned on poles, still others crucified, as

1. Acts II, 14; V, 29.
2. Galatians II, 11-19.
3. I Peter V, 13.

is said to have happened to Peter. But many Christians maintained correctly that "the blood of the martyrs is the seed of the Church." These people were serious about their business of being Christians. They gladly gave up their lives for the cause of Christ. For us they are an object lesson. We are now living in times of religious indifference. A Christian is not persecuted any more for his religion. At the same time, the missionary zeal possessed by such men as Peter and Paul is also gone for the most part. This is no doubt the reason why so little is done today for the Church of Christ, and why the world is so full of unrest. Let us hope that this present chapter may help you understand how much you owe to the first martyrs and missionaries. They have enabled you to read Christian books and to learn about the kingdom of Christ.

Student Activities

1. With the aid of a dictionary write out definitions for the following words: *martyrdom, gentiles, notorious.*
2. Give the reasons why the Christian Church spread so rapidly.
3. Why do so many people refuse to accept Jesus Christ?
4. Who wrote the Acts of the Apostles?
5. You have heard the story of Annanias and Sapphira; in what way does that story fit in with the practices of the early Christian Church?
6. List the books of the New Testament.
7. Why was Antioch an important city in the history of the Church?
8. Write a 100 word essay on the Apostle Paul.
9. Where did John write the Apocalypse?
10. What is meant by religious indifference?
11. Why were the Christians willing to give up their lives for Christ?
    Note: One of the early Christian symbols besides the cross was the fish. It is interesting to note that the Greek word for fish is IXTHUS; when each letter is taken separately, the following sentence can be built: JESUS CHRIST, SON OF GOD, THE SAVIOUR.
    The century we are living in is the Twentieth Century. We have many things to help make life comfortable, and yet the twentieth Century is perhaps the unhappiest century in the history of the world. Why is there so much misery in this age?

CHAPTER 15

The Christians Conquer the Greek and Roman Worlds

JESUS SEEKS NO POLITICAL CONQUEST. If Jesus had gone at the head of an army, as His disciples had always wanted Him to do, and had set the Jews free from the rule of the Romans, He would have become a very important person in Roman history. All the textbooks of ancient history would have devoted a great deal of space to Him. Let us suppose for a moment that He conquered Palestine, then Asia Minor, then the Balkan Peninsula, and finally Italy and the capital of Rome itself. Thus He could have founded His Church in the great capital of the Roman empire and then He could have dictated to the people throughout the Roman world what their religion should be. Even the conquest of a little province would have made it necessary for the public records of the Roman empire to mention His name frequently. But as it was, during His own life He was never mentioned in the dispatches of any of the Roman officials. We may say at least that none of them, if there were any, have been preserved. There are even large textbooks of Roman history which do not mention His name a single time. History books are often like our newspapers in that they will pay a great deal of attention to the actions of very foolish or very bad persons. Anyone can have his name printed on the front pages of our great newspapers, and even have his picture shown there, by doing something very queer or very criminal. So it could have been with Jesus and the early Christians.

HOW ITALY WAS CONQUERED BY THE CHRISTIANS. They quietly went about their business and gradually extended the power of the Church, so that nineteen hundred years later, in our present century, Christ rules Italy and Rome more effectively than any king has ever done. The teaching of the Christian religion is compulsory in all the public schools of Italy today, not only in the elementary but also in the high schools. Whatever you may think

110

of Italy and the Fascists, you must admit that the constant study of the Christian religion in all the public schools of Italy is something of great-importance. Jesus and His followers were indeed real conquerors who in the end defeated all the religions of the ancient world, and made both the Greek and the Roman provinces of the empire Christian, at least in name.

The Christians in Palestine. After the destruction of the city of Jerusalem in the year 70, most of the Christians fled to the region east of the Jordan River, where their congregations were small and poor. In the first half of the second century, Palestine became more Greek than Jewish. But in the cities along the coast there lived many Christians. The centers of the Christian congregations was the great city of Caesarea with its famous school and library. At the Church council at Nicea in 325 there were present nineteen bishops from Palestine. In Phoenicia, which was located directly to the north of Palestine, there were also Christian congregations, which were for the most part located along the coast of the Mediterranean Sea. Their great center was the city of Tyre, the famous port of antiquity. Ten bishops from Phoenicia attended the Church council of Nicea. Directly to the south of Palestine, in northern Arabia, Christian churches were founded in fairly large numbers, so that in a certain synod of the year 244 there were fourteen bishops present from this region.

The Churches in Syria. As we have seen before, in the great city of Antioch the apostles founded a flourishing church. Antioch was the capital of western Syria, and one of the greatest ports in the world. A synod was held there in the year 268, and there were present eighty bishops. You may be interested to know that in the history of the early Church a distinction was made between a church council which included representatives from a large section of the world, and a synod, which was attended by delegates from a much smaller region. The synod held in Antioch in the year 268 was intended only for the clergymen living and working in western Syria, that is, the region to the north of Phoenicia. During the second century the Christian religion was also preached and spread in eastern Syria, where was located the famous city of Edessa. From Edessa the Christian missionaries went east into Persia and northern Mesopotamia, where in the middle of the third century there were several bishoprics. In one of the oldest Church histories written, which dates from about the year 550, it is said that about the year 225 there were in Assyria and Mesopotamia seventeen bishoprics. We know also that there were numerous Christians in Persia, for during a persecution in the fourth century we are informed that martyrs died by the tens of thousands.

THE CHRISTIANS IN PARTHIA, SCYTHIA, AND INDIA. In distant Parthia and Scythia Christian churches were founded during the second century. Both of these regions lay outside of the Roman empire, Parthia being east of it, and Scythia north of it, namely, north of the Black Sea in southern Russia. According to many old sources, which may or may not be correct, the Apostle Thomas preached the Gospel of Christ in northwestern India, and died a martyr there. It is true, however, that there are many Christians living in western India today who call themselves "Thomas-Christians." They claim to be descendants of the early Christians of the first and second centuries, but we are not certain whether their opinion is reliable or not.

THE CHURCH IN ALEXANDRIA. Next to Rome and Antioch, Alexandria was the largest and most important city in the Roman Empire. In the second century it had a population of nearly one million, and 300,000 of those were Jews. It was only natural for the missionaries to come to Alexandria soon after the death of Christ. Eusebius, who was the first important Church historian, tells us that Mark, who wrote the second Gospel, was the founder of the Church in Alexandria. But we find no reference of any importance in the Bible to the work done in Alexandria by the Christian missionaries. From Alexandria the Christians spread their Gospel to southern Egypt and westward into Libya. When in the year 321 a synod was held in Alexandria, there were present about one hundred bishops. At the opening of the fourth century the Christians in Egypt numbered about one million.

THE CHURCHES IN ASIA MINOR. As a result of the very successful work done by Paul and John in the provinces of Asia Minor, an extremely large number of churches grew up in this great peninsula. One of the provinces there was called Asia, and its capital was Ephesus, where about the year 170 a synod was held, and where 26 bishops were present. Another important city where the Christians were active, was Smyrna on the west coast of Asia Minor. At the Church council of Nicea in 325 about one hundred bishops represented Asia Minor. In the eastern section of Asia Minor there was located the independent kingdom of Armenia, where Christian missionaries coming from Edessa and Antioch and Cappadocia preached the Gospel of Christ at a rather early time. Armenia was the first country of any considerable size that may be called a Christian land. At the end of the third century there ruled in Armenia a king called Tiridates, who made himself independent of Persia, and was baptized a Christian. He had a large number of heathen temples destroyed and declared Christianity as the state religion of Armenia. During the third and fourth centuries about four million Armenians became Christians, and there were in their country twelve important bishoprics.

THE CHURCHES IN MACEDONIA, CYPRUS, AND CRETE. We have seen how active the Apostle Paul had been in Macedonia, which included ancient Greece. Most important of all the congregations founded by him was that in Corinth, and that we have also seen. In the ports along the Greek coast, large numbers of Christians continued to preach the Gospel to their heathen neighbors. Especially important became the Church in the great city of Constantinople, which, in the first, second, and third centuries was still called Byzantium. During the fifth and sixth centuries Constantinople became the chief center of the Christian Church in the East. At the same time Rome became the greatest center in the West. The language of the churches in the regions mentioned thus far was Greek, except in those countries that lay beyond the frontiers of the Roman Empire, such as Scythia, Parthia, and India. We must now turn to that part of the Roman Empire where the Latin language prevailed, and where the important writings of the Christians were written in the Latin language.

THE CHURCHES IN ITALY. In Rome, of course, the Christians were numerous from the middle of the first century onward. But unfortunately we know very little about this Roman church of theirs. We have said above that when Peter talked about the church in Babylon, he must have referred to this Roman church. We are certain that Paul was in Rome for several years. Because of the very important place occupied by Paul and Peter in the early church, it was but natural that the church in Rome was considered so very important. We know that at a synod held in Rome during the year 251, there were sixty Italian bishops present. The Roman historian Tacitus relates that during the persecution of the Christians under Emperor Nero, a "vast multitude" was killed because of their faith. At the beginning of the fourth century there were between sixty thousand and one hundred thousand Christians in the city of Rome, who had more than forty churches of their own. At that time most of the important families still refused to accept the Gospel of Christ. Another important center was Naples in southern Italy, but in northern Italy the Christians were very slow in making converts. The oldest bishopric in northern Italy is Ravenna, and next to that is Milan.

THE CHRISTIANS IN NORTHERN AFRICA. When you consider how few people live in northern Africa today, you may be surprised to learn that during the second and third centuries of our era this part of the Roman Empire was very thickly populated, like Asia Minor, which also is a thinly-populated country today. Although the great port of Carthage had been totally destroyed by the Romans in the year 146 B.C., it had revived again, and in the second century of our era, it was once more a mighty city. It was the greatest center of Christianity in northern Africa at that time. During the first half of the fourth century there were about 250 bishoprics in northern Africa. The famous Church Father Cyprian tells that about the year 240 a certain heretic was condemned by ninety bishops, showing how many Christians there were already in Africa at that time. Christianity spread most rapidly among the Greek, Roman, and Carthagian inhabitants in northern Africa. The native population, called Berbers, remained for the most part pagan.

THE CHURCHES IN GAUL. Little is known about the spread of Christianity in the great province of Gaul during the course of the second and third centuries. Naturally the first bishoprics were established in that part which was closest to Italy, namely, the southeast. On the Mediterranean coast was located the famous port of Marseilles, while also in the city of Lyons many Christians were to be found by the year 300. At that time there were about twenty bishoprics in Gaul.

THE CHURCH IN GERMANY. As we have seen, the western and southern parts of Germany belonged to the Roman Empire, and along the great Roman roads there were to be found a number of Christian congregations. Among the great cities in this region we may mention Cologne, Mainz, and Strasbourg. At the end of the second century there seems to have been about ten thousand Christians in western and southern Germany, and immediately to the west of the Rhine River.

THE CHRISTIANS IN GREAT BRITAIN. Since Great Britain was separated from the Continent by the English Channel, the Christians did not come to Great Britain at a very early time. It seems that the missionaries went all the way from Asia Minor by sea to the British Isles, and when in 314 a synod was held in Arles in southern France, there were present three bishops from Great Britain, namely from the bishoprics of York, London, and Lincoln.

WHICH PERSONS WERE MOST EASILY CONVERTED TO THE CHRISTIAN FAITH. Since most of the travelers went to the cities first, the number of Christians in the cities was far greater than in the rural districts. Women were more easily converted than the men were. It seems that in all ages women have been more easily inclined to become religious, as you may have already noticed yourselves. Until the opening of the fourth century, most of the Christians were poor, and many of them were slaves and freedmen. But after the middle of the second century it became more fashionable for wealthy persons to join the church also. A certain emperor in the year 258 issued a separate decree against the Christians among the senators and several important governmental officials in the Roman Empire. There were also great scholars among the early Christians, some of whom we will discuss presently. But before the fourth century the Christian religion was not taught in any of the public schools, and for that reason scholars in general despised the new religion. In the Roman army there were many Christians. Among the soldiers, and even among the officers it was held by the Christians that the career of a soldier is a profession, and that a Christian may well serve his government in the capacity of a soldier. Some of the leaders of the Christians, however, thought that Christians should not take up arms in defense of the government, but they were in the minority. It is interesting to note that the great persecution of the Emperor Diocletian was first directed against the Christians in the army.

THE EARLY PERSECUTIONS. The first general persecution began under Emperor Nero, as we have seen before. On July 19, in the year 64, a terrible fire broke out in Rome, which destroyed ten of the fourteen sections of the city. It lasted six days, and most people suspected that it had been started by the emperor himself. For that reason, he, anxious as he was to free himself from this accusation, placed the blame upon the Christians, and for that reason he started persecuting them. Many strange things were told about the Christians, and the people in general were very glad to see the Christians tortured and killed. Nero opened the garden of his great palace to the public, and thousands of the Roman citizens derived great delight from seeing the poor martyrs burned upon poles, where they were sometimes covered with pitch or tar. In that way the gardens of the emperor were illuminated by the Christian martyrs at night. Many of them were thrown before wild beasts, and we also read in an early source that some of the prominent Christian women were compelled to take part in plays where they played the roles of victims who were actually being murdered. The persecutions were also probably carried on in the provinces, and they did not end until the year 68 when Nero died.

LATER PERSECUTIONS. The next persecution occurred in the year 95, when the Emperor Domitian, who openly called himself God, turned against the Christians, partly because they refused to join in the ceremonies of the Roman religion, and partly because he wanted to force them to pay a tax to the government which was to be a continuation of the money contributed to the pagan religion worship in Rome. This persecution lasted only one year. Under the capable emperors who ruled between 98 and 180 there were many persecutions of the Christians, although the emperors themselves were men of great ability and power. These emperors often complained that not only in the cities, but even in small villages, the temples were often empty, and the festivals in which the Roman gods were honored often had to be discontinued, because so few people attended them. Especially cruel was the great emperor Trajan, who ruled from 98 to 117. Among the martyrs who died during his reign is the famous Church Father Ignace. About fifty years later, under another great emperor, the well-known martyr Polycarp was killed. He died in the city of Smyrna. The last great persecution occurred in the reign of Emperor Diocletian, who ruled from 284 to 305. Many Christian churches were destroyed, and in many cases graves were opened and bodies of dead Christians removed.

THE CATACOMBS. At this time the Christians in Rome used to worship in the subterranean passages known as the catacombs. They had also worshiped here in earlier days, and many of the graves of the Christians can still be seen there today. About the year 304 the Christians in Rome hastily closed the openings that led to the passages, in order to protect the graves that had been dug there before. Many thousands of the Christians were killed, many other thousands were banished. In many cases also, the Christians were subjected to terrible torture, or had some of their limbs removed. But in the year 305 Diocletian finally gave up his throne. He realized that his persecutions had all been in vain.

THE PERSECUTIONS COME TO AN END. In the year 306 the famous ruler Constantine started his reign in the western part of the Roman Empire. Five years later several of the rulers issued a decree stating that from now on the Christian religion would be officially tolerated by the government of the Roman Empire. This decree was issued in a city of Asia Minor called Nicomedia, and was signed by four important governmental officials, including Constantine himself.

THE EDICT OF MILAN. In the year 312 Constantine made himself master of the western half of the Roman Empire. In the next year he and his partner Licinius issued the famous Edict of Milan, since they were at that time in that great city. Eusebius tells us that when Constantine was about to fight his great battle for the conquest of the western half of the Roman Empire, he saw above the setting sun a vision of a cross, together with these words: "In this sign shalt thou conquer." During the following night in a dream Christ appeared to him, and commanded him to make the cross his standard in war and conquest. Whatever may have been the nature of this dream or vision, it is certain that Constantine at this time became favorable to the Christians and that after the year 313, with a few short exceptions, the Christians were officially tolerated by the Roman government.

POWER AND EXTENT OF THE CHRISTIAN CHURCH IN THE REIGN OF CONSTANTINE. About the year 313, when the Edict of Milan was issued, there were altogether about seventeen or eighteen hundred bishoprics, nine hundred in the East, and between eight hundred and nine hundred in the West. The expansion of the Church was extremely rapid in the second half of the third century. This may partly have been due to the fact that between 258 and 303 there were very few persecutions, and of limited size. But you must not imagine that during the times of the persecutions the Christians became cowards, and that few dared to join them. It is indeed true that the "blood of the martyrs was the seed of the Church." Christianity was most successful in the following parts of the civilized world: Antioch, the greatest city in the East, Egypt, Rome, with a part of south and central Italy, the coasts of Greece and Macedonia, southern Spain, the south coast of France, and several cities in southern France. In the following regions Christianity was fairly well represented, but not very successful: Palestine, Phoenicia, Arabia, Mesopotamia, the interior of Greece and Macedonia, northern Italy, and Great Britain. Relatively few Christians were to be found in central and northern France, Belgium, and Germany.

INFLUENCE OF THE CHRISTIANS UPON THE HEATHEN. Even those who refused to join the ranks of the Christians were often strongly affected by the Christian faith. Owing to the official attitude of the Church, it became customary to consider slavery as an evil institution. In many circles marriage was now looked upon with greater respect, and many thousands of persons regarded it as something sacred. It also became customary for many Romans to practice the Christian idea of love towards one's neighbor and to lead more decent lives.

Student Activities

1. With the aid of a dictionary write out the definitions for the following words: *compulsory, bishopric, heretic, career, subterranean.*
2. What weapon did the Christians use to conquer the Roman Empire?
3. Who are the "Thomas-Christians?"
4. Who was Eusebius?
5. Name the different parts of the world where Christianity was spreading?
6. Who were the Roman emperors that persecuted the Christians?
7. What were some of the accusations which were made against the Christians?
8. Which persons were more easily converted to the Christian religion?
9. Who were some of the famous Church Fathers?
10. When was the last great persecution of the Christians?
11. What were the catacombs?
12. Write a fifty word statement on Constantine.
13. What was the Edict of Milan?
14. In what way did Christianity influence even those poeple who did not become Christians?
    Note: The Church of God will endure until the end of time. Empires, kingdoms, and republics come and go.

> *In the cross of Christ, I glory*
> *Towering o'er the wrecks of time;*
> *All the light of sacred story*
> *Gathers round its head sublime.*

CHAPTER 16

The Internal Development of the Christian Church

WHO THE APOSTLES WERE. Since Judas Iscariot betrayed his Master, and since afterwards he also committed suicide, he was no longer considered one of the twelve disciples. The remaining eleven disciples, as has been explained above, became the eleven apostles. In the place of Judas the apostles chose by lot Matthias. So there were originally twelve apostles. But it is customary to consider Paul also as an apostle, because he was appointed by Christ Himself, although it happened after the Ascension. Another Christian missionary who is often called an apostle is Barnabas. Christ gave those apostles the command to preach His Gospel wherever they could find people to listen to them, to heal the sick, to found churches, and to watch over new congregations.

THE GOVERNMENT OF THE LOCAL CHURCHES. We read in the Acts of the Apostles that in the congregation in Jerusalem it was found necessary to appoint certain persons as deacons. Their duty was to manage the finances of the congregation, to take care of the poor, and to assist the local pastor in various minor duties. Above the deacons were the *presbyters* (elders), and *episcopi* (bishops), or supervisors. You will learn in a later chapter that one important Protestant church has been named after presbyters, the Presbyterian Church. On the other hand, the great church of England is called the Episcopal Church. In the Presbyterian Church much emphasis is laid upon the work performed by the elders, or presbyters; whereas in the Episcopal Church there are bishops, but no officials called presbyters. The Presbyterian Church, on the other hand, has no bishops. At first the terms *presbyter* and *episcopus* (the singular, whereas *episcopi* is the plural) could be applied to the same person, whom we would call the pastor or the minister of the local congregation. During the second century of our era it became customary to apply the term *episcopus* to a real bishop, who was in charge of an important congregation or of a number of smaller congregations. It seems that during the first century each congregation was ruled by more than one person, and these persons formed a committee and shared in the management of the whole congregation, except that they were above the deacons, who assisted them. It became the custom gradually to *supplant* the committee by one person, for it was seen that each congregation would need a person of considerable authority, who would be in charge of all the important work, especially the preaching that was to be done. The pastor was often assisted by both elders and deacons.

How the Churches Remained in Touch With Each Other. During the first hundred years after the death of Christ, the apostles and their successors spent much of their energy in founding new churches and afterwards in maintaining contact with them. Although Jesus had said to Peter that he was to feed His sheep, it cannot be proved that Peter actually governed all the congregations that were in existence during his own lifetime. Neither can we say that Paul was the ruler of all the congregations that he himself had founded. To a very large extent the distant congregations were independent of each other. But at the same time they also were in contact with each other. It was customary for the leaders in the churches to write letters to each other and their respective congregations. It also happened frequently that members of one congregation moved to another church. Gradually the churches were drawn together, owing to the fact that they had to fight a common enemy in *paganism,* and later another common enemy in the heretics. Gradually the churches drew up a creed, and it was necessary, in order to become a full-fledged member of a church, to prove that a person did accept that creed.

The Patriarchs and Archbishops. Among the hundreds of churches in the Roman Empire during the third and fourth centuries, a few became leaders, and their respective bishops were called patriarchs, or archbishops. The word patriarch was used particularly in the East, and was applied to a bishop who was in charge of a number of other bishops. The churches in Alexandria had a patriarch to rule over them, and the same was true of the churches in Antioch and later of Constantinople. On the other hand, the bishop of Rome was seldom called a patriarch, or even archbishop. During the period from 300 to 800 his title gradually was recognized as being equivalent to a "father of the Church." He was called the Pope, meaning the father of the church. In the Church Council of Nicea in the year 325 it was decided that, in accordance with an old custom, some of the bishops in the churches would be called patriarchs, and that they were to have a supervision over all the bishops in their particular area, namely those of Alexandria, Antioch, and Rome. In all of these three cities the churches claimed that they had been founded by the Apostle Peter. The fourth city to have a patriarch of its own was Constantinople. Beginning with the middle of the second century the bishops in certain important local areas used to come together to make common decisions for all their churches, especially because of the fact that there were so many heretics in the church. These meetings were called *synods*, and often ordinary church members were present to listen to the discussions. But only the bishops had a vote. The Church Council of Nicea gave orders that in the different provinces of the whole empire there should be synods held from time to time. Each province would have its own synod. But the whole of the church would send its delegates to a meeting called a church council.

THE RULE OF THE BISHOPS AND THE PRIESTS. Each bishop had a diocese, or bishopric. He exercised a large amount of power, although he did consult the pastors or ministers of the congregations under him. Soon it became customary to use the name "priest" instead of presbyter. The priests were like the pastors in the Protestant churches of our own time. But not all the priests were pastors. It was the duty of the bishop to maintain the purity of the doctrine of the churches in his diocese. In several instances the apostles appointed bishops, but afterwards the bishops were chosen by the congregation at large, which was assisted by neighboring bishops. Very likely the clergymen in the local churches would recommend a certain person for the office of the next bishop. They would consult the opinions of important members in the local congregation, and also they would ask the advice of other bishops in the neighborhood. After that the election would take place, and sometimes the congregation could choose from among two or three candidates, or otherwise could either say that it approved or rejected the one person that had been recommended to them. The Church Council of Nicea decided that at least three bishops should be present at such an election, and that one bishop should confirm the election and install the new bishop. It was customary for priests and deacons to be appointed by the bishop, after he had secured the advice of important members of the local congregation. When these priests and deacons were installed, the other priests and deacons showed their approval by placing their hands upon the head of the new official. Many priests were merely assistants of the bishops. In the meetings of their congregation they would sit near him, and they would assist him in the church services. They would also instruct the young people in the catechism and they would help with the administration of the Sacraments. At the time when there was no bishop, they would perform the duties of the bishop. But, as we have said above, many of the priests became pastors of congregations. Certainly not every pastor was a bishop.

How the Clergy Were Paid for Their Services. In the twentieth chapter of the Acts of the Apostles and in the fourth chapter of the First Epistle to the Corinthians we read that the apostles very often were engaged in some occupation of their own, such as tent making. In that way they took care of their financial needs. But when it became customary for the clergy to spend all their time in performing religious duties, their congregations naturally would present gifts to them. Very early in the history of the Church the people in the congregation would assemble on the first day of the week (Sunday) and would leave their gifts in the local churches. The farmers would often donate to the church the first part of their crops, and in many cases people would give one-tenth of their income to the church. This practice was called tithing, and the money that they gave was the tithe. The word "tithe" means one-tenth. In the second half of the second century the custom arose in many churches to give salaries to the clergy once a month. It would not seem like salaries such as are paid today, however, for the people would often present goods instead of money. But the result was about the same.

Celibacy of the Clergy. You probably have learned before that the Apostle Paul, unlike Peter, was not a married man, and that he thought a person could serve God more successfully if he remained single than if he were married. Paul said that a married man would seek to please his wife and would be busy with his family, while a single man could devote all his time and services to God and the Church. As for the other apostles, we have no evidence to prove that they were married or single. Some of the older Christian writings say that they were all married, but others leave the question unsolved. Most of the Jews and the pagans despised unmarried persons. Some of the Roman laws even prohibited the custom that we call celibacy, meaning that a person would refuse to become married. That many of the bishops in the early church were married men, you may gather for yourselves by reading I Timothy III, 2-4, and the Epistle to Titus, I, 6. Here Paul insists that bishops, priests, and deacons must be the husband of one wife only. This may mean that they could be married only once, or more likely it means that they could have only one wife at one time. During the third century a great many clergymen came to the conclusion that it would be best for them to follow Paul's example. Later on the same custom began to spread in the East.

THE SACRAMENT OF BAPTISM. A sacrament is a sacred institution or practice in the Christian Church, founded directly by Jesus Christ Himself. Although in the course of the first three or four centuries a great many persons believed that Christ had instituted seven sacraments, Martin Luther in the sixteenth century and practically all the Protestants after him have reasoned that there are but two sacraments, namely, baptism and the Holy Supper. No real Christian would doubt that baptism is a sacrament, because Jesus was not only baptized Himself by John the Baptist, but He also gave instructions to His disciples to baptize those persons who were converted to the Christian religion. Baptism was a sacrament that a Christian needed in order to become a member of the Church. It meant that the Christian would follow Christ and would suffer with Him and for Him. It took the place of circumcision among the Hebrews in the times of old. In the first two centuries most of the Christians who were baptized were bold enough to make a confession of their faith. A synod held at Carthage in the year 252 decided that there was no reason why children could not be baptized. But when we study the sources we do find that at first a great many persons were of the opinion that no one should be baptized until he was old enough to understand the principles of the Christian faith. In a great many cases a person would be baptized almost immediately after having publicly confessed his belief in Jesus Christ. But later on it was felt necessary by the leaders in the Church to give instructions to those who wanted to join the Church. At first baptism meant complete immersion, or in other words, the person would be completely covered with water, unless he were ill. In that case sprinkling of water would be deemed sufficient. There are, however, many scholars who believe that in the West persons were baptized only up to their knees, but that water was sprinkled over the head three times by the bishop. But gradually the custom was established that sprinkling should be considered sufficient for everybody. Furthermore, opposition to the baptism of children disappeared very largely in the period between 500 and 1500.

THE SACRAMENT OF COMMUNION, OR HOLY SUPPER. Like the sacrament of baptism this sacrament was accepted from the beginning by the disciples and the apostles of Christ. In the second chapter of the Acts of the Apostles we are told that the Christians remained steadfast in the doctrine of the apostles and in the breaking of the bread. This means that, as is the custom of the churches today, the members of the church would receive Holy Communion. Perhaps you have seen a picture of a famous painting showing Christ at a large table surrounded by His disciples, ready to give them both the bread and the wine. That wine was used in the early church appears very clearly from the first Epistle to the Corinthians by the Apostle Paul in the eleventh chapter. He also refers to this sacrament in the tenth chapter of this same Epistle. When Christ pointed out to His disciples the bread that they were to eat and the wine they were to drink, He stated that these elements were His body. He said: "This is my body." Both the Roman Catholics and the Lutherans have always accepted these words to mean that the bread and the wine actually were the body of Christ. The Calvinists, on the other hand, have always thought that the word *is* means *signifies*. But all real Christians agree that the following words of Christ must be emphasized especially: "Do this in remembrance of me."

Holy Days. Instead of the Sabbath day of the Hebrews and Jews, the Christians introduced a new day of rest, which from about the year 50 was the first day of the week. It is remarkable and also unfortunate that the name "Sunday" is still given to this day both in the English and the German languages. But this is not the case in the French language and some other languages as well. In the original sources we often read of the phrase "the Lord's Day." This is the name we should all apply to the first day of the week, instead of calling it Sunday. But the custom of naming it after the sun has been established so long that it probably will be impossible to change it. As we have seen in an earlier chapter, three days out of the seven have been named after the sun, the moon, and Saturn. It seems that at the beginning the Christians merely assembled for worship on the first day of the week, and that several hundred years later it became a regular custom to refrain from doing work on that day. The Christians also for a long time considered the old Hebrew festival called *pascha* worthy of imitation. But the Christians gave another meaning to this festival than the Hebrews had done. Unfortunately, as was the case with the day called Sunday, this festival also was named after a pagan festival, namely the festival of spring named after a goddess called Eastre (Eostre). There have been enemies of the Christian Church who tried to prove that both Sunday and Easter day were derived merely from heathen customs, instead of Christian institutions. But those who are familiar with the history of the Christian Church know better than that. You may have wondered why Easter is never on the same day for two or three years in succession. Christmas day is always on December 25, but Easter day depends upon the time when the moon is full. From the middle of the second century onward it became customary to fast for some time before Easter in order to emphasize the importance of Christ's suffering which occurred shortly before His resurrection, which in turn preceded His Ascension by forty days, and Pentecost by fifty days. In many countries these latter two days have also become holidays. That many of the Christians thought it a good custom to fast also on Fridays, since the crucifixion of Christ occurred on Friday, seems quite natural. But this custom did not become universal, and it was not taken over by the Protestants, owing to the influence of Martin Luther.

DAILY LIFE OF THE CHRISTIANS. Upon the whole it was difficult to distinguish between the Christians and the pagans, because the Christians obeyed all the laws of the government except those few which commanded them to do things contrary to the will of God. For example, they refused to worship the emperor of the Roman Empire. Christians often occupied important positions in the government. Many of them, as we saw, became soldiers. But they refused to attend the pagan festivals in Rome, such as the plays or games that were performed in the great outdoor theatres. But where the Christians differed from the heathens was in their private actions. They prayed, they sang hymns, they read the Bible, they went to church on Sunday, they fasted often, they gave alms to the poor, and they spent a great deal of their time thinking about Christ and about God in heaven. What the pagans noted in particular was the purity of the lives of the Christians, and the love that they showed toward their neighbors. As one of them said: "Look how they love each other." Another custom that surprised the pagans was the highly organized system of maintaining the poor in the churches. This proved to be such a great success that one of the pagan emperors tried to imitate it.[1] The Christians upon the whole were against idleness, and they did not approve of the custom of begging for a living. Instead of supporting beggars, they provided work for persons in need of money. The Christians took great care in maintaining widows and orphans.

---

1. This was Emperor Julian.

THE ATTITUDE OF THE CHRISTIANS TOWARD MARRIAGE. Unlike the peoples of the ancient world, especially the Greeks and the Romans, the Christians placed women upon an equal footing with men. This was one of the reasons why the Christian religion spread so rapidly in the Roman Empire. Marriage was looked upon as something very sacred, and among the Roman Catholics it was considered a sacrament, because Christ was present at a wedding, where it is said he performed His first miracle.[1] Very few of the Christians were opposed to marry a second time after a person's wife or husband had died. But there was one important group that did prohibit this.[2]

WHAT THE CHRISTIANS THOUGHT OF SLAVERY. It cannot be said that the Christians directly attacked the institution of slavery. There are several passages in the New Testament that show how the Apostles Paul and Peter regarded slavery. They argued that it was a necessary institution for the time in which they were living, although they naturally did not praise it.[3] Athenagoras even said: "We also have slaves." Two other leaders among the Christians said the same thing. They were Justin and Tatian. The leaders in the Church persistently said that it was not permitted for slaves to leave their masters. They were to obey their masters, as both Paul and Peter had said in their epistles. The chief function of the Christian Church was not to preach social reform, but to make the people more religious and to prepare them for eternal life in heaven. The influence which the Christians exerted upon social institutions was indirect rather than direct. Nevertheless, there can be no doubt that the Christians helped greatly to destroy slavery in the Roman Empire. They saw very clearly the evil aspects of the institution. They deeply regretted the cruelty often inflicted upon the slaves by their masters. Consequently, in a great many cases the masters of slaves were urged by the leaders in the church to treat their slaves with greater kindness and if possible to regard them as their equals. Although among the heathens slaves were not permitted to get married, the Christians regarded the marriage of slaves as perfectly legal and proper.

CHURCHES AND CHURCH YARDS. During the first two centuries of our era the Christians did not yet have their own church buildings, but conducted their services in the homes of the rich members of their congregations. Unfortunately, the churches that were

---

1. This was the wedding of Cana.
2. These people were called Montanists.
3. See I Corinthians VII, 20-22; Col. III, 22; Eph. VI, 5; I Tim. VI, 1; I Peter II, 18.

erected during the third century were probably all destroyed in the terrible persecutions of Emperor Diocletian. It is likely that most of them were decorated with pictures, because in the years 1933 and 1934 one old church was discovered beneath the sand wastes in Mesopotamia. It had been built in a city that had been destroyed in the year 256. In this church there were found pictures of the Good Shepherd, the women at the grave of Jesus, and some scenes from the Old Testament. These pictures did not differ very much from those in a Jewish synagogue in which there were about one hundred similar pictures. But of course, the Jewish pictures did not make any reference to Christianity. At an early time it became customary to bury the Christians in what was regarded as holy, or sacred, ground. For hundreds of years this custom was maintained, and the word church yard in English literature refers to such a cemetery. The Roman Catholics still maintain this custom today, but many Protestants have discontinued it. Among the oldest places of worship, as we have seen, were the catacombs under Rome and its vicinity. Here and there among the passages there would be found a large intersection where lamps would be placed, and where services were held. Most of these catacombs were constructed by the Christians themselves, for it was permitted under Roman law for a Christian to have such subterranean passages dug on his own property and intended for graves. Altogether there were about sixty of these, almost all of which were constructed under ground surrounding the city of Rome, rather than Rome itself. Some of them date from the very first century. In several of them we may still study the paintings that were painted upon the walls (frescoes). Some of these pictures are very interesting, referring to some of the parables of Jesus, the worship of the little baby Jesus by the Wise Men, the mother of Jesus with the little baby boy, the Good Shepherd with a lamb on His shoulders, Daniel in the lion's den, and the other famous Hebrew leaders, such as Noah, Abraham, David, Jonah, and Job. Since Jesus had said that He was the vine and the Christians were the branches, there are numerous vine stalks portrayed in these paintings. The dove stands for the Holy Spirit, as well as the Christian peace of soul. The anchor stands for hope, the fish for the Savior, and the peacock for immortality. Most of the early churches above the ground were imitations of the Roman basilica, which building has been mentioned above. Because of its importance a separate paragraph is devoted to the Roman basilica.

THE CHRISTIAN BASILICA. There was one important difference between the pagan basilica and the Christian basilica. In order to make the building in the shape of a cross, the Christians added a long hall at the end of the building, which they called the transept. Beyond the transept was a small semi-circular room called the apse. Here as a rule the altar was placed. The great central hall leading from the front door to the apse way in the back was called the nave. It was flanked on both sides by beautiful columns supporting the roof. The nave was higher than the walls to the right and the left, called the aisles. The nave was lighted by windows above the roofs of the aisles. Beginning with the fourth and fifth centuries it became customary to add small rooms at the side, which were called chapels.

HERETICS AND HERESIES. Almost from the very beginning there were certain persons in the Church who refused to accept the faith of the Christians. You have already heard of the story of Judas Iscariot, who betrayed his Lord, and who may be called a heretic in a certain sense. But the word "heresy" is usually applied to a person who does not accept all the articles of faith in the Church. He may reject them all, or he may reject some of them, but he does not accept all of them. We may consider the first heretic to have been the man mentioned in the Acts of the Apostles as Simon the Magician. He asked the apostles how much they would charge him for giving him spiritual power such as they possessed, in order that he might also be able to cure the sick and raise the dead. But the apostles told him that spiritual powers were not for sale. He taught a sort of heresy. The first real group of heretics were called Gnostics. They mixed Christian teachings with the doctrines of Persian, Greek, and Egyptian philosophers and experts in religion. They showed a tendency to go too far in despising material things, especially human bodies. They talked a great deal about the mysterious element in religion and the necessity for people to go through certain peculiar ceremonies. Simon the Magician was one of these people. The Gnostics appealed to a great many books that were in circulation, and which were said to be just as much inspired as are the books that now make up our Bible. For that reason the leaders of the Christian Church assembled and drew up a list of what are called the canonical books, meaning the accepted books that belong in the Bible. It was during the second century that this list was officially made up. Until the middle of the second half of the second century, therefore, there was no real Bible, such as we know it today.

THE MANICHEANS. This particular heresy was founded by a Persian religious leader whose name was Mani, and who in the year 276 or 277 was beheaded at the command of a Persian king. His religion was a mixture of the older religions of Babylonia, Persia, and India. He made much of the supposed contrast between spiritual and material things. His followers were constantly talking about the conflict between material and spiritual forces. They thought they could gain a great deal by much fasting and much suffering on the part of the physical body. Many of them were against marriage, swearing of oaths, and military service.

ARIANISM. This heresy was taught by its founder named Arius. He lived at the end of the third and the beginning of the fourth centuries, and taught that Christ is not eternal like God the Father, and that He is not of the same substance either. In his opinion God the Father was God, but neither the Son nor the Holy Spirit were divine, such as He was. You can easily understand that such a heresy was very dangerous, because it really tried to destroy the most important element in the Christian religion. You could not call anybody a Christian if he refused to believe that Christ is the eternal Son of God, and like God a part of the Trinity. For that reason Arius was strongly attacked by some great leaders in the Church, especially by Athanasius. At the great Council of Nicea in the year 325 the heresy of Arius was officially condemned, and the creed of Athanasius accepted by the Church. Later on the Athanasian Creed was accepted by the leaders in the Protestant churches.

THE APOSTOLIC FATHERS. The Church Fathers were the leaders in the early Christian Church, up to about the year 600. Those who lived in the first century of our era are called the Apostolic Fathers, because they were either the apostles themselves, or they had been taught directly by the apostles. Among these we may name Clement of Rome, who died about the year 100, and was one of the important leaders among the Christians in the city of Rome; and Ignace, the third bishop of Antioch, who was seized by Roman officials and taken to Rome, where he was thrown before the wild beasts in the circus (107). On his way to Rome he wrote seven letters to seven important churches, including those at Ephesus, Rome, Philadelphia, and Smyrna.

THE GREAT CHURCH FATHERS OF THE NEXT THREE CENTURIES. The first of these is Polycarp, the bishop of Smyrna, who was a pupil of the Apostle John, and became a martyr in the year 154, when he was taken to Rome and in the next year killed. The greatest defender of the Christian Church during the second century was Justin Martyr. He was a great scholar and converted a large number of people to the Christian faith. He wrote books in defense of the same, and he even founded a school in the city of Rome, where many pagans received instruction in the Christian religion. He died a martyr's death in Rome about the year 165. One of Justin's pupils was an Assyrian called Tatian. He is also considered a Church Father. The most famous Christian leader to attack the heretics during the second half of the second century was Irenaeus, bishop of Lyons. He wrote powerful books against the heretics and did much useful work in checking the different heresies of his time. During the third century we meet the great Clement of Alexandria, a very learned writer, who was born in Athens as the son of pagan parents. About the year 190 he became a teacher and about ten years later the president of the great Christian school in Alexandria. He spent much of his time in explaining the great differences between Greek philosophy and Greek religion on the one hand and the Christian religion on the other hand. A still greater scholar was Origen, who wrote more than eight hundred works. He made use of seven stenographers to whom he dictated many of his writings, which include valuable commentaries on the various books of the Bible. Both Clement of Alexandria and Origen wrote their works in the Greek language. The chief Latin writer of their time was Tertullian, who is well-known as a very successful enemy of the heretics. He was less liberal and less tolerant than the other two writers we have just mentioned. One of the most saintly leaders in the Church during the third century was Cyprian, the bishop of Carthage, who was martyred in the year 258. The most influential Church Father of the fourth century was Ambrose, the bishop of Milan. He had the courage to reprimand the Emperor Theodosius for having been responsible for cruel massacres. He was a great speaker, and he converted many influential persons, including the famous Augustine, whom we shall mention in another chapter.

THE BEGINNINGS OF MONASTICISM. During the second and third centuries a large number of Christians came to the conclusion that they could serve God most perfectly by withdrawing themselves from the busy world. In their opinion it was not good for them to be in contact with sinful persons. So they moved away from cities and villages, and retreated into secluded places. Some went to live in the desert, some were hermits, and some even lived on the top of old pillars in Egypt. One of the most famous leaders among these Christians was Anthony, who lived in the Egyptian desert for about fifty years. He died there about the middle of the fourth century. Gradually it became customary for a group of Christians to live together in buildings of their own, which were called monasteries. The persons who lived in them were called monks, if they were men, and nuns, if they were women. The word "monk" means a person who lives alone, while the word "nun" is derived from an old language in Egypt (Coptic), and means pure or chaste. These monks and nuns lived an organized life which was regulated by a number of rules. The greatest founder of monasteries in the Near East was Basil, who was a bishop in Asia Minor at the end of the fourth century. He drew up a monastic set of rules called the Rule of Basil. The chief organizer of monasteries in the West was Martin of Tours, who worked in Gaul during the fourth century. In the following century the famous St. Patrick moved from Gaul to Ireland, where he established flourishing monasteries.

Student Activities

1. With the aid of a dictionary write out the definitions for the following words: *supplant, paganism, synod, immersion, persistently, aspects, basilica, hermits.*
2. Explain the terms, *patriarch* and *bishop.*
3. Does your church have a bishop?
4. What was the chief duty of the bishop in the early days of the Christian Church?
5. In what manner did the Christian congregations pay their pastors and bishops?
6. What is celibacy?
7. What are the two sacraments which Christ instituted? What is a sacrament?
8. What is the Calvinistic view regarding the words of Christ, "This is my body," and "This is my blood?"
9. In what manner were the Christians distinct from the pagans in their daily life?
10. What is the business of the Church of God here on earth?
11. Is it proper for the church to be in politics? Why not?
12. What were some of the early heresies?
13. Read the Nicene Creed which you may find in your hymn-book. Note that it has three articles; why? Note which article is the longest; why?
14. How did Ambrose, bishop of Milan, show his great courage?
15. What is *monasticism?*

CHAPTER 17

The Germanic Peoples Invade the Roman Empire

WHO THE GERMANIC PEOPLES WERE. The Germanic tribes belonged to those Indo-European peoples called commonly the Nordics. They were characterized by large bodies, fair complexion, and blue eyes. We cannot record their history before their occupation of the lands along the southern shores of the Baltic Sea about 1500 B.C. But we know that for some centuries they were content to dwell in what is now Denmark, southern Norway, southern Sweden, and northern Germany, where they kept cattle, fished, hunted, and carried on a primitive system of cultivation.

THEY PUSH SOUTHWARD. As their needs for more lands increased, they began to push southward, and came in contact with the Celts and various Slavic peoples. The Celts were darker of complexion than the Teutons, and their frames were somewhat smaller. We may assume that they belonged to the Alpine race of peoples who between 2000 and 1000 B.C. were living in central Europe. Some of these people, as we have seen, moved into Italy, where they constructed their homes upon poles.

THE CELTS. About 500 B.C. the Celts settled in what is now called France; their country was Gaul and they themselves were named Gauls. In England they were known as Britons, and in Scotland, Wales, and Ireland the name *Gaels* was applied to them. The great majority of the ancient Celts were absorbed by the Roman and later Germanic inhabitants of Gaul, though in the extreme west, in the peninsula called Brittany, they were able to retain their racial characteristics. A similar process occurred in the British Isles, where the Angles and Saxons settled in such large numbers that they overwhelmed the Celts. The latter held their own in Ireland, Wales, and western Scotland; but in England and the lowlands of Scotland on the east coast Germanic settlers absorbed the Britons.

132

WHERE THE SLAVS LIVED. The Slavs originally occupied the eastern slopes of the Carpathian Mountains. They were once closely related to the Alpine peoples, but preferred to settle in the plains of eastern Europe rather than the regions to the north and west of the Alps. After 500 B.C. various distinct tribes occupied lands of their own, thus becoming the ancestors of the Russians, Poles, Czechs, Slovaks, and other Slavic peoples. For a time they were to be rivals of the Germans even in northern Germany, as we shall see presently.

THE GERMANS MEET THE ROMANS. How long the Germans waited before they were dissatisfied with the swamps and heaths and woods of the Baltic lands, we cannot say. But by 200 B.C. they began their migrations southward, and not so very long after that date a number of tribes appeared near the northern frontiers of the Roman Empire. Julius Caesar was the first important writer to mention some of them, and about 150 years later the great Roman historian Tacitus studied their way of life and finally wrote a booklet about them (the *Germania,* 98 A.D.). From these literary sources and from the implements left by the Germans themselves we may derive a fairly accurate picture of their habits and customs.

EVERY DAY LIFE OF THE GERMANS. Before the Germans reached the Rhine and the Danube in their southward movements of migration, they knew nothing about the use of money and practiced barter. They made their living by keeping cattle, growing grain and vegetables, and hunting and fishing. The men despised the necessary work in the fields and domestic employments, which tasks were given over to the women. Their simple homes were constructed of wood and were usually located in a village, for the Germans did not like to live on separate farms. The house of the average free German consisted of but one room together with an annex for the housing of the cattle. For heating and cooking purposes a fire was kept in the fireplace in the rear of the room. Benches and one or more tables comprised nearly all the furniture; beds in the modern-sense of the word were not yet available, for the Germans were content with a little pile of straw for their bedding. Those who were of noble rank maintained more elaborate homes, decorated with weapons and game trophies.

CLOTHES WORN BY THE GERMANS. Some tribes maintained the custom of wearing skins for clothing, but others made use of clothes that were little inferior to those worn by the Greeks and the Romans. Men and women both were partial to linen for inner clothing, while in cold weather the men were dressed in short jerseys or jackets, covered with cloaks of woolen cloths or skins. The women often wore garments that resembled the classical patterns of Roman or Greek matrons. The men covered their legs with cloth wound round in a careless fashion. Since some of the German tribes used to bury their dead in hollowed trunks of trees and carefully dressed the bodies for preservation, many of these bodies have recently been found in an excellent condition; they show clearly what were the clothes worn by the primitive Germans nearly two thousand years ago.

THEIR FOOD. The food and drink consumed by them was simple and wholesome. Oats and barley were popular; after having been ground by hand, the grain was eaten in the form of porridge. Wheat and rye were also grown, and after the Romans had taught the Germans how to bake bread, the latter naturally raised more wheat and rye. But, since rye can profitably be grown on poor, sandy soil, the consumption of rye bread became much greater than that of wheat bread. Beer was brewed from barley, and sometimes the men would get drunk from drinking too much of it. Cows and sheep were pastured, while hogs were allowed to roam freely through the woods, where they lived on acorns and beechnuts.

HOW THE TRIBES WERE GOVERNED. Much has been written about the political institutions and the social customs of the Germanic peoples, for it is recognized that they were the forefathers of the dynamic peoples who built such great nations as Germany and England. Those who are interested in the rise of modern democracy naturally inquire as to what were the contributions made by the primitive German tribes. They had kings of their own, as well as tribal and national assemblies, the word "national" referring to a group of closely related tribes. The kings were limited in power, for not only did the priests serve as judges, but the assembly of all the freemen always had to be consulted by the king. The assembly elected the officials (magistrates) who were to decide suits in the counties and villages. Some of the tribes were divided into *hundreds,* that is, land units of about one hundred families. While the Saxons used the word "hundred" for such a unit, the Franks called it the "mark." These local units enjoyed their own form of government within their respective tribes. Undoubtedly they bequeathed to posterity some measure of local self-government and some traces of personal liberty for which the Anglo-Saxon race afterward became noted over the whole world.

MARRIED LIFE. The Germans appear to have strongly supported the practice of monogamy. Tacitus reported that each bride was carefully instructed as to her duties. She became "the partner of her husband's labors and dangers, and was destined to suffer and to share with him alike in peace and in war." He also stated that adultery occurred very rarely, and as a rule was followed by severe punishment.

GERMANIC RELIGION. The Germans resembled other pagan peoples in that they venerated sacred animals, such as birds and horses. They also collected images in sacred groves. They worshiped forces of nature, including the sun and the moon. Woden, or Wodan, was the chief god; Thor was the god of thunder; Tiu was the god of war; Freya was the goddess of fertility. Consequently, the English words for the days of the week, with the exception of Saturday (which is named after the planet Saturn), have all been derived from the names of these German gods.

WHY THE GERMANS WERE EASILY CONVERTED TO CHRISTIANITY. Originally the Germans did not believe that death separated soul and body, as did the Christians. In their opinion a person's life after death was similar to that lived upon this earth. Their heaven was called *walhalla*. Here their great men were said to enjoy themselves immensely in drinking wine from the skulls of their defeated enemies. Some of the Germanic tribes worshiped under sacred oak trees, and when Christian missionaries appeared among them and cut down such trees without experiencing any harm, the Germans often were quickly converted to the Christian religion.

GAMBLING AND SLAVERY. We learn from Tacitus that the men were very fond of gambling. They often gambled with such recklessness that not seldom would a man lose his property, then his personal liberty, and finally that of his wife and children. This practice will account in part for the institution of slavery among the Germans. Most of their slaves, however, had formerly been members of hostile tribes who had been defeated by their new masters. There were also to be found persons who were neither slaves nor freemen. Their condition resembled that introduced among the Romans along the frontiers of the Roman Empire, where Germanic settlers received grants of land. These settlers were called *coloni;* they were bound to the soil, but they were not slaves.

THE FRANKS MOVE INTO THE LOWLANDS (NETHERLANDS). The great migrations of the Germanic peoples occurred in the fourth and fifth centuries of our era. However, many tribes had attempted from time to time to occupy the fertile and well cultivated lands to the west and south of the Rhine and the Danube. During the third century the Franks had occupied nearly the whole of what is now the kingdom of the Netherlands and Belgium. From this region they steadily moved southward. During the fifth century they conquered the northern part of Gaul.

HOW GREAT BRITAIN BECAME ANGLO-SAXON. The Angles, Saxons, Jutes, and Frisians moved across the North Sea from Denmark, northwestern Germany, and the Netherlands into England. Little is known about their early invasions, but we are reasonably certain that these occurred during the fifth century. As we have just seen, the Germanic invaders absorbed the Britons in England and pushed others into Wales, Ireland, and Scotland. Gradually the Angles, the Saxons, and the other tribes intermarried and adopted from each other their racial qualities and elements of their respective languages.

THE GOTHS MOVE SOUTHWARD. While the Franks were occupying the Netherlands and northern Gaul, other Germanic tribes migrated southward into central and southern Germany and the regions located directly to the north of the Balkan Peninsula and the Black Sea. The most important migration was that of the Goths, who moved from Scandinavia to the region just mentioned. They were soon divided into two groups of tribes, or nations, those to the east being called Ostrogoths (or East Goths), the others, Visigoths (or West Goths). During the fourth century they were suddenly disturbed by the Huns, who moved with great rapidity from northern Asia into Europe. They killed thousands of Ostrogoths, and pushed the majority of the Visigoths into the Balkan Peninsula. So desperate were the Visigoths that in a momentous battle with the Roman legions they defeated both the Emperor Valens and his army. This was the battle of Adrianople (378).

THE GOTHS AND VANDALS MOVE STILL FARTHER. After a brief invasion to the south, as far as Athens and Corinth, the Visigoths turned to Italy, and in 410 they sacked the city of Rome. But still they were not ready to make a permanent settlement.

Within a few years they crossed southern Gaul and entered Spain. It was in Spain that they maintained a kingdom of their own which lasted from 420 to 720. Similar were the experiences of the Vandals, who also crossed Gaul and then invaded Spain. But they went still farther, and in 429 founded a kingdom in northern Africa.

SUDDEN RISE AND FALL OF THE EMPIRE OF THE HUNS. About the middle of the fifth century the dreaded Huns migrated into central Europe, and in 451 invaded Gaul under the leadership of Attila. But their great empire speedily collapsed upon his death, which occurred in 453.

THE KINGDOM OF THE OSTROGOTHS. Far different was the fate of the kingdom set up by the Ostrogoths. Under King Theodoric they occupied northern Italy. Here they defeated the barbarian Odoacer, who had assisted in the overthrow of the Roman Empire in the West (476). Now that the last emperor in the west (Romulus Augustulus, or "Little Emperor") had been deposed, the Germanic invaders were free to fight among themselves for the mastery of Italy and Gaul. Nearly the whole of Italy was conquered by the Ostrogoths, whose kingdom lasted until 555. In that year it was overthrown by a great general representing Emperor Justinian of the East Roman Empire. The same general also was responsible for the destruction of the Vandal Kingdom in northern Africa (548).

THE LOMBARDS ALSO ESTABLISH A KINGDOM. Another Germanic kingdom of considerable importance was that of the Lombards, who conquered northern Italy about the year 600, but who in turn were defeated by the Franks in 774. It was after them that Lombardy was named.

WHICH TWO GERMANIC KINGDOMS LASTED A LONG TIME. We have seen that on the continent of Europe only two Germanic peoples were able to construct a kingdom that lasted for a considerable period. That of the Visigoths in Spain was not overthrown until the eighth century, while that of the Franks continued its existence in Gaul until 987. It is to the history of this latter kingdom that the next chapter will be devoted.

Student Activities

1. With the aid of a dictionary write out the definitions for the following words: *characterized, absorbed, barter, elaborate, wholesome, posterity, venerated.*

2. List the various Germanic tribes mentioned in this chapter.
3. Which peoples of Europe are descended from the Slavs?
4. Who was the first Roman writer to mention the Germans?
5. Describe the clothing worn by the Germans.
6. Which peoples of Europe are the descendents of the Germanic tribes?
7. Which methods did Christian missionaries sometimes use to convince the Germans of the foolishness of worshipping idols?
8. How did Britain become Anglo-Saxon?
9. Who were the Huns?
10. Which Germanic tribe overthrew the "Little Emperor" of the Roman Empire?
11. Which two Germanic kingdoms lasted a long time?
12. You have read about the Franks. Of which nation were they the founders?

CHAPTER 18

The Rise and Fall of the Frankish Empire

WHY THE FRANKS BECAME SO POWERFUL. The Franks were fortunate in that they were not compelled to seek for fertile lands far from their original settlements. Consequently, they could strengthen their gains from time to time. They also were favored by the head of the Christian Church in the West, the bishop of Rome, who came to be called the Pope, that is, the father of the Church. The Franks, unlike the Goths and other Germanic peoples, had adopted the orthodox Christian faith; but the Goths were deemed heretics by the Church leaders. (The Goths had originally been converted by Ulfilas (d. 381), who was a follower of Arius.)

KING CLOVIS ENLARGES THE KINGDOM. The first great king of the Franks was Clovis (481-511), who not only seized the northern portion of Gaul (France), but also defeated a rival Germanic tribe living along the west bank of the middle Rhine. Near the end of his reign he added central Gaul to his kingdom, and finally he extended the frontiers to the river Garonne in the south.

THE FRANKS GET A CODE OF LAW. It was about this time that Frankish scholars drew up the famous code of law called the Salic Law and named after the Salian Franks. It displaced Roman law in northern Gaul and the Netherlands, where it was developed in order that the cruel and primitive mode of seeking revenge for harm inflicted upon anyone might come to an end. The Salic Law provided carefully tabulated punishments for various crimes committed. For example, when a person had been killed, the murderer had to pay to the family of the deceased a sum of money or equivalent based upon the importance of the dead victim. According to this law the value of a Frank's life was twice as great as that of a Roman's, and that of an official in the king's court three times as great as that of an ordinary freeman. In case of wounds inflicted upon a human being, his age and the value of each wounded member was noted; and in cases of cattle stealing the age and condition of the animal and various other factors were duly considered.

The Salic Law was important in the history of France (which was named after the Franks), for it specified that females could not inherit real estate, so that no woman was ever permitted in France to inherit the throne in her own right.

FRANKISH AND ROMAN CUSTOMS CHANGE EACH OTHER. Everywhere in Gaul the Roman and Frankish manners tended to fuse. The invaders gradually intermarried with the more cultured inhabitants, but in what is now southern Belgium and France they did not settle in sufficiently large numbers to alter the language of the people. To the north of this region, however, they did this, and the modern Flemish and Dutch languages are versions of the Frankish tongue. Unfortunately, as barbarians mixed with highly cultured peoples, the high level of civilization formerly maintained in Gaul was lowered. On the other hand, it must not be imagined that, after the Franks had settled in Gaul and the Visigoths in Spain, the newcomers continued to fight against the Roman inhabitants. They lived peacefully among them for the most part, and they learned much from them.

FRANKISH GOVERNMENT. Although the national assemblies continued to function, the kings gladly took over from the Roman emperors their exalted conception of a monarch's position in the state. The king learned to depend more and more upon subordinate officials, the greatest of whom was the Mayor of the Palace. The *counts* administered local units for the king, and the *dukes* controlled with military forces the various districts near the frontier. Taxation was not well understood by the Franks, and so the king had to be satisfied very largely with revenues from royal domains and from fines levied in local courts. The army was self-supporting, for the king relied upon his nobles to furnish troops at their expense. In return for this they were rewarded with grants of land.

THE MAYOR OF THE PALACE BECOMES KING. Between 640 and 750 the kings were noted for a remarkable lack of personal ability, so that the Mayors of the Palace assumed the real reins of power. One of these was Charles Martel, or Charles the Hammer, for he successfully defended the Frankish kingdom against the Mohammedan invaders from the south, whose history we shall mention in another chapter. Charles Martel was a member of a house called Carolingian. He was succeeded as Mayor of the Palace by his son Pepin, who in 751 was recognized by the Pope as the real king of the Franks. He now received his title of Pepin I.

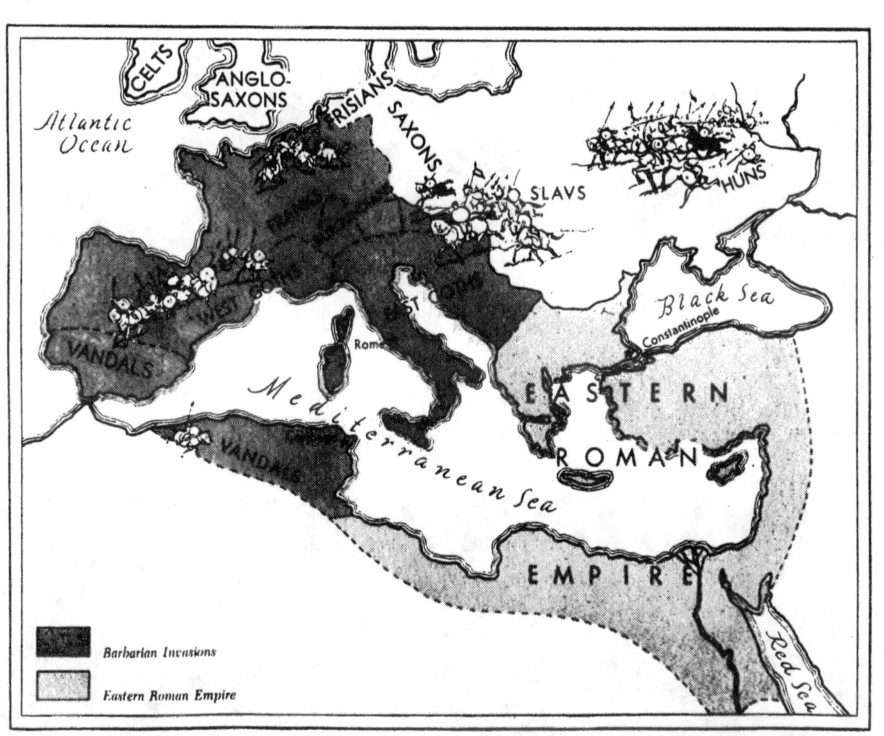

Adapted from *The Church Through the Ages,*
Courtesy Concordia Publishing House

LOCATION OF TRIBES AFTER THE BARBARIAN INVASIONS

A VIEW OF CHARLEMAGNE'S RESIDENCE, THE FALCON PALACE
It formerly stood at Nijmegen, The Netherlands.

INTERIOR OF IMPERIAL
CATHEDRAL, AACHEN, GERMANY
This portion was built in the eighth century.

A PAGE FROM ULFILAS' TRANSLATION
OF THE BIBLE
From a manuscript known as the *Codex Argenteus*
at the University of Upsala, Sweden.
The Bettmann Archive

Pepin was able to reward the Pope in 754, when he aided the Pope in obtaining independence of both the Lombards in the north of Italy and the East Roman Empire to the east of Italy. In this manner the so-called Papal States, or States of the Church, were founded, which were to remain an important state in central Italy until 1860.

CHARLEMAGNE, THE SON OF PEPIN I, BECOMES EMPEROR. The greatest ruler of the Franks was Pepin's son Charles, known as Charles the Great, or Charlemagne. He subdued the Lombards, as we have seen, subjugated the warlike Saxons in northwestern Germany; and even annexed a region in northern Spain, called the Spanish March. He also assisted the Pope, who in 799 had to contend with a riot in the city of Rome. The grateful Pope in 800 crowned Charlemagne emperor. Now the Roman Empire seemed to be restored in the West and Italy freed from the domination of the emperor in Constantinople. But how long would the Franks be able to keep intact their huge empire, which now stretched from northern Spain and central Italy to the North Sea and central Germany? All was well as long as Charlemagne lived, but when he passed away in 814, many enemies of the Franks were waiting in the north, the south, and the east to pounce upon the rich dominions held by the Franks. Before we take up the story of decline, however, let us first examine the basic elements of Frankish civilization and its contribution to the rise of modern civilization.

HOW THE FRANKS WERE GOVERNED. Charlemagne was noted for the institution of the *missi dominici,* or messengers of the king (lord), who extended the king's power into all local districts. Going usually in pairs, one representing the Church, of which Charlemagne was the head, and the other the civil power of the king, they supervised legislation and the administration of justice throughout the realm. In the *capitularies,* or royal decrees, the king set forth his desires as to how the country should be governed, how education should be improved, how churches should be constructed, and how the army should become most effective.

HOW CRIMINALS WERE BROUGHT TO TRIAL. In spite of the Salic Law, much of the old criminal procedure continued to function. *Compurgation* was the custom for witnesses and the accused person to "swear together," as the word implies; thus they were to prove his innocence. If this were deemed inadequate, trial by *ordeal* followed, and the accused person had to carry a piece of hot iron, walk upon hot iron, have a part of his body immersed into hot water, or be cast into cold water. If he received only minor injuries, or if he did not float in cold water, he was declared innocent. Sometimes *trial by battle* was used to see which person was guilty.

FRANKISH BOARDS OF JUDGES.   Under Charlemagne, however, a great improvement was made in criminal and civil procedure. Boards of judges were frequently appointed by the counts in the local districts, who would be called together from among the more wealthy and reliable landowners. They would testify and act as judges. Afterward they were only witnesses, and the real judge would preside over the board. It was from these Frankish boards that our jury system developed, as we shall see.

FARMING AND BUSINESS.   In the eighth century agriculture, commerce, and industry expanded. Such vegetables as peas, beans, carrots, cucumbers, and radishes were grown with marked success, while grain was produced in better quantity and quality than among the earlier Germanic tribes. Butter, cheese, honey, mustard, and vinegar were also manufactured with improved skill. Trade with the Near East flourished in the reign of Charlemagne, and from Asia the Franks obtained pepper, cloves, and cinnamon. The Jews were welcomed by the Franks, and Greek and Syrian traders were also well treated. A silver coinage was maintained, but the mass of the people continued to make use of barter rather than of money. The estates in the country were nearly self-sufficient, though the owners were often obliged to buy iron, sand, clay, grindstones, wine, salt, and fish, or some of these.

EDUCATION IS IMPROVED.   Charlemagne was greatly interested in the field of education and art. He established a palace school at Aachen (Aix-la-Chapelle), where he spent much of his time, owing to the fact that warm baths were to found there. He had a beautiful church built in this city, and he assembled about him learned scholars and educators, such as Alcuin, the English pedagogue and writer; and Einhard, the chaplain and the emperor's biographer.

CHARLEMAGNE IS SUCCEEDED BY A WEAK SON.   Unfortunately for the Franks, Charlemagne was succeeded by Louis the Pious, his well-meaning but inefficient son. The latter was unable to prevent the invasion of the empire from the north by Germanic sailors (the Northmen, whom we shall meet later), from the south by Mohammedans (Saracens), and from the east by Slavs and Magyars or Hungarians. He in turn had three sons who quarreled among themselves for the future division of the empire, and he was not tactful in his relation with the Pope. Hardly had he died in 840 when civil war broke out, which in 843 was followed by the Treaty of Verdun. Lothair, the eldest son, obtained the central portion running from the North Sea along the Rhine and then across the Alps into Italy; together with the imperial title. His two brothers received respectively the lands to the east and the west of this strip in the middle.

A BOUNDARY IS ESTABLISHED BETWEEN FRANCE AND GERMANY. In 870 was signed another treaty, that of Meersen, which established for centuries to come the boundary between Germany and France. The middle region to the north of the Alps disappeared, but the earlier division had left a tradition of a disputed zone between East Frankland (later called Germany) and West Frankland (France). Here many wars were to be fought between Germans and Frenchmen, to determine who was to have the Rhine Valley.

THE FRANKISH EMPERORS AFTER 870. Lothair, the son of Louis the Pious, and the grandson of Charlemagne, bequeathed the imperial title to his son, Louis, who ruled Italy only. In 876 it went to Charles the Fat, who was for a few years the ruler of all the Frankish lands (884-887). After his death it was held by one of his nephews in Germany. But after 900 the title was disputed and gradually lapsed. The Carolingian House became extinct in Germany by 911, and in France by 987, while Italy was divided among many rulers.

WHY CHARLEMAGNE AND HIS EMPIRE WERE SO IMPORTANT. Thus ended the empire constructed by Charlemagne and his illustrious predecessors. But their work had not by any means been in vain. A time was to come when peace was restored and the invaders were driven out of France and Germany and the Netherlands. The career of Charlemagne would be heralded in song and storybook. His institutions were revived and the imperial title restored. The chaos of the ninth century was duly followed by a great revival of commerce and industry. The churches and palaces, though partly in ruins, reminded the statesmen and scholars of later days of the great work begun under the Franks. Both France and Germany claimed Charlemagne as their national hero, — and both nations built their institutions upon the foundations so securely laid by this extraordinary personage.' Thus the Franks became for many people and generations a source of inspiration and wonder; their empire reappeared in another form and thus remained imperishable.

Student Activities

1. With the aid of a dictionary write out the definitions for the following words: *consolidate, displaced, intermarried, intact, decrees, self-sufficient, illustrious.*
2. Why were the Goths heretics?
3. What were some of the provisions of the Salic Law?
4. Who were the Mayors of the Palace?
5. Write a 100 word essay on Charlemagne.
6. How was the guilt or innocence of accused persons determined in the Frankish kingdom?
7. Why did the empire of Charlemagne fall apart after his death?
8. When was the first boundary between Germany and France established?
9. Why is Charlemagne considered a great man?
   Note: Charlemagne could not write. He tried to learn the art of writing when he was quite an old man, but lost patience and gave it up. But he was determined that the young in his empire should learn to read and to write, and with that purpose in view he caused numerous schools to be established for the education of the young.

CHAPTER 19

Europe and the Orient in the So-called "Dark Ages"

IN THE PERIOD FROM 500 TO 1100 THE BYZANTINE EMPIRE AND THE SARACEN WORLD CERTAINLY WERE NOT IN THE "DARK AGES." At the very time that Germanic warriors fought over Italy and other parts of the Roman Empire in the West, the East Roman Empire, which is also called the Byzantine Empire, received new strength under the able emperor Justinian (527-565) and some of his successors. A little later Mohammed founded a new religion in Arabia, and soon after his death, which occurred in 632, his followers conquered Syria, Palestine, Persia, northern Africa, Sicily, and Spain. These Arabs came to be called Saracens. They constructed a marvelous civilization at the moment when in western Europe the "Dark Ages" were in full swing. Moreover, as the Saracen merchants and scholars spread over western and southern Asia, they learned that great progress had been made there in many fields of human enterprise. For these reasons you must be very careful with the use of the term "Dark Ages."

IN THE REIGN OF JUSTINIAN THE EAST ROMAN EMPIRE BECAME VERY WEALTHY AND POWERFUL. It was in the reign of Justinian that the famous code of Roman law called the code of Justinian, or the *Corpus Juris Civilis* (meaning the Code of Civil Law), was drawn up. This great work was not only a collection of laws but it contained also important decisions and opinions by Roman jurists. At the same time the East Roman Empire was considerably enlarged by the great general Belisarius, who destroyed the Vandal kingdom in Africa, while in Italy he conquered the Ostrogothic kingdom.

THE GREATNESS OF CONSTANTINOPLE. In the period from 565 to 1095 Constantinople was the largest city in the world with a population of about 800,000, an enormous foreign trade, a large number of industrial establishments, and two famous universities, one conducted by the civil government and the other controlled by the Church. Since Constantinople was formerly called Byzantium, the state of which it was the capital is often called the Byzantine Empire.

THE WEALTH AND POWER OF THE BYZANTINE EMPIRE. In the so-called "Dark Ages" this empire led the world in commerce, scientific agriculture, the methods employed in warfare, many of the arts, and government. In the second half of the sixth century two Christian monks brought from China cocoons of silk worms and seeds of the mulberry tree. These enabled the empire to secure in Europe and western Asia a monopoly of the trade in raw silk for five hundred years. The tremendous flow of commerce brought into the imperial treasury vast revenues, for a ten percent tax was levied on imports and exports in Constantinople. In this manner the government could build up a magnificent bureaucracy, which assisted the autocratic emperor. Its army was the finest in the world, and numbered about 120,000 men; while during the seventh century and from about 850 to 1050 the navy was the strongest to be found anywhere.

TAXATION AND THE GOLD STANDARD. The state maintained a regular system of taxation, unlike the former Roman Empire and the contemporary states. It established the first important use of the gold standard in the history of Europe and the western world. The gold coin which formed the basic unit was first called *solidus* and later *bezant*. It was kept pure from about 325 to 1075. The government, unlike those of the western countries in the Middle Ages (the period from 500 to 1500), permitted bankers to loan money freely to merchants and all others who needed capital.

THE BYZANTINE EMPIRE WAS VERY HIGHLY CIVILIZED. Learning and art were highly developed, and the services rendered by the Byzantine Empire to the growth of western civilization were of the greatest importance. Not only did Constantinople check the attacks of the Saracens in eastern Europe, but its scholars preserved Greek culture when the western countries knew almost nothing about it. Moreover, the Byzantine Empire spread civilization among the Slavic peoples. The enlightment of the government may be seen in the free instruction offered by the state university in the liberal arts, philosophy, and the classics. A fine example of Byzantine architecture is the Church of Saint Sophia (Holy Wisdom), built in the reign of Justinian. We shall refer to this church again in our chapter that deals with medieval art.

THE SARACENS WERE IMITATORS. Compared with the glory of Constantinople, the civilization of the Saracens seems little more than a reflection of what the Byzantine Empire had already produced. The Saracens were for the most part Arabs, that is, Semites, like the Jews; and under the leadership of Mohammed (570-632) they formulated one of the world's most powerful systems of religious thought. They were good pupils of the Byzantines, and of the Hindus in India, but they surpassed them both in their ambition to conquer distant lands and to extend their own commerce.

MOHAMMED AND THE KORAN. Mohammed was born and brought up in the holy city of the Arabs, called Mecca. He carefully studied the religions of the Hebrews, the Christians, and the Persians; from these he derived his own, though he added some elements which distinguished Islam, that is, Mohammedanism, from all other religions. His most important thoughts were collected by his followers and written down in the form of a book, the famous Koran. This tells of the great Hebrew prophets, who were said to be on a par with Jesus Christ. There was but one god, Allah, and one supreme prophet, Mohammed. The description of the Mohammedan heaven and hell resembles in a few respects those mentioned in Christian writings. But one curious feature of the Mohammedan religion is that in this life a person may not consume alcohol, while in heaven he can drink barrels of it without experiencing any trouble. Polygamy was permitted, prayer deemed necessary at least five times a day, pork and other unclean meats forbidden, and a pilgrimage to Mecca strongly urged. A priesthood was not developed.

CAUSES OF SARACEN POWER. The causes of the swift conquests achieved by the Mohammedans are (1) the simplicity and brevity of their creed, (2) the clever way in which the Saracens won over the subjects of the Byzantine Empire by offering them lower taxes, (3) the divisions within the Greek, or Orthodox Church, which weakened the churches, and (4) the economic pressure caused by poor crops and dried up pasture lands in Arabia, which impelled the Arabs to seek better lands.

THE CHIEF CENTERS OF SARACEN CULTURE. Among the great centers of Saracenic culture may be mentioned Mecca, the holy city; Medina, to which town Mohammed moved in 622 from Mecca, (this event is called the *Hegira,* and the date is the first year of the Mohammedan era); Cairo, in Egypt; Damascus, in Syria; Bagdad, constructed by the Saracens in Mesopotamia; and Sevilla and Cordova, in Spain.

WHAT THE SARACEN SCHOLARS AND ARTISTS ACCOMPLISHED. The Saracens brought to Spain a number of new flowers and shrubs. They opened new schools there and founded fine libraries. Their beautiful buildings, such as the Alhambra Palace in Granada, and their lovely gardens compared favorably with the poor cities of other regions in western Europe. Their churches were called *mosques,* and were noted for the slender towers named *minarets.* The Saracens borrowed much from the Greeks and the Christian scholars in Syria and Mesopotamia, while from India they brought the system of numbers called erroneously the Arabic numbers. They made excellent progress in astronomy, and surpassed all others in their knowledge of physics and chemistry. Among their literary works may be mentioned the well-known collections of stories, *The Thousand and One Nights.*

How Far the Saracens Spread Their Religion. Saracen merchants traveled far and wide, venturing into the heart of Russia, and they followed the course of the Vistula River to the Baltic Sea. They sold oriental products to the Scandinavian countries and traded with all the regions along the shores of the Mediterranean Sea. They also entered India and had contact with China and Japan, though much of its was indirect. Today over seventy million inhabitants of India are Mohammedans, while the overwhelming majority of the population of seventy millions in the Dutch East Indies also belong to their faith. Northern Africa, Asia Minor, Syria, Persia, Mesopotamia, and Arabia have remained Mohammedan to this day. Altogether there about 210 million Mohammedans in the world.

The Peoples of Ancient India. Before the Mohammedans entered India, this country had been subject to various invasions from the north. The earliest inhabitants appear to have been the Dravidians, who had arrived between 2500 and 1500 B.C. In recent years some of the leading scholars have come to the conclusion that these people were closely related to the Sumerians of about 3000 B.C. Subsequently Aryans entered India from the north in successive invasions. They brought with them the advanced culture of ancient Babylonia. Their oldest writings are called the *Rig-Veda.* The word *Veda* means knowledge, especially religious knowledge, and it is not surprising to note that the *Rig-Veda* were religious poetry written by the priests. They speak of gods who were known as great powers of nature and who affected human beings. Several classes of superhuman beings and evil spirits were also distinguished. In the early period there were no temples, but sacrifices were offered at the hearth in private homes. It was believed that diseases were caused by demons and that the dead continue to exist in a ghostlike form. Afterward a new form of religion was introduced, which was called *Brahmanic,* for it dealt with the one supreme god, Brahma, who out of his own substance was said to have created the world. Salvation was the union of the individual soul with the universal soul.

RELIGIOUS BELIEFS AND CUSTOMS. The doctrine of the transmigration of souls also was widely held. According to this a person may inhabit a body for a time and in another life inhabit another body, sometimes even an animal body. The caste (that is, the position in society), the sex, and one's fortune were said to be determined in advance by previous acts. The word *Yoga,* which was very old, signified the means of uniting the individual soul with the godhead. Thus was formed the Hindu religion, which ever since the beginning of our era has been the popular religion of India, though, as we have just seen, seventy million out of 350 millions later adopted the Mohammedan faith. The great Bible for the Hindus is the *Bhagavad-Gita,* which has gone through hundreds of editions. It is considered a masterpiece of religious writing by the Theosophists of our day. Since it was composed about the year 150 A.D., it would appear that some of its teachings have been derived from the Christian religion, especially so since the idea of a God who forgives sins and demands love as does the God of Christians, was unknown in ancient India.

COMPARISON BETWEEN HINDUISM AND CHRISTIANITY. The great Hindu book agrees with the New Testament in that both are opposed to what we might call the materialistic spirit; they both accept the idea of an almighty God who continues to sustain the universe and who is always perfect and will last forever; the New Testament and a large part of the Hindu book are opposed to the doctrine of *pantheism,* which means that everything is a part of God. But Hinduism tolerates both good and evil; it ignores individual personality and knows nothing of the fatherhood of God; it has developed a terrible caste system; it encourages the idea that women are inferior to men; and it includes the worship of idols and sacred animals.

THE RELIGION CALLED BUDDHISM. The system of religion called *Buddhism* also originated in India, but it was not accepted by many inhabitants, so that it is now extinct in India, having migrated to China. The person who founded this religion called himself Buddha, that is, the Enlightened One. He lived from about 560 to 480 B.C., and his native country was the region now called Napal, near the foothills of the Himalayas. He did not write a book, which was also true of Jesus and Mohammed; nor is there to be found a satisfactory biography of him written in his own time. His disciples handed down his oral sayings, which were later collected in books. Buddhism is a way of salvation, and it must be achieved by each person for himself. The supreme goal is the *Nirvana,* that is, the "blowing out" of one's individuality. The highest state attained in this life is that of a Saint, who has given up all moral infection, all desires of the flesh. Today Buddhism flourishes in China, Japan, Burma, Siam, and Ceylon. Altogether there are about 150 million Buddhists in the world today.

CONFUCIUS. China, however, also developed a religion of its own, which was founded by Confucius (551-478 B.C.). History cannot record what was the culture of the first inhabitants of China except that they lived in the western portion and steadily pushed eastward along the Yellow River. It is clear to us that they had removed from the lands directly to the east of Mesopotamia and had brought with them much useful knowledge. But it is not clear what they did with this knowledge. At first there were a number of independent kingdoms, but afterward the kings acknowledged the rule of the Chinese emperor. Between 900 and 650 B.C., however, the power of the emperor declined and China was ruled by a loose confederacy of state governments. Finally, about 200 B.C., a more strongly centralized government was set up under the rulers of the Han dynasty, and now China entered upon a period of great prosperity and a high level of civilization.

THE INFLUENCE OF CONFUCIANISM. Between 600 and 400 B.C. nine books were composed to which the name of Confucius became attached, although he did not do much more than transmit some of them. They comprised the five Canonical Books and the four Classics, and were so highly regarded by the Chinese that they affected their thinking more than the Bible affected the Christians in some of the European countries. There are about 350 million Confucianists today. This orthodox religion of China was called Confucianism by the scholars in the western world, but the Chinese named it the School of the Learned. It was a combination of nature and ancestor worship. The emperor, called the Son of Heaven, was the head of the state religion. Heaven was thought of simply as a personal god who determined the length of each person's life. There has been no doctrine of creation, but the beginning of things has been accepted as a matter of fact. High moral standards have been maintained, especially the respect shown by children for their parents and ancestors. The Chinese believe that man is good, but tends to deteriorate as he grows older.

CHINA REMAINS A SECLUDED COUNTRY.   North of China lived the wild Tartars, who, like many of the Chinese, belonged to the great Mongolian race. In order to keep them out of China, the emperor about 220 B.C. had the famous Great Wall constructed, which is the largest monument ever raised by man, surpassing by far in size even the Great Pyramid in Egypt. For many centuries the Chinese were suspicious of foreigners, which accounts in part for the fact that their civilization was not subject to rapid changes nor to the influence of the western nations. The Chinese contributed but little to the making of western civilization. We did learn, however, that the art of manufacturing silk was carried from China to the Byzantine Empire. It is likely that the invention of printing in Europe, which occurred during the fifteenth century, was partly the result of the spread of Chinese methods of printing that had been established during the eighth century. The use of gunpowder likewise originated with the Chinese. The Europeans also learned from the Chinese the art of making porcelain, and perhaps the mariner's compass. Examinations for positions in the civil service were held in China for centuries before the Europeans dreamed of using them.

THE SARACENS WERE FRIENDLY AND TOLERANT.   Neither the Hindus of India nor the Chinese were greatly interested in expanding their foreign trade. This was left largely to the Saracens, who were willing to please their clients in many ways. Christians living among them received the privilege of worshiping in their own churches, and in Palestine they were freely permitted to worship at the holy spots where Jesus had trod. The Saracens were polite and cultured, interested in the promotion of commerce and industry, and until the second half of the eleventh century they enabled the Europeans to trade with the peoples of the Far East.

THE COMING OF THE SELJUK TURKS.   But it was during the eleventh century that a tribe of barbarians came from northern and central Asia, conquered Asia Minor, and occupied Palestine (the Holy Land). Although they adopted the faith of the Saracens, they were unwilling to extend the hand of friendship to the Christians. They became fanatical Mohammedans, and disturbed the Christian pilgrims in the Holy Land. The result was that the emperor of the Byzantine Empire became thoroughly alarmed and appealed to the Pope for aid against the Seljuk Turks, as the newly converted Mohammedans were called, in distinction from the Semitic Saracens. In this manner the Crusades were started near the end of the eleventh century. Before we take up their history, however, we must make a study of the growth of the Christian Church.

Student Activities

1. With the aid of a dictionary write out the definitions for the following words: *enterprise, jurists, monopoly, transmigration.*
2. Who was Justinian?
3. How did cocoons of silk worms get to Europe?
4. What were some of the teachings of Mohammed?
5. Name some things which we have obtained from the Saracens?
6. What is meant by the caste system of India?
7. Who founded the religion of the Chinese?
8. Why did the Chinese build the Great Wall?
9. What two things probably originated among the Chinese?
10. What does the phrase, "Fanatical Mohammedans," mean?
11. In what ways did the Seljuk Turks differ from the Saracens in their dealings with the Christians?
12. List the chief countries and important men that you read about in this chapter.
    Note: This chapter deals mostly with the Eastern world or the Orient. That means all of Asia and the eastern part of the Balkan peninsula in Europe. Europe and the Americas are known as the Western world. Note also that the center of the Christian Church was Europe. Asia, Africa, and the Americas (not yet discovered) were in the grip of heathen religions.

CHAPTER 20

The Early Medieval Church and the Crusades

THE RISE OF THE PAPACY, OR THE TITLE AND OFFICE OF THE POPE. The Christian Church remained united for about a thousand years, but the western Church, which came to be called the Roman Catholic Church (the word "Catholic" means "Universal"), was ruled by the Pope, and the eastern Church (the Greek, or Orthodox, Church) was directed by the Patriarch in Constantinople. The Pope derived his authority partly from the fact that Rome, of which he was the bishop, was for hundreds of years the capital of the Roman Empire. Besides, an ancient tradition recorded that the Apostle Peter was martyred in Rome, where he had lived for several years as the pastor of the whole Church. Thus the theory arose that Peter was the first Pope, or representative of Christ upon the earth. The first important Pope to emphasize these facts was Leo I, who lived in the fifth century.

AUGUSTINE AND JEROME. Among the great Church Fathers of the period from 325 to 600 may be mentioned St. Augustine (d. 430), the author of two famous books. In his autobiography (*Confessions*) he tells of his conversion to the Christian faith and other interesting events, while his other work, *The City of God*, explains the superiority of the Christian religion when contrasted with the religions of Greece and Rome. Another outstanding Father was Jerome, who translated the Bible into Latin from the Hebrew and Greek. His version, called the Vulgate, became the official version of the Roman Catholic Church, and it was also the basis of the Protestant Bibles. The eastern Church, on the other hand, clung to the Septuagint version of the Old Testament, which had been used by the disciples and the apostles, as well as the early Church Fathers. The oldest copy of the Bible extant today dates from the fourth century and contains the Septuagint version of the Old Testament in the Greek language.

BENEDICT FOUNDS THE BENEDICTINE ORDER. Shortly after the year 500 the most famous of all monastic orders was founded in

153

Italy by St. Benedict, and is named after him, the Benedictine Order. It officially established the three monastic vows of poverty, chastity, and obedience, and, although it was not originally noted for learning and agricultural skill, these characteristics were acquired during the Middle Ages. The order provided education in many regions where there were no schools except those of the order, and it also offered food and shelter to pilgrims and travelers of various kinds.

THE CAREER OF GREGORY THE GREAT. Another Italian churchman who achieved much for the Church was Gregory the Great, who ruled as Pope from 590 to 604, and is considered the last of the great Church Fathers. In his time Rome was almost deserted and many of its buildings in ruins. He restored order and prosperity in the city, preached powerful sermons, and wrote excellent books, of which his *Pastoral Care* was popular among the clergy, because it contained valuable advice for them.

MISSIONARY WORK PREVIOUSLY DONE IN ENGLAND AND IRELAND. Perhaps even more important was the fruitful missionary zeal of this industrious and pious Pope. He was very anxious to convert the Germanic peoples in the British Isles and Germany. Although in the fifth century many of the Irish had been won over to the Christian religion by St. Patrick, little had been done in England. The Irish missionaries under the leadership of Columba (d. 597) had established numerous churches and monasteries in western Scotland and western England. They had opened schools and libraries, and they had won fame for their beautifully decorated manuscripts. Some had even gone to Gaul and preached the Christian faith there.

GREGORY SENDS THE MONK AUGUSTINE TO ENGLAND. But Gregory I was not satisfied with this work. He entrusted to a prior in one of his own monasteries, whose name was Augustine, the task of introducing the Christian religion into southern and central England. In 597 Augustine arrived in England, and he founded there the archbishopric of Canterbury. During the seventh and eighth centuries the English in turn sent out their own missionaries, of whom the best known is St. Boniface, the "Apostle of the Germans." In 754 he was killed in the northern regions of the Netherlands by some barbarians who chose not to become Christians.

THE CHURCH IN THE EAST AND THE SCHISM OF 1054. It must not be imagined, however, that only in western Europe was missionary work performed among the heathen. The eastern Church, as we have seen, also contributed a large share in converting the Slavic peoples. This church also had its own monastic orders, and, what is highly significant, its own university, before western Europe had a single institution of higher learning. Since the Byzantine Empire was very wealthy and powerful, and since the Church had originated in the Near East, the Patriarch in Constantinople opposed the claim of the Pope to universal dominion over the Church. The difference in language (Roman versus Greek) increased the friction, while some minor disagreements made it difficult to come to an understanding. For example, the eastern Church taught that the Holy Spirit proceeds only from God the Father, and not from the Father and the Son both. The Patriarch said that the Pope erred grievously in this respect. Finally, in 1054 the leaders came to the conclusion that the two branches of the Church could no longer remain united, and so they have ever since constituted two separate churches. This momentous split in the Church was called the *schism*, from the Greek work *schisma*.

THE POPE FACES NEW TROUBLES. Shortly after 1054 the Pope encountered fresh difficulties. In Germany, France, and England ruled monarchs who were becoming very ambitious in their desires to check the power of the Pope and of the clergy in general. As long as western Europe had remained in chaos and there was no strongly centralized government left that could maintain order and promote commerce and industry, and as long as the clergy operated almost all the schools that were in existence, the people naturally looked up to the Church as the real government. The clergy had taught the peasants improved methods of agriculture, had signed documents, had built new libraries, had preserved the records of the past, and had prevented crime from spreading too much. The Church still had its own courts and taxed everybody. Practically all inhabitants (only Jews and Mohammedans were excepted) were born into the Church and had their lives organized by the clergy, so that the Church had become by far the most important institution in western Europe.

RIVALS OF THE POPE. But in the tenth and eleventh centuries, strong kingdoms arose which gradually began a contest with the Pope for a share in the government of the people. The king in Germany was since 962 also emperor, and by the middle of the eleventh century this emperor was Henry III, a man of such power that he had been able to control the election of several popes. He had also supported a reform party which had sought to improve conditions in the monasteries and in the papal court in Rome. In 1095, for example, it was decided that hereafter only *cardinals* could elect a Pope. Thus Henry's own friends had added new power to the papal chair in making it more independent of the civil rulers. But Henry was dead by this time, having been succeeded in 1065 by his son, Henry IV.

GREGORY VII AND HENRY FIGHT THE INVESTITURE STRUGGLE. Henry IV is remembered for his unfortunate struggle with Pope Gregory VII (1073-1085), who proved to be a strong opponent. Not only did he succeed in abolishing marriage of the clergy (thereby upholding *celibacy*), but he also limited the abuse called *simony*, that is, the sale of church offices. More than that, he determined to deprive the civil, or secular, rulers of the right of *investiture*, which was the practice on the part of these rulers to confer upon important members of the clergy certain lands that belonged to the Church, together with the office in the Church that went with them. Whenever a bishop or abbot or prior died these lands belonging to his bishopric or monastery were granted anew to his successor. Gregory did not object to this, for he realized that real estate was under the jurisdiction of the civil government, especially in his age, the age of feudalism, which we shall describe presently. But he disliked the fact that a king felt empowered to bestow upon a bishop the symbols of his ecclesiastical office, namely, the ring and the staff.

HENRY IV IS DEFEATED. In 1075 Henry IV was informed about the Pope's attitude, but he took no immediate action, thinking that he might thus prepare himself for the coming struggle. The Pope grew impatient and *excommunicated* the emperor, which means that the emperor was no longer permitted to attend the Communion Service (Mass) in the Church, and also was deprived of other privileges, besides the obedience of his subjects. The latter for the most part now turned against him, so that he was forced to go to Canossa in Italy, where the Pope was staying, and beg the Pope to forgive him. But no definite settlement was made until the Concordat of Worms was drawn up in 1122, which was a compromise, similar to those agreed upon in the first decade of the twelfth century between the Pope and the kings of England and France. The emperor received the power which he had enjoyed before, namely, that of conferring upon churchmen their lands, but not the symbols of their office, while he kept some control in the election of bishops.

INTERIOR OF A MEDIEVAL
BAKESHOP
A miniature from the *Codex Picturatus*
(fifteenth century).

A MEDIEVAL TAILOR'S SHOP
From a fourteenth-century miniature.

A MEDIEVAL SCRIBE AT WORK
By Jean Miclot, secretary to Philip the Good,
Duke of Burgundy (1419-1467).

A SIXTH-CENTURY IVORY PLAQUE
Scenes from the life of Joseph.

The Bettmann Archive

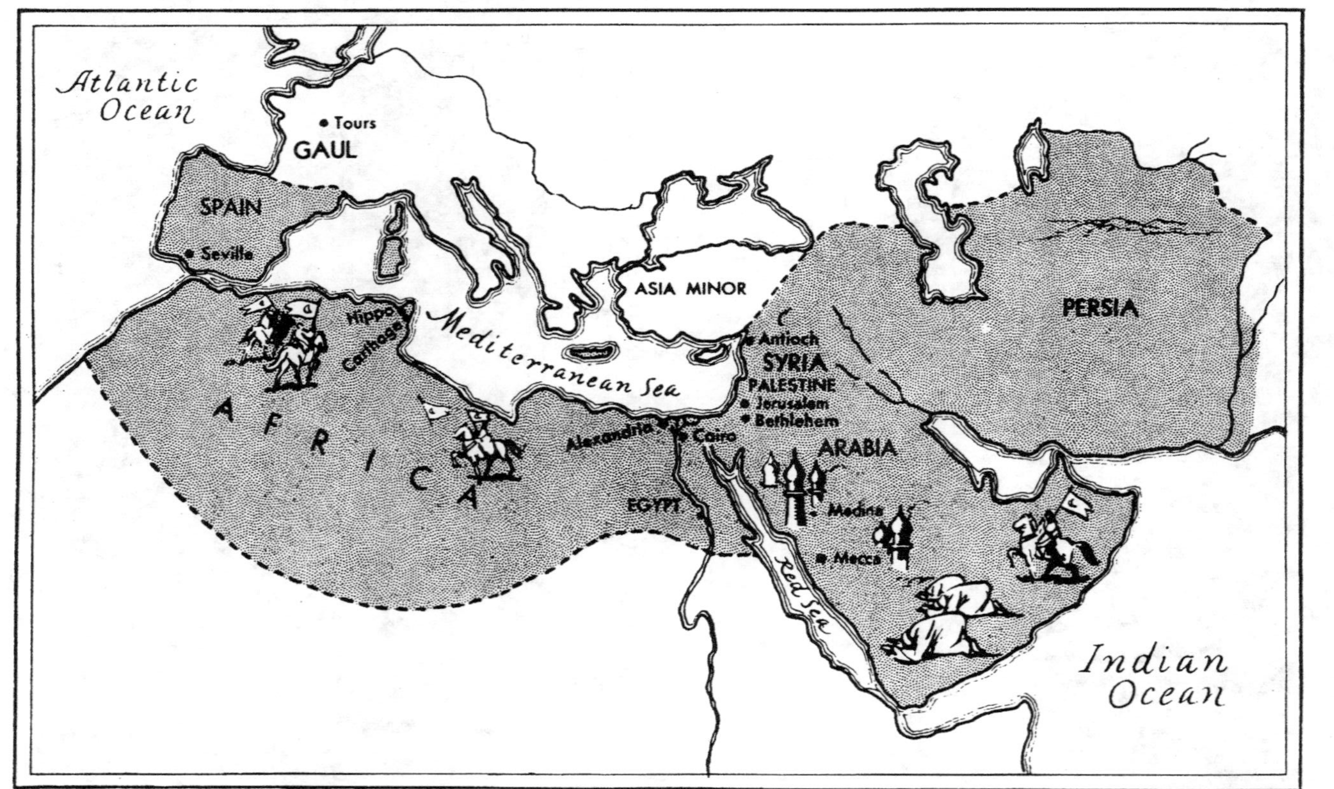

Adapted from *The Church Through the Ages*, Courtesy Concordia Publishing House

THE CONQUESTS OF MOHAMMEDANISM (A.D. 632-732)

INNOCENT III IS THE MOST POWERFUL OF THE POPES. The papacy reached its greatest power under Innocent III (1198-1216). He firmly ruled the Papal States and controlled some of the policies of several kings, especially those of England, Portugal, Aragon, Hungary, Poland, and Denmark. He had his ward, Frederick II, elected emperor in Germany, and he made even the powerful king of France (Philip II) take back his wife, whom he had deserted for another woman.

THE FRANCISCAN AND DOMINICAN ORDERS ARE FOUNDED. It was in the time of Innocent III that two important monastic orders were founded. They were called mendicant or begging orders, for their members originally begged from house to house for food and clothing, exactly as did those disciples of Jesus whom He sent out two by two to heal the sick, comfort the poor and preach the Christian religion. These mendicant monks or friars did much for the revival of true religion. The Franciscans, founded by St. Francis of Assisi, were noted for this kind of work; while the Dominicans, named after St. Dominic, devoted themselves more to the work of teaching and preaching, and the suppression of heresy.

THE FIRST CRUSADE IS UNDERTAKEN. Religious fervor was also seen in the labors of the crusaders, who continued on an enlarged scale the pilgrimages to the Holy Land that had begun centuries before 1100. The First Crusade was the result of an urgent request for aid against the Seljuk Turks sent by the emperor of the Byzantine Empire to Pope Urban II. The latter in 1095 addressed a large crowd of devout men in central France, who at once promised to go to Palestine and rescue the holy places from the *infidels,* as the Turks were called. Two different groups of men, led by distinguished dukes and counts, went along different routes to Constantinople, but only one of them succeeded in marching through Asia Minor, taking Antioch, and finally Jerusalem. The latter city fell in 1099, and now the Kingdom of Jerusalem was established. Three other Christian states reached northward along the Syrian coast and thence eastward to the upper Euphrates River.

THE SECOND AND THIRD CRUSADES FOLLOW. But the joy of the crusaders and their supporters in Christian Europe did not last long. When in 1144 the state in the extreme north was seized by the Mohammedans, the Second Crusade followed in 1147. Though led by the emperor of Germany and the French king, it accomplished nothing. The fall of the kingdom of Jerusalem in 1187, when taken by the great Mohammedan statesmen Saladin, aroused the Christians to renewed zeal. So the Third Crusade was organized in 1190 by three famous monarchs in the West, the emperor, the king of France, and the king of England. However, the Holy Land could no more be recovered; all the Christians were able to conquer were three cities on the coast, including Antioch.

IN THE FOURTH CRUSADE CONSTANTINOPLE IS PLUNDERED. The Fourth Crusade is more important, for it led to the taking of Constantinople by the crusaders under the guidance of the Venetians, who were to carry them to the Holy Land, but made them go north to the wealthy capital of the Byzantine Empire (1204). The city was partly sacked and plundered; it never recovered from this terrible blow and declined rapidly after 1204.

SOME OTHER CRUSADES. Altogether seven important crusades were distinguished by number from one to seven. But there were many others of lesser importance. One of these was the Children's Crusade of 1212, in which about 50,000 boys and girls under twelve participated. They had expected that God would permit them to do what their elders were unable to accomplish. Had not the Savior said that of "such is the kingdom of heaven?" They had no doubt that at their approach the waters of the Mediterranean would be laid dry *at their feet*. But no such thing happened, and thousands perished along the way, either from exposure to the weather or from hunger. A large number found a place on some vessels going southward, but instead of being taken to the Holy Land, they were sold to Mohammedans as slaves!

THE RESULTS OF THE CRUSADES. The results of the crusades have been variously estimated. There is no doubt that more than a million lives were lost in them and that immense sums of money were spent on them. Secondly, the absence of tens of thousands of wealthy landowners together with a multitude of laborers produced beneficial changes in the relation between the owners of the land and the tillers of the soil; the latter received better pay for their work and more social importance. Thirdly, the Christians noted with some surprise that many of the Mohammedans were highly cultured and also religious, so that both Christians and Mohammedans became more tolerant of each other. Fourthly, the contact between Europe and Asia was greatly extended and commerce expanded, particularly in Italy. The Europeans were more interested than before in the spices of the Orient, the carpets and rugs, the glassware, sugar, tea, coffee, and dates imported through and from the Near East. The donkey and the mule were brought to Europe, rice and cotton were more widely cultivated in Spain and southern Italy, and more extensively consumed in the other European countries. Finally, literature was enriched and scholarship improved. But Palestine, Syria, Egypt, and Asia Minor remained in the hands of the Mohammedans.

Student Activities

1. With the aid of a dictionary write out the definitions for the following words: *universal, schism, infidels, exposure.*
2. Who was the missionary called Augustine?
3. How old is the oldest copy of the Bible that we have?
4. Who is known as the "Apostle of the Germans"? Why?
5. Why did the eastern Church and the western Church split?
6. Which kings were not willing to let the Pope at Rome have all power?
7. Which pope had the most power?
8. Describe the mendicant orders.
9. What were the crusades?
10. Give the causes of the crusades.
11. What did the Europeans get from the Orient as a result of the crusades? Note: Christ has established His Church on earth to bring people to faith and to feed them with the Word of God. God has also established the state. The business of the state is to establish and keep law and order by force if necessary. These two institutions (Church and State) must take care of their respective duties. It is very bad when the Church tries to do the work of the state and vice versa. The result of such intermingling has always been bloodshed and misery. Read the first amendment to the Constitution of the United States.

CHAPTER 21

Feudalism Spreads in the States of Western Europe

THE SECOND PERIOD OF INVASIONS IN WESTERN EUROPE. The Christian countries of western Europe, as you have seen, were often invaded by barbarians and Saracens when the Byzantine Empire and the Mohammedan world were becoming rich. Shortly after Charlemagne's death the fierce Northmen arrived in their boats from Norway and sacked the thriving towns of western Germany, the Netherlands, France, and Spain. At the same time the Saracens established a foothold in Sicily, from where they attacked the mainland of Italy and southern France. They even plundered Rome at one time (846), while the year before the Northmen (also called *vikings*) sacked the city of Paris. To make matters worse, the Magyars (Hungarians) and the Slavs invaded central Europe and central Germany with considerable success.

FEUDAL GOVERNMENT IS BORN. Amidst the chaotic conditions of the ninth and tenth centuries a peculiar system of government arose which is called *feudalism*. The national government lost nearly all of its power, and the national armies, courts, systems of taxation, capitals, and currencies disappeared. Although there were still kings, these rulers possessed little more than the mere title of king. The dukes and counts now had their own armies, courts, and coinage; while they in turn had to surrender some powers to lesser nobles and clergymen.

WHAT THE LORDS AND VASSALS DID FOR EACH OTHER. Even more remarkable was the way in which the ownership of land was changed to meet the new conditions. Vast numbers of landowners, when they saw that they could not defend their property against the invading enemies, made arrangements with their more powerful neighbors for their mutual advantage. The lesser man received protection from the greater man on condition that he share with his *lord* the title to his property. He became the *vassal*. Although he

160

remained in his own home, and continued to work his own fields, he owed the lord certain services. Oiiginally these were of a military nature and required about forty days out of each year.

WHAT THE VASSALS DID FOR THEIR LORDS IN TIMES OF PEACE. In times of peace these duties assumed another aspect, and the vassal would be obliged to render to his lord financial assistance. Occasionally he would be called upon to perform personal services, either in the lord's court or his home. For example, he might help his lord in dressing himself, or when he was hunting Upon the death of a vassal, his son had to pay an inheritance fee. When a bishop, abbot, or prior was elected to his new position, he was expected to present to his lord the return from the lands he administered for the bishopric or monastery. He would do this for a period of one year or half a year. In addition to the payment of fixed charges, the new person who received the land, called the *fief*, rendered *homage* to his lord by kneeling before him and holding his hand and promising him respect and service.

WHO COULD NOT BECOME VASSALS. In the period of disorder that caused the rise of feudalism, not all men who needed protection against the invaders were fortunate enough to become vassals. Those who were members of the poorer classes and owned little or no land did receive protection from the lords, and they also had homes of their own, but the nature of the services they performed was very different from those which the vassals had to render. Though some of them remained freemen and worked on the lord's fields as tenants, most of them were or became *serfs*, that is, they were like the *coloni* in the Roman Empire whom we have mentioned before. Only a few of them were employed in business or private homes.

HOW THE SERFS DIFFERED FROM THE SLAVES. Unlike the slaves, the serfs remained attached to their particular services. They could not be bought and sold individually, though they were often inherited or sold together with the land upon which they worked. Their lord, or master, as a rule owned an estate called the *manor*. Sometimes the name "vill" was also used to refer to the estate upon which the serfs worked. In England it was the custom to distinguish between various types of serfs, and those who were called villeins enjoyed a slightly better status than the average serfs.

WHAT KIND OF DUTIES THE SERFS OWED THEIR LORDS. It was the duty of the serf to render many services to the lord of the manor, for which he received no pay. He would work on the land of the manor at stated times, two or three days a week in normal seasons and a little more in busy times. Occasionally he had to give to the lord a few chickens or his best calf, or some of his vegetables and grain. He also paid a fee for grinding his grain at the lord's mill, for baking his bread in the lord's oven, and for pressing his grapes in the lord's winepress. Moreover, he had to keep the roads and the lord's buildings in good repair. He was distinctly inferior to his lord, whereas the relations between the lord and vassal were honorable, that is, the vassal and the lord belonged to the same social class. Many a lord was also the vassal of another lord, but no serf was ever a vassal and no lord was ever a serf of another lord. Feudalism and manorialism are indeed two distinct institutions, and in hundreds of instances one would exist without the other.

WHY CASTLES WERE BUILT. In case the manor house was exceptionally large and fortified with thick walls and towers, it would be called a *castle*. In such a building the lord would assemble the cattle and the serfs in times of war. Hard though the lot of the serf was, he gratefully remembered the circumstances under which he or his ancestors had been saved by the powerful lord with his soldiers and his castle or manor house. The best sites were usually selected for the castles, either on top of a prominent hill, or on the slope of a mountain overlooking a river, or at the confluence of two or more rivers. Wherever the grounds were low, a wide ditch was constructed around it called the moat, and when the castle was attacked, the drawbridge in front was pulled upward. The defenders would hide themselves behind battlements or small windows, and shoot arrows at the enemy forces, or throw stones at them, or pour melted lead on them. The opposing forces would often make use of battering rams, similar to those employed formerly by the Romans. The invention of gunpowder and the use of cannon after 1350 made it much more difficult to defend castles, but they continued to be built even as late as the sixteenth century.

WHO THE KNIGHTS WERE. Noblemen in the Middle Ages generally were *knights*. They were not born knights, however, since knighthood was deemed an honor that could only be acquired through training and character building. The young son of a nobleman as a rule was employed in the home of another noble, where he served as a *page*. He learned the art of *chivalry*, which was a way of life practiced by refined nobles. The page was taught to ride a horse well (the word *chivalry* was derived from the French word for horse, *cheval*). He had to be polite to the ladies;

handle the sword, lance, and battle-axe; assist his lord in make-believe battles called *tournaments;* participate in social entertainments, such as dances, singing to instruments, and games of chess. His business was to be a gentleman, cultured, polite, refined, graceful, and courteous. When he had finished his course of training, he was knighted in an elaborate ceremony. He received the stroke of the sword upon his shoulder, and an experienced knight pronounced him capable of his new station in life. Often a member of the clergy was present to bless him and remind him of his exalted position and responsibility.

WHAT THE THREE FEUDAL AIDS WERE. The knights of the Middle Ages engaged in much fighting and hunting, for they deemed it below their dignity to work for their living. Fighting was regarded as a pastime, and usually the knights did not indulge in much bloodshed, for their main purpose was to capture another knight and thus exact from him a ransom, which the vassals of the captured knight had to pay for him. It was also the duty of the vassals to give their lord money for the dowry, when his daughter was married, while the ceremony of knighting was such an expense for the father of the new knight that also in this case he asked his vassals to make their contribution. These three forms of financial assistance were called the three feudal aids.

WHAT THE WORD "LADY" MEANT. The noble ladies, unlike the Greek women, shared in the social life of their husbands and sons. They nursed the sick and the wounded, and had charge of the servants in the manor house or castle. They supervised the spinning and weaving in their homes. Whenever the weather was suitable and the local situation favorable, the women went out to hunt with the aid of falcons. These birds were perched on the ladies' wrists and sent out to capture smaller birds. The ladies also spent much of their time playing chess, checkers, and dice. They resembled the women of antiquity in painting their cheeks, dying their hair, using false hair, and taking immense pride in their luxurious garments. Not seldom did the local priest reprimand them and induce them to turn their thoughts a little more to spiritual things.

HOW SOME NOBLES BEHAVED AT HOME. Unfortunately, the nobles often were gluttonous and undignified in the manner they treated their own wives. They would scold them and sometimes beat them brutally. Their banquets were often elaborate and lasted a long time. Heavy eating and drinking were common, and after everyone had eaten and drunk plenty, the host would call in some jesters called *fools,* who would tell funny stories.

WHAT KIND OF CLOTHES THE NOBLES AND LADIES WORE. The clothing worn by the nobility had originally been spun at home, but the crusades had caused an increased demand for finery that was manufactured in the cities and brought to the country homes by peddlers. Sometimes the nobleman would buy cloths and other needed articles in town. The men wore by preference a belted jacket and tights, the women a gown that extended from the upper part of the neck to their feet. In cold weather hoods and mantles were worn over these clothes.

FARMING DONE BY THE SERFS. The peasants lived together in a little village. Their homes and their food and their clothing were very similar to those of their forefathers, which have been described above. They used the three-field system of cultivation, leaving one-third of the tillable soil lie idle each year. Oxen were used for plowing and pulling the carts. Cows were kept very largely for their milk, but in winter the majority were killed, because the peasants did not yet know how to grow root crops for their cattle, so that they became skinny and could not be kept alive unless a large proportion were butchered. The serfs worked small strips of land upon which they raised their own crops; the woods and pasture lands were held in common or else the lord would charge a fee for the use of them. On the heaths sheep and goats were pastured under the care of a shepherd. Peat was dug for fuel and some of the plants were used for thatch on the roofs of the humble homes, though reed was more frequently employed for this purpose.

DAILY LIFE OF THE SERFS. It is customary in many circles to describe the lives of the medieval peasants in such a light as to exaggerate their misery and burdens. They worked from twelve to fourteen hours a day in summer, sometimes even longer. They had no window panes and the smoke of their fires had to escape through an opening in the roof or the door. Their food was indeed simple and not well balanced. They could not read or write. Many of their lords were unreasonable in their demands. But you must not overlook the fact that serfdom was far superior to the form of slavery employed in the United States till 1865, even by highly cultured and refined personages. Moreover, the serfs of the Middle Ages were better treated than multitudes of laborers in the first half of the ninteenth century. Chivalry was certainly not an empty name, and the tremendous power of the Church caused the great majority of lords to regard the serfs as equals before God. The number of holidays was much larger than those of modern times, with the result that the peasants could often attend church or rest at home. Finally, their tasks were not so laborious as many scholars can imagine today, in our age of hurry and bustle and speed. In western Europe plants grew slowly, the weather was mild, the manner of living wholesome. When the weary peasant did come home late some nights he slept as well as do our workmen who have rushed to and from their factories, and who must have their trips, funny papers, radio entertainment, and numerous strikes before they feel that they get their share out of life. Contentment and happiness were easily achieved by the serfs of the Middle Ages, strange though this may seem to thousands of modern interpreters.

WHAT HAPPENED TO THE EASTERN PART OF THE OLD FRANKISH EMPIRE. In the feudal age (1000-1300), the kings and emperors who ruled in their respective states were as a rule of slight importance. We shall mention only a few of them, beginning with Germany. East Frankland gradually developed into what was called at first the Germanic-Roman Empire, and after 1250, the Holy Roman Empire. Here were to be found four great states, namely, Saxony, Franconia, Swabia, and Bavaria; each was ruled by a duke. The first kings belonged to the Saxon house, and it was one of them, Otto I, or Otto the Great, who in 962 was crowned emperor by the Pope. He was noted for checking the Hungarians and the Slavs, who had been invading Germany from the East, and for ruling firmly over the great dukes. The kingdom in Italy had fallen to pieces in the first half of the tenth century, and since Charlemagne's empire had included northern Italy, it was natural that Germany and northern Italy were united in one empire. In the preceding chapter we have noted the reigns of two other emperors, Henry III and his son, Henry IV. After the death of Henry IV in 1106 the imperial power in Germany and Italy declined, owing in part to the fact that the emperors had to be elected by the leading princes, who took care in each case to limit his power in order to protect their own.

HOW FRANCE BECAME UNITED INTO A STRONG KINGDOM. In West Frankland feudalism had made an early start, but the power of the king steadily increased at the very time that the emperor in

Germany saw his power decline. In 987 a new royal house commenced its rule in a small region around Paris that came to be called the "Island of the Franks." This *Isle de France* was the beginning of France. Under the firm hands of the kings that belonged to the Capetian House, or the House of Capet, numerous counties and duchies were annexed to the royal domains. The strongest of these kings we have noted before, Philip II, or Philip Augustus (1180-1223). He was a contemporary of Pope Innocent III, and joined the Third Crusade. He annexed Normandy and several counties to the crown, so that before his death the kingdom of France was firmly established as the first of the new national states in the West. The dukes and counts, together with the other nobles, were gradually being deprived of their rights to hold courts of their own and to organize armies within France. Before long a national legislature would be called together to assist the king in making France a unified country.

THE BEGINNINGS OF THE ENGLISH NATION. While France was rapidly becoming the most powerful state in western Europe, England remained poor and backward. Before the ninth century a number of kings ruled in several kingdoms, but about 830 King Egbert of Wessex united the various states into one kingdom, called England. During the next forty years England was repeatedly invaded by the Northmen, who were called the Danes by the English. The illustrious English king, Alfred the Great (871-901), set aside a region in the north for the Danes, called the Danelaw, where they ruled in their own power. In the meantime Alfred codified the laws of England, translated important Latin works into the Anglo-Saxon language, and entertained learned men from abroad. In his reign the *Anglo-Saxon Chronicle* was partly completed; it contains much information about the English people of that time.

THE ENGLISH GET A LIMITED MONARCHY. In the tenth century England was divided into *shires,* and each of them was put under a *shire reeve* (sheriff), who represented the king. In the central government the king was assisted by a council of great nobles and clergymen, called the Great Council. It was out of this council that Parliament developed in later centuries. Although the leading nobles had the power to elect their kings, they were bound to restrict their choice to one family, that is, the royal family. Both the division into shires or counties, and the system of limited monarchy were with a few exceptions maintained for many centuries, so that even today England still has the same counties and the limited monarchy.

THE NORMANS CONQUER ENGLAND. Shortly after the year 1000 England was ruled by a Danish king, but after a quarter of a century of Danish rule, an English king by the name of Edward the Confessor held the royal power. He died in 1066, and soon after his death William, the duke of Normandy, invaded England, defeated a rival candidate for the throne at Hastings, and seized the whole English kingdom. By granting huge estates to his followers under feudal tenure, he introduced the basic principles of feudalism into England. Other results of this "Norman Conquest" will be noted in the next chapter.

SPAIN IS NOT YET UNITED. In Spain a number of Christian kingdoms were established during the tenth and eleventh centuries, when the Mohammedans were slowly driven back to the south. Among these were Castile and Aragon, which would some day play an important role in the expansion of Europe. To the west of Castile was founded the kingdom of Portugal.

THE FOUNDING OF LESS IMPORTANT KINGDOMS. In central and northern Europe the feudal age also gave birth to a number of kingdoms, including the three Scandinavian countries, Denmark, Sweden, and Norway, which were united under one king in 1397. Other new kingdoms founded between 800 and 1000 were Poland, Bohemia, and Hungary. Furthermore, Swedish statesmen established a new state around Moscow, called Muscovy. The natives called the Swedes "Ross" or "Russ," and thus it happened that the modern word "Russia" originated.

FEUDALISM FINALLY DISAPPEARS IN WESTERN EUROPE, BUT LINGERS LONGER IN GERMANY AND EASTERN EUROPE. Feudalism became so strong in Germany and Poland that the state called Holy Roman Empire gradually was divided into more than two hundred little ones, while Poland was ruined by its nobility, so that it later disappeared as an independent nation. However, France, Spain, and England were soon in a position to get along without feudalism and to institute a strongly centralized form of government. Thus the change to the modern state was slowly accomplished in western Europe, while Germany and the countries of eastern Europe advanced very slowly, and in this manner failed to take part in the great race for world dominion.

Student Activities

1. With the aid of a dictionary write out the definitions for the following words: *sacked, mutual, turmoil, status, reprimand, gluttonous.*
2. Explain feudalism in your own words.
3. Who were the serfs? In what way were they different from slaves?
4. Describe how castles were built.
5. How were the castles defended against enemies?
6. What were the activities of a medieval "gentleman?"
7. How did the "ladies" occupy themselves?
8. We have many kinds and types of amusements; what type of amusements was in vogue during the Middle Ages?
9. Describe the life of the "serfs."
10. What was the "Isle de France?"
11. How did William of Normandy become king of England?
12. How did the word, "Russia," originate?

Note: Feudalism cut up almost all of Europe into small sections. Each section was ruled by a lord, and the land was worked by the serfs. Thus there were no nations in the sense that we understand the word, "nation," now. The kings were supposed to be overlords, but they had very little power, because the lords in their strong castles could snap their fingers at the king.

CHAPTER 22

England and Scotland in the Middle Ages

THE NORMAN CONQUEST BRINGS NEW CUSTOMS TO ENGLAND.
After the Norman Conquest the English people were subject
to the powerful and beneficial civilization of the French. William
the Conqueror (William I) not only introduced into England the
principles of feudalism as practiced in his native Normandy, but he
and his associates also brought with them the use of the French
language, French customs, and the knowledge of French architects. Although Normandy had been settled in the ninth century
by Northmen, after whom it had been named, these invaders had
not been numerous enough to impose upon the earlier inhabitants
of Normandy their speech and racial characteristics. Normandy
was as much a part of medieval France as was the region around
Paris. Its people were speaking a French dialect when William the
Conqueror added England to his original domain.

HOW THE ENGLISH LANGUAGE WAS FORMED. For generations
the masses of the people were but slightly affected by the language
and the customs of the nobles from Normandy. However, their
Anglo-Saxon speech gradually merged with the French language
employed by the king and the majority of his nobles, so that the
simpler and more common words remained Germanic, while the
words used almost exclusively by the upper classes became largely
Romance, that is, like the speech of the ancient Romans. In this
manner the English language was formed from two radically different tongues, so that approximately one-half of the English vocabulary is of Germanic origin, and the other half is derived very
largely from French.

THERE WAS NOT ENOUGH FEUDALISM IN ENGLAND TO WEAK-
EN THE CENTRAL GOVERNMENT. The introduction of feudal customs into England was not on such a large scale that it resulted in
the decentralization of the government. On the contrary, the English nobility, which before 1066 had become unruly, was firmly
ruled by William I and his younger son, William II. The system

of local government was also but little affected, though we observe that the name "county" was given to the shires for a time, and some of the English nobles were called counts. However, the name "count" was not long retained in England as a title, except when applied to foreign counts. The jury system was undoubtedly of foreign origin, as we shall see presently.

ENGLISH TRADE WITH THE CONTINENT NATURALLY EXPANDS. The intimate contact between England and Normandy resulted in an increased flow of commerce and the exchange of many ideas and customs. The English also grew more interested in Flanders, which was becoming the most thickly populated and the most wealthy region for its size in western Europe. Flanders lay directly to the north of Normandy and was near England. Consequently, those English cities which were nearest to the southeast coast grew more rapidly than those situated farther inland. London, Dover, and Norwich profited greatly from the Norman Conquest. Moreover, the whole of England and Scotland were benefited by the close contact with the highly-gifted people of medieval France and Flanders. Chivalry, monastic reform, new types of architecture, and new forms of literature were well received by the English. We shall refer again to this important section of medieval history when studying the more important features of medieval civilization.

ENGLAND AND NORMANDY ARE RULED TOGETHER BY THE HOUSE OF PLANTAGENET. Although William the Conqueror upon his death in 1087 bequeathed Normandy to his oldest son, Robert, and England to William II, the two countries were not to remain separated long, for Henry I, the younger brother of William II, ruled over both. Besides, England soon had another French king. Since Henry I had left no male heir, the throne passed to his daughter, Matilda. She married a French count called Geoffrey Plantagenet, and when she died in 1154, her son, Henry II, inherited Normandy, England, and several French counties. Henry II was the first in the line of Plantagenet kings of England. But having been brought up in France, and having married a French princess, who ruled a large part of France in her own name, Henry II spent little time in England and never learned the English language. Nevertheless, he was one of the greatest of English kings, and even extended for the first time the rule of the English monarch over Ireland. While Scotland developed a monarchical form of government of its own, Ireland became subject to the rule of English kings.

HENRY II IMPROVES THE LOCAL GOVERNMENT. Henry II (1154-1189) is noted for having improved the King's Court, instituted by Henry I. This body was made up of a small number of trusted officials who assisted the king, among them the chancellor, or royal secretary; the justiciar, or chief of the judiciary; and the treasurer. Henry II also made use of traveling judges who would travel through the counties and hold court sessions for the king, thus extending throughout the realm the king's justice. It was their practice to meet with the sheriff, who also represented the king, as we saw.

ENGLISH COMMON LAW IS FOUNDED. Even more important was the foundation of English Common Law, for which Henry II was largely responsible. He had found the system of law in a chaotic condition, owing to a civil war that had preceded his reign, and to the custom of earlier monarchs who had neglected to organize the various systems of Anglo-Saxon, feudal, and manorial law. Moreover, the Norman kings favored French and Roman laws, so that all was chaos before the reign of Henry II. Assisted by legal experts, who carefully studied Roman law and the decisions of courts of past centuries, he had a new code assembled which was flexible, for it was made up of the accepted local legal customs and the decisions of the royal courts, to which afterward were added the measures passed by Parliament. Unlike the countries on the Continent, England developed a system of its own, independent for the most part of Roman law.

HOW THE JURY SYSTEM WAS STARTED. Henry II also introduced the jury system, which was originally very similar to the boards of judges used formerly by the Frankish kings. The word "jury" is derived from the French verb *jurer,* to swear, for the witnesses who were called together swore under oath that they were telling the truth. Henry II decreed that twelve men should constitute such a board in his country, as well as in various parts of France and the Netherlands, where the Frankish custom was still continued. For more than three hundred years after his reign the witnesses were not kept apart from the jury, for it was the duty of the board to investigate and to pass judgment. On the continent the verdict was left to the judge, but in England and the United States the institution finally developed as it now operates, leaving the decision largely with the jury.

KING JOHN LOSES NORMANDY AND HAS TO GRANT THE MAGNA CHARTA. Far different from Henry II was his younger son, John, who was decisively defeated abroad by the king of France, and lost Normandy and most of the other territories he had inherited from his father in France. He was also defeated in a conflict with Pope Innocent III, and had to surrender England to the Pope, who returned the kingdom to him as a fief of the papacy. Finally, he had to sign the famous document, Magna Charta, or the Great Charter, dated June, 1215. It was not unlike earlier charters, such as that signed by Henry I on his accession to the throne in 1100. But it was more extensive and was granted under more spectacular circumstances, for the king had been surrounded by his nobles and forced to sign it.

WHAT THE GREAT CHARTER (MAGNA CHARTA) DID FOR THE ENGLISH PEOPLE. The charter stated that "no freeman may be taken, or imprisoned, or outlawed, or banished, except by the lawful judgment of his peers,[1] or by the law of the land." It devoted much attention to feudal dues and duties, and it protected the merchants from royal injustice. It also provided that the king was to issue letters of invitation to the archbishops of Canterbury and York, the bishops, and abbots (the *lords spiritual*); and to the earls and chief barons (the *lords temporal*), to attend the Great Council, which soon was to become the beginning of Parliament. The Magna Charta still forms a part of the British constitution, for this constitution is made up of the important decrees of the royal courts, the Great Council, and Parliament. The importance of Magna Charta must not be exaggerated, however, for in 1679 Parliament found it necessary to pass the *Habeas Corpus Act,* which provided that no one could be imprisoned without a fair trial, showing plainly that Magna Charta had failed to do that for the English people. The main feature of the document is the limitation of the king's power.

IN THE FOURTEENTH CENTURY PARLIAMENT BECOMES VERY POWERFUL. To indicate how powerful Parliament became in the fourteenth century, we must mention the fact that in 1327 it deposed Edward II, because he had been defeated by the Scotch at the Battle of Bannockburn (1314), and because he had not ruled efficiently in his own kingdom. Before the end of the fourteenth century, Parliament had taken away from the king the power to impose direct taxes (such as an income tax) without its consent, and it had also restricted his power to levy indirect taxes (such as a sales tax). But this remarkable growth of parliamentary power in England was a bit too fast. Between 1485 and 1640 many

---

1. This word means "equals."

kings and at least one queen (Elizabeth) were to make Parliament weaker than the monarch. On the other hand, even in the darkest days of attempted absolutism the subjects of the king could point to Magna Charta and to the developments of the fourteenth century, for they were precedents that could never more be fully ignored.

WHY THE HOUSE OF LORDS LOST MUCH OF ITS POWER. As soon as feudalism declined, and the clergy and the nobility had to give up much of their power, the House of Lords, in which they had seats, yielded a large portion of its power to the House of Commons. This lower house was made up of the representatives of the middle class, and later also of the masses of the people. Today the House of Lords serves merely as a check upon excited members of the House of Commons by delaying legislation. Unlike our Senate, the House of Lords can no longer prevent any legislation which has passed in the House of Commons from becoming the law of the land. For, unlike our Senate, the House of Lords does not represent the masses of the people but is made up of men with titles who retain their seats for life. England, like all other nations in the western world, had to learn much from other peoples before it could pass on the torch of learning and liberty to less enlightened countries.

THE ENGLISH KINGS ANNEX IRELAND AND WALES, AND TRY TO SEIZE SCOTLAND. Since England formed the largest political unit in the British Isles, its kings attempted to annex the others. The first king to succeed partly in this task was Henry II, who extended his rule over Ireland. In 1284 Edward I conquered Wales, and introduced there the system of English law and county government. In 1301 his oldest son received the title of Prince of Wales, which title has ever since been conferred upon the heir to the English throne. Not content with the conquest of Wales, Edward I also determined to seize Scotland. But the Scotch defended themselves with great courage, and their kings found a useful ally in the kings of France. Thus, with French aid, the rulers of Scotland were able to maintain, with a few short interludes, the independence of Scotland. It was not until 1707 that England and Scotland were united, and even then it could hardly be said that England had annexed Scotland. For more than a century England had been ruled by Scotch kings, and it seemed advantageous to both countries that they should be united and have a common parliament. We shall learn more about this union in a later chapter.

Student Activities

1. With the aid of a dictionary write out the definitions for the following words: *beneficial, vocabulary, decentralization, flexible, ally.*
2. What is the English language made up of?
3. How did it happen that England and France were united under one king?
4. How did the "jury" system begin?
5. Write a paragraph on King John. Note: there has only been one King John in the History of England. What do you think could be the possible reason for that?
6. What was the Great Council?
7. What does the term, "Habeas Corpus," mean?
8. Why was Edward II deposed by Parliament?
9. What was the English House of Lords made up of?
10. How did the title, "Prince of Wales," originate?
11. When were England and Scotland united?

CHAPTER 23

How Several Great Nations of Modern Europe Are Born

FEUDALISM AND SERFDOM DECLINE, AND NATIONAL STATES MAKE THEIR APPEARANCE. During the thirteenth and fourteenth centuries both feudalism and serfdom rapidly declined in western Europe. For one thing, the cities were growing fast, and many workmen were needed there from the country. So serfs would run away or ask for better living conditions. Often they were now given wages instead of a share in the crops, and the moment they began to work for wages, or a part of the crops without having to do the old servile work, they ceased to be serfs. Moreover, the powerful businessmen in the cities began to seek ruling power for themselves, and thus the nobles lost much of theirs. The city folks, often called burghers, combined with the king against the clergymen and the nobles. In this way the lords of the manors became less important than they used to be. The dukes and counts also were weakened, while the king got stronger all the time. He took many old rights away from these great nobles, and transferred them to the national government. Instead of having a large number of little courts, controlled by nobles, the king would send his own judges through the country to hold court sessions for him. The people were drawn together in this way, and they felt themselves to be part of a *nation*. The little feudal states disappeared, and in their places came the large national states, such as France and Spain.

WHAT MAKES FRANCE SO IMPORTANT IN THE MIDDLE AGES. First of all, we should discuss the meaning of the term "Middle Ages." Some peoples, like the French, speak of the "Middle Age," but we use this term in the plural. We follow the old custom of putting the period from 500 to 1500 between the "ancient ages" and the "modern ages." The ten centuries that separate ancient from modern history are regarded as a middle period, just as we put the "middle class" in society between the "upper class" and the "lower classes." During the first half of the Middle Ages, France did not do so well. The Roman Empire had been smashed in the West, and France had been overrun by many Germanic tribes. Furthermore, in the second period of invasions France had suffered a great deal again. This was the time when the Frankish Empire went to pieces (814 to 987). But when in the year 987 a powerful line of kings began their rule under the name of the House of Capet, or the Capetian House, conditions soon improved. Most of the Capetian kings were able men, and each of them until about the year 1300 left a male heir to succeed him. This cannot be said of the English kings, while the German people were still more unfortunate, as you have seen. Besides, France was highly favored by its location, soil, and climate. France had a long coastline on the Atlantic Ocean and the English Channel to the West, and a fine coastline on the Mediterranean Sea to the South. That helped to increase trade. France had also four long rivers which provide means for water transportation. Moreover, much of the soil was very fertile clay land, and the weather was mild, the rainfall sufficient for most crops, and the growing season very long (from eight to twelve months a year). So you can easily understand why it was that France at the end of the Middle Ages had a population of fifteen million, while England had only four, Spain only eight, and Germany ten million.

How Philip Augustus, or Philip II, Strengthens the King's Power and Weakens the English King. France owed much to Philip II (1180-1223), who was named Philip Augustus, because he was such a powerful king in an age when most kings were still very weak. He fought a successful war against poor King John of England, and took from him the important duchy of Normandy and several counties besides. He also weakened the great nobles of France and added to the power of the Royal Council. In this council much work was done by friends of the king in ruling France as a whole. Instead of employing the services of nobles in this council for the most part, he tried more and more to put in members of the middle class, especially in all positions of influence.

Why the Waldensians and the Albigensians are Persecuted by Philip II and Pope Innocent III. In southern France lived two groups of religious persons who were not satisfied with all of the doctrines of the Church, while they also complained that the government was not democratic in the Church. They wanted the leaders in the Church to return to the simple conditions that prevailed in the early Christian Church. In that respect they resembled the Protestants of a later age. The Waldensians were named after an eloquent preacher called Peter Waldo, and the Albigensians were named after the town of Albi. A certain count was very friendly to them, and this gave King Philip II a chance to annex his county. The Pope assisted the king, because some of these religious folk were accused of being heretics. Many of them were killed, and nearly all of them lost their real estate property, which went to the king and his court.

Louis IX Continues Much of the Work Done by Philip II. This king was called Saint Louis, because he was deeply religious and was a leader in the last two crusades. With his death in 1270 the crusades came to an end. He greatly strengthened the king's power, and he also did much for the growth of business. Furthermore, he helped to improve the schools in his kingdom, and he encouraged those who were willing to set the serfs free. In his reign a new institution was founded which was called the *Parlement*. You must note carefully the spelling of this word, and compare it with *Parliament*, the English institution. Although these two words look so much alike, their meaning is very different, for the French assembly was not a law-making body, as was the English Parliament, and is our Congress. Its purpose was to examine laws that were to be made, in order that they would not conflict with those that had already been passed before.

The Reign of Philip IV and the Beginnings of the Estates-General. It was in the reign of Philip IV (1285-1314) that the French legislative body was begun. This body was called the Estates-General, for in it were represented the three Estates of France, namely, the clergy, or First Estate; the nobility, or Second Estate; and the middle class, or Third Estate. At about the same time (around 1300) the courts of the nobles lost much of their power and were replaced largely by royal courts. Besides, their local armies ceased to function and the royal military forces took their place. A system of national taxation was now introduced, and the local taxes of the nobles were abolished for the most part. Finally, the king defeated the most boastful of all popes, Boniface VIII, so that after his reign the papal power was never again what it had been in the days of Innocent III or Gregory VII.

A New House Occupies the Throne. If the French kings could only have continued on this road to national prosperity, their country would have become the outstanding nation in the West for centuries to come. But it was not to be, for in 1328 the House of

Capet at last came to an end when the king died without leaving a male heir, and was succeeded by his nephew. The new house was called "Valois," though in a sense the old house still continued. In the meantime Edward III of England laid claims to the French crown, because his mother was the daughter of a former king of France. Other factors added to the rivalry, such as the alliance between France and Scotland which we have discussed in the preceding chapter, the question of fisheries in the English Channel, and the situation in Flanders, a country supposedly belonging to France, but tied to England economically because the Flemings bought a large quantity of English wool for their textile manufacturers. Thus the Hundred Years' War broke out, which really was a series of wars lasting from 1337 to 1452.

THE ENGLISH WIN THE FIRST PART OF THE HUNDRED YEARS' WAR. In the first period the English were very successful and defeated the French in several important battles, because they used better bows and arrows, and depended less on the old-fashioned cavalry. They also seem to have been the first to use gunpowder, which frightened the horses of the French. But the French cause was by no means lost when the fourteenth century drew to a close. For several decades there was but little fighting, and even a great victory achieved by the English in 1415 was not in itself decisive. But soon after that the powerful duke of Burgundy joined the English. He ruled an important duchy in eastern France, as well as Flanders and about ten other wealthy duchies and counties in the Netherlands, or Low Countries. He was called Philip the Good, but he did no good to France, and it seemed for a time as if all was lost. The English overran northern France, took Paris, and finally stood before the gateway to southern France, the city of Orleans (1429).

WHAT JOAN OF ARC ACCOMPLISHES FOR FRANCE. But suddenly there appeared upon the scene the most remarkable woman of the Middle Ages, the peasant girl, Joan of Arc. She had come from Champagne in eastern France, where she thought that she had heard spirit voices and had seen spirit lights. She had been instructed to save France from the treacherous Burgundians and their English allies, and had received the command over a small band of soldiers. Her long locks of hair had been cut off and she had put on the armor commonly worn only by men. Such was her confidence that both soldiers and statesmen began to rely on her as the future savior of the unhappy nation. She journeyed to the city of Rheims, which was the Church center of France, just as Canterbury was that of England. Here she spoke to the heir to the throne, whose official title was the *dauphin*, corresponding to that of the Prince of Wales in England. He hardly knew what to do or to say at first, but when she told him of the guidance she had received from spiritual beings and convinced him of her honesty, he was willing to be crowned king of France and let her relieve the city of Orleans.

The English Are Defeated, But Joan Is Burned. As soon as the English were forced to withdraw from Orleans, the French took new courage and the Burgundians deserted their allies. In a few years Paris opened its gates to the French soldiers and then northern France was quickly given up by the English. However, the English held Joan as prisoner and had her burned at the stake in Rouen, the capital of Normandy, because she was considered a witch and a heretic for having consulted with spirits. Whatever may have been the faults of the judges who unfairly tried her, the Roman Catholic Church has recently seen fit to declare Joan of Arc a saint rather than a witch. This significant step was taken after able scholars had studied all the known details of her life and concluded that she had been assisted by spiritual powers of no small importance.

The War Has Greatly Injured France. The wars ended in 1453 without a treaty of peace. England retained none of her lands in southwestern France and kept only Calais and its immediate vicinity in northern France. But that was lost in 1558, as we shall see later. Though France had come out of the war as the victor, her fair lands lay in ruins, and many of her cities had been destroyed, so that in some of them no inhabitants were left, and in others but a few dozens or hundreds. French commerce and industry were paralyzed, and her name abroad was poorly regarded. England, on the other hand, was benefited by the loss of lands that were of no advantage to the nation as a whole. Now the king could concentrate upon domestic developments, and the foundations could be laid for the great kingdom of Great Britain and Ireland.

Germany and Italy are Drifting Apart. While France and England were becoming national states with a strongly centralized government in each of them, Germany was subject to very different developments. Germany and northern Italy were still believed to be united, and several emperors frittered away much time and energy in trying to hold the unruly Italian towns in subjection. But it proved wholly in vain, and after 1350 the emperors in Germany had to leave Italy to its own destiny.

No National Union Is Possible in Germany. The Holy Roman Empire, as we have seen, was made up of more than two hundred little states, of which about sixty were imperial cities. The cities were independent except that they recognized the emperor as their ruler. The older states had ceased to be of great importance, though Bavaria and Saxony were still fairly large. Bavaria had lost the border region called Austria, and curiously enough, this latter region would some day become far more important in European history than Bavaria itself.

The House of Hapsburg. In Austria ruled the most illustrious house in the history of Europe, namely, the House of Hapsburg, which held Austria with its dominions from before 1300 until 1918. The first member of this family to become emperor was Rudolph, who added Austria to his original domains in northern Switzerland. When he died in 1291, the leading princes refused to elect his son, because they had become jealous of this upstart family. Rudolph had used the imperial title to gain control of Austria and three other little states which were later added to Austria. But by the middle of the fifteenth century the Hapsburgs were in a different position. They were now needed to protect Germany against powerful enemies, and, with the exception of three years in the eighteenth century, the members of their house retained the imperial title until the Holy Roman Empire came to an end in 1806.

Who the Seven Electors Were. For about three hundred years (1356-1648) there were seven *electors* in the Holy Roman Empire, whose duty it was to supervise with the emperor the general control of the whole collection of states and to elect the emperor upon the death of his predecessor. Usually one or more years passed before they made their choice, during which time the ruler was merely the King of the Romans. Three of the electors were archbishops in western Germany, of whom the archbishop of Mainz was the chief, just as in France the Archbishop of Rheims was the most important. The king of Bohemia was also one of the electors, while a duke and two counts completed the number seven. The electors took great care to limit as far as possible the powers of the emperor, who had to sign a sort of contract with them upon his accession.

THE GOVERNMENT OF THE HOLY ROMAN EMPIRE. There was no national army in the empire, nor a national capital, nor a national coinage, nor a national court, though near the end of the Middle Ages a supreme court was instituted in order to establish a vague authority over quarreling princes and to declare what were the laws of the empire. The Diet, or *Reichstag*, was the national assembly, in which the princes and the imperial cities were represented, but not the people. This arrangement was continued in Germany even after the Holy Roman Empire had come to an end. It was not until after 1867 that the people could elect delegates to represent them in the national assembly or legislature. And even then there still remained a body, now under a different name, which continued to represent only the princes and the municipal councils or some of the old cities. This custom was continued until the fall of the German Empire in 1918.

BRANDENBURG BECOMES AN IMPORTANT STATE. It must be said, however, that even in Germany the process of nationalism was developing, for not only did Bavaria and Saxony continue to be important states with their own armies, coinage, and courts, but a new state rose to power that was some day to rank with first-class nations. This was Brandenburg in central Germany, with its capital Berlin, which is still the capital of Germany today. In 1415 Brandenburg became the property of the House of Hohenzollern, and its ruler received the title of Elector. Another member of the same house was grand master of the Teutonic Knights, a military order that had been founded in the Holy Land during the Crusades. After the crusades were over, this order had received grants of land on the south and east shores of the Baltic Sea. Here its members labored among the heathen and established colonies of German settlers in what was later called East Prussia and the region to the northeast, including Lithuania, Latvia, and Estonia. In 1525 the grand master dissolved the order, because the majority of its members became Protestants, who did not favor monastic or semi-monastic orders. He became Duke of Prussia, and when in 1618 his house died out, the other branch of the House of Hohenzollern, that is, the ruler of Brandenburg, annexed East Prussia. Later the name "Prussia" was given to the whole of the new state, and eventually the ruler was made king, and the kingdom of Prussia was established, which certainly was one of the leading national states of the eighteenth and nineteenth centuries.

SWITZERLAND BECOMES A NATION. At the same time another new state was carved out of the dominions of the Holy Roman

Empire. This was Switzerland, which began in the fourteenth century with a group of little republics and won its independence of the Hapsburgs in the fifteenth century. In 1648 Switzerland was officially declared independent of the empire as well. The little country was made up of tiny states called *cantons*, which were joined together into a federal state with a republican form of government. It became a real nation, though some of the cantons were preponderantly German (those in the north and east), others French, and one was Italian. National states need not depend entirely upon one race and language to keep all the people together, but rather a willingness to work together and to be subject to a common form of government. A good example is Canada, where two distinct races live peacefully side by side under the same government and body of national laws.

THE LOW COUNTRIES OR NETHERLANDS ALMOST BECOME A NATION. It seemed for a time as if not only what was later called Belgium would be a nation, but the whole of the region called the Netherlands. Here, as we saw, ruled Philip, the duke of Burgundy (1419-1467), who was succeeded by a son, and the latter by a daughter called Mary of Burgundy. Mary married Maximilian of Hapsburg, who in 1493 became emperor. They in turn had a son, who was known as Philip of Hapsburg, and would undoubtedly have become emperor in turn, as well as prince of the Netherlands. Furthermore, he had married the heiress of Spain. But he died a young man, and was succeeded by his son Charles. Thus Spain and the Netherlands were for a time united under one ruler. The Netherlands would have become a separate state in the course of time, if both the northern and the southern regions could have agreed upon a common policy against Spain. But in the sixteenth century they drifted apart, with the result that Belgium and the Kingdom of the Netherlands were from 1839 to 1940 two separate states.

THE SPANISH KINGDOMS ARE UNITED. In the Middle Ages there really was not a country called Spain, but, as we saw, the Visigoths ruled the Iberian Peninsula, and then the Mohammedans held it. However, in the twelfth and thirteenth centuries Castile, Aragon, and Portugal became independent states, each ruled by a king. In 1469 Ferdinand of Aragon and Isabella of Castile were married, and when in 1479 Ferdinand became king of Aragon, the most important steps had been taken in the unification of Spain. In 1492 Ferdinand conquered the Mohammedan state in the south called Granada. His daughter, Joan, married Philip of Hapsburg, and thus it happened that her son Charles became king of Spain upon the death of his grandfather Ferdinand (1516).

THE SPANISH GOVERNMENT BECOMES AUTOCRATIC. Isabella and her husband pursued a policy of absolutism, that is, they deliberately deprived the nobles, the clergy, the parliaments (*cortes*) of Castile and Aragon, and the great municipal councils of much of their political power. Their policy was continued by Charles, their grandson, so that Spain was one of the first countries in modern times to have an autocratic form of government. The Spanish government was also noted for its policy of persecuting Jews, Mohammedans, and Protestants. In 1492 the Jews were ordered to leave the country or else be converted to the Christian religion. Subsequently, the same was done to the Mohammedans. The Inquisition was founded in 1478 by the Queen of Castile as a royal court intended as a means of destroying heresy. Both in Spain and the Netherlands it had thousands of Protestants burned at the stake, and also in the American colonies it was in operation for a time.

THE ITALIANS ARE NOT YET UNITED. Italy, unlike Spain, was not united until after the middle of the nineteenth century. The chief reason of this peculiar development is that Italy was not ruled by kings, except in the south. Its leading states were three republics Venice, Florence, and Genoa; the duchy of Milan; the Papal States; and the kingdoms of Naples and Sicily. Venice was the most wealthy and powerful of them all, but in the first half of the fourteenth century it experienced some difficulty in trying to keep ahead of Genoa, its great rival in commerce. Florence was at first only an industrial city of some importance, but after 1350 it also became a commercial town, as we shall see in the next chapter. Milan occupied an important position in the rich Po Valley, where it was the leader among numerous other towns. Rome was the capital of the Papal States, and was ruled by the Pope until 1870. Naples was a great city and possessed, as did also the other cities just mentioned (except Rome), much territory in its vicinity. But unlike these city-states of northern Italy, Naples was a kingdom. Sicily, unlike all of the others, was not dominated by one city. Its capital was the beautiful city of Palermo, which was for centuries the largest city in Italy (about 900-1300), with a population of 150,000.

FREDERICK II IS CALLED THE WONDER OF THE WORLD. For about half a century (1197 to 1250) Sicily was ruled by one of the most famous and romantic kings of the Middle Ages. This was Frederick, who was elected emperor in 1211 as Frederick II, owing to the influence of his guardian, Pope Innocent III. He had inherited Sicily from his mother, who was the wife of an emperor in Germany, and for that reason he could claim the imperial title there. Having been brought up in the midst of the Saracen atmosphere in his native Sicily, he was naturally "broad-minded" and taught Christian Europe a significant lesson by appointing in his newly founded University of Naples both Christian and Mohammedan professors. In Sicily he abolished serfdom and feudalism, promoted scientific agriculture, and enlarged commerce by signing trade treaties with various Saracen powers. He set up a magnificent form of government in Sicily and he also did much for the advancement of science. Long before the kings of France dared to rise against a Pope, he defied this official openly and often he laughed the Pope to scorn. That such things were possible in the thirteenth century is an indication of the position occupied by Italy in the Middle Ages. It was a land of marked contrasts, of diversity of talents, of new currents of thoughts, and of strange ideas.

THE COUNTRIES OF NORTHERN AND EASTERN EUROPE REMAIN BACKWARD. Very different from Italy were the countries in northern Europe, where civilization and Christianity were introduced rather late. The Scandinavian kingdoms were even more backward than was England, for they were far removed from France and Italy. Moreover, the cold climate and the large expanse of mountainous country in Norway and Sweden did not favor the spread of commerce and industry, nor the promotion of agriculture. The same is partly true of Russia, which from about 1250 to 1450 was ruled by a Mongolian people and thus was unable to come into much active contact with the peoples in western Europe or with the Byzantine Empire. Moreover, the Slavic peoples which inhabited the western regions of the Balkan Peninsula likewise failed to share in the great outburst of commercial activity and of learning which was to make Italy once more the chief center of western civilization.

Student Activities

1. With the aid of a dictionary write out the definitions for the following words: *prevailed, textiles, concentrate, deliberately.*
2. Give some reasons why France was so important during the Middle Ages.

3. Who were the Waldensians and the Albigensians? Why were they persecuted by the pope and the king?
4. Write a 100 word account on Joan of Arc.
5. Although France won the Hundred Years' War, yet can it be said that she *won* in the strict sense of the word? Why?
6. Why was it impossible for the Germans to unite in one nation?
7. Who were the Seven Electors? Why were they called "Electors?"
8. You will note that much of European history is concerned with Royal families. Name some of the leading ruling families mentioned in this chapter.
9. Who united the Spanish kingdoms?
10. What was the purpose of the "Inquisition?"
11. Why was Frederick II called the "Wonder of the World?"
12. Why did Russia and the countries near her, remain backward for so long a time?

CHAPTER 24

Medieval Towns and Town Life

WHY THE CITIES ARE SO IMPORTANT. As we follow the course of civilization from the ancient world to the end of the Middle Ages, we find that the cities played in it a part altogether out of proportion to the small number of people that lived in them. During the Middle Ages only about one-tenth of Europe's population was in cities, but it was that one-tenth which produced most of the principal elements of medieval civilization. The peasants, who formed nearly nine-tenths of the inhabitants, spent their lives in comparative ignorance, little aware of the new ideas in education, religion, art, and science. Not even the nobles, in spite of their high position in society, contributed much to the making of western civilization.

HOW TOWNS GROW. The towns owed their rise to commerce and industry, though in some instances they originated on spots where was located a prominent castle, or where a bishop held an important court, or where pilgrims came to worship at some famous shrine. No town could grow to great proportions without these two vital forces, commerce and industry. Some were founded near the mouth of a large river, or if the river were not very long, it might still be important as the highway for a thickly populated region. The greatest of all European cities, London, was located near the mouth of the humble Thames. As commerce with France and the Netherlands increased, the region around London profited from it and London itself expanded. In the United States, New York surpassed all other cities, not because the Hudson River was the longest stream, but because its valley and the surrounding regions were best located to attract large numbers of settlers. At the mouth of the long Danube there never was a great port, but the Rhine gave birth to several large cities, some along its banks, like Cologne (the largest city of medieval Germany), and at least one near its mouth (Rotterdam, while Antwerp also owed much to the Rhine). The confluence of rivers usually provided an excellent site for a town, such as that of the Seine and the Marne, where Paris was located, and of the Rhone and a branch, where Lyons was built. Sometimes an easy crossing of a river encouraged people to found a town, as was the case with Rome on the Tiber.

WHAT MAKES CONSTANTINOPLE GROW SO LARGE. Constantinople, the largest city of medieval Europe, held a double advantage, for it was the only important stopping place between the Black Sea and the Aegean Sea, and it was also conveniently located to catch much of the trade between European and Asiatic countries. For more than two thousand years the main artery of world commerce ran from the Far East through the Near East to Italy and the lands beyond, and it was not until the end of the Middle Ages that this vast current of commerce was turned away from its old course. Much of this commerce flowed through Constantinople, though between 1200 and 1500 Alexandria received a slightly larger share.

WHICH GOODS WERE BOUGHT AND SOLD IN CONSTANTINOPLE. Even after the Saracen conquest of Syria and Egypt, Constantinople continued to grow. Its monopoly of the silk trade, its enormous fleet, its immense wealth, and its capable rulers combined to add to its power. Here the merchants of Venice brought from the West the lumber, raw wool, linen, iron, amber, grain, furs, fish and oils. They exchanged these goods for oriental luxuries, such as spices, glassware, beads, precious stones, carpets, sugar, tea, coffee, dates, currants, oranges, and raisins. Great mercantile and craft corporations in Constantinople were engaged in the purchase of raw materials and the manufacture of highly prized cloths, furniture, manuscripts, bindings for books (manuscripts), and metalware. They sold these at the public market place, which was vastly superior to anything that Athens or Sparta had ever seen.

WHAT THE GOVERNMENT DOES FOR BUSINESS. The great corporations were controlled by the prefect of the city, who issued the *Book of the Prefect*, establishing for all the guilds a definite set of rules. The industries were so regulated that middlemen were not required, food prices were kept within reasonable bounds, and unemployment was reduced to the vanishing point. Those who were without work received employment from the government or from charitable organizations. Corporations were founded which sold stock in shares, very much as is done in the western world today. Interest charges on loans were 12 percent on sea-borne enterprise, 8 percent to professional moneylenders, 6 percent to ordinary persons, and 4 percent to the wealthy, who borrowed the most and who could put up the best security. A large number of inspectors were kept busy seeing that weights and measures were correct, that buildings were constructed properly, that bankers, notaries, and lawyers obeyed the laws, and that foreigners were well treated.

ALEXANDRIA. Next to Constantinople ranked Alexandria in Egypt. Owing to the fact that the most convenient route to the Spice Islands was by way of Egypt and the Red Sea, Alexandria not only captured much of the rich spice trade but also of the trade in precious stones, ivory, glassware, tropical fruits, and gums. The Saracens granted to the Venetians and Genoese merchants the right to worship in their own churches and to be tried in their own courts. They themselves were highly cultured and knew much about accounting and banking. They passed their information on to the clever Italians, who also learned much at Constantinople.

TRADE BETWEEN ITALY AND THE NEAR EAST. The Italians established trading posts along the coasts of the eastern Mediterranean. From these quarters (called factories) in various important ports they opened up trade with the regions of the interior. Before 1300 some Venetian merchants even reached the very heart of China, and then Japan. But the coming of the Ottoman Turks in the fourteenth century meant disaster for the Italians. In 1453 they seized Constantinople and extinguished the Byzantine Empire. Although the Venetians regained special privileges from the Turks, these were mere scraps of paper as far as the Turks were concerned. Gradually the Venetians lost some of their colonies along the eastern shore of the Adriatic Sea, so that at the end of the Middle Ages their glory was rapidly passing.

FLORENCE BECOMES A GREAT INDUSTRIAL CENTER. Florence, as we saw, also gained a share in the extensive trade of the eastern Mediterranean. It had over two hundred establishments where woolen cloths were manufactured, and also numerous craft guilds. A learned writer near the end of the Middle Ages reported that in Florence there were between 8,000 and 10,000 children who could read (out of a total population of 100,000), which signifies that many adults also could read. He also noted that about six hundred young people attended high schools, and that there were in the city 110 churches, 30 hospitals with 1,000 beds, 80 banks, 80 judges, and 60 doctors. If he had lived long enough, he would have observed that nowhere in western Europe between 1500 and 1700 were there any towns half as large as Constantinople and Alexandria had been in the "Dark Ages."

THE NAVE OF CANTERBURY
CATHEDRAL

FACADE OF THE CATHEDRAL AT
ROUEN, FRANCE

THE CATHEDRAL AT CANTERBURY, ENGLAND

THE GERMAN CITIES ARE ALSO PROSPEROUS. From Italy, Spain, and France the flow of commerce reached central and northern Europe. Venice had derived much of its importance from the fact that the lowest pass over the Alps, the Brenner, was situated near this city, and that the Adriatic Sea extended northward almost into the center of Europe. So Germany was easily reached from the Mediterranean region, and its greatest cities lay along the road from the Alps to the North Sea. Besides, the herring fisheries in the Baltic Sea and the grain trade in that region had given birth to many flourishing towns, which combined into the celebrated Hanseatic League. At one time nearly one hundred cities were members of it. They protected their merchants and wrested from various governments important trading privileges. Lübeck was the capital, and Hamburg and Bremen ranked among the most important members.

MERCHANTS AND CRAFT GUILDS REGULATE BUSINESS. In most of the cities in western Europe merchant and craft guilds developed, in order to control prices of goods manufactured and of products brought in from the country or from other cities. The merchant guild supervised commerce, while the craft guilds were each in charge of a certain craft, such as shoemaking, carpenter work, or cloth manufacture. All the carpenters would belong to the guild of the carpenters, all the wool manufacturers would live in a certain street or quarter and have a monoply of the making of woolen goods. It was customary to protect both the public and the manufacturers by agreeing that only those who made the goods should be permitted to sell them. So the master of a shop sold his products in front of his store or in the store or at the market. There was nothing new or unusual about this procedure, but now the guilds had a better organization than before.

THE THREE CLASSES OF WORKERS. It was stated in their regulations that a person should first serve as an *apprentice* without wages (usually for a period of seven years) before he could become a *journeyman* and receive wages. After he had finished his course of training and had produced some *masterpiece,* he would become a *master* and set up his own shop. The masters would hold regular guild meetings, where they decided their future course of action, and they also engaged in much feasting. The guilds protected members and provided for the needs of widows, orphans, and sick persons. In the larger towns of Italy and Flanders the workmen formed the lowest class, while skilled masters were the aristocracy. Often a conflict would break out between these two classes, and actual civil war would prevail for a time. Like feudalism and serfdom, the guild system began to disappear at the end of the medieval period. Middlemen made their appearance, and the national government interfered with the guilds, while large corporations imported goods from foreign countries or undermined the numerous little establishments.

The Towns Get Their Own Governments. Originally the towns had been for the most part under the control of local feudal lords, who owned the land upon which the town had been built. But gradually the towns freed themselves and worked with the king, from whom they received a charter. This stated that the town was independent in many ways, and would not have to pay taxes except in a lump sum. The charter also provided as a rule that serfs who had run away from their manors to the town would be considered freemen after they had lived in the town for a year and one day. As soon as a town had received its judicial and administrative independence, the citizens would choose a board of officials to govern the town as the municipal council. The presiding officer was usually called the *Mayor*, or *Burghermaster*.

Population Figures. Paris was the largest city in western Europe from 1200 and 1500, attaining a population of about 300,-000 by the fifteenth century. Cologne, the largest city in Germany, had only about 50,000 inhabitants, and London about the same number, while Florence, Milan, Venice, and Rome had from 75,000 to 100,000. At the end of the fifteenth century the greatest port of western Europe was Antwerp, but its population did not exceed 75,000.

Daily Life in the Cities. The typical medieval city in western and central Europe was compactly built, though often enough space had been included within the walls to permit the citizens to raise food for themselves during the siege. The streets were usually narrow and crooked. Many of them were also unpaved, showing clearly that human beings have a way of turning to barbarism after they have learned to do better. London of the seventeenth century was a sorry sight compared with the magnificent city of Alexandria in 200 B.C. or 1200 A.D. Many of the houses had thatched roofs and often a fire would wipe a whole city away, as happened to nearly the whole of London in 1666. Few houses were provided with windows of glass panes, the majority of them having only oiled paper, linen, or pigskin. Manure piles were often to be found in the front of the houses, and the filth was heaped up in the streets until washed away by the rain or carried away by some official. Pigs, geese, and children played merrily in the dirt. Protection against fire and robbers was almost non-existent; street lights were practically unknown. Late in the evening the curfew rang to notify the citizens that the streets were no longer safe till daybreak. Silence reigned in the streets all night, although occasionally parties of armed citizens would be seen on their way to some meeting.

WHY CONTAGIOUS DISEASES SWEEP THROUGH THE CITIES. It is not surprising that the absence of hygiene should have been accompanied by scourges such as the terrible Black Plague of the year 1348-1349. This was one of the Bubonic plagues that were carried from the Orient by rats and fleas. It was a highly contagious disease, and often spread through the cities of medieval Europe. In the fourteenth and fifteenth centuries Germany was visited by more than thirty such plagues. That of 1348-1349 swept away more than one-third of the population of western Europe. Moreover, every summer the heat, though not excessive, caused food to spoil and water to become impure. Many a summer one-tenth of the population in a city was wiped away by the unsanitary conditions and the improper care of mothers and children. This will explain in part why the cities of the Middle Ages did not grow very fast, and why the population of England was only five millions after the Middle Ages had come to an end.

Student Activities

1. With the aid of a dictionary write out definitions for the following words: *shrine, guilds, enterprise, thatched, curfew.*
2. At what kind of places did towns originate? Why?
3. What kind of goods were bought and sold at Constantinople?
4. Name the famous commercial towns of Italy during the Middle Ages.
5. What was the Hanseatic League?
6. Explain the terms, "apprentice," "journeyman," "master." In what trades is a similar system used even at the present day?
7. Describe a typical medieval city.
8. Why were there so many plagues?
9. What was the purpose of the curfew ringing in a medieval town?
10. What is our chief means of keeping food wholesome during summer?
11. Make a table showing the advantages that we enjoy, which the people during medieval times did not have.
    Note: Commerce and trade, which means the exchange of goods, is the means whereby people are enabled to obtain and enjoy more and more of the goods of this world. Commerce is carried on in cities and towns where people congregate. The more business there is, the more wealth is amassed. Some of this wealth is used to establish schools, to erect fine buildings, to buy luxuries. This provides employment for teachers, artists, architects, etc. These things taken together make what is called a higher "civilization."

CHAPTER 25

Scholars, Writers, and Artists in the Middle Ages

Why So Little Progress Is Made in Western Europe Dur-ing the Early Middle Ages. In the period between the fall of the Roman Empire (476 A.D.) and the twelfth century, the Christian countries of western and central Europe were extremely slow to develop a high civilization of their own. Although they were in contact with the Byzantine Empire and the Mohammedan world, the means of communication were so poor that only a few merchants and learned men derived much advantage from this contact. The countries to the north of the Pyrenees and the Alps had acquired but a small amount of the culture bequeathed by the Roman Empire. Classical civilization was foreign to them, and even the Christian religion had been imported from another land. Both classical civilization and the Christian religion were for that reason slow to penetrate into the northern countries.

Improvement Suddenly Comes in the Twelfth Century. However, the twelfth century brought to western Europe not only a great revival of commerce and industry, but also an outburst of learning, a new school of architecture, monastic reforms, and the beginnings of great national literatures. During the twelfth and thirteenth centuries a fairly large number of new languages developed, and excellent literature was produced.

The Romance Languages Develop Out of Medieval Latin. Classical Latin (Latin as written by the Romans) and the Greek language had been employed by practically all the scholars of the civilized world in the West. While the knowledge of Greek almost entirely disappeared in the countries of western Europe, classical Latin continued to be employed by scholars. In Italy, Spain, and Gaul the people gradually modified the language that had been employed in the Roman Empire. Like all living languages, the classical Latin was subject to many changes. It naturally happened that the inhabitants of Italy developed a language of their own,

192

which came to be called Italian. The people of Spain perfected another language, which is called Spanish, while the Portuguese developed the Portuguese language. In France, which used to be called Gaul, the people at first used two different languages, that of the north and that of the south, but during the thirteenth century these two languages were gradually merged into one. In this manner the French language originated. Another language that was derived from classical Latin was the Rumanian tongue.

MEDIEVAL LATIN IS STILL WIDELY USED. However, it must not be imagined that the use of the Latin was dropped altogether. The scholars still continued to use the Latin language, but it no longer was exactly the same as that which had been employed in the Roman Empire. This new Latin we usually call medieval Latin, which may be distinguished from the classical Latin in the word order, the vocabulary, and in the spelling of various words. Many of the documents issued by the medieval governments were drawn up in medieval Latin, while the Church also employed the same language. Beautiful Church hymns were written in medieval Latin. Moreover, some of the finest historical writings of the Middle Ages were drawn up in medieval Latin.

THE RELIGIOUS DRAMA APPEALS TO MANY MEDIEVAL PERSONS. A very interesting form of medieval literature is the religious drama, that is, plays which were enacted upon the stage, both within the church buildings and elsewhere. While some of these plays were based upon stories of the Gospels, others were drawn from the lives of the saints, and still others were written for the improvement of the moral standards of the people. Most of these plays were written by the clergy, and many were also enacted by the clergy upon the stage.

THE WANDERING STUDENTS WRITE LATIN POETRY. The university students also wrote literature of their own, which is a part of medieval Latin literature. One type of students was called the wandering students, for, although many students attended more than one university before they graduated, the wandering students were noted especially for the manner in which they wandered from place to place in search of higher education. They composed a rather amusing literature in the form of poetry, in which they glorified their own lives, and sang of beautiful ladies, romance, and wine-bibbing. A stanza is reproduced below.

At the mandate, go ye forth,
Through the whole world hurry!
Priests tramp out toward south and north,
Monks and hermits scurry,
Levites smooth the Gospel leave,
Bent on ambulation;
Each and all to our sect cleave,
Which is life's salvation.

ROMANCE LITERATURES. The languages that were derived from the Latin are usually called the Romance languages. The literatures produced in Italy, Spain, Portugal, France, and Rumania are called the Romance literatures. One of the early specimens of Romance literature was written in France, and was called the *Song of Roland*. It is a beautiful piece of epic poetry, and it tells of the career of a mythical nephew of Charlemagne, whose name was Roland. The story opens with a remarkable description of Charlemagne himself, who is considered the most powerful Christian king in the western world. The reader is told how Charlemagne with his army entered Spain and defeated there the Mohammedans. But before his return to Gaul, a Mohammedan ruler attacked the Frankish troops that had been left behind in charge of Roland. The Franks were hopelessly outnumbered but they continued to fight bravely. One by one they fell dead upon the ground and Roland himself, after having broken his lance, drew his sword and cut through the helmet of his opponent. The bravery of the Franks is described in the following:

The Franks strike on; their hearts are good and stout.
Pagans are slain, a thousandfold, in crowds,
Left of five score are not two thousand now.
Says the archbishop; "Our men are very proud,
No man on earth has more nor better found.
In chronicles of Franks is written down,
What vassalage he had, our emperour."[1]

CHARLEMAGNE THE HERO IN THE SONG OF ROLAND. After almost all the Franks have died, Roland blows his magic horn, and Charlemagne, who is thirty miles away, hears it, and rushes back. And when he arrives upon the battlefield, he finds that Roland has also fallen. Charlemagne now takes revenge upon the Mohamme-

1. From C. K. Scott-Moncrieff's edition of *The Song of Roland* (London: Chapman & Hall, 1920).

dans, and annexes the northern part of Spain. This was called the Spanish March, as we have seen in a preceding chapter.

LYRIC POETRY. In addition to the exciting themes recounted in the epic poetry, we also note beautiful lyric verses. Some of these verses were sung to music by the *troubadours,* who were not only great singers, but also poets and composers of music. Nearly all of these writers, of whom about four hundred are known to us, were Frenchmen, for which reason we apply a French name to them. They used the French language by preference, because their audiences could no longer understand Latin.

THE ROMANCES. Very popular were the so-called *romances,* which were long pieces of poetry, and for that reason they were not sung to music. They described the thrilling love-affairs of noble lords and beautiful ladies, to which were added exciting stories of travels, adventures, the killing of dragons and other terrible beasts, the rescue of lovely young women from the clutches of tyrants, including cruel husbands, and the extraordinary performances of magicians.

KING ARTHUR AND HIS MEN SEARCH FOR THE HOLY GRAIL. In many of the medieval romances the story was told of King Arthur and his knights, who were said to be searching for the so-called Holy Grail, that is, the cup that Jesus had used during the ceremony of the Last Supper. The theme was taken up again by Tennyson in his famous *Idylls of the King.*

THE TOWNSPEOPLE ALSO GET A LITERATURE OF THEIR OWN. But a large part of the reading public soon began to clamor for a type of literature that was more realistic, that is, more true to actual life. After all, the nobles and their lovely ladies formed but a small part of the population. The merchants, artisans, lawyers, and government officials lived exciting lives of their own, and they loved to read about the adventures of their own class. Consequently, a new type of literature made its appearance in which the townsmen are the heroes. They make fun of the peasants, and they despise the priests and the monks. They suspect the latter of many wicked deeds.

THE THREE BAD CHAPS OF MEDIEVAL LITERATURE AND THE MORALITY PLAY. Like the popular fables of Aesop, the Greek writer, the composers of literature in the Middle Ages loved to depict adventures of Reynard the Fox Bruin the Bear, and Isengrin the Wolf, the "three bad chaps" of medieval literature. Morality plays were also in great demand. They assisted the preachers in their efforts to render religion more acceptable to the masses of the people. One of these plays was called *Everyman*. It was so attractively written that even today it still has many admirers.

The Play Called the Mystery of Adam. It was during the thirteenth and fourteenth centuries that much of the religious drama was presented in the Romance languages. One of the most popular of these plays was entitled *The Mystery of Adam*. In this play Adam was shown at one end of the stage, where he was busily at work, so that he failed to see Satan, who approached Eve and whispered something pleasant into her ear. She was informed that Adam was a poor match for her. He had neglected to notice her ravishing beauty. So the Devil continued that she should no longer be deprived of the fruit of the tree that would bring her the knowledge of good and evil. It was in this manner that Eve fell from grace in Paradise.

How the Germanic Languages Were Developed. From France and Italy the cultivation of literature spread into the countries inhabited by the Germanic peoples. These peoples had just begun to develop a written language of their own. The Germans spoke and wrote two different languages, the High German, used in the south where the land was high, while the Low German was the language of the people in northern Germany. Other Germanic languages were Swedish, Danish, and Norwegian, or the three Scandinavian languages; and the Dutch and the Flemish, used in the Netherlands, which were nearly identical, since they both had been derived from the Frankish tongue.

Early Germanic Literature. Among the earlier examples of Germanic literatures may be mentioned the epic called *Beowulf*, which was written in the eighth century in Anglo-Saxon alliterative verse. This work was probably based upon one of the numerous sagas that were recited in the Germanic countries of the north long before the people knew how to write. Similar in content to *Beowulf* are the *Eddas*, which were composed in Icelandic verse. You may note in this connection that Iceland had been settled by the Northmen, so that the language of its inhabitants was Scandinavian. Another important work is the *Anglo-Saxon Chronicle*, which was the first important literary work composed in Germanic prose of an original character. It gives an excellent history of the reign of Alfred the Great, as well as an account of English history to the year 1154.

The Song of the Nibelungs. In southern Germany several famous pieces of epic poetry were written during the twelfth and thirteenth centuries. One of these tells of the exciting adventures of Attila the Hun, Siegfried, the great hero from the lower Rhine Valley, and a brave Frankish queen. Naturally there is a great display of slaughter and fierce passions. The great composer Wagner found in this work a theme for some of his finest operas.

RENAISSANCE LITERATURE WILL BE DISCUSSED IN THE NEXT CHAPTER. The fourteenth and fifteenth centuries form a transition period in the history of European civilization. This period is often called the Age of the Renaissance, because a great awakening (*renaissance*) of learning took place in Italy and spread into the other countries of western Europe. The literature of the period is not generally classified with purely medieval literature, so that we shall mention it in the next chapter, which will be devoted to the dawn of modern civilization.

COMPARISON BETWEEN MEDIEVAL AND MODERN CIVILIZATION. The learning of the Middle Ages is a subject that has often caused in the minds of modern readers a feeling of pity for the persons who were unfortunate to live at that time. People are said to have been exceptionally superstitious. But it seems that they were merely superstitious in their own way, and not more so than many persons are today. Comparatively little attention was then paid to the study of science, while even in the universities history, geography, political science, sociology, and anthropology were sorely neglected. On the other hand, much more attention was paid to theology, philosophy, and religion than is done today. The curriculum was more restricted, but what there was of it was thoroughly digested. The students were trained to think for themselves, regardless of what many modern writers have said. They certainly knew how to work out problems for themselves, and they were skilled in the art of concentration, which is very little practiced in our time.

BEGINNINGS OF PUBLIC EDUCATION. Since the western countries were slow to take advantage of the culture bequeathed by the Greeks and the Romans, it is not surprising that education was not made available to the masses of the people. Even a large number of noblemen never learned to read. Church schools continued to operate, but they were not numerous enough to give instruction to more than one-tenth of the children. However, in Italy and the Netherlands many public schools were founded by the municipal governments. And at the end of the twelfth century the universities originated in the western countries. They were not the first in the history of Europe, but they did start a definitely new system of higher education.

MANY NEW UNIVERSITIES ARE FOUNDED. Many universities developed out of monastic and cathedral schools, as was the case with the University of Paris. This was the outgrowth of the school attached to the cathedral of Notre Dame (about 1175). Here, at the beginning of the twelfth century, the eloquent Abelard had taught with immense success. The institution in Paris grew to large proportions, and at the close of the Middle Ages it had a student body of about six thousand. But the oldest universities were those at Salerno and Padua in Italy, while Bologna, in Italy, was also earlier than Paris. Oxford was founded about 1180 and Cambridge in 1209. Naples was established by Emperor Frederick II, and Salamanca by a king in a little Spanish country (Leon). The oldest university in the Holy Roman Empire was that of Prague (1348), but that was in Bohemia, not in Germany. Among the German universities may be mentioned those at Cologne, Leipzig, and Heidelberg.

HOW INSTRUCTION IN THE UNIVERSITIES WAS GIVEN. In each university the liberal arts were taught. This course led to the degree of the Bachelor of Arts, and next to that of Master of Arts. Many of the universities also had graduate departments in theology, medicine, and (or) law. In all of them Latin was the language used by the professors and students. The professors dictated much of the time to the students, who were seated on benches or the floor, which in that case was covered with straw. The students used to write their notes on wax tablets, but in the fifteenth century the use of paper became very common. The earlier manuscripts had often been written on parchment, which is made from the skin of animals, but this proved to be so expensive that the Christian peoples eagerly took over from the Saracens the manufacture of paper from rags and plant fiber. The word "paper" has been derived from the word "papyrus," which, as we saw, was made from the pith of the papyrus plant. It was but one step from the making of papyrus to that of paper. Pens were made of quills from feathers (the quill is a large feather). Ink was first made from water mixed with vegetable gum and soot from blackened pots; but afterward from mixtures of animal and vegetable dyes. Today it is manufactured from chemicals.

TEXTBOOKS USED IN THE MEDIEVAL UNIVERSITIES. Among the most widely used textbooks were several works by Aristotle, the Code of Justinian, Euclid (for geometry), Ptolemy (for astronomy and geography), and Hippocrates and Galen (for medicine). Unfortunately, too much reliance was placed upon the word of Aristotle and other authorities, and not enough attempts were made to investigate nature. Experimentation was not widely used, though you must be careful not to assume that there was none of it. Moreover, it would be a gross error to think that the students and the professors did not have keen minds.

THOMAS AQUINAS IS A VERY GREAT THINKER. Thomas Aquinas, for example, was a great expert in the field of theology, philosophy, political science, and economics. It would take the average senior in an American university several years to understand his masterpiece, the *Summa Theologica,* which is available in English translation.

ROGER BACON PREDICTS THE COMING OF AIRPLANES. Another great scholar of the Middle Ages was Roger Bacon, who constantly made use of the experimental method. He asserted that, after having listened for forty years to some of the outstanding philosophers of his time, he still had learned nothing. It was his opinion that the Bible should be studied in the original languages, for he argued that the Vulgate was full of mistakes. It was his habit to examine plants and animals wherever he could find them; he traveled from country to country, and he freely conversed with other travelers. He devoted twenty years to the study of chemistry, physics, and medicine. He even perfected some microscopes of his own, and he worked with many other instruments. Bacon was also known for his fertile imagination. At one time he predicted that in the future, ships would be equipped with "machines without rowers, guided by one man, borne with greater speed than if they were full of men. And flying machines are possible, so that a man may sit in the middle turning at something by which artificial wings may beat the air in the manner of a flying bird."

GREAT ADVANCES ARE MADE IN MEDICINE. During the thirteenth century a great advance was made in the practice of medicine. A large number of hospitals was founded, some of which are still in operation. Contagious diseases were beginning to be studied and treated. Quarantine and segregation were freely employed. Operations for gallstones, hernia, and cataracts were very skillfully conducted.

MEDIEVAL SUPERSTITIONS. Most people in the Middle Ages were much more credulous than we are today. Many of them dabbled in the science, or so-called science, of alchemy, thinking that they could make gold out of other metals. They were also very much interested in astrology, for it was their opinion that the different stars affected various persons, so that each of them could predict many details in his future life. It also was customary for large numbers of persons to depend more upon magic than on the services of reliable physicians. Thousands of pilgrims used to travel to some famous shrine, where they worshiped the saint that lay buried there. In many cases it was believed that sick people were cured in this manner. It has become fashionable in our time to laugh at these "simple" folk, but the testimony of millions of persons in our century seems to prove that the people of the Middle Ages were not nearly so superstitious as they are depicted in many of our older textbooks of history.

BYZANTINE ARCHITECTURE IS WELL WORTH STUDYING. Whatever may have been the defects of medieval civilization, it must certainly be admitted that in the field of architecture, sculpture, and painting, the Middle Ages made great contributions. The first important style of architecture to be noted is that which is called Byzantine. The Byzantine churches were characterized by their dome, their mosaics, and their magnificent paintings and sculpture. We have mentioned in a preceding chapter the fine church in Constantinople called Santa Sophia. This church building also has a dome and it was famous for its beautiful mosaics, which, after the Ottoman Turks conquered Constantinople, were covered with whitewash. It is only in the last few years that the Mohammedans have at last decided to uncover these great works of art, and they have changed the church building into a public museum. The famous church which was built for Charlemagne in Aix-la-Chapelle, (Aachen), was also an example of Byzantine architecture. This type of architecture spread into Russia and various countries of northern Europe. Even the famous church of Saint Mark's in Venice is an example of Byzantine architecture.

TYPICAL FEATURES OF ROMANESQUE ARCHITECTURE. Another important type of architecture is the Romanesque. This type was derived in part from the Roman, and for that reason the name Romanesque has been applied to it. But many of its elements have been developed from eastern styles, and also from the Byzantine architecture. Romanesque architecture is featured by heavy walls, thick pillars, round windows, round arches, predominating horizontal lines, and the absence of very high and splendid towers. This type of building was constructed during the tenth, eleventh, and twelfth centuries. Among the most important examples may be mentioned the cathedrals of Worms, Mainz, and Speyer, in the

Rhine Valley. A famous Romanesque church in Italy is that at Pisa, which was built at the end of the eleventh century. In England this style was called Norman, and one example is the famous cathedral at Durham. The cathedral at Canterbury is also in part a Romanesque structure, but the building as a whole also partakes of a later type, which came to be called Gothic.

GOTHIC ARCHITECTURE IS VERY BEAUTIFUL. The finest architecture of the Middle Ages is the Gothic style, which was first perfected in northern France in the beginning of the thirteenth century. Some of these churches, like that of Notre Dame in Paris, are a combination of Romanesque and Gothic styles. Gothic architecture has the following features: Its predominating lines are vertical, rather than horizontal, which is the case in Romanesque architecture; its arches are pointed, not round; its walls are high and not so thick as those in the Romanesque buildings; there are more windows, and the windows are larger than those in the earlier buildings; the pillars are more slender, and the towers are much taller. Another important difference between the two types of architecture just mentioned is that the later type has more profuse decorations, and gives expression to the joyful feeling of religious ardor that was prevalent in the thirteenth century.

IMPORTANT EXAMPLES OF GOTHIC ARCHITECTURE. The cathedral at Rheims, that at Cologne, the Westminster Abbey in London, and the cathedral at Milan are among the most famous examples of Gothic architecture. It should be noted that Gothic architecture was not restricted to church buildings, for some of the most famous town halls in Germany and the Netherlands were Gothic buildings. In many of the great cities it was customary for the citizens to take pride in their great city halls, as well as in their famous cathedrals. Some of these buildings were characterized by profuse sculptural decorations and by a lofty tower that contained the municipal bells. Such a building was called a belfry.

THE PAINTINGS OF THE MIDDLE AGES. Medieval painting resembles medieval sculpture in that it is strongly affected by the religious fervor of the artists of the time. Innumerable pictures of the Madonna and her child are to be seen in the churches and the museums of Europe today. Unlike Greek art, the painting of the Middle Ages is not characterized by the widespread desire to display the human body exactly as nature had made it. In practically all cases men and women are fully clothed. The thirteenth century was not ready for that great revival of the Greek spirit in art and literature that was to dominate the civilization of the Renaissance.

Student Activities

1. With the aid of a dictionary write out the definitions for the following words: *revival, romances, sagas, segregation, credulous, abstract.*
2. What great change took place in Europe during the twelfth century? (The Twelfth Century takes in the years from 1101-1200 A.D.)
3. Classical Latin is the Latin language as the Roman authors used it. What do you understand by the term, "Medieval Latin?"
4. Which are the Romance Languages, and why are they thus termed?
5. Give a summary of the contents of the "Song of Roland."
6. Who were the three bad chaps of medieval literature?
7. Do you think that people were more superstitious during the Middle Ages than at present? Why?
8. How were the students taught at the medieval universities?
9. What is meant by "experimentation?"
10. Why is Roger Bacon considered an important man?
11. Name the various styles of architecture mentioned in this chapter. Note: We are near the end of the so-called Middle Ages or Medieval times. We are about to begin the study of the beginning of Modern times. The Modern Age was ushered in by great discoveries in new lands, and by the Reformation of Luther, just to mention a few. The church had become very corrupt during the long centuries since Jesus Christ ascended into heaven, and numerous people were dissatisfied with the way things were going in the Church.

CHAPTER 26

The Dawn of Modern Civilization

GREAT CHANGES OCCUR IN THE FOURTEENTH AND FIFTEENTH CENTURIES. Not only did the fourteenth and fifteenth centuries produce the great revival of learning that is commonly called the Renaissance, but it was in the same period that the Portuguese explored the coast of Africa and finally reached India; and before the close of the period, as we all know, Columbus discovered America. Moreover, in the field of science, philosophy, theology, literature, and in education in general great changes occurred which constitute the transition from medieval to modern civilization.

THE EUROPEANS SUDDENLY WANT TO CONQUER OTHER LANDS AGAIN. From the fall of the Roman Empire in the fourth and fifth centuries until the beginning of the fourteenth century, the peoples of Europe seemed content with their own land, and felt little desire to occupy the countries of Asia or Africa. How different was the situation in the days of Alexander the Great and of the Romans! Even the Crusades were far from successful, largely because the governments of the medieval countries were not sufficiently interested in driving the Mohammedans out of the Holy Land. But in the fourteenth and fifteenth centuries occurred some of the most important geographical discoveries, while at the same time feudalism and serfdom disappeared. Although all these changes were very gradual, there is no doubt that a great transition was made.

WHY THE RENAISSANCE BEGAN IN ITALY. It is not surprising that the Renaissance should have begun in Italy, because Italy was now an exceedingly wealthy country and in constant contact with the great nations around the Mediterranean Sea. The financial power that had resulted from the expansion of commerce and industry was used by patrons of art and learning. In Florence and Venice great banks were founded, and the gold standard introduced. From Italy this gold standard spread over many of the countries in the western world. Furthermore, it was in Italy that the civilization of the ancient world had reached its climax. Both the cultures of classical Greece and classical Rome had their height in Italy, when Rome was the center of the civilized world. It was but natural for the scholars of Italy to remember what Italy had once done for the human race.

WHAT MADE THE ITALIANS SO TOLERANT AND INQUISITIVE. Very stimulating also was the contact with the Saracen world. It was there that great universities had been founded before there were any in the Christian countries of western Europe. The great city of Venice was but a dependency of the Byzantine Empire when it first rose to power. Its fleets regularly called at the port of Alexandria, and from Alexandria scholars of Italy received much useful information. The Italians were tolerant and inquisitive; they were not afraid to study the Mohammedan works, nor did they scruple at a frank desire for more money. Not seldom were the Italian merchants criticized by the higher clergy for having evaded some of the regulations in the church law, but the merchants continued on their course just the same.

REASONS WHY MEDIEVAL FOLK HAD DONE LITTLE WITH CLASSICAL CULTURE. Medieval Europe, it is true, had paid comparatively little attention to the civilization of classical antiquity, partly because that civilization was heathen. For that reason, many of the Christian scholars were hesitant to become fully acquainted with it. Scholars of the Renaissance, on the other hand, gladly revived the interest in the great heathen writers of the ancient world. In the second place, most medieval scholars had thought so much of the life everlasting and the world of the spirit, that they had been responsible for the neglect of worldly things. Many medieval scholars had looked upon their own bodies with feelings of contempt, and a large number of pious souls had actually tried to hurt their bodies with the intention of thereby improving the condition of their souls.

THE ITALIANS BECOME INTERESTED MORE IN THE THINGS OF THIS WORLD. But the Italian scholars of the fourteenth and fifteenth centuries began to look upon human nature with an entirely different eye. They were of the opinion that it was not sinful nor harmful to take good care of the body, to eat excellent food, to attend plays occasionally, and to enjoy the things of this world.

THE EUROPEANS START THE GEOGRAPHICAL DISCOVERIES. As the inhabitants of Italy and the adjoining regions became more interested in commerce and industry, and as they continued to heap up wealth, it naturally followed that both the scholars and the mer-

SIXTEENTH-CENTURY MERCHANTS RECKONING THEIR ACCOUNTS

From a woodcut of the period by Jost Ammann. It was chiefly the search of the traders for new markets and sources of supply that led to the age of voyage and discovery.

VIEW OF A SIXTEENTH-CENTURY PRINTING ESTABLISHMENT

From an engraving of the period.

The Bettmann Archive

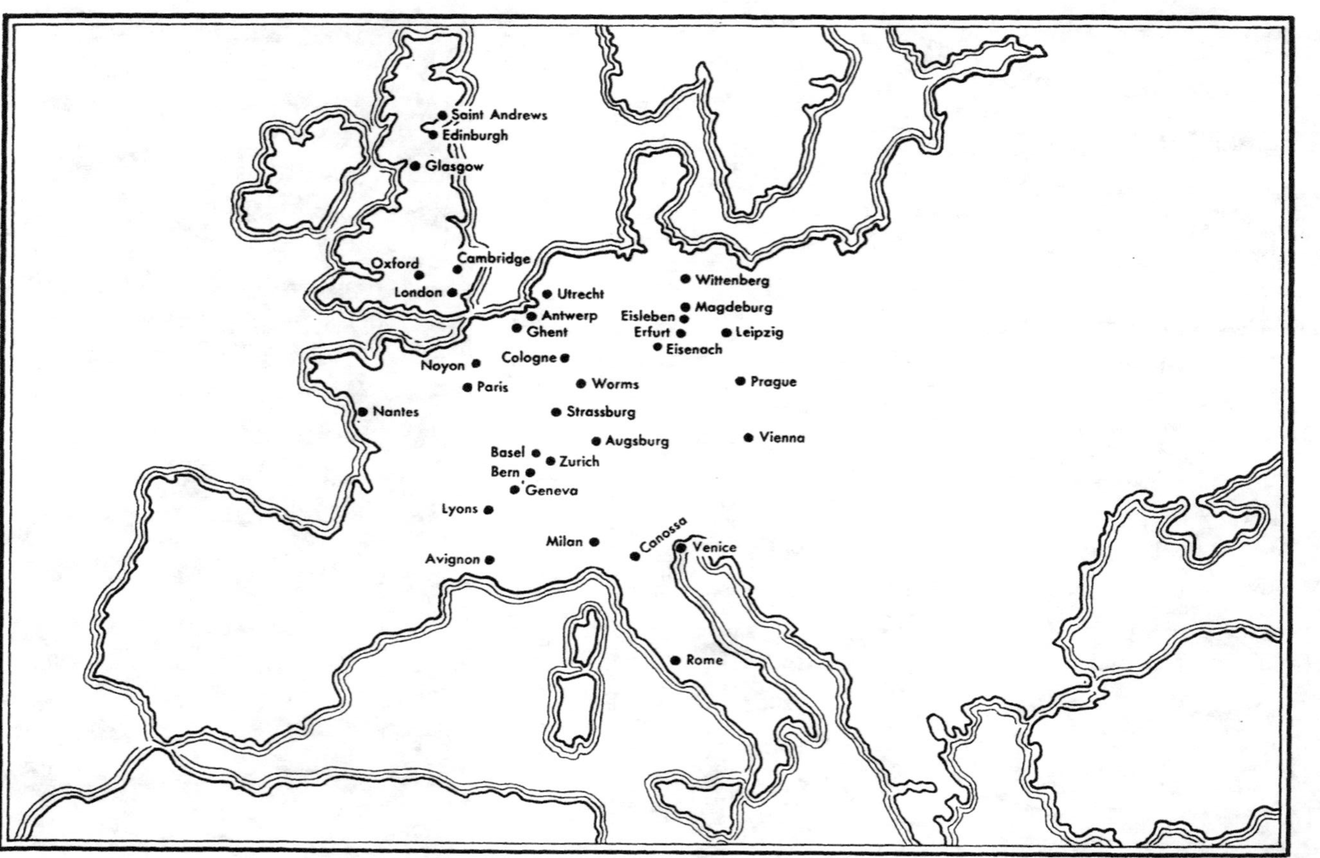

From *The Church in History*, Courtesy National Union of Christian Schools

CITIES OF THE REFORMATION

chants began to look beyond the narrow horizons of the Middle Ages. They wondered about what might be done for the expansion of European commerce. New instruments were made for the benefit of the navigators. The most valuable of these was the mariner's compass, which contained a magnetic needle pointing always to the North. Another was the *astrolabe,* which showed the position of the stars and planets. New maps were also drawn, indicating the position of rocks, sandbanks, and various other dangerous places that should be avoided. The distance between the various ports and between islands and important landmarks along the coast were also carefully pointed out.

MANY SCHOLARS WONDER IF GOVERNMENTS COULD NOT BE IMPROVED. It also became fashionable to study and criticize the political institutions of the various European countries. No longer did people assume that all of these institutions were perfect simply because they happened to be in existence, but the question was asked constantly as to how they might be improved for the benefit of both ruler and subjects. On the other hand, it was in the same period that absolutism, or autocratic government, originated in Spain, France, and England.

WHAT HUMANISM WAS. One of the first scholars in Italy to reveal the new attitude toward both classical civilization and medieval customs and institutions, was Petrarch, who lived in the beautiful city of Florence. He gave perfect expression to what was called *Humanism,* which was a system of thought and an attitude toward life revealing a definite break with much of the culture of medieval Europe. He and hundreds of his followers eagerly read the works of Cicero, Aristotle, Plato, and Homer. They admired the human body and the human mind, as contrasted with the soul or spirit. It is for this reason that they were called Humanists. They also showed a renewed interest in the beauties of nature; they spent much of their time traveling from country to country in their search for lost works of the ancient world and in the attempt to study the physical features of their own countries.

PATRONS OF ART AND LEARNING HELP HUMANISM. It was also in Florence that one of the outstanding patrons of art and learning lived. He belonged to the wealthy banking family called the house of Medici.[1] He had a library of eight thousand volumes collected, and he kept forty-five copyists busy copying the most important books from other libraries.

---

1. Cosimo de Medici.

GREAT PROGRESS IS MADE IN EDUCATION. In the field of education also great progress was made. The leading educators planned to provide for their pupils a harmonious development of mind, body, and morals, such as had been attempted before by the Greeks, two thousand years ago. The leading educators of Italy in the fifteenth century emphasized the practical and social side of the student's life. The studies consisted of classical literature, preceded by Greek and Latin grammar, the study of the Church Fathers, and the seven liberal arts. And in addition to those regular subjects, the educators of the Renaissance gave attention to physical and moral education, though they kept the religious instruction that had been given in the schools attached to the churches and the monasteries.

WHAT ONE ENLIGHTENED EDUCATOR SAID. For example, one of these educators said that he called those studies liberal which are worthy of a free man; those studies by which we attain and practice virtue and wisdom; those which call for, train, and develop the qualities in mind and body that ennoble men, and which are rightly judged to rank next to virtue only. He said that he gave the first place to history, because it was both effective and useful, which would make history appeal equally to the scholar and to the statesman. Next to history ranked moral philosophy, which he said was really one of the liberal arts, for its purpose was to teach men the secret of true freedom. History, he concluded, gives us a concrete example of the precepts that are taught by philosophy. The latter shows what men should do, the other what men have said and done in the past.

THE HUMANISTS IN THE NORTH PREPARE THE WAY FOR PROTESTANTISM. The various elements of the Renaissance spread quickly from Italy to the northern countries, where a large number of influential scholars eagerly took over the most important and the most useful principles. The greatest among these was Erasmus, who taught that one should combine religious zeal with sounder scholarship. In his amusing book, *The Praise of Folly*, he makes fun of the old-fashioned theologians, philosophers, and educators. He also exposes many abuses in the Church, and he shows that people ought to emphasize religious living more than empty formality. He and his friends in the northern countries prepared the way for the coming of Protestantism, because they undermined the respect of the people for the higher clergy, and they also pointed out a number of practices which they ridiculed so effectively that ever since in Protestant countries they have been dropped. For example, they claimed that monasticism was unnecessary, that clergymen need not remain unmarried, that there was no use in praying or talking to saints, that pilgrimages, shrines, and relics were also useless, and that the whole sacramental system of the Church should be reformed. They even made fun of fasting on Fridays and in the springtime, before Easter, so that this attitude was also carried over into Protestantism. Erasmus found many admirers in England, of whom John Colet, of the university of Oxford, was the most effective in the early years. But after his death his role was taken over by the famous writer, Thomas More, who composed *Utopia*.

RENAISSANCE ART IS A COMBINATION OF CLASSICAL AND MEDIEVAL ART. Although it has been customary to regard the Renaissance also as a revival of art, it is more to the point to say that the artists of the Renaissance movement combined the best principles of medieval art with those left by the classical peoples, so that they formed an entirely new school of art, which is called Renaissance art.

AN EXCELLENT EXAMPLE OF RENAISSANCE ARCHITECTURE. One of the most important examples of Renaissance architecture is the celebrated Church of Saint Peter in Rome. One of the leading architects who was responsible for this building was Michelangelo, who is considered the greatest artist of the whole movement. He was also a famous sculptor and painter.

THE WORK OF LEONARDO DA VINCI. Another important figure in the Renaissance art is Leonardo da Vinci, the versatile thinker, who was a mathematician, a scientist, as well as a painter and a sculptor. He painted the famous portrait called *Mona Lisa*.

RAPHAEL AND MICHELANGELO. In Florence worked also Raphael, who is best known for his beautiful painting entitled the *Sistine Madonna*. It brings to our minds the magnificent fresco painting upon the ceiling of the Sistine Chapel, in the Vatican Palace in Rome. Here Michelangelo painted scenes from the Old Testament, being employed by the Pope in this work. He added also characters from ordinary history, and from sacred and pagan traditions. He was assisted in his work by Raphael.

OUTSTANDING FEATURES OF RENAISSANCE SCULPTURE AND PAINTING. Some of the more important characteristics of Renaissance painting and sculpture are the extraordinary combinations of *realism* (which means showing things just as they are), and religious feeling. The members of the Renaissance school paid careful attention to the anatomy of their models, as may be seen particularly in the two celebrated statues by Michelangelo, called *David* and *Moses*.

GERMAN AND FLEMISH ART. In Germany and Flanders also a great deal of beautiful painting and sculpture was produced. In Flanders worked the two brothers, John and Hubert van Eyck, who were known far and wide for their magnificent altarpiece known as the "Adoration of the Lamb." The two outstanding artists in Germany were Alfred Dürer and Holbein. The latter drew the illustration for one of the Erasmus's masterpieces, *The Praise of Folly*. He settled in England, where he worked for King Henry VIII.

THE GREAT ITALIAN POET DANTE. The most important figure in the field of literature is the Italian poet, Dante, who spent much of his life in his native town of Florence. He wrote the greatest work ever produced in the Italian language, the celebrated poem entitled *The Divine Comedy*. In this poem he described the three great places or states known as Heaven, Purgatory, and Hell. His work is marked by intense religious fervor, as well as by beautiful style and artistic work throughout. But it cannot be said that Dante, who lived in the earlier years of the fourteenth century, was actually a part of the Renaissance movement. He is generally classified with the poets of the Middle Ages, although in some ways he resembled men like Petrarch and Erasmus. He gave free expression to his romantic feelings, but naturally in this respect he was not unlike many of the poets who had preceded him, both in Italy and in other countries of western Europe. The fact that he wrote his great masterpiece in the Italian language, shows that he was not so anxious, as was the real humanist, to glorify the Latin of a former age. He was thinking more of the common people, who would not be interested in Latin literature. But he resembled the great men of the Renaissance in that he criticized the Pope, whom he gave a very uncomfortable place in Hell, with his head downward. Like many other great scholars of the Middle Ages, he favored a great empire, to be ruled by the emperor in Germany.

CHAUCER AND WYCLIFFE ARE LEADERS IN ENGLISH LITERATURE. The outstanding writer in England during the fourteenth century was Chaucer, the author of the *Canterbury Tales*. In this fascinating work the author described the habits of individuals in various walks of life, such as the knight, the physician, the friar, the nun, the scholar, and the merchant. He wrote in the English language, and was one of the great founders of English literature. Another important writer of the fourteenth century in England was John Wycliffe, who was for some years professor in the University of Oxford, but owing to some of his "heretical" beliefs, he was silenced. He was very much interested in the common people, and he supported their cause in every possible way. He and some of his associates translated the Bible into English, for which reason he is often called the "father of English prose." But the English government suppressed this work.

Two English Writers Try to Help the Poor. Near the end of the fourteenth century there occurred a great uprising among the peasants of England, with whom John Wycliffe frankly sympathized. Their grievances were explained by William Langland, the author of a widely read work entitled, the *Vision of Piers Plowman*. Both Wycliffe and Langland complained that the wealthy suppressed the poor, but they also knew that many of the poor tried to withhold their rent and their services from the lords, because those lords were living openly in sin. Both writers warned the poor to be very careful in rising against their masters, while at the same time admitting that the masters were very much at fault. Wycliffe said: "Lords many times do wrong to poor men by unreasonable dues and taxes, and take poor men's goods, and sometimes beat them when they ask for their pay. And thus lords devour poor men's goods in gluttony and waste and pride and the latter perish from maltreatment and hunger and thirst and cold, and their children also. And, so in a manner they eat and drink poor men's flesh and blood."

Preparation for the Invention of Printing. The cause of education was greatly aided by the invention of printing, which occurred about the middle of the fifteenth century. It was caused in part by the increased demand for books, and partly by the knowledge of printing that had spread westward from China. John Gutenberg appears to have been the most important figure in the process which we call the invention of printing. You should note that it was not a very simple process, but that many different persons took part in it. For a long time before the middle of the fifteenth century printers in the Netherlands and adjoining regions had printed books from wooden blocks, a whole page at one time.

Gutenberg Invents Printing by Movable Type. But it was Gutenberg who seems to have been the first one in Europe to use movable type. He placed separate letters side by side, so that they might be moved at will to form different words. These letters were made of metal, not of wood. From Germany this new way of printing rapidly spread to Italy, the Low Countries, France, Spain, England, and so forth. In Germany alone, about one million volumes were printed each year throughout the sixteenth century. After the demand for books increased, prices fell. One advantage resulting from this invention was the greater degree of accuracy secured by the new process. In the Middle Ages it had been very difficult to find two copies of any book that were exactly alike. The invention of printing was undoubtedly one of the most important, and perhaps the most valuable of all modern inventions and discoveries.

Student Activities

1. With the aid of a dictionary write out the definitions for the following words: *dependency, versatile, fascinating, maltreatment.*
2. What is meant by a "revival of learning?"
3. What do you understand by the term, "Humanism?"
4. Who was Erasmus?
5. Name some of the leading artists mentioned in this chapter.
6. Why is Dante considered a great author?
7. What important work did Wycliffe do?
8. Why was the invention of the printing press such an important event in human history?
9. Who appears to have been the inventor of the printing press?
10. Write out five outstanding statements from this chapter.
    Note: In this chapter you have read how Europe began to spread out to other parts of the world. The Europeans were no longer satisfied to remain on their own continent. You have also read how great works of art were produced in painting, sculptoring, and literature. The invention of the printing press was a great help in getting ideas across to the people by means of the printed page.

CHAPTER 27

The Commercial Revolution and the Rise of Modern Capitalism

The European Businessmen Cause the Demand for Explorations. During the fourteenth and fifteenth centuries, as we observed in the preceding chapter, commerce and industry expanded on an enormous scale. The merchants and owners of industries constantly sought more markets, more raw products, and a greater supply of materials. Thus they indirectly led to the geographical discoveries, for it was their demands for the spices of the Far East, for the precious metals of India and China, and for the luxuries of the Near East that inspired men like Columbus to find routes of trade that would most quickly and most easily bring new products to the doors of the merchants of Europe.

Importance of the Spice Trade. Especially important was the spice trade, because the food of the average family in western Europe was far from attractive. Vegetables were used very little, and fruits even less. Agriculture had not yet advanced sufficiently to provide the people of Europe with a proper supply of wholesome food. Coarse bread was eaten in large quantities, but potatoes were as yet unknown. The meals usually consisted of oatmeal, dark bread, and buttermilk porridge mixed with barley. Occasionally an egg and a small piece of meat were added for each member of the family, and a glass of beer, but no tea and no coffee as a rule. Only in the summer time were vegetables commonly used. Since the peasants did not complain, it was the middle class and the upper class whose demand for spices and for more fruit led, in part, to the geographical discoveries, which form a part of the Commercial Revolution.

Which Spices in the East Appealed Most to the Europeans. Spices did indeed make up for a poor daily diet. The most popular of all the spices was pepper, which was grown on the west coast of India. For many years the merchants of Venice used to buy the pepper in the port of Alexandria. Then they would sell the pepper at a great profit in the various fairs and markets of western and central Europe. Nutmegs and cloves were raised in a group of small islands, called the Spice Islands. Cinnamon bark grew in the interior of Ceylon and on the west coast of India.

PRECIOUS METALS AND OTHER GOODS WERE ALSO WANTED. Since for centuries the European nations had bought their spices and other precious articles from the countries in the Far East, the latter countries had acquired an immense amount of gold and silver, which had been the payment for the said luxuries. Ambitious travelers such as the Venetian merchant, Marco Polo, had returned from China and India with extraordinary tales of the wealth accumulated there. They not only aroused the curiosity of their friends at home, but the latter hoped to be able to recover some of these metals. Precious stones, fragrant gums, sugar, tea, coffee, carpets, glassware, cloths, and especially the spices, were all in great demand.

WHAT WERE THE THREE GREAT ROUTES OF COMMERCE TO THE EAST. Three great routes of commerce traversed western Asia. One was entirely a sea route, and connected China with the countries along the Red Sea. The most important port at the western end of this route was Alexandria. Another route crossed a part of the mainland of Asia and was also partly a water route, because it ended at the Persian Gulf, and from there it was customary to bring the products to the Red Sea and then over land and along the Nile to Alexandria. This will explain the importance of the great Egyptian port at the mouth of the Nile River. The third route went all across the center of Asia and westward to Constantinople. When the Ottoman Turks in 1453 conquered the city, this route was rendered practically useless, and the southern route became all the more important.

WHY THE TRADE ROUTES SHIFTED TO THE WEST. The question is often asked why it was that the great trade routes at the end of the Middle Ages changed so much. Was it perhaps because of the Ottoman Turks, or was it for other reasons? It would seem that a combination of circumstances was responsible for this remarkable development. The Ottoman Turks were undoubtedly responsible for much destruction and devastation. They caused in part the downfall of Venice as a great commercial power. But it was not so much what they had done as what they might do that became the great cause of the change in the routes of world commerce.

THE CHRISTIANS AND THE TURKS CANNOT GET ALONG WITH EACH OTHER. After Constantinople had fallen, many merchants and owners of industries in Italy and other countries of the West were wondering what the Turks would do next. The enmity between the Mohammedans and the Christians was also an important factor in the whole drama. It was not for nothing that the Pope asked constantly for new crusades against the infidels. Nor was it for nothing that the literature of the time is filled with thousands of references to the "Unspeakable Turks." When zealous preachers and great reformers criticized abuses in the State or the Church, they would often say that a bad clergyman, or a bad, deceitful merchant was almost as wicked as a Turk. When references were made to devastation, bloodshed, and robbery it was often said that only a Turk could do worse. Reformers who preached against usury and graft often remarked that a usurer was even more detestable than a Turk.

THE SUEZ CANAL WAS ALMOST COMPLETED, AND SUCH A CANAL WOULD HAVE POSTPONED THE DISCOVERY OF AMERICA. The Venetians had rightly argued that the best way to maintain the trade with the Orient was to preserve the old routes of commerce. They had even begun to dig a canal that would have become the Suez Canal. If the Turks had shown proper interest in this undertaking of the Italians, it appears that the discovery of America would have been delayed for at least a hundred years. But it was the terrific pressure for the finding of new routes to the Far East that brought Columbus in 1492 to America. As late as 1609, Henry Hudson still was trying to do the very same thing when he went along the Hudson River, hoping in this manner to find a passage to the Orient. Many an explorer tried to sail around the earth by way of the North Pole. Everybody thought at first that the New World was more a hindrance than a value to the merchants of the West.

THE PORTUGUESE GO AROUND AFRICA TO INDIA. In the meantime, the Portuguese had gradually explored the west coast of Africa, and in the year 1486 Diaz reached what is now called the Cape of Good Hope. Twelve years later, in 1498, Vasco da Gama landed at Calicut, in southern India. Portugal was indeed very favorably located for exploration, because it was situated at the extreme southwestern tip of Europe. There seemed to be little sense in trying to expand eastward into Spain, because the rivers that flowed through Portugal were very shallow and, as a rule, had little water in them. Furthermore, the interior of Spain back of the Portuguese frontier, was extremely high and dry. For this reason the Portuguese continued to go southward, hoping to find valuable products in western Africa, to check the Mohammedan faith, and finally to reach in this manner the coast of India, and the Spice Islands.

THE PORTUGUESE OBTAIN A MONOPOLY OF THE SPICE TRADE. After Vasco da Gama had reached southern India, the Portuguese began to occupy the most valuable places. Here they bought directly from the producers the spices. After a lengthy journey these were put up for sale at Lisbon, where the merchants of Flanders, Italy, Spain, and England would purchase them at a fairly high price. But they were glad to obtain them this way. For about one hundred years the Portuguese enjoyed a practical monopoly of the spice trade, for they had occupied the lands along the southern part of the Red Sea and along the Persian Gulf, as well as the west coast of India.

THE LINE OF DEMARCATION IS DRAWN FOR SPAIN AND PORTUGAL. It was not long before the Spaniards and the Portuguese began to quarrel about the division of the heathen lands. Both wanted to go to the same places, which naturally was impossible, since each power wanted to have a monoply of the trade of its own colonies. Consequently, in 1493 Pope Alexander VI decreed that a line of demarcation be drawn to separate the colonies of Portugal and Spain. In 1494 this line was slightly altered and the Pope now decreed that all heathen lands lying three hundred and seventy leagues west of the Cape Verde Islands should become Spanish territory, and the other Portuguese.

THE ENGLISH ALSO ENTER THE FIELD. THE WORK OF CABRAL AND MAGELLAN. John Cabot, who was an Italian navigator, secured financial aid from the king of England, and in 1497 he reached the coast of North America somewhere near Cape Breton Island. In the year 1500 Cabral, the Portuguese explorer, discovered Brazil, and in 1513 Balboa crossed the Isthmus of Panama and beheld the Pacific Ocean. It was generally believed that a few hundred miles to the west lay the mainland of Asia, until Magellan crossed the Pacific Ocean in 1520 and observed how wide that body of water actually was. Though he himself did not return to Spain, some of his ships did so in the year 1522, thus completing the first circumnavigation of the world.

THE BEGINNINGS OF MODERN CAPITALISM. It was during the century of the geographical discoveries that the modern way of doing business originated. Just before the end of the Middle Ages,

Italy and Germany enjoyed the leading position in the world of finance. Many of the Italian merchants had become bankers, and they loaned money to other merchants, as well as to monarchs and princes, at fairly high rates of interest. The first banks which were established in Florence were merely banks of deposit. Here people would leave their money as savings accounts. But gradually their business grew larger, and the banks of Florence then began to lend money on interest. This example set by the bankers of Florence was followed by those of Venice and Genoa.

GERMAN BANKS. NEW CURRENCIES. In Germany there were also several wealthy families that became leading bankers. They had branches in many cities, not only in Germany, but also in Italy, France, and the Netherlands. The most important house in Germany was that of the Fuggers, for they corresponded to the Medici in Italy. The most popular currency of western Europe was the *florin,* which originated in Florence, and is still used in the Netherlands. The Germans used both the florin and mark. The English and the people of the Netherlands made use of the *pound,* which was a pound of silver, and divided into twenty shillings, while each shilling was divided into twelve pence.

BILLS OF EXCHANGE AND CHECKS ARE MORE WIDELY USED. During the thirteenth century Italians developed the bill of exchange to take the place of the shipping of coins. From Italy these bills of exchange were introduced into other countries, partly by bankers and partly by the revenue agents of the Pope. But it remained a custom in many of the countries, at least in part, to ship valuable goods in payment of debts incurred. It was also before the end of the Middle Ages that checks replaced much of the metal currency. Since the bankers had begun to receive money on deposit and also to loan money on interest, it was a simple thing to turn to the writing of checks. For example, if A owed B, and if both had money in the same bank, A would give B a check for the amount.

MORE MONEY IS LOANED AT INTEREST. Another advantage to the merchants was the changed attitude adopted since 1500 by the leading scholars and clergymen toward the loaning of money on interest. Business simply had to have more capital all the time, and if the merchants were not permitted to borrow money and pay a reasonable rate of interest on their loans, trade and industry could not expand rapidly enough. Before long stock markets were established, and stocks of great commercial companies were bought and sold. In this manner modern capitalism grew from infancy to maturity.

BOOKKEEPING IS INTRODUCED. It was also in Italy that bookkeeping and other systems of accounting were developed. Owing to the highly advanced methods invented by the Italians, it became customary for the merchants in Germany, the Netherlands, and England to send their sons to Italy to study there accounting and general business methods. In those times a banker was often called a *Lombard,* because the Lombards had at one time ruled northern Italy. This in turn accounts for the fact that the great business street in London was called Lombard Street, and has retained that name to this day. It corresponds to Wall Street in New York.

THE IMPORTANCE OF ITALY IN THE ECONOMIC HISTORY OF EUROPE. Thus it follows clearly that Italy remained, until the beginning of modern times, a great power in the world of business and of capitalism in general. But with the change in the world routes of commerce, and with the hostile attitude of the Ottoman Turks in the eastern Mediterranean, it was natural that Italy had to share its advanced position with the powers situated along the Atlantic Ocean. And the time was not far away when Italy would cease to be an important factor in economic development.

AT THE END OF THE MIDDLE AGES ITALY BEGAN TO DECLINE. Much of the same may be said for the fields of learning, art, literature, and education. The Mediterranean Sea, which for more than three thousand years had been the center of civilization, finally lost its favorable position. After the close of the fifteenth century Portugal, Spain, France, the Netherlands, and England built colonial empires, established great commercial companies, founded new universities, developed national schools of art and literature, and led the way in political, social, and economic experimentation. For many years these countries had been looked upon by the cultured Greeks and Romans as barbarous, but the time came at last when the worm turned, as you might say, until by the opening of the twentieth century it had become fashionable for the so-called Nordics to look with scorn upon the peoples of the Balkan peninsula, Asia Minor, Mesopotamia, Egypt, and even Italy.

Student Activities

1. With the aid of a dictionary write out the definitions for the following words: *usury, demarcation, depredations.*

2. Why were spices such an important item of trade during the fourteenth and fifteenth century?
3. Name as many spices as you can.
4. What other products besides spices did the Europeans want from India?
5. Draw a map showing the trade routes between the Italian cities and India.
6. How did the Portuguese try to reach India?
7. What were the two most powerful nations of Europe at the time when Columbus discovered America?
8. Who were Cabral and Balboa?
9. Why is Magellan famous in history?
10. What are "Bills of exchange?"
11. Why were the bankers called, "Lombards?"
12. Why did Italy lose its position of importance during the Age of Discoveries?
    Note: The Mediterranean Sea lost its great importance, and the center of gravity moved to the Atlantic Ocean. The rich and powerful cities of Italy gradually went down, and new centers of wealth developed in northern and western Europe. Portugal became the center of trade, and in turn was supplanted by Spain. Spain was displaced by the Dutch, and the Dutch in turn were ousted from their leading position by the English.

CHAPTER 28

The Western World Is Being Prepared for the Reformation

WHAT THE REFORMATION WAS. In the first half of the sixteenth century occurred a great reform movement within the Church, which we call the Reformation. It resulted in the development of several Protestant churches, and also partly in a reformation of the Roman Catholic Church. This reformation in the Catholic Church is sometimes called the Counter-Reformation, because it has often been assumed that it was caused almost entirely by the Protestant movement itself, that is, the Reformation. But a more satisfactory term is the Catholic Reformation, because it was older than Protestantism.

SOME CAUSES OF THE REFORMATION. The Reformation was caused by many factors, some of which we have studied in earlier chapters. Throughout the Middle Ages there were men and women who criticized the Church, or objected to some of the doctrines preached by the clergy. Such people were called heretics, and in many cases they had been excommunicated. After the opening of the thirteenth century a large number of "heretics" had been burned at the stake, or imprisoned. One of the most influential "heretics" was John Wycliffe, who labored in England, as we saw. Another reformer was John Huss, who spread his doctrines in Bohemia, and was burned at the stake.

MANY HUMANISTS AND REFORMERS WANT TO IMPROVE THE CHURCH. Humanism was also an important cause of the Reformation, because the humanists pointed out abuses in the Church, and clamored constantly for reform. Equally important, perhaps, is the work of those reformers who were not heretics, nor humanists, but faithfully attempted to purify the Church. History, like the newspapers, has a tendency to emphasize the exciting and dramatic episodes, for which reason these noble reformers have often been sadly neglected. We shall meet a few of them in our treatment of the Catholic Reformation.

218

THE BABYLONIAN CAPTIVITY AND THE GREAT SCHISM. The demand for reform increased greatly during the fourteenth century, when the so-called Babylonian Captivity occurred. From 1309 to 1377 the Pope was living at Avignon, instead of in Rome. Although Avignon at that time was not a part of France, strictly speaking, the city was across the frontier, and every one of the Popes of Avignon was of French birth, and obedient to the French king. This episode is called the Babylonian Captivity, for it resembles the exile of the Hebrews in Babylonia, where they lived for about 70 years. What was still worse, the Great Schism followed in 1378, and lasted until 1418, when there was not only a Pope at Avignon, but another in Rome. For forty years the Church was divided between the supporters of the Pope at Avignon and those who favored the Pope in Rome. The schism was healed in 1418, at the Council of Constance, which was held from 1414 to 1418.

THE COUNCIL OF CONSTANCE FAILS TO REFORM THE CHURCH. Another task performed by the council was the execution of John Huss, who was burned at the stake for heresy. But as far as the reformation within the Church went, practically nothing was accomplished in addition to the healing of the schism. Other church councils followed during the course of the fifteenth century, but in none of them was anything worth while achieved.

HOW POWERFUL THE ROMAN CATHOLIC CHURCH WAS. Nevertheless, the Roman Catholic Church at the opening of the sixteenth century was still a very powerful institution. In order to suppress heresy, the Church continued to make use of the Inquisition, and frequently it excommunicated both unruly monarchs and influential heretics. Furthermore, the Church also wielded another tool, which was called the Interdict, and which resembled a wholesale excommunication, in that it was laid upon a whole country. As a result of this interdict, all the inhabitants of the affected country were under the ban of the Church. The Pope also continued to make use of the so-called papal bulls, which were decrees addressed either to members of the clergy or to governments of various countries. Besides, a tax was laid upon every family, called the Peter's Pence, and members of the clergy were required to pay to the Pope the equivalent of the first year of the income of their particular office in the Church.

THE SEVEN SACRAMENTS. But the greatest cause of the strength of the Roman Catholic Church was to be found in the sacramental system. The Church acted as a *mediator* between God and men, and its seven sacraments were considered a necessary means of acquiring salvation for every human being. Baptism was the sacrament which was thought to cleanse the child from original sin, because every human being upon birth was subject to eternal damnation, due to the fall of Adam and Eve in Paradise. But baptism could be depended upon to wash away this so-called original sin. For this reason parents were always very anxious to have their children baptized as soon as possible. Confirmation was also administered to everybody. When boys and girls reached the age of about twelve years, the bishop would welcome them into the he was the male heir. Being the son of Anne Boleyn, who was the them. Marriage was the sacrament that sanctified the ties between husband and wife. The sacrament of penance was instituted to enable persons to obtain absolution, or forgiveness, for the sins committed by them after baptism. It was called penance, because it required that after a person had confessed his sins to the priest and had been forgiven, there still were some penalties attached to the sin, and it was held that by doing penance, that is, by performing some good work, the penalties might be removed.

How Important the Sacrament of Penance Was. During the twelfth and thirteenth centuries a custom had originated whereby persons might be helped in doing penance. It was felt that a substitute for penance offered by the church would be acceptable to God. In this manner *indulgences* came into use They were intended to remove the temporal guilt or punishment remaining after a sin had been forgiven. *Purgatory* was a place or state in which the soul was believed to live before it was considered fit to enter Heaven. As the name implies, here the soul was purified, while it also received an opportunity to remove the last of the penalties that remained after forgiveness of sins. Consequently, indulgences could also be applied to the stay in Purgatory. They would shorten such a stay.

The Mass, or Communion Service. The mass was the sacrament in which the bread and wine were used to represent the body and blood of Jesus Christ, who died upon the cross in order to save the human race from eternal damnation. The Roman Catholic Church taught and still teaches that during the sacrament both the bread and the wine undergo a miraculous change into the body and blood of Christ. Although the physical elements in the bread and wine are not altered, it is the substance, or the spiritual essence that is back of the material thing, that is changed. For this reason the name *transubstantiation* is applied to the process. In a certain sense Christ was believed to be offered anew for the sinner.

TWO OTHER SACRAMENTS. Extreme unction was the sacrament which was administered to the person who seemed to be at the point of death. He would be anointed with holy oil, in order that his condition might be improved upon and he might be more fit to go to Heaven. Holy orders, or ordination, was intended for the members of the clergy when they were ordained and received their office in the Church.

WHAT THE MYSTICS THOUGHT OF THE SACRAMENTS. One of the most widely debated questions of the Middle Ages had been whether the sacraments had power in themselves to help the sinner, or whether grace and faith were the only important elements in the process. In many countries there had been *mystics*, who had claimed that everything depended upon the union between the individual soul or spirit and God Himself. The mystics objected to much of the formalism in the Church and they said that empty formalism can do nobody any good. For that reason they emphasized the spiritual union between themselves and God, rather than the attendance in church and the administration of the sacrament. But it must not be assumed that the mystics refused to go to church or to take the sacrament, for they did that, as well as others. But they simply stated that such acts were not as important as a certain way of thinking. The sinner ought to show real repentance for his sins and he ought to feel real love in his heart before he went to church.

THE BOOK CALLED THE IMITATION OF CHRIST. One of the most famous books written in the fifteenth century emphasized this teaching. This work, called the *Imitation of Christ*, was the most widely read book ever written in Europe. It went through more than ten thousand editions and has been translated into almost all the languages in the world. In this little book the reader is shown how he may become a real mystic and attain the union between God and himself. But somehow, nothing seemed to cause any important change until suddenly Martin Luther appeared upon the scene to become the hero of the Protestants and the villain to the Roman Catholics.

Student Activities

1. With the aid of a dictionary write out the definitions for the following words: *influential, episodes, reform, mediator, moderate, checked, grievances, toleration, commentary, ritual.*
2. How did the Church punish "heretics?" Was that proper and right?
3. Who was John Huss?
4. What are the Seven Sacraments which the Roman Catholic Church teaches?

CHAPTER 29

The Beginnings of Protestantism and the Catholic Reformation

Luther's Youth. Luther was the son of a fairly wealthy miner, and was enabled to secure an excellent education in the University of Erfurt. It had been his intention to become a lawyer, but suddenly, frightened one day in summer by a terrible thunderstorm, he promised to become a monk. While he was in the monastery he began to wonder about the question of salvation, and finally came to the conclusion that a sinner cannot obtain salvation without faith. He reasoned that good works were of little use to anybody, for everything depended upon faith. He objected especially to the sale of indulgences, a practice that had been going on for some time near his own city.

His 95 Theses. He was now, that is, in 1517, a professor of theology in the newly founded University of Wittenberg. Although indulgences were not being sold in Saxony, where he was living at that time, people from Saxony had come to buy them, and this annoyed him very much indeed. So on the last day of October, 1517, he posted his celebrated Ninety-five Theses on the door of the Castle Church in Wittenberg, in which he told scholars what he thought of the sacramental system, indulgences, and faith. Although his theses were written in Latin and intended only for the scholars, they were almost immediately translated into German and spread over the whole of the Holy Roman Empire. Within three years Luther became the most famous person in all Europe.

Luther Has a Debate With John Eck. In 1519 he held a debate with a noted Catholic theologian, called John Eck, and in this debate he frankly stated that in his opinion not only a Pope but also a church council might make serious mistakes. In 1520 he wrote his most effective little work, entitled, "Address to the Christian Nobility of the German Nation." He pointed out the enormous wealth of the Church, and he recommended that much of the money that flowed to Italy should remain within Germany.

In this manner he appealed to many of the German princes, who had held similar views on the subject. He was immediately excommunicated by Pope Leo X, but he paid no attention to the excommunication and when the papal bull arrived in Wittenberg, he had it burned in a bonfire, amidst the applause of his joyful students. In 1521 Luther appeared before the Diet of Worms, where in the presence of the emperor and many bishops and princes he repeated his former teachings. While on his way back to the university he was kidnapped and taken to the castle called the Wartburg, because the elector of Saxony was afraid that Luther would experience the same fate that had befallen John Huss at the Council of Constance.

LUTHER BEGINS TO TRANSLATE THE BIBLE. At the Wartburg, Luther began the translation of the Bible into the German language, which, although it was not the first translation into that language, was by far the most important. He felt and he said that all the people should be enabled to read the Bible for themselves, and naturally in their own language. For hundreds of years most of the church members had relied almost entirely on what the preachers told them in church. Many priests had said that the people could not understand a large number of verses in the Bible. If they should read those, and if they misunderstood them, that would be worse for them than if their pastor had read them and had explained the difficult statements for them; or else, if they had never heard about them. But Luther reasoned that all the people should by all means read the Bible. If there were passages that they failed to understand, why could they not ask their pastors for an explanation? The Bible was the only inspired Word of God, reasoned Luther. It was intended for reading by all members of the churches. Luther took great pains to find out just what were the best German words and sentences to take the place of the original Hebrew in the Old Testament and the original Greek in the New Testament. He succeeded so well in this task that he practically made the literary language of modern Germany. Since he lived in the center, between the north and the south, also between the east and the west, his language was easily understood in almost all parts of Germany.

WHY LUTHER SUDDENLY LEAVES THE WARTBURG CASTLE. Shortly after Luther was taken by his friends to the Wartburg, he heard that in the university town of Wittenberg some of his followers were preaching radical doctrines. Now Luther was not a radical thinker. He wanted a *reformation* in the Church, and not a *revolution*. Changes that had to be made should be very gradual; they should also be *moderate*. So he rushed back to Wittenberg, worrying more about the Church than about his own safety.

LUTHER'S MARRIED LIFE. Three years later, in 1525, he heard that a young lady of noble birth had left a convent near Wittenberg, and was interested in meeting some religious leader whom she might perhaps marry. Her name was Catherine von Borah. Luther proposed to her, and they soon were married. They lived in Luther's own monastery, which the elector of Saxony donated to the married couple. You will understand of course that Luther was no longer a monk by that time, and the building was no longer a monastery. His wife was a devoted mother of several healthy children. She had a large restaurant or boarding-room in the basement of her home, where she could seat three hundred students. She made a handsome profit this way, and also kept cattle in the country. As a result, Luther was worth at the time of his death, about one hundred and fifty thousand dollars. As one Lutheran professor once said to the writer of this chapter, Luther proved the truth of these words of Jesus in the Sermon on the Mount: "Seek ye first the kingdom of God, and all these (material) things shall be added unto you."

LUTHER AND THE PEASANTS' WAR. In 1525 occurred the terrible Peasants' War, which checked the spread of Lutheranism in Germany. Luther was misunderstood by both nobles and peasants, because he had tried to help them all. The peasants of southern and western Germany had risen against their masters, because they had many grievances against those lords. They wanted to be relieved of some of their servile burdens, while they also wished to be able to choose their own pastors. It seemed as if Luther at first favored the cause of the peasants, because he criticized the selfish nobles. All of this was true, but at the same time he objected to the rash measures adopted by some of the leaders of the peasants, who attacked the homes of the nobles, burned many of them, and killed a large number of the lords. Luther argued that the lords should be willing to meet the peasants part way, while he also encouraged the peasants to remain quiet and faithful. Consequently, those who have said that Luther was inconsistent have done so simply because they have not read the original works.

HOW THE NAME "PROTESTANTS" WAS STARTED. In 1526 the national Diet was held in the city of Speyer, where it was agreed by the leading princes of the Holy Roman Empire that the Lutherans should be placed on the same footing with the Catholics.

However, three years later, in the same city, at another Diet, the Catholic princes suddenly shifted their position and determined to grant no further toleration to the Lutherans. For this reason, the Lutheran princes complained about the action of their opponents, and issued a protest, with the result that hereafter the Lutherans were called the Protestants. Since that time all other denominations that broke away from the Roman Catholic Church in the western world have been called Protestants.

WHAT HAPPENED IN 1530 AT THE DIET OF AUGSBURG. The next Diet was held in the city of Augsburg, in the year 1530. Here the Lutherans presented their official creed, which was drawn up partly by Luther and partly by his intimate friend, Melanchthon. The Confession, which is called the Confession of Augsburg, has ever since that year 1530 remained the official creed of the Lutheran Churches. The emperor of the Holy Roman Empire, who had been elected in 1519 as Charles V, was a faithful son of the Roman Catholic Church. He strongly objected to the Confession of Augsburg, and prepared for actual fighting against the Lutheran princes. Unfortunately, however, for the emperor, he was unable to destroy Protestantism in Germany, partly because he had to contend with a rebellion in Spain; besides he had to fight four wars against the King of France, and he also spent much of his time and energy in trying to check the Ottoman Turks who were crossing Hungary and finally, in the year 1529, besieged the city of Vienna in Austria. So the Lutherans continued on their march to victory, and although from 1546 to 1555 actual civil war was fought in Germany, the Roman Catholics were unable to stop the spread of Protestantism. In 1555 the Treaty of Augsburg was signed, in which the Catholics granted the Lutheran princes official recognition.

LUTHERANISM SPREADS RAPIDLY IN THE THREE SCANDINAVIAN COUNTRIES. Protestantism was even more successful in Scandinavia than it was in Germany. All of the three Scandinavian countries—Sweden, Denmark, and Norway—became thoroughly Lutheran. But in the countries to the west of Germany, Lutheranism did not succeed in gaining the support of the masses of the people. In these countries, as we shall see, another form of Protestantism took a better hold. In England still another type of Protestantism was introduced. And while the three new denominations were becoming firmly established in the western countries of Europe, a number of smaller denominations made their appearance, which we shall also discuss in the present chapter.

WHAT ARE SOME IMPORTANT DIFFERENCES BETWEEN LUTHERANISM AND CATHOLICISM. But before we take up these other denominations, we must point out the most important differences between the teachings of the Roman Catholics and the Lutherans. (1) Luther taught that human beings are entirely corrupt, owing to the fall of Adam and Eve in Paradise. The Catholics, on the other hand, though they admitted that man was almost totally corrupt, believed that nevertheless he had retained a certain amount of divine power, so that he was able to cooperate with God in the process of salvation. Luther, as we have seen, said that everything depended upon God, and that human beings were in no way able to perform any good works, unless they were aided by grace, through faith in Jesus Christ and the power of the Holy Spirit. (2) The Lutherans in Germany, though not in Scandinavia, objected to the institutions of bishops in the church, and especially to having an archbishop to rule over the ordinary bishops. All of the Lutherans refused to accept the Pope as the head of the Christian Church. In Germany the bishops were displaced by officials called superintendents. (3) The Lutherans did away with monasticism, shrines, rosaries, indulgences, pilgrimages, the veneration, or at least, the invocation of saints, a large number of holy days, or holidays, five of the seven sacraments (retaining only the Holy Supper and Baptism), the compulsory refusal of the clergy to get married, and the doctrine of transubstantiation.

ZWINGLI SPREADS PROTESTANTISM IN SWITZERLAND. Protestantism made rapid progress in Switzerland under the leadership of Ulrich Zwingli, who, like Luther, believed that man was totally corrupt, and that salvation depended entirely upon the grace of God and justification by faith. He also rejected all the practices that we have mentioned a moment ago, when discussing the differences between the Lutherans and the Catholics. He even went further than Luther in refusing to permit his followers the use of crosses, altars, paintings, and sculpture in the churches. Zwingli is noted particularly for his peculiar interpretation of the doctrine of the Holy Supper. It was his opinion that Christ was not present officially in any capacity, either physically or spiritually, during the sacrament of the Holy Supper. He thought that the words in the Bible, "This is my body," which were spoken by Jesus when He presented the bread at the last supper at Jerusalem and said that the bread signified the suffering that He was to undergo upon the cross — these words did not mean that the bread was the flesh of Christ, but simply meant the flesh. In other words, the word "is" stood for "signified," and Zwingli held that the purpose of the sacrament of the Holy Supper was simply to commemorate the suffering of Christ for sinners. In 1531 Zwingli died upon the battlefield, where he served as chaplain of the Protestant forces who were fighting against the Roman Catholics.

CALVIN SURPASSES ZWINGLI. Zwingli's work in Switzerland was ably continued by John Calvin. Calvin was undoubtedly, next to Luther, the greatest Protestant figure of the sixteenth century. The religious movement which he caused was of even greater historical importance than Lutheranism, because it spread into the countries that were to become great colonizing powers, notably England and the Dutch Republic. Calvin was born in 1509 in a small town in northern France, and for four years he attended the University of Paris (1523-1527). He was a serious thinker, and a good student. Unlike Luther and Zwingli, he was slow to accept Protestantism. At first he was greatly affected by humanism, and his first work published was a commentary on the Roman philosopher Seneca. In 1536 he published the first edition of his great masterpiece, *The Institutes of the Christian Religion*. The first edition was in Latin, but in 1541 a French translation was published. Calvin's work was largely based on some of the more important works by Luther. But he also followed some of the other leaders among the Protestants, including Zwingli. He agreed with Zwingli that all decorations should be removed from the church buildings, but he disagreed with Zwingli in the interpretation of the Holy Supper. Although he did not think that Christ was present in any physical manner, he did insist on the spiritual presence of Christ in an official capacity during the Holy Supper.

WHAT ARE THE IMPORTANT DIFFERENCES BETWEEN CALVINISM AND LUTHERANISM. We may note the following differences between Calvinism and Lutheranism: (1) The Calvinists insisted that during the church services only psalms and the few hymns in the New Testament might be sung, for all other hymns, being the work of men, should not be considered on the same plane as the psalms, which were a part of the Word of God. (2) While the Lutherans thought that Christ was present during the Holy Supper in a physical manner of some sort, the Calvinists denied this altogether. (3) The Calvinists, as we have observed, insisted on bare walls and ceilings, the removal of all crosses, and the abolition of confirmation, which the Lutherans still regarded as an important ceremony. (4) The Calvinists, unlike the Lutherans, were more interested in long sermons than in music and other formalities.

(5) The Calvinists were also more strict in the regulations of their own lives. They objected to dancing, worldly literature, and unnecessary fun in general.

WHAT CALVIN DID IN GENEVA. Calvin spent the last years of his life in the city of Geneva in western Switzerland. Here he founded the University of Geneva, presided over the establishment of several Calvinistic churches, and addressed hundreds of letters to his followers in various countries. Like the Lutherans in Germany, he abolished the institution of bishops, but instead of using superintendents in their places, he revived the institution of elders, or *presbyters*. It is from this word *presbyters* that the name "Presbyterian Church" has been derived. The official title of the Calvinistic churches on the Continent was the Reformed Church. This title was retained in Switzerland, Germany, and the Netherlands. But in France the Calvinists were generally called Huguenots, while the Calvinistic church in Scotland and England was called the Presbyterian Church. Calvinism became an important factor in the making of American civilization, because through the influence of the Puritans, who were for the most part Calvinistic in doctrine and in the idea of church government, Calvinism spread through New England and affected even the Baptists.

THE GROWTH OF PROTESTANTISM IN ENGLAND. Protestantism in England owes its rise to many factors, and it took a course somewhat different from that followed by Lutheranism in Germany and Calvinism in the other countries. English Protestantism was, in a way, a compromise between Roman Catholicism and Protestantism as it was developed on the Continent. Protestantism received indirect support from King Henry VIII (1509-1547), who had a dispute with the Pope over an attempted divorce which the Pope would not grant. For that reason Henry VIII refused to recognize the Pope any longer as the head of the Christian Church, and made himself the head of the Church in England. Seeing that many people in England objected to monasticism, as the result of the work of the Humanists, he took advantage of the situation and dissolved all the monasteries in England. But this did not make him a Protestant at all, for in 1521 he had defended the Roman Catholic faith against Lutheranism, for which reason the Pope had called him officially "The Defender of the Faith." This title Henry VIII retained until the end of his life, and all later monarchs, though nearly all of them were Protestant, clung to this title. About twenty years later, Henry VIII once more indicated his position by publishing a booklet against the Lutheran faith.

But since he broke with the Pope and abolished monasticism, he gave a certain measure of encouragement to the Protestants in England. In a following chapter we shall discuss the reign of Henry VIII in more detail, as well as the reign of his three royal children who succeeded him.

ENGLISH PROTESTANTISM SPREADS RAPIDLY UNDER QUEEN ELIZABETH. After the death of Henry VIII in 1547, Protestantism spread rapidly throughout England, and although for a few years under his Catholic daughter Mary, Protestantism was held in check, it was under Queen Elizabeth, who ruled from 1558 to 1603, that England finally became Protestant.

SOME IMPORTANT FEATURES OF THE CHURCH OF ENGLAND, OR ANGLICAN CHURCH. Queen Elizabeth considered herself the head of the Church in England. The official title of the new church was the Church of England, or the Anglican Church. This Church retained the institution of bishop, and since the Latin word for "bishop" is *episcopus,* the name Episcopal Church is often applied to the Church of England. Unlike the Calvinistic churches, the Church of England had from the beginning a prayer book of its own, which was called the *Book of Common Prayer.* This book prescribed the order of worship in the Church.

WHY THE PILGRIM FATHERS LEFT ENGLAND. Queen Elizabeth decreed that those who did not attend services had to pay a fine, and the ministers who refused to conform to the creed and practices of the Church were punished. It is partly owing to this measure adopted by the Queen in the so-called "Act of Uniformity of Common Prayer," of 1559, that near the close of her reign many hundreds of Protestants who refused to conform to her policies, removed to the Netherlands. The Pilgrim Fathers belonged to these peoples. The doctrine of the Church of England was very largely Calvinistic. But the Church government, as we have seen, as well as the order of the services and the keeping of the decorations, indicate the compromise between Catholicism and Continental Protestantism.

HOW MANY PERSONS BECAME PROTESTANTS. Before the death of Queen Elizabeth, Protestantism had spread to such an extent in England that more than 80 per cent of the population had become Protestants. This percentage remained stationary during the seventeenth century. One reason why Protestantism had become so popular was the use made of the "Great Bible," that is, a translation of the Bible published in 1539 that was based very largely on Protestant versions. The Catholics finally were compelled to issue a translation of their own. But by that time Protestantism had been so firmly established that no amount of action on the part of the Catholics could change the proportion between Catholics and Protestants.

WHO THE ANABAPTISTS AND THE BAPTISTS WERE. In the second half of the sixteenth century a number of new denominations were founded. The first of these was that of the Anabaptists, who were so named because they had to be baptized all over again, and so they received the name "Anabaptists," or "Again-Baptists." A great variety of beliefs were held among the Anabaptists on the Continent, but after the middle of the sixteenth century many of the peculiar elements disappeared, and finally, in 1575, the Anabaptists were given toleration in the Dutch Republic. Gradually the name "Anabaptist" was dropped, and the new name of Baptist was put in its place. The great Baptist Church of England and the United States had its origin for the most part in the Dutch Republic, where large numbers of English Protestants sought refuge in the reign of Queen Elizabeth and of her successor, James I.

THE CHURCH OF THE QUAKERS IS FOUNDED. Similar to the early Baptists were the Quakers, who called themselves "Friends." Like the Baptists, they refused to swear oaths, insisted on simple ceremonies, and believed in religious toleration. Most of them also objected to the use of arms, and generally they refused to fight for their governments.

THE INDEPENDENTS WERE MOSTLY CONGREGATIONALISTS. The name "Independent" was given to those denominations who believed that each congregation should be entirely independent. The Baptists and the Quakers were "Independents." Other Independents were the Congregationalists, who gave that name to their own denomination, because they believed in the independence of each congregation. The Pilgrim Fathers were Congregationalists. It is partly through the influence of the Pilgrim Fathers, the Quakers, and the Congregationalists in general, that democracy and religious toleration came to America. The Congregationalists, like the Calvinists on the Continent, refused to allow a great deal of authority to the pastors, and reserved much of it for their deacons. In this manner they encouraged the growth of democracy.

WHO THE ENGLISH PURITANS WERE. The Congregationalists were closely related to the so-called Puritans who, although they remained within the Church of England, tried to reform and purify the church from within. They objected, as a rule, to the use of the Prayer Book, the bishops, and elaborate ceremonies in the services. Nearly twenty thousand of them went to the English colonies in America between 1620 and 1640.

ROMAN CATHOLIC REFORMERS HAVE AN EARLY START. In the meantime the leaders in the Roman Catholic Church had by no means been idle. Not only had great scholars and preachers within the Church done much for reform even before the close of the fifteenth century, such as was done by Cardinal Ximenes in Spain, but in the first half of the sixteenth century a new religious order was founded by a Spaniard, Loyola, called the Society of Jesus or the Jesuits. The members of this order exercised great influence in educating statesmen and other influential persons. Loyola had also written a valuable book, which was a guide for those who tried to lead a holy life upon this earth. It was called the *Spiritual Exercises,* and indicated how, during four weeks, a person might become more saintly.

THE INDEX AND THE COUNCIL OF TRENT. Another weapon used by the Roman Catholic Church was the *Index,* which was a list of books condemned either entirely or in part by the leaders of the Church. Finally, from 1545 to 1563 a great Church council was held in the city of Trent, where, under the leadership of the Jesuits and the Dominicans, a number of reforms were introduced into the Church. The official creed of the Church was carefully drawn up in writing, so that hereafter everyone could tell exactly what the Church taught. Moreover, this council also issued a new translation of the Bible, still called the Vulgate, but much improved over the older version. It was indeed most encouraging for the Roman Catholics to note that the Church did not feel obliged to change any of its important doctrines.

WHY ITALY AND SPAIN REMAINED ROMAN CATHOLIC. Italy remained thoroughly Catholic, partly because here was the seat of the papacy, and partly because Italy was largely dominated by the kings of Spain. But there were also other reasons why Italy refused to accept Protestantism. The Italians were too much attached to the memory of such men as St. Francis of Assissi, who certainly had known what vital religion was. They could not give up monasticism so easily as the Germans. They loved their ritual and their beautiful church buildings. The same may be said of the Spaniards, who had started a church reform of their own, as we saw. The Portuguese remained Roman Catholic for similar reasons.

WHY ONLY LESS THAN ONE-TENTH OF THE FRENCH PEOPLE BECAME PROTESTANT. Although Calvin was a Frenchman and for a time nearly one-tenth of the French were Calvinists, the king refused to accept the new faith, partly because he was satisfied with the arrangements that had been made in 1516 by the king and the Pope, allowing the king and the clergy a considerable amount of independence and the king himself some influence in the election of bishops. Moreover, France was a country with a Latin civilization, which favored the Roman form of Christianity.

WHY AUSTRIA, POLAND, IRELAND, THE RHINE VALLEY IN GERMANY, AND SOME OTHER REGIONS REMAINED ROMAN CATHOLIC. Austria, though a Germanic country, was near Italy, and its rulers were faithful to the Roman Catholic Church. In southern Germany and the lands of the Rhine Valley Catholicism also recovered much lost territory after 1530, because of the work of the Jesuits and other members of the clergy. Learned Catholic scholars added much to the power of the Catholic Church in these regions. Poland remained Catholic largely because the Poles were hostile to the Germans. The Irish refused to follow the lead of the English for a similar reason. The southern Netherlands chose to remain under Spanish rule, as we shall see, and so naturally remained also Roman Catholic in religion. Bohemia was recovered by the Catholics in the seventeenth century, as will be indicated presently.

WHAT WERE THE RESULTS OF THE REFORMATION. The results of the Reformation have been variously estimated. It is generally agreed that it caused a split in the Church that has not yet been healed. It also led indirectly to the religious wars of the period from 1546 to 1648. The Bible was much more widely read by the masses of the people, and in Protestant countries it was regarded as the only reliable authority in the realm of faith and morals. The Calvinists and many of the Lutherans, in common with most of the other Protestants, were also guided by the teachings of the Bible in their business relations and in their attitude toward the civil government. The study of the Bible replaced part of the curriculum of the universities in the Protestant countries, and especially in the elementary schools it received much more attention than had been the case before. The Reformation in Germany led to a great expansion in elementary education; Luther and Melanchthon set up the first system of public elementary schools in the modern world. But it cannot be proved that the Reformation established either autocracy or democracy, for it was too complicated a movement to do that. Finally, it did not lead to the rise of capitalism, though many scholars used to think that this was the case. The Reformation was for the most part a religious movement of a conservative nature, and indirectly it assisted the movement for reform within the Roman Catholic Church. It has played a role of the utmost importance in the development of American civilization.

Student Activities

1. Write a 100-word essay on Luther as a child and as a young man.
2. What prompted Luther to post his Ninety-Five Theses?
3. Why is Luther's translation of the Bible a very excellent one?
4. On what points did Luther differ from the Roman Catholic Church?
5. Why did the peasants rebel against their masters? What methods did the peasants use? Were those methods lawful? Why not?
6. How did the name "Protestant" start?
7. Who was Melanchton?
8. Why was Charles V unable to stop the spread of Lutheranism?
9. Which countries of Europe did not become Protestant? Why not?
10. What was the chief difference between Luther and Zwingli?
11. Who was Calvin?
12. Why did the Pilgrim Fathers leave England?
13. Who were the Anabaptists?
14. Who was Ignatius of Loyola? How did he help the Roman Catholic Church?
15. What were some of the results of the Reformation?
16. What was and still is one of the official creeds of the Lutheran Church? Note: A Reformation is a peaceful change, but a Revolution is a quick and violent change. You have been studying a good deal of the things which have happened in the past, but always bear in mind that God is the Supreme Ruler Who guides events in the world for the benefit of His believers here on earth.

CHAPTER 30

The So-called Christian Nations Fight Numerous Religious Wars

WHICH WERE THE LEADING COUNTRIES IN EUROPE DURING THE SIXTEENTH CENTURY. If you could have taken a trip through Europe four hundred years ago, you would have visited numerous countries that were still there in the year 1939. You would probably have taken a small ship of some two hundred tons which was moved by the power of the wind blowing against its sails. After six or more weeks you would have landed in England, at the port of Bristol or London perhaps. At that time there was not yet one kingdom called Great Britain, but there were two separate kingdoms, namely, those of England and Ireland, including Wales, as we saw before; and Scotland to the north of England. England had about four or five million inhabitants, who were not greatly interested in their political rights but let the king have a great deal of power. The average Englishman wanted above all peace at home and a chance to make a decent living. Parliament was not strong, because the people did not care much about the amount of power which Parliament had at that time. Across the English Channel there was the great and powerful kingdom of France, whose monarch in the first half of the sixteenth century was even more powerful than was the king of England. But in the second half of the century, as we shall see, France was hurt badly by civil wars, called the religious wars. You would not have enjoyed living in France very long. In Spain you would have found similar conditions, but no civil wars. In Italy you would have seen foreign armies invading the peninsula several times. First came the armies of France, and later those of the king of Spain, who was also emperor in the Holy Roman Empire (called Charles I in Spain and Charles V in the Empire). You might have taken a trip with him from Italy through the republics of Switzerland into Germany. A good prophet would have told you that after the

Thirty Years' War (1618-1648), Switzerland would be given absolute independence of the Empire. But the Holy Roman Empire would be ruined by that terrible war, because Germany could not keep foreign armies away. How different has the situation been in Germany lately, hasn't it? You would have seen another importance between conditions as they were then and as they are now. Turkey was then the largest state, while today it is very insignificant. The reverse was true of Russia, which was then very backward and weak. In northern Europe you would have found the three Scandinavian countries, of which Sweden would win its independence from Denmark in the year 1523. Perhaps you would have been interested the most in the rise of a new republic, which fought a mighty battle for freedom, and won it after eighty years of war. That was the Dutch Republic, or the United Netherlands.

FRANCE AND SPAIN FIGHT SEVEN WARS IN A ROW. In the reign of King Charles I of Spain, the French and the Spaniards fought four wars. Both countries were anxious to get territories that only one of them could have, and when Charles finally gave up his throne in 1556, his son was ready to fight the fifth one. This was Philip II, who at the end of his reign fought another war with France. The seventh war followed in 1635, and lasted 24 years. You might well wonder why these European kings refused to be satisfied with what they already ruled over, and why they could not think of more useful things to do than to fight for land in Europe or beyond the seas. But, although they called themselves Christians, they paid little attention to the teachings of Jesus. No wonder they caused their peoples so much misery and poverty!

EIGHT CIVIL AND RELIGIOUS WARS ARE FOUGHT IN FRANCE. Now that there were both Catholics and Protestants in France, the two churches began to imitate the wicked rulers and fight wars between them. Besides, the king of France and his family were sometimes at war with nobles who were Catholics, just like the royal family. So you must not think of these eight wars from 1562 to 1593 as religious wars entirely, but as being rather mixed. Among the French Protestants, who were called Huguenots, as we saw, there was one great leader who would some day be king himself. In the year 1572 he married the sister of the young king. His name was Henry of Bourbon, and his wife was Margaret of Valois. The bride belonged to the old royal house which in 1589 came to an end, because the last king in that house left no male heir. The next house was the house of Bourbon. We remember the marriage of 1572 because at the time it was being celebrated, several thousand Huguenots were suddenly murdered by the Catholics, who had the power to do so, being in the majority. The massacres occurred for the most part on August 24th, which was called among the Catholics St. Bartholomew's Day, that being the day when this particular saint was honored by them. On that day thousands of prominent Huguenots were in Paris to attend the royal wedding. They were attacked while they were asleep, suspecting nobody of evil plans.

KING HENRY IV ISSUES THE EDICT OF NANTES (1598). In order to become king himself, Henry of Bourbon, after having become a Catholic to save his life in France and after having turned Protestant again when he felt safer, turned around once more. He saw that over 90 percent of the French subjects were Catholics, and he realized correctly that a Protestant could not be a king in France. But he also wanted to satisfy the Huguenots, and thus in 1598 he gave them religious toleration, and the right to hold offices in the government. But he did not want to lessen his own power, and for that reason he never called a meeting of the national legislature, called the Estates-General. Upon the whole you may well consider him an autocratic ruler, like the king of Spain at that time.

THE KINGS OF SPAIN ARE VERY INTOLERANT IN RELIGION. Charles I and his son Philip II persecuted Protestants, Jews, and Mohammedans. Thousands of Jews and Mohammedans had to leave Spain in their reigns. Moreover, the two kings also suppressed the national legislature, not so much by refusing to have it hold meetings, as by taking most of its powers away. They did the same to the courts of the Church, and to the great nobles. They continued the work done before them by Ferdinand and Isabella, whom we have mentioned in a preceding chapter.

THE DUTCH RISE AGAINST SPAIN. The inhabitants of the northern Netherlands are called the Dutch people, for the English gave them that name, confusing the Hollanders with the Germans, who really should have been called the Dutch, for the German name for Germany is *Deutschland*. The Dutch greatly disliked Philip II, who was their king, for their country, as we have seen, was ruled by the king of Spain, since he was a descendant of Ferdinand and Isabella. There were several reasons why the Dutch were displeased. Not only did Philip II give orders to have thousands of Protestants killed, but he introduced a very burdensome sales tax, and he also tried to take away from the Hollanders some valuable political rights, such as having local officers of their own in towns and rural districts. At first Catholics rose with Protestants, but later on the war was fought mostly by the Protestants against Spain.

WILLIAM THE SILENT BECOMES THE FOUNDER OF THE DUTCH REPUBLIC. One of the nobles in the Netherlands who led the Dutch in their revolt, was a German prince from the country called Nassau. He had inherited a little state in southern France called Orange, and he also owned much land in the Netherlands. He is called William of Nassau, and also William of Orange. He and many other rulers after him in the Netherlands have belonged to the House of Orange-Nassau. One day, when he was in France, an important Spanish official told him what the king of Spain was going to do to the rebellious Hollanders, and he wondered what William would say about it. But he kept still, and so he is known in history as William the Silent. He spent his time, his money, and his blood for the Dutch, and when he was assassinated in 1584, his last words were: "My God, have pity on my poor people." His two sons continued the fight with marked success, and in 1648 the Dutch Republic was recognized as an independent state.

WHAT WAS HAPPENING IN ENGLAND AT THIS TIME. While the Dutch were shaking off the yoke of Spanish absolutism, the English people were preparing themselves for the task of developing representative government. However, before 1603 it seemed very much as if they were going into the opposite direction, for, under the House of Tudor (1485-1603), Parliament was deprived of much of the power it had acquired in the fourteenth century. The English had favored a strong king in 1485, because they had grown very tired of the quarreling nobles, who had kept up a civil war for thirty years (the War of the Roses, 1455-1485). Henry VII had taken advantage of this situation by enlarging the powers of the crown. His son, Henry VIII (1509-1547), had married Catherine of Aragon, the daughter of Ferdinand of Aragon and Isabella of Castile. But when he had wanted to get himself another wife, largely because Catherine had failed to produce a male heir, the Pope, as we saw, refused to grant him permission. He had altogether six wives, and he was succeeded by three children, as the table below indicates.

THE HOUSE OF TUDOR

Henry VII (1485-1509)
|
Henry VIII m. (1) Catherine of Aragon
           (2) Anne Boleyn
           (3) Jane Seymour

(3)	(1)	(2)
Edward VI	Mary	Elizabeth
(1547-1553)	(1553-1558)	(1558-1603)

EDWARD VI AND MARY TUDOR. Edward VI ruled first, because he was the male heir. Being the son of Anne Boleyn, who was the wife the Pope would not let Henry VIII marry, he was a Protestant. Mary Tudor was the daughter of Catherine, and so was a Catholic. She married Philip II of Spain and made her country the ally of Spain in a war against France. It was in this war that England lost Calais in France (1558).

THE REIGN OF ELIZABETH. Elizabeth was the only child who enjoyed a notable reign. She fought Spain, whose government in 1588 sent to England the fleet called the *Invincible Armada,* but it was easily defeated by the English and the Dutch. Spanish sea power was temporarily broken, but the battle won by England was of greater importance in the minds of the English than in reality. The English found renewed energy, but in the next two reigns, they were weak on the sea, as well as on land. In one war against Spain, they were decisively defeated (1625-1626). So it will not be wise to make too much of the defeat of the Armada. The same is true of other battles which are often singled out for undue attention.

THE THIRTY YEARS' WAR BREAKS OUT. The most important war in the period from 1500 to 1650 is the Thirty Years' War (1618-1648), which, like the Hundred Years' War, was in reality a series of wars. It began in Bohemia as a contest between the Catholic emperor, who was king of Bohemia, and one of the Protestant princes of Germany. The prince was defeated in 1620, and had to flee to the Dutch Republic. Most of the Bohemians now were forced to become Catholics, and war ceased in Bohemia.

DENMARK AND SWEDEN TRY TO HELP THE GERMAN PROTESTANTS. But in 1625 the king of Denmark wanted to strengthen his position in the Baltic area and secure for his son some of the

German territories. He was promised help by the English government, which was never sent. So he was also defeated in a short time. Peace was made in 1629, but in 1630 another war began, this time having been started by Gustavus Adolphus, the king of Sweden. He invaded Germany, partly to save Protestantism. He received money from France, which was the rival of the Hapsburg House. You should note that in 1556 Ferdinand, the brother of Charles I of Spain, had become emperor, and that both Germany and Spain were ruled by members of the house of Hapsburg in the period we are discussing in this chapter.

FRANCE ALLIES WITH SWEDEN AGAINST THE EMPEROR. The Swedish king was the first Protestant ruler to defeat the Catholics in Germany. He was killed, however, at Lützen (1632), where his troops defeated the most able general of the Catholic forces—Wallenstein. Once more it seemed as if Protestantism would be destroyed in Germany. But in 1635 France entered the war against Spain, while in 1638 France also made war on the emperor. Aided by Dutch sea power, the French and their allies achieved notable victories, so that the balance between Catholics and Protestants in the Holy Roman Empire was restored.

THE TREATY OF WESTPHALIA ENDS THE WAR. Peace was signed in two cities of Westphalia, in western Germany, for which reason it is known as the Treaty of Westphalia. In addition to Lutheranism, the faith called Calvinism was given official recognition and toleration in the empire. Sweden received valuable regions in northern Germany, which gave her the control of the three most important rivers in this part of Europe—the Elbe, the Oder, and the Weser. On the Elbe is located the great port of Hamburg, on the Weser the city of Bremen. Brandenburg-Prussia, whose ruler, the Great Elector (Frederick William), had fought on the winning side near the end of the war, obtained large grants of lands. France secured the major part of Alsace, but not the city of Strasbourg. Switzerland and the Dutch Republic were declared independent of the empire. Within the empire each prince could determine what should be the religion of his subjects, but this clause must not be taken very seriously, for such a provision could not be enforced. It simply implied that, as in England, the ruler tried to make his subjects conform to the state church. What was more important, each prince was free to make war or peace within the empire without having to consult the emperor. So low had the central government fallen that parts of the "nation" were permitted to ally with foreign powers against other states within the empire.

GERMANY IS RUINED BY THE WAR. But the most dreadful thing for Germany were the social and economic effects of the war. For nearly thirty years many districts had been devastated several times in a row. Thousands of persons had literally starved to death. Parents had eaten their children and prison wardens had devoured their prisoners. The most terrible crimes imaginable were committed by the soldiers from time to time. They plundered the peasants, ruined homes, destroyed whole cities, and removed the cattle. Germany had been absolutely at the mercy of a whole host of foreign armies, whose soldiers had come from Switzerland, Poland, Savoy, Italy, Spain, France, Sweden, and the Netherlands. Many of them had been without discipline except when actively engaged in combat. Since years went by in certain parts of Germany without fighting, the soldiers often took the law into their own hands, and plundered everybody within reach. In some respects this war was the most terrible of modern times, and neither the Middle Ages nor many periods before the Middle Ages can show any other that was more inhumane or unreasonable. The Thirty Years' War would seem to mock those stupid admirers of mankind who are of the opinion that human beings have within themselves the power to make definite progress in spiritual as well as in temporal and material affairs. Germany required a century and a half to recover from this war!

Student Activities

1. With the aid of a dictionary write out the definitions for the following words: *massacres, autocratic, rural, notable.*
2. What was the St. Bartholomew Massacre?
3. How did Henry IV of France try to satisfy the Huguenots?
4. Which European country was the most intolerant in religious matters?
5. Which people fought eighty years for their independence?
6. Why is William of Orange a very important person in Dutch History? Look up the story entitled, *Fugitive,* in the Bobbs-Merrill Seventh Reader. Who were the "Beggars" in that story?
7. Where did the Thirty Years War begin?
8. Name the nations involved in the Thirty Years War.
9. What three religious groups received official recognition in the Treaty of Westphalia?
10. What were some of the evil results of the Thirty Years War?
11. Is it possible for human beings to better themselves without any help? Note: The Thirty Years War and all the other wars show how wicked mankind really is. Greed and pride control so much of all human activities.

CHAPTER 31

France Once More Becomes a Leader Among the Nations of Europe

THE FRENCH KING TRIES TO RULE AS AN ABSOLUTE MONARCH. During the second half of the seventeenth century, France was a very powerful country, although its government was not democratic. You must not imagine that just because a certain country has a democratic government, it is more prosperous and more powerful than it might otherwise be. Democracy alone will not make a country great and strong and rich. When in the year 1940 France was totally defeated by Germany, the democratic country lost the war. We read too much in our newspapers and magazines about the blessings of democracy, and far too little about the need of more Christianity. Democracy and Christianity must go hand in hand. A country may for a time be powerful without being Christian, as was the case with ancient Persia, but worldly power alone is also not enough, and that will never last very long. So you must study the history of each country as we come to it, and ask yourself if you can understand what made it so great or so weak, and why it could not last more than a certain length of time.

WHAT HAPPENED TO THE LEGISLATURE OF FRANCE, CALLED THE ESTATES-GENERAL. We have just seen that King Henry IV of France refused to call a meeting of the Estates-General, for he wanted to keep as much power as possible for himself. He was assassinated in 1610, and his widow became regent for their little son, called Louis XIII. She called a meeting of the Estates-General in 1614, but in a few weeks she dismissed the members, because they seemed unable to accomplish anything worth while. The next meeting came 175 years later, at the outbreak of the French Revolution, when absolutism in France finally and suddenly received its deathblow. During these 175 years the king of France was the master throughout the realm.

WHAT THE GREAT MINISTER RICHELIEU DID FOR HIS KING. Much was done for the establishment of absolutism in France by a

242

brilliant statesman who was more powerful than the king, but whose efforts tended to increase the royal power and prestige. This minister was called Cardinal Richelieu, and he guided the destinies of the French people from 1624 to 1642. He deprived the nobles of political power, checked the Huguenots, and entered the Thirty Years' War, in order to weaken the House of Hapsburg, as we saw. Thus he prepared the stage for the so-called Grand Monarch — Louis XIV (1643-1715).

WHAT MAZARIN DID FOR LOUIS XIV. When the young king was still unable to rule for himself, he was fortunate to be assisted by a worthy successor of Richelieu, who was also a cardinal in the Roman Catholic Church and whose name was Mazarin. But upon the death of Mazarin in 1661, the king took over the reins of government and firmly held them until his own death in 1715. He took his task most seriously. It was said that with the aid of an almanac you could tell what time of the day it was by finding out what Louis XIV was doing. He conferred with the governors of the provinces and the ambassadors from foreign powers. He gave directions to his own ambassadors. He also supervised the work of the law courts, the management of the army and navy, the commerce and industry of the nation as a whole, and the colonial affairs. He is sometimes referred to as the Sun King, because he took the glory of the sun as a symbol of his personality and power in Europe.

KING LOUIS XIV HAS A FINE PALACE BUILT FOR HIMSELF AT VERSAILLES. In order to keep the nobles usefully but not dangerously engaged, the king invited thousands of them to live in the city of Versailles, which is now a suburb of Paris. There he had a palace built for himself and there he established the French capital, though Paris had formerly been the capital. Various nobles performed duties connected with the royal home and court. Some of them waited upon him as he got out of bed and prepared himself for the tasks of the day. One would present his shirt to him, another would help him get washed. At the dinner table he was the center of attraction, just as the sun rules over its satellites. He loved the glory of the royal court and of the battlefield, where he often led the armies in person.

FRENCH TRADE AND SEA POWER INCREASE. For some years the king wisely accepted the advice of Colbert, who was one of the ablest ministers in the service of the monarch. Colbert argued that France ought to have more commerce and industry, which could only be accomplished with the support of the government through protective tariffs and subsidies. He increased the size of the merchant marine and of the navy, and he encouraged men like Cadillac, La Salle, and Marquette to explore the region of the Great Lakes in North America. They and many others extended New France from Quebec through the valleys of the St. Lawrence and the Mississippi to New Orleans.

THE FRENCH KING NEGLECTS THE COLONIES. If only the king could have continued upon this course of favoring the labors and plans of Colbert, he would have been responsible for the founding of a huge colonial empire. France was allied since 1662 with the mighty Dutch Republic and in North America the Indians were more friendly to France than to England. The Dutch held New Netherlands, which would not have become New York, if the French and the Dutch had worked together at this critical period between 1665 and 1685. Not only was France nearly twice as large as England and had a population about three times as great as had England; but France was favored with a better climate, had a coast line on both the Atlantic and the Mediterranean, and possessed vast natural resources in its fertile soil and its industrious inhabitants. But Louis XIV was interested more in conquests in Europe than in the expansion of New France in America. Three times before the French had tried to establish an East India Company, in order to gain a share in the lucrative spice trade, but the Dutch had been able each time to stop their efforts. Louis XIV stubbornly continued the narrow-minded policy of gaining some lands in Europe at the expense of the Hapsburgs.

LOUIS XIV FOOLISHLY FAVORS LOUVOIS AND VAUBAN ABOVE COLBERT. After 1670 the king chose as his trusted ministers Louvois, the minister of war; and Vauban, who was in charge of the fortifications and military engineering in general. The first two wars in his reign were directed against Spain, from which country he wrested a few small provinces in what are now respectively northern and southern France. From 1672 to 1678 he sought to destroy the Dutch Republic, but, though he was allied with the English, the Dutch lost nothing. The ally of the Dutch, that is, Spain, had to surrender a county to the east of France (1678). Now the king had reached the height of his ambition, and he decided to annex more territory to the east of France. But in doing this, he overlooked what he was losing in America and India. He should have thought more about the future importance of America and the Far East, instead of trying to add small bits of land to France in Europe.

Louis XIV Would Have Been Wise if He Had Allied With the Dutch. The Dutch Republic was the outstanding power in the field of sea power and trade. This country was very wealthy during the time of Louis XIV. It possessed the Hudson Valley in North America, while France owned important colonies in the Mississippi Valley and to the north of New England, in Canada. Moreover, the Indians were more friendly to the French than to the English. The Dutch colony called New Netherlands separated New England from the English colonies to the south. So you can see how easily the French and the Dutch could have defeated the English in North America. Besides, the Dutch were the most successful traders in the Far East. From 1641 to 1859 they were the only Europeans permitted by the Japanese government to trade in Japan. They also possessed the Malay Archipelago, Ceylon, and South Africa. By helping the French, they could have driven the English out of North America and out of India.

What Louis XIV Did Instead. But the Sun King could think only of conquests near France. First he annoyed the Germans by annexing some German districts near the Rhine (1680-1681), and then he made all the Protestants very angry by repealing the famous Edict of Nantes which, as you have seen, was granted to the Huguenots by King Henry IV (1598). Some two hundred thousand industrious French Protestants left France, and instead of being permitted to go to the French colonies in North America or elsewhere, they had to go to those countries where Protestants were welcome. These countries were naturally England, the Dutch Republic, or Holland (for Holland was the largest of the states that formed the republic), Brandenburg, and the Dutch colony of South Africa, called at that time Cape Colony. Here the Huguenots told the people how cruel the French king was. As a result the English, the Germans, and the Dutch became very much displeased with the French king. The English and the Dutch peoples were ruled by one person (William III) in the period from 1688 to 1702. How that happened you will learn in the next chapter. But here we must mention the alliance between the English and the Dutch which really lasted a long time, namely, from 1674 to 1756. During that time France lost several important wars to the English. The first of these was fought from 1688 to 1697, but France lost no territory this time. It was the fifth war in the reign of Louis XIV.

What Happened in the Last War of Louis XIV. In 1701 began the last war waged by the Sun King. It is called the War of the Spanish Succession, because it was fought over the Spanish kingdom and its possessions. In 1700 the last Hapsburg king of Spain died. He had stated in his will that all the Spanish lands should go to Philip of Bourbon, the grandson of Louis XIV, and the grandnephew of the Spanish king. The English and the Dutch combined with the Austrian Hapsburg to prevent the execution of this will. Fortunately for Louis XIV, a number of circumstances caused a change in the English ministry and a sudden desire for peace. In the Treaty of Utrecht (1713) it was provided that Philip receive Spain, Austria the Spanish Netherlands and some Italian states, and Great Britain Gibraltar in Spain and some colonial territories. To satisfy the British, it was also stated that France and Spain could never be ruled by the same member of the House of Bourbon. But it was only natural that in the next generation or two the French and the Spaniards would be closely allied. They would probably fight together against England each time there was a war.

COMPARISON BETWEEN FRANCE AND ENGLAND. To the peoples of Europe it seemed in 1715 that France was still the outstanding state. The royal court at Versailles had been and remained the model for most of the other courts, including that of the English monarchs. It was in fact the attempt of two Stuart kings in England to imitate French absolutism that caused the two revolutions in England during the seventeenth century. In each case the king was defeated, which was fortunate for the English people, for if one king could ruin so great a nation as France had been in the seventeenth century, it would have taken less effort to render England helpless also. Whatever France still possessed was hers by birthright, not because of the work of her absolute monarchs. The English, on the other hand, would begin as a second-rate power and climb to a position that even France had never acquired.

WHY FRANCE AND SPAIN HAD BEEN AHEAD OF ENGLAND. Both France and Spain had held a tremendous advantage over Great Britain. Spain had led the way in exploration, colonization, and unification at home; but the kings had exhausted the country through their foolish policies at home and abroad. France was subjected to the same treatment, but France was much more wealthy than Spain, and it had ministers like Richelieu and Colbert. Great Britain also began with royal absolutism. But in spite of the attempts of four Stuart rulers in succession to follow in the footsteps of their relatives across the sea, they could not stop the middle class from rising against them in the end. Spanish civilization was short-lived in Europe at least; French civilization was a great force in Europe, and bore rich fruit in North America; but British civilization became a world factor, even where New France had once been.

Student Activities

1. With the aid of a dictionary write out the definitions for the following words: *regent, absolutism, destinies, satellites.*
2. What is an *absolute* monarch?
3. Why was Richelieu an important person in French history?
4. Who was the "Sun King," and why was he thus called?
5. What did Colbert wish to do for France?
6. Write a 100-word account of Louis XIV.
7. What are some of the mistakes that Louis XIV made?
8. Make a list of the important characters of this chapter.
9. What possessions did France have in America?
10. What did the repeal of the Edict of Nantes mean to the French nation?

CHAPTER 32

Representative Government Is Established in England

A NEW HOUSE BEGINS ITS RULE IN ENGLAND. You will remember that at the end of the sixteenth century Queen Elizabeth, the Protestant daughter of King Henry VIII, governed the kingdom of England, while her cousin, Mary Stuart, was queen of Scotland. The Scotch queen had a son named James, who in 1603 became king of England, for at that time Queen Elizabeth passed away. This king was known in Scotland as King James VI, and in England as King James I. He was the first member of the House of Stuart who ruled England.

KING JAMES I GETS INTO TROUBLE WITH THE PURITANS AND WITH PARLIAMENT. The new king could not get along well with the many Puritans who were living in England during his reign, because they wanted a more democratic church government than was to be found in the Anglican Church, and the king wanted to remain head of the church and maintain the bishops. He also became angry when the Puritans said that they did not want the Prayer Book any longer, which in the Anglican Church was used during the services. He annoyed the leading members of Parliament, because he wanted too much power in the government. So they complained bitterly about this proud king from Scotland. The situation became so unpleasant for a time — from 1614 to 1621 — there were no meetings of Parliament at all. It looked as if James I was going to be as autocratic as were the kings of France and Spain.

THE KING JAMES VERSION OF THE BIBLE. Since King James I was very much interested in religion, he ordered that the whole Bible should be carefully translated into the English language by the best scholars he could find in the two universities at Oxford and Cambridge. Altogether 54 men were selected, and they were divided into six groups, each of which translated a certain part of the Bible. When this work was finished the different groups examined the parts that the others had done, and thus they made a wonderful translation, which is known as the Authorized Version, or the King James Version. Until recently this was the translation used by the great majority of the Protestants in this country, but now there is also another one called the American Revised Version.

KING CHARLES I ALSO HAS TROUBLE WITH THE PURITANS AND WITH PARLIAMENT. During the last four years of his reign (1621-1625), James I was not very active and let much of his work as king be done by his son and a certain nobleman whom we call the Duke of Buckingham. These two young men were hostile to the Puritans and friendly to the Catholics. For a time they expected that Prince Charles, the son of King James I, would marry the daughter of the Spanish king. How do you think the Puritans would have liked that marriage? But the prince and his friend were not well received in Spain, and they returned home without the Spanish princess. Now the English prince did exactly what others often do when they are in love and cannot get the person whom they want. He turned around immediately and married the sister of the French king, who was also a Catholic. He declared war against Spain and allied himself with the French king. Few Englishmen liked their Catholic queen, and they also did not like the war they had to fight for their king.

THE PURITANS ARE PERSECUTED. Finally, the new king of England, who in 1625 succeeded his father, made life so unpleasant for the Puritans and other Protestants outside of the Anglican Church, or Church of England, that some twenty thousand of them came to America, where they founded New England. Among them were the Pilgrim Fathers, who in 1620 landed at Plymouth. Several thousand English Protestants lived for years in the Dutch Republic, where they found religious liberty. You probably know already that some of the Pilgrim Fathers had first gone from England to Holland.

THE PURITAN REVOLUTION. In 1640 the Puritan leaders started a rebellion against King Charles I. They were assisted by the Independents, who received that name because their congregations were independent units in their church. Greatest among the Independents was Oliver Cromwell, who fought against the king, had him imprisoned, and finally persuaded his friends to have him executed. In 1649 the king died, and Cromwell took over the reins of government. He in turn persecuted the Catholics and the Anglicans. Before long most Englishmen became opposed to this new form of tyranny. The English people had grown weary of the power exercised by both Puritans and Presbyterians (1640-1648), and then by the Independents under Cromwell (1648-1658). If these well-meaning folk had been more moderate in their attempted reforms, they might have succeeded. But they "overplayed their hand." One excellent measure introduced, however, by Cromwell must not be overlooked. He permitted the Jews to return to England, where they had not been allowed to live for more than 300 years. He and his followers, both Puritan and Independent, had also been responsible for a great increase in personal piety and a more serious way of life. Besides, they had taught the royalists that the time was gone for the sway of absolutism. Parliament must remain to represent the people.

WHAT SORT OF A RULER CHARLES II WAS. Charles II was in the Dutch Republic when he accepted the English crown. Here lived his sister, who had married the president (called *stadhouder*) of the Dutch Republic. She was now engaged as his widow in bringing up her son, who later became known as King William III of England. The new king who in 1660 restored both the monarchy and the Church of England, was the son of a French princess and was secretly a Roman Catholic, while his brother, James, was openly a Catholic. Charles allied with the French against the Dutch Republic, but in 1674 the Protestant leaders in Parliament forced the king to make peace with the Dutch. Important also in English history is the Test Act of 1673, which provided that no Catholic could hold a position in the government. James, the king's brother, who was the Duke of York, was now deprived of his post as admiral; and hereafter the foreign policy of England favored the Dutch and the Protestant cause.

THE ENGLISH CONQUER NEW YORK AND GAIN A FOOTHOLD IN INDIA. Charles II was shrewd and did not dare to oppose Parliament. He found a way of bribing many members with French gold, paid by Louis XIV. And thus it happened that he could rule England until the day of his death. In the early years of the reign, when the English were still hostile to the Dutch, they conquered New Netherlands and named it New York (1664). They also obtained the great port of Bombay on the west coast of India (1662). Now the East India Company, which had been founded in 1600 and had secured some land in India in 1613, could make more definite progress in the colonization of this great country.

WHY THE REIGN OF JAMES II WAS SO SHORT. England was becoming a first-rate power at last, and if a prudent king had succeeded Charles II in 1685, the English government would have remained nearly autocratic for a long time to come. But James II (1685-1688) differed from his brother in that he was stubborn and conceited. He was at once opposed by the parliamentary leaders, for they did not wish to have a Catholic king rule over them, nor could they tolerate the undisguised practice of autocracy. So they invited his son-in-law, William III, to accept the English throne, which the latter was happy to do, because he saw a chance of checking France with the help of England. The revolution of 1688 is called the Bloodless Revolution, since it was not followed by a civil war. James quietly left Engand, and William ruled in his place till his own death in 1702.

WILLIAM INTRODUCES THE BILL OF RIGHTS.   One of the first things that William III did in England was to provide religious toleration for the large number of Protestants who did not belong to the Church of England. But still more important is the Bill of Rights of 1689, which ranks with Magna Charta and the Petition of Right in giving Englishmen valuable political rights. It has been incorporated in the first ten Amendments to the American constitution. Among the privileges granted by the monarch to the people were the right to present petitions in Parliament, to receive proper treatment when accused of crime or misdemeanor, to elect members of Parliament regardless of the king's wishes, and to be more fully represented by Parliament. The king could no longer levy any taxes for his own benefit, but was to receive a regular appropriation from Parliament.

WHAT THE GLORIOUS REVOLUTION OF 1688 ACCOMPLISHED FOR ENGLAND.   The nature of the Glorious Revolution may easily be misunderstood. It does not imply that William III and his wife, Mary, were monarchs of England because Parliament had made them monarchs. On the contrary, Parliament merely continued to do what even the nobles did in England before the Norman Conquest of 1066. They could only remove one monarch and appoint or elect another within the same family. It was still assumed by Parliament, as it is done today as well, that God alone could decide who was to be king of England. He alone determined who would be the children of the king and queen. For that reason the coins of Great Britain and Canada continue to state that the monarch is "king by the Grace of God." All that the revolution did was to restore ancient customs and to end absolutism, which was an innovation imported from abroad.

POLITICAL PARTIES MAKE THEIR APPEARANCE. During the reign of William and Mary much was done to prepare the way for the rise of the cabinet system and democratic government. Two political parties originated, called respectively the Whigs and the Tories. The latter stood for a strong king and supported the landed nobility. The Whigs favored the expansion of commerce and industry, and increased political power for the merchant class. Since William was first of all interested in checking the French, he paid little attention to Parliament, so that within this body certain ministers acquired powers formerly exercised largely or entirely by the monarch.

THE REIGN OF QUEEN ANNE. Queen Anne succeeded William III, since she was his wife's sister, and since he left no heir. Anne noticed the growing might of Parliament, and since 1707 neither she nor any other monarch of England has ever vetoed any bill passed by Parliament. Because she also left no heir to the throne, a new house (of Hanover) acquired it in the person of George I, who was the son of the elector of Hanover.

WHO WAS THE FIRST KING OF THE HOUSE OF HANOVER. This state had recently risen to an important position in northwestern Germany and its ruler had received the title of Elector. George's father had married the grand-daughter of James I, and thus his son had an excellent claim to the throne, not because the English Parliament had made it for him, but because God had provided it.

THE BEGINNINGS OF THE CABINET SYSTEM. George I never learned to speak English fluently, and so he left the parliamentary leaders to their own plans. It gradually became customary to form a "cabinet," which was made up of men in control of the majority party in Parliament. The chief of these leaders became the Prime Minister, who would retain his office only as long as his followers commanded a majority of the members in the House of Commons. The latter were elected, while the members of the House of Lords sat for life and received their seats by inheritance or appointment. The first person to become almost a Prime Minister was Walpole, who headed the Whigs and enjoyed his exalted position from 1721 to 1742.

ENGLAND AND SCOTLAND ARE UNITED. Another important political development in the first half of the eighteenth century was the union of England and Scotland to form the united kingdom of Great Britain (1707). Scotland gave up its own parliament, but received proper representation in the British Parliament, as well as free trade in England. Ireland, on the other hand, remained under the domination of the British government and British landlords. The British government retained the right to veto or modify the measures adopted by the Irish parliament, and the English landlords charged high rents from the tenants in Ireland but spent the money in England.

WHY GREAT BRITAIN IS SO IMPORTANT IN MODERN HISTORY. Great Britain was the first country to develop the cabinet system combined with the idea of having two houses in the national legislature. Its system of national government became the model for most of the great nations of the nineteenth and twentieth centuries, until the period after the First World War. At the same time Great Britain established the largest colonial empire, the strongest navy, and the greatest merchant marine that the world had ever seen. It transplanted European civilization in North America and in many other parts of the world. It provided the United States with its language and a number of important political institutions, and became the foremost economic power of the nineteenth century.

SPAIN AND HOLLAND DECLINE, AND FRANCE CANNOT KEEP UP WITH ENGLAND. At the same time Holland and Spain declined, while Portugal never recovered from the colonial losses sustained when it was a province of Spain (1580-1640). France, as we saw, had lost its chance to keep pace with Great Britain, but on the Continent she was to exert great influence through her royal court and the writings of her scholars.

Student Activities

1. With the aid of a dictionary write out the definitions for the following words: *royalists, prudent, innovation, vetoed.*
2. Why was James I disliked by many people in England?
3. Who were the Puritans?
4. What are some of the things that Cromwell did for England?
5. Why was the rule of James II so short? Note: James II was Duke of York before he became king of England. While he was Duke of York, the Colony of New York was named after him. In the English royal family, the oldest son is generally the Prince of Wales, and the next oldest is the Duke of York.
6. When did the English get a foothold in India?
7. What was the Bill of Rights?
8. What is meant by the phrase, "King by the Grace of God?"
9. How did the Hanover Family become the ruling family of England?
10. Why is England so important in modern history?
    Note: When people elect the men to make the laws, then political parties begin to form, because not all people have the same ideas on how the nation should be run.

CHAPTER 33

Great Britain and France Fight a Duel for World Empire

BRITISH GAINS IN 1713. In Great Britain the merchants began to get an increasing share in the foreign policy of the government. William III had profited by their desire to secure more markets abroad and more colonies beyond the seas, for the middle class had supported him in his war with France (1688-1697). In the War of the Spanish Succession (1702-1713) the British had taken care that Spain would not have any longer an opportunity to exclude Englishmen from the trade with her colonies. So in 1713, at the conclusion of the war, the Assiento Treaty had been signed between Great Britain and Spain, which permitted the British to import Negro slaves from Africa into the Spanish colonies in America, together with one shipload of merchandise each year. From France the British obtained Newfoundland, Nova Scotia, and the Hudson Bay region. In America this war was called Queen Anne's War, because it fell in the reign of Queen Anne (1702-1714).

WHAT HAPPENED IN THE WAR OF THE AUSTRIAN SUCCESSION. The next war between Great Britain and France was the War of the Austrian Succession (1740-1748). In North America it was called King George's War, for at that time George II was king of England (1727-1760). When Emperor Charles VI of the Holy Roman Empire died in 1740, he left no male heir, and hoped that his daughter, Maria Theresa, would inherit his domains and the imperial title. In the same year a new monarch ascended the throne in Prussia as King Frederick II, who is better known as Frederick the Great. He proceeded to invade Austrian territory and thus started the war, in which Great Britain chose to support Austria, and France aided Prussia. At the treaty which ended the war in 1748, Frederick II secured Silesia from Austria, but otherwise there were no important changes.

FRANCE LOSES CANADA AND HER COLONIES IN INDIA. The next war was called the Seven Years' War (1756-1763), but on the American side of the Atlantic it was the French and Indian War, because the English had to fight against the French combined in some regions with the Indians. Once more Prussia attacked Austria, and once more kept Silesia. But this time France sustained terrific losses in North America and India. Wolfe captured Quebec for the British (1759), and now the French rule in Canada collapsed. At the same time France lost the contest for the control of India, where the British had enjoyed a distinct advantage ever since the year 1613. In addition to Bombay on the west coast, the British held Madras on the east coast, and Calcutta in the northeast. At first the French scored some initial successes under their able governor, Dupleix. But later the British won a great victory at Plassey (1757), where the brilliant Robert Clive defeated native troops who had been supplied with French arms and advice.

WILLIAM PITT OBTAINS A FAVORABLE PEACE. At home the British were nobly served by their capable Prime Minister William Pitt the Elder, who subsidized the armies of the Prussians, in order to keep the French busy in Europe. He also inspired parliamentary leaders into strong action against France. When peace was signed at Paris in 1763, the French surrendered all their land on the North American continent, and the right to fortify any region in India, keeping only a few trading posts. Great Britain received Canada and the region to the east of the Mississippi, while Spain obtained the lands to the west of that river, partly to make up for having given Florida to Great Britain.

REASONS WHY THE FRENCH WERE SO BADLY DEFEATED. If at this time the French people had been guided by a monarch who sincerely sought to increase the naval power of his nation, much might still have been accomplished for France. But the king was just as blind as the majority of his subjects. They were so well satisfied at home that they preferred their native soil to adventure upon and beyond the seas. On the other hand, William Pitt encouraged the ambitions of the English. They had been fortunate in that their monarchs, when they were absolute rulers, had given their subjects permission to go to the English colonies in America, though they did not belong to the State Church. We may add here the fact that the French were widely scattered over a vast territory, while the British held relatively small regions with a compact population. While the English colonies in North America had a population of nearly two million, New France counted but one hundred thousand European settlers. In 1700 the figures had been respectively 150,000 and 15,000.

COMPARISON BETWEEN THE FRENCH AND THE BRITISH. Many thousands of Englishmen were literally forced to seek a living on the seas and in the colonies, while the French were most comfortable at home. The fertile soil of France kept the vast majority of the inhabitants employed upon the land, with the result that a powerful middle class did not make its appearance there until the nineteenth century. The English merchants and manufacturers, on the other hand, compelled their king and Parliament to recognize their class interests and so to direct the foreign policy as to secure more markets for their manufactured goods and more raw materials for the domestic industries. They entertained the same aims as Colbert had had; in Colbert's case they are called *mercantilistic*, but that term could just as well be applied to the policies of the British government in 1756 and of the American government in 1939.

THE BRITISH DO NOT GIVE THEIR COLONIES PROPER RIGHTS. Where the British merchants made a mistake was that they looked upon the colonies as mere dependencies of Great Britain, which could be freely exploited. Moreover, the English subjects in America were for the most part the descendants of persons who had left England for reasons that had made them look upon England with feelings of little respect. About twenty-five thousand of them altogether had emigrated because they could not enjoy religious toleration in the mother country. Many other thousands went because of poverty, class struggles, or political reasons. They and their children could not see what was good in a government made up in part of the higher clergy and the nobility. How could these lords represent the people, they asked. And why could not the farmers and the merchants find anyone to represent them, as they *were* represented in the colonial legislatures? As long as both mother country and colonists faced the common enemy — the French — the differences between them were not seriously regarded. But after 1763 conditions were greatly altered.

THE BRITISH ADOPT NEW MEASURES WHICH ANNOY THE COLONIES. New measures adopted by the British Parliament increased the feelings of resentment in the colonies. The Stamp Act of 1765 and the renewed enforcement of the navigation acts led to considerable dissatisfaction. What was worse, King George III (1760-1820) was for the time being almost an absolute monarch and used many members of Parliament as his tools. That is the reason why he was able to get the Stamp Act passed. This act stated that in the English colonies in North America a tax would have to be paid on newspapers and magazines. The money paid by the Americans was to be used by the British government. Immediately the Americans resisted this new measure, with the result that in the next year (1766) the tax was canceled by the British. But the Americans continued to ask themselves, What right does the British government have to tax us when we are not represented in the Parliament?

THE BOSTON TEA PARTY IS FOLLOWED BY BRITISH PENAL LAWS. Another tax that made the Americans very angry was that on tea sold to the American colonies. The tea came from India, and the tax was of great value to the British government as well as to the merchants of the English East India Company which imported it. But the enraged inhabitants of Boston in Massachusetts looked upon the tax from another standpoint when they saw the English ships bringing the tea to their great port. Some of them got on board and dumped a large amount of the tea into the water. That of course led to more trouble, for the British government declared that the port of Boston must remain closed until the Americans were ready to pay for that wasted tea.

THE AMERICAN REVOLUTION BEGINS. Massachusetts was joined by the other twelve colonies in the rebellion that followed in 1775. The Continental Congress was called together in that year, and it took quick action. It appointed George Washington of Virginia as commander of the troops, and in 1776 it issued the Declaration of Independence. At first the British thought that this revolution would not last long. They occupied the great cities along the coast, such as Philadelphia, New York, Boston, and Charleston. Now what could the poor rebels do after having lost those important towns? Thus reasoned the British. But they did not understand that the colonies were very large and the people in them could very well continue fighting even after they had lost all their ports along the Atlantic seaboard. Washington did go through many sad and weary days of hardship and defeat, but his courage and the help of many other brave leaders enabled him to win a tremendous victory. In 1777 the British army at Saratoga was badly defeated, and in 1781 a British army under Cornwallis surrendered at Yorktown.

THE AMERICANS ARE AIDED BY THE FRENCH AND THE SPANISH. The War of the American Revolution was in a sense another conflict between Great Britain and France. Both France and Spain aided the colonies, and at last Great Britain was humbled. In the peace of 1783 (signed at Paris) the thirteen colonies were declared independent, and in the same year Spain received Florida from Great Britain. France obtained only the island of Tobago in the West Indies, but was satisfied in having revenged itself upon the British.

WHY THE CANADIANS DO NOT CARE TO RISE AGAINST THE BRITISH. The question is often asked why Canada did not side with the French in this war, since most of the white inhabitants were French and Roman Catholic. You may note here that under the French government the population had not received proper attention. The officials had been marked generally by inefficiency and graft. But in 1764 the British civil government was established under a governor who ruled with the advice of a nominated council. In 1774 the Quebec Act was passed, which allowed the French subjects and priests many privileges, so that an able scholar was later moved to say that the act "was a just and generous measure . . . to the credit of English good sense." In 1791 the Canada, or Constitutional, Act followed, and gave to Canada a form of representative government that was in force for nearly fifty years. In short, the people in Canada could not see what they would gain by returning to former conditions under French rule, or by securing independence.

AFTER THE WAR THE BRITISH REFORM THE GOVERNMENT OF THEIR COLONIES. The War of the American Revolution taught the British a valuable lesson. They immediately set to work to change the government in India. The India Bill of 1784 provided for a greatly improved administration of the great colony. The new system was so satisfactory that it governed India for twenty years. Moreover, Ireland, from 1782 to 1800 enjoyed the privilege of making its own laws. The commercial policy of Great Britain also underwent a change for the better. Gradually the mercantilist theories were dropped and free trade was established.

IN THE TWENTIETH CENTURY FREE TRADE HAS TO BE GIVEN UP. But in the twentieth century, as we shall see, it became impossible for the British to maintain free trade in the face of the tariff walls raised by other powers. It would be well for all of them if they would learn to cooperate a little better with each other, though one can scarcely blame the British alone for this unfortunate condition. Since 1783 Great Britain has been a leader in enlightened colonial government and in commercial policy.

FURTHER RIVALRY BETWEEN GREAT BRITAIN AND FRANCE. In the meantime France continued to seek glory upon the battle fields of Europe. From 1793 to 1815 Great Britain and France fought desperately on land and sea, and when at last Napolean was exiled to the island of St. Helena, Great Britain obtained further colonial gains, though not so much from France as from the Holland, which had foolishly sided with the French during the French Revolution. It was not until 1904 that the old rivalry between Great Britain and France was finally ended, and as a result the two countries could become allies in the Great War (World War).

Student Activities

1. With the aid of a dictionary write out the definitions for the following words: *dependencies, exploited, resentment, inefficiency.*
2. What advantages did England receive from the Assiento Treaty?
3. What territories did France lose at the end of the Seven Years War?
4. Why were the French so badly beaten in the Seven Years War?
5. What were some of the causes of the American Revolution?
6. Why did France help the Americans during their war for independence?
7. Why did Canada remain with England instead of siding in with the Americans?
8. What lesson did the British learn from the American Revolution?
9. When did the rivalry between France and England end? Note: It began again in 1941 when France was defeated by Germany.
   Mercantilism is an idea that the colonies are there only for the benefit of the mother country.

CHAPTER 34

Prussia and Russia Become Great Powers

WHY RUSSIA AND PRUSSIA WERE SO SLOW TO BECOME GREAT POWERS. At the opening of the eighteenth century it was not yet noticeable to the peoples of Europe that Prussia and Russia were about to take their places among the first-rate nations. Both countries had been very slow to make definite progress in scientific agriculture, commerce, and industry. They had been out of touch with the great thought movements as well. So poor was their location that they had experienced great difficulty in deriving much benefit from the Renaissance or the Commercial Revolution. And when Portugal, Spain, France, England, and Holland founded colonies beyond the seas, Prussia and Russia merely were spectators of a great drama.

THE BEGINNINGS OF PRUSSIA. But the time came at last when Prussia and Russia entered the circle of the great European powers, surpassing before long Spain, Portugal, and Holland. It was in the reign of the Great Elector (1640-1648) that the foundations were laid of the largest state in modern Germany. He annexed three valuable districts in the lower Rhine Valley, which were situated in a valuable position near the Dutch Republic. Moreover in the Treaty of Westphalia (1648) he received almost enough territories to double the size of his country. Among these was Eastern Pomerania on the south shore Baltic Sea.

THE GREAT ELECTOR ESTABLISHES ABSOLUTE MONARCHY IN BRANDENBURG-PRUSSIA. Once having extended the frontiers of Brandenburg to the Baltic Sea, the Great Elector set about to increase his own personal power at the expense of the local legislatures. In Brandenburg itself he met with very little opposition, for his subjects were aware of the advantages to be derived from the exercise of absolute executive power by a ruler whose aim clearly was to make his country strong and prosperous. The inhabitants of Brandenburg preferred prosperity under a despotic ruler to poverty and possible invasion under a constitutional government.

But the subjects of the Great Elector in East Prussia and in the lower Rhine looked upon him as a foreigner who could hardly be expected to be interested in their welfare. Yet even in these provinces the Great Elector succeeded in extending his power by completely suppressing the local legislatures. In 1660 he made East Prussia[1] entirely independent of Poland. Until that year he and his predecessors had recognized the king of Poland as their feudal lord, but after 1660 East Prussia ceased to be a fief of Poland.

GREAT PROGRESS UNDER THE GREAT ELECTOR. Frederick William, the Great Elector, was now able to merge the three separate parts of Brandenburg, East Prussia, and the lower Rhine region into one centralized national government. He reserved for himself the appointment of the most important officials. He was especially interested in the promotion of agriculture, commerce, and industry; and he had a canal constructed connecting the Elbe River with the Oder River, which proved to be of great commercial advantage to the city of Berlin. During his reign the population of this city grew from 8,000 to 20,000. He had swamps drained, roads repaired, and foreign workmen invited to settle in Brandenburg. When in 1685 Louis XIV revoked the Edict of Nantes, Frederick William encouraged 20,000 Huguenots to remove to Brandenburg, where he offered them exemption from taxes for ten years, and funds for the building of their own churches.

FURTHER IMPROVEMENTS, 1688-1740. Between the death of the Great Elector and the opening of the reign of Frederick the Great in 1740, much work was done by the rulers of Brandenburg-Prussia in continuing the plans of the Great Elector. At the Treaty of Utrecht in 1713 the ruler was officially recognized as "King in Prussia." Between 1713 and 1740 the army was increased from 38,000 to 80,000, and the method of appointment was reformed so that from that time the King insisted upon merit instead of upon a large amount of money possessed by those who wanted positions in the army. He also ignored the connection of the candidates with important families in the realm. In the place of the local legislatures he instituted officials who made up the bureaucracy. This new system of government proved so efficient in Prussia that it was retained until 1918.

FREDERICK THE GREAT ENLARGES PRUSSIA. As we have seen, Prussia annexed Silesia in the War of the Austrian Succession (1748). Although in the Seven Years' War the Prussian King

---

1. In the year 1618 the House of Hohenzollern in Brandenburg, to which the Great Elector belonged, inherited East Prussia.

Frederick the Great faced the combined armies of Russia, France, and Austria, he was able to retain Silesia. Not only was he supported by the British in his desperate fight, but he was also exceedingly fortunate in that the ruler of Russia who opposed him, died in 1762, and was succeeded by a czar who happened to admire him. Not content with the annexation of Silesia, Frederick made an alliance with the ruler of Russia in 1772, in order to take away from Poland some valuable territories. This was called the First Partition of Poland, in which Austria also shared. Frederick the Great obtained West Prussia, which connected Brandenburg with East Prussia; and after 1772 it was no longer necessary to speak of Brandenburg-Prussia, for now the whole country which was ruled by Frederick the Great could be simply called Prussia.

FREDERICK BECOMES AN "ENLIGHTENED DESPOT." But what was still more important for his subjects was that he showed real interest in their welfare. In his reign more than 15,000 acres of waste lands were improved. He increased the size of his army from 80,000 to 160,000, while the population of Brandenburg-Prussia grew from 1,250,000 to 4,000,000. He filled the royal treasury, reformed the system of taxation, opened many new schools, abolished cruel torture, and introduced religious toleration. He also improved the judicial department of the government by reducing the number of courts, and speeding up the trials. However, he refused to introduce the elements of democracy. Although he called himself "the first servant of the State," yet he distrusted the masses of the people and he continued to rule as an absolute monarch. But he served them well, and it was not until after the World War in 1918 that the inhabitants of Prussia questioned the wisdom of his policies.

WHY RUSSIAN HISTORY IS SO IMPORTANT FOR US TODAY. Even more important for the student of history is the expansion of Russia into the huge empire that covered nearly all of eastern Europe and the whole of northern Asia, with an area twice as large as that of the United States. Although today it is no longer an empire, Russia continues to be a state of great importance. It possesses immense resources which have scarcely been touched. Moreover, the people are undergoing a very significant experiment in social reconstruction; and that nation may some day surpass our own in economic and political power. In order to understand the nature and the history of Communism, and in order to become familiar with the present-day government of Russia, it will be necessary to study carefully the growth of Russia and its peculiar kind of government during the seventeenth and eighteenth centuries.

Russia Is an Oriental Nation, and Is Very Different From Western Europe. The first thing that strikes the modern reader in the Western world, is the fact that Russia, although it began as a European state, is in reality an Oriental nation. This does not imply that its people, the Slavs, were originally of Asiatic stock. The Slavs lived on the eastern slope of the Carpathians when they first entered history, but what made Russia an oriental state is the fact that it was never able to get into close contact with the nations of the western world. Not even the Byzantine empire could establish intimate contact with Russia. One distinguished Russian historian has aptly said: "A thousand years of the hostile neighborhood of the Asiatic nomads will by itself justify many times over the absence of the European spirit in the history of Russia." Another Russian scholar has written these significant words: "The nomads not merely attacked Russia, but they cut her off from the shores of the Black Sea and destroyed her communication with Byzantium . . . Asiatic barbarism strove to deprive Russia of all the roads and all the breathing spaces opening upon cultivated Europe."

Migrations of Asiatic Peoples Into Eastern and Central Europe. The first important invasion from the East was that of the Huns in the fourth century. The next was that of the Magyars, or Hungarians, which crossed Russia and finally settled in the central valley of the Danube. In the eleventh century occurred the invasion of the Seljuk Turks, who, instead of turning westward, moved to the south and occupied Asia Minor and the region beyond. During the thirteenth and fourteenth centuries Russia was occupied by a host of Mongolian invaders. They established the greatest empire the world had ever seen, including not only northern Asia, but also China and European Russia.

Finally Russia Is No Longer Disturbed By These Migrations. It was not until the end of the fifteenth century that Russia was at last free from the threat of invasion from Asia. About the middle of the sixteenth century Russia was ruled by the able Ivan IV, who was also called Ivan the Terrible, and was the first ruler to adopt the title of "Czar." In 1613 the House of Romanov commenced its long rule, which lasted until 1917. The first member of this ruling house was called Michael; he fortified western Russia against Sweden, while his son annexed eastern Ukraine and pushed the western frontier of Russia up to the Dnieper River.

AT LAST UNDER PETER THE GREAT RUSSIA BECOMES A GREAT
POWER. Not until the time of Peter the Great did Russia become
a first-rate power in Europe. Peter the Great was Czar of Russia
from 1689 until his death in 1725. He possessed a remarkably alert
and inquisitive intellect, and as a young man he took great pleasure
in leading bands of his companions in riotous pranks. In 1690
he became intimately acquainted with a Swiss adventurer who was
a heavy drinker but aroused his interest in western civilization.
Peter had always been fond of making boats and other toys, and
when his Swiss friend suggested that he should build a ship, he
eagerly seized upon the idea and launched one on the White Sea
in northern Russia. He reasoned that some day he would have a
real fleet, in which plan he was not to be disappointed. Seeing that
the waters of the Arctic gulf were frozen over during nine months
of the year, he turned to the Black Sea in the south. But here he
met the Turks and hostile Asiatic peoples. Undaunted by their
hostility, he constructed a fleet and made war upon the Turks, from
whom he seized for a time the important port of Azov.

PETER THE GREAT TRAVELS AND WORKS IN THE WESTERN
COUNTRIES. In 1697 a group of fifty young men of best families
in the Russian capital of Moscow, left for the western countries,
where they hoped to learn the arts and sciences, as well as shipbuilding and military engineering. The young men were led in
person by Peter, who acquired much information in Prussia about
the training of troops. From Prussia he went to Holland, where
he worked for several months as an ordinary laborer in order to
learn the secrets of Dutch shipbuilding, and where he also studied
engraving and anatomy. Next he went to England, where he
familiarized himself with shipping and industry. Wherever he
went, he faced the realization that the foreigners were superior to
his own countrymen, for which reason he decided to have his subjects adopt the customs of his western neighbors.

THE RUSSIANS ADOPT WESTERN WAYS OF LIVING AND WORK-
ING. Unfortunately for Peter the Great and Russia, his trip was
cut short in 1698 by a rebellion of his bodyguard in the capital.
Upon his return to Russia, he caused the rebellious troops to be
executed and he himself took part in the execution of hundreds
of them. He displayed great physical strength and dexterity in
slicing off their heads, and he also revealed that he still remained
a barbarian at heart. Now the czar began his reform. He ordered
that the men should have their long, flowing beards cut off and that
they should shed their oriental garments. He introduced the use

of tobacco, and he compelled the women to leave their separate apartments and to mingle freely with the members of the opposite sex. Peter also reorganized his army and constructed a powerful navy. In imitation of the ruler of Prussia, he centralized the govern ment, although in the administration of it he also followed the Swedish pattern. Local self-government practically disappeared in Russia, and all the provinces were united into eight large units, called governments, each of which was ruled by a governor and an advisory council.

THE CZAR BECOMES THE HEAD OF THE CHURCH IN RUSSIA. Peter also made himself the head of the Church in Russia, which, having been established through the guidance of Byzantine missionaries, was a part of the Greek Catholic, or Orthodox, Church. He did not abolish the title of the Patriarch of Moscow, but this official lost much of his former power in the Church. Now the czar of Russia was in a position to dictate to the clergy what they should preach and which men they should appoint to offices in the Church. The army, the navy, the police system, the governors, the council of officials which was called the Senate, and finally, the clergy, had become tools of the monarch. This form of government generally remained in force until the revolution in 1905.

BUSINESS AND FARMING ARE GREATLY IMPROVED IN RUSSIA. Peter the Great also made great exertions to improve the economic situation in Russia. When he traveled through Prussia, Holland, England and northern Italy in 1697, he induced several hundred skilled artisans to imigrate to Russia and to teach his subjects the principles of western civilization, to create new industries, and to foster trade. He also encouraged young Russians of good families to go abroad and to study there the languages and sciences of Western Europe. He himself had learned to speak Dutch and German. The new industries of Russia were supported by the State; great iron mines were opened in the Ural Mountains; thousands of serfs were drawn from the rural districts to work in the new industries, and active commercial contacts were established with the western countries.

RUSSIA GETS A "WINDOW TO THE WEST." Peter said that he wanted a "window to the West." And so he founded a new capital near the Baltic Sea, which was called St. Petersburg. Although the city was built on swampy, soggy ground, the iron will of the czar made it possible for Russia to obtain one of the finest capitals of modern Europe. In the course of time St. Petersburg surpassed in size and population such capitals as Rome, Madrid, Lisbon, Brussels, and Amsterdam.

THE COMMUNISTS LATER CHANGE THE NAME OF ST. PETERSBURG. It was only after 1917, when the Communists obtained power in Russia, that St. Petersburg, first called Petrograd and next Leningrad, ceased to be the capital and the most important city in Russia. This change, introduced recently by the Communists, indicates that the Communists were returning to the conditions that had prevailed before the reign of Peter the Great.

THE WAR BETWEEN SWEDEN AND RUSSIA. Peter the Great carried on an important war against Charles XII, the youthful king of Sweden, who ruled from 1697 to 1718. Although the Swedish king was at first successful, he made the serious error of penetrating Russia as far south as the region nearest the Black Sea, where, in 1709, he was defeated by the Russians at Poltava. After this battle the tide turned against the Swedes, and their forces were practically wiped out. When in 1721 Russian signed a treaty of peace with Sweden, it secured four states on the eastern shore of the Baltic Sea.

WHAT HAPPENED IN RUSSIA BETWEEN THE REIGNS OF PETER THE GREAT AND CATHERINE THE GREAT. The period between the reign of Peter the Great and that of Catherine the Great, that is from 1725 to 1762, saw no important changes in the foreign and domestic policies of the government. During the Seven Years' War, as you have learned, Frederick the Great was opposed by the Russian ruler, Elizabeth, who was offended by the Prussian king partly because he had written some verses in which he made fun of her. But when she died in 1762, she was succeeded by Peter III, who at once made peace with Prussia. Moreover, when a palace revolution resulted in his death in the same year, Catherine II, or Catherine the Great, took over the reigns of government, and adopted a policy of neutrality.

THE WORK DONE FOR RUSSIA BY CATHERINE THE GREAT. Catherine was a German princess and had been the wife of the czar who in 1762 was murdered. It is possible that Catherine was responsible for his death, for we know that she was one of the most wicked women who have ever sat upon a throne. Under Catherine the Great (1762-1796) further reforms were introduced in the Russian government. A new code of laws was drawn up for Russia. Catherine publicly condemned intolerance, religious persecutions, and cruel punishment. She was very much interested in the cause of education, and labored incessantly for the expansion of the school system of Russia. She also was in touch with the great scholars of western countries, and she even invited some of them to come to Russia and to teach her people western manners. In 1783 the Russian Academy was founded, and patterned after the French Academy.

CATHERINE REALLY REFUSES TO HELP THE MASSES OF HER PEOPLE. But Catherine, like Frederick II, had no intention of introducing democracy. Nor did she even abolish serfdom. On the contrary, she actually made the condition of the serfs worse than it had been before. One day she wrote to the governor of Moscow, "The day when the farmers wish to become enlightened, both you and I will lose our places." She deprived the Church of its real estate holdings. But you can scarcely say that this was a reformation. Her aim was chiefly to increase the power of the ruler, to weaken Sweden, Poland, and the Ottoman Empire, to enlarge Russia at the expense of her neighbors, and to maintain a large army and a powerful navy.

THE RUSSIANS DO NOT BECOME WESTERNIZED IN THEIR LIVES AND HEARTS. It is evident that neither Catherine the Great nor Peter the Great actually made Russia resemble the powers of the western world. All that these rulers did was to cover the heart or soul of the Russian nation with a thin veneer of western culture. During the seventeenth and eighteenth centuries there was practically no middle class in Russia, commerce was largely controlled by foreigners, and there was no industry in the modern sense of the word.

POLAND IS DESTROYED AND PARTITIONED BY RUSSIA, AUSTRIA, AND PRUSSIA. Russia, as you saw, took advantage of the weakness of Poland, as well as of that of the Ottoman Empire. In the first Partition of Poland in 1772, Russia took a large slice of territory on the western frontier of Russia. In the second partition in 1793 and in the third partition in 1795, Russia in each case took some more land, so that by 1795 she had seized more than that taken by Austria or Prussia. Poland had easily been destroyed as a nation, because this country, like Russia, had not yet developed a great middle class. The nobles had seized almost all of the powers of government, while they remained exempt from taxation and the other important duties performed by the other people. The serfs in the country and the laborers in the cities paid almost all of the taxes, performed most of the duties, but received very few privileges. In the national legislature it was possible for one nobleman to block any measure which was introduced by the other three hundred. The king was deprived of power, because at the time of election he had to sign a contract with the nobility, which always took care to limit his power to the utmost. Thus it happened that the three greedy neighbors of Poland were able in a few years to destroy Poland completely. It was not until after the World War in 1918 that Poland became an independent nation again, although it was then not as large as it used to be. Unfortunately, as you know, Poland was partitioned once more in the year 1939.

THE OTTOMAN EMPIRE ALSO DECLINES. At the same time that Poland was destroyed as a nation the Ottoman Empire declined rapidly. It lost all of Hungary to Austria before the middle of the eighteenth century, and in 1774 it gave up to Russia the territory around the city of Azov. The Russian government also received the right to protect the Christian churches in Constantinople. Moreover, Russian merchants were in the future to trade freely on the Black Sea and the straits which connect the Black Sea with the Mediterranean. If it had not been for the fact that Russia was so busy in annexing a large slice of Polish territory, the Ottoman Empire would probably have experienced greater losses than it did during the eighteenth century. And the only reason Russia did not annex the large region of the Balkan Peninsula during the nineteenth century is the opposition of Austria, Great Britain, and Germany. Thus it happened that the great city of Constantinople, which had been for centuries a Christian center of culture, remained in the hands of the Mohammedans.

RUSSIA EXPANDS EASTWARD UNTIL ITS FRONTIERS TOUCH THE PACIFIC OCEAN. If Russia experienced difficulty in annexing land in Europe to the south of Russia proper, it had little trouble in expanding eastward beyond the Ural Mountains. Between 1600 and 1800 Russia annexed practically the whole of Siberia, so that by the opening of the nineteenth century it was twice as large as the United States is today. What Russia might have become under a form of government such as ours, is difficult to say. At any rate, there is not a great government in the world which is not anxiously watching the foreign and the domestic policies of the Russian government. In a following chapter we shall study the economic changes which have recently been accomplished under the government of the Communists. We shall see that Russia made some great advances during the quarter of a century up to 1939.

Student Activities

1. With the aid of a dictionary write out the definitions for the following words: *apparent, despotic, exemption, merit, artisans.*
2. Draw a map of Russia and Prussia.
3. How did the Great Elector of Prussia increase his own personal power?
4. What good things did the Great Elector do for Prussia?
5. Why is Frederick the Great such an important person in European history? Give three reasons.
6. What does the statement, "Russia is an Oriental nation," mean?
7. Who were the two famous Russian rulers mentioned in this chapter?
8. Describe Peter the Great.
9. Why was it a bad thing for Peter the Great to take control of the Church?
10. What is meant by the "Window to the West" that Russia has always desired?
11. What do you think of Catherine the Great?
12. What nations took part in the Partition of Poland?
    Note: Poland really destroyed herself, because of her inefficient system of government. When a nation becomes weak, cowardly, and inefficient, then greedy neighbors will soon take it over.

CHAPTER 35

Cultural Developments in Early Modern Times

THE EUROPEAN BACKGROUND OF AMERICAN HISTORY. In the period from 1500 to 1700 the first European settlers arrived in North America. They brought with them their own languages, their ways of living, their forms of government, their ideas about religion, and their plans for the education of the young folk. In this way they transplanted European civilization in North America. The civilization of the English and French and Spanish colonies on our continent before the year 1700 was little more than a new form of English, French, and Spanish culture. But you must note this difference between Europe and America: The Europeans were brought up in the Old World, where distinct classes of people had lived side by side for centuries. It was difficult in Europe to rise from one class into another. Many of the customs of the Middle Ages were still in existence, while in America the settlers founded their homes in a new country. Here they removed the Indians and then could build upon what you may call "virgin soil." As we shall see in the next chapter, the Americans did a great deal for the growth of modern democracy and for religious liberty.

THE EXTENSION OF HIGHER EDUCATION IN WESTERN EUROPE. The spread of knowledge was greatly assisted by the work of the universities. Many of them had been founded before the year 1500, as you saw, and during the sixteenth century several others were established. England still had only the two universities of Oxford and Cambridge, but in Scotland a new university was founded at Edinburgh, and Ireland acquired one in Dublin. One of the greatest universities of the early modern times was that founded at Leyden in the Dutch Republic. It became for a time the foremost center of learning in the Protestant countries. And such was the intellectual progress made in the Dutch Republic that four other universities were established there besides that at Leyden. They were all in a sense state universities, and they undoubtedly contributed much to the development of modern civilization. In some

270

of these Dutch universities a large number of English Puritans studied and it is not surprising that the first president of Harvard University was an alumnus of one of these universities.

The Universities in Spain, France, and Other Countries. On the other hand, Spain showed just as much interest in higher education. Although Spain was governed by an absolute monarch, this does not necessarily mean that higher education was stifled. During the sixteenth century nine universities were established in Spain. It is also worth noting that the University of Salamanca at one time during the sixteenth century had almost seven thousand students. In France little progress was made in this period, and we may say the same of Germany and Italy.

Courses Given in the Universities. Few changes were made in the universities. The curriculum remained almost unchanged from one generation to the other until we reach the second half of the nineteenth century. The study of history, geography, mathematics, science, and modern languages was seriously neglected. But the study of ancient Greek and Latin, besides theology and philosophy, was still extensive. Until the eighteenth century the language of instruction was Latin.

What Was Done in the Elementary and Secondary Schools. In the field of elementary and secondary education the progress attained was tremendous. Not only were large numbers of public schools founded in the great cities, but also private schools were established. Among these private schools may be mentioned the two famous institutions at Eton and Winchester in England. One of the outstanding educators in England was Roger Ascham, who was for a time the tutor of Princess Elizabeth (later Queen of England). He published a book entitled *The Schoolmaster*, in which he emphasized the value of Latin and Greek, and the importance of a more humane treatment of the pupils in school. Another important school in England was that of St. Paul's Cathedral in London. The English grammar schools, up to the year 1700 at least, continued to follow the pattern of this school in London. These grammar schools were little more than preparatory schools for the colleges. They continued to stress the importance of Latin and Greek, and they also neglected the study of the sciences, history, mathematics, and practically the whole field of the social sciences. The same may be said of the Boston Latin School, which was founded in 1635. It was one of the earliest to be established in the American colonies.

WHAT LUTHER AND MELANCHTHON DID FOR THE ELEMENTARY SCHOOLS. As you have seen, Luther and Melanchthon were responsible for a considerable improvement in education. Although they neglected the liberal arts in the universities, they more than made up for this defect in emphasizing the need of education for the masses of the people. In Saxony they established the first public school system of the modern world. Luther composed a lengthy work on education, which was called *Sermon on the Duty of Sending Children to School.* In this sermon Luther said: "The civil authorities are under obligation to compel the people to send their children to school." It was owing to efforts of men like Luther and Melanchthon that universal education was finally made possible in all the countries of the West. Luther insisted that the Bible should be studied in all the schools, higher, secondary, and elementary. He also felt that excellent instruction in rhetoric and argumentation was a great help to the people. He showed great liking for the study of history and the natural sciences. He even recommended the practice of teaching gymnastics in the schools, reasoning that such work would strengthen both the body and the soul, and he recommended the study of music in the belief that it would help to drive away sadness. The study of the modern languages owes a great deal to Luther, partly because he issued his famous translation of the Bible in the German language. As you have seen he practically created the modern literary language of German. He also insisted that in the elementary schools the children should learn to read and write in their own language.

THE WORK OF MONTAIGNE. Another important educator of the sixteenth century was the French scholar, Montaigne, who wrote an essay entitled *On the Education of Children.* In this work he effectively made fun of the narrow form of training, commonly known as the humanistic type, that we have discussed in a preceeding chapter. He wrote: "We only toil to stuff the memory, and in the meantime we leave the conscience and understanding undeveloped and empty. As the birds fly about to pick grain and carry it untasted to their offspring, so the teachers of our day go about picking knowledge which they hold at their tongue's end and so hand it out to their pupils. The worst of it is that their pupils are no better educated than they themselves." Montaigne insisted that the pupils should do much more than memorize their books. They should become polished, refined, courteous, and eager to learn the realities of life and nature.

WHAT COMENIUS DID FOR EDUCATION. The outstanding educator of the seventeenth century was Comenius. He discovered a simplified system of teaching the Latin language, and he also issued the first illustrated reading-book of modern times. He perfected a system of general education from the first grade up, which was designed to prepare a person most profitably for the duties here on earth, as well as for the life everlasting in heaven. His system included advice to the parents of the children in school, and it instructed them as to how they could properly equip their children until they had reached the age of six.

COPERNICUS BOLDLY TEACHES THAT THE EARTH MOVES AROUND THE SUN. It was in the sixteenth century that the study of astronomy was greatly enriched by the pioneer work of Copernicus, who founded the so-called Copernician system. He had studied in Italy from 1495 to 1507, and it was here that he prepared his famous theory that the earth moves around the sun. Knowing what the opinion of the leading clergy was on this subject, he did not dare to publish his treatise until the year of his death, that is, 1542. The clergy had argued that the earth was the center of the universe, and that it was more precious to God than the sun. Therefore it was thought impossible that the earth should revolve around the sun. But Copernicus was more interested in the truth than in the arguments of the professors in the universities and the clergy in the Church.

THE WORK OF GALILEO. His work was ably continued by the famous astronomer, Galileo. The latter in 1608 perfected a telescope with which he discovered the mountainous character of the surface of the moon, and the moons of Jupiter. He also discovered that the Milky Way is made up of an enormous number of stars, and he did all in his power to spread the theory advanced by Copernicus. But in 1633 he was taken before the Tribunal of the Roman Inquisition. He was forced to recant, and he had to sign a document in which the following words appeared: "After I had been notified that the said doctrine was contrary to the Holy Scriptures, I wrote and printed a book in which I discussed this doctrine already condemned, and added arguments of great force in its favor without presenting any solution of these. Therefore I give up, curse, and detest the aforesaid errors and heresies."

PROGRESS IN MEDICINE. In the field of medicine much progress was achieved by Vesalius, who lived in the Netherlands during the sixteenth century. He made great contributions to the science of surgery and to the study of anatomy. Instead of depending too much upon book learning, he carried on personal observations and experimentation. He published important books on anatomy, in which a large number of useful illustrations were included. In England lived Harvey, who in the first half of the seventeenth century became famous for his work in anatomy. His studies on the circulation of the blood in the human body were of great importance.

WHAT FRANCIS BACON DID FOR THE STUDY OF SCIENCE. Another Englishman of note was Francis Bacon (1561-1621). He was Lord Chancellor under James I, but he devoted most of his attention to the study of science. Bacon made much of the need of experimentation. He showed great reverence for the Greek scientists, to whom he devoted much attention in his famous work, *Novum Organum*. In Bacon's opinion the methods used in the universities of his time were still too much like the system of the Middle Ages. He said that too much time was spent on argumentation and on mere book learning, and not enough on experimentation.

THE WORK OF THE LEADING DUTCH SCIENTISTS. During the seventeenth century the Dutch also made important contributions to the study of science. Significant is the work of Christian Huyghens, who was the first to produce a pendulum clock. He also perfected the so-called "gun powder machine," which was in a sense a predecessor of the steam engine. Dutch scientists were also noted for their work in the study of electricity, for it was in the University of Leyden that the Leyden jar was discovered in which the students were able to store static electricity. Huyghens was the first scholar to present the viewpoint that light is a form of vibration. He came to the conclusion that there is in the universe a certain substance that carried these vibrations of light, and he called that substance, "ether."

SPANISH SCIENTISTS ALSO ARE VERY ACTIVE AND SUCCESSFUL. It is interesting to observe that Spain during the sixteenth century was one of the most enlightened countries in the world. Nothwithstanding the Inquisition, Spanish scholars were not nearly so backward as has often been assumed in this country. For example, long before Galileo was silenced by the clergy in Italy, the theory of Copernicus was accepted widely by Spanish scholars. It was they who were consulted by the pope in 1582, in order to produce a new calendar. This is the famous Gregorian Calendar, which was named after Pope Gregory XII. In the first half of the sixteenth century the Spaniards drew the finest maps of the time. They also published important books about travel, proper colonial government, and international law.

How International Law Was Drawn Up. As a matter of fact, the Spaniards were the first to produce a satisfactory system of international law. The most important work in the field of international law was that done by Vitoria. His work was used by the celebrated Dutch authority of the seventeenth century, who was called Hugo Grotius, and wrote the famous work entitled, *On the Law of War and Peace*. Although Grotius is commonly called the "father of international law," a title which he deserved fully, it must not be forgotten that he owed a great deal to his Spanish predecessors.

Progress in Mathematics. During the seventeenth century the study of mathematics was encouraged by a large number of scholars in various European countries. They were led by the French scholar, Descartes, who evolved what is known as analytical geometry. The decimal point was introduced about 1585 by a Flemish scholar, who became famous for his work called *The Decimal*. Although the use of the decimal point had been introduced in India about one thousand years before it was adopted by the Europeans, Simon Stevin, the Flemish mathematician just mentioned, deserves much credit for his work.

Advancement in Philosophy. Modern philosophy really was born in the seventeenth century. Although at the end of the fifteenth century and in the first half of the sixteenth century certain writers in Italy had achieved notable fame for their work in this field, it was not until the seventeenth century that the great names of early modern times appeared. The two most important among the latter are Descartes and Spinoza. Descartes was famous for his maxim which implied that it was only through doubting that a person could learn much about life. He said that matter and mind were of equal importance, while Spinoza reasoned that God is the only true substance, and that mind and matter are merely manifestations of God. Near the end of the seventeenth century we meet the outstanding German philosopher and scientist, the great Leibnitz. He had much to do with the invention of the calculus.

The Law of Gravitation. Another scholar who assisted in developing the theory of calculus is Sir Isaac Newton (1642-1727). He became famous for his theory of the law of gravitation, which implies that the attraction which one particle of matter has for every other, is proportionate to its respective mass. And it was in this manner that Newton explained how the planets are kept in their course. The study of science was advanced in England during the second half of the seventeenth century as a result of the establishment of the Royal Society for the Advancement of Science.

THE IMPORTANCE OF ENGLISH LITERATURE. During the sixteenth and seventeenth centuries literature was enriched by writers in all the important countries. But there is no doubt that the British made greater contributions than those of any other contemporary nation. As everybody knows, the outstanding writer of the times was William Shakespeare, who during both the reign of Queen Elizabeth and of her successor, James I, wrote his immortal plays.

THE KING JAMES VERSION OF THE BIBLE. In the reign of King James, as we saw, the Bible was translated into English, which translation is the famous King James translation, or the Authorized Version. Since James I was a scholar and realized that the older version contained many errors, he asked the Archbishop of Canterbury and some of the professors of Oxford and Cambridge to prepare a list of Greek and Hebrew scholars. At the end of three years their task was completed, and in 1611 it was possible to publish the complete translation. It did much to establish the literary language of modern England.

WHO THE MOST FAMOUS ENGLISH WRITERS OF THE SEVENTEENTH CENTURY WERE. In the seventeenth century we note John Milton, the author of *Paradise Lost*, which is the greatest of all English epics. Milton also wrote a number of important pamphlets in which he defended the religious and political theories of the Puritans in England. The two great classical poets of the second half of the seventeenth centuries were John Dryden and Alexander Pope. Swift, who wrote *Gulliver's Travels*, made it his task to support the Tories during the reign of Queen Anne, and his book is in a sense a political satire. In 1719 Daniel Defoe published *Robinson Crusoe*, which was the first English novel that became world-famous. It was also in the first half of the eighteenth century that Joseph Addison and Richard Steele founded the well-known periodicals called *The Tatler* and *The Spectator*. These two magazines ably discussed public and social affairs.

WORKS DEALING WITH POLITICS. In the books and pamphlets of the time much attention was paid to religious and political questions, while society in general was also criticized. The outstanding supporter of representative government was John Locke, who devoted several world-famous treatises to the subject. His writings were very popular among the colonists in North America, and they had a great deal to do with the coming of the war of the revolution in America.

RELIGIOUS BOOKS.   Although since the Restoration in 1660 Puritanism gradually died out in England, the number of popular religious works continued to appear.   Among these is the far-famed work of John Bunyan — *Pilgrim's Progress* (1678).   It seems that the Puritans were largely responsible for the remarkable absence of writers like Shakespeare, who delighted in providing the public with plays.   The Puritans, as we have seen, were opposed to the attendance at theaters, and they detested all "stage plays."   The result was that English writers between 1630 and 1720 wrote but a few of such plays.

THEATERS AND PLAYS.   The theaters had to depend for the most part upon plays that had been produced in France, and translated into the English language.   Not until late in the eighteenth century, when Oliver Goldsmith and Richard Sheridan wrote their comedies, was England once more a leader in the field of drama.

THREE GREAT FRENCH WRITERS OF THE SEVENTEENTH CENTURY.   It was in the century between 1630 and 1730 that France led in certain forms of literature.   Both Corneille and Racine lived in this period, and they were among the greatest writers of tragedy. The plot in these plays is rather simple, and the admirer of Elizabethan drama is likely to be disappointed in them by the absence of exalted romance, as well as by the lack of realism.   But these two writers made up for this neglect by presenting to the reader perfect workmanship, excellent organization of the material, and an almost faultless imitation of the supreme tragedies of the Greeks. Molière was famous for his satires, in which he criticized the middle class folk who had suddenly become rich, and who were characterized by vulgarity.

A FAMOUS SPANISH BOOK BY CERVANTES.   In the same period Spain continued to make her contributions to literature as well as to the sciences.   One of the outstanding writers in Spain was Cervantes, who became immortal through his novel, *Don Quixote*. But you should notice that Cervantes died in 1616, which is before the century we have just mentioned (1630-1730).   He published his novel in two parts, the second of which appeared in 1616.   The first part was almost immediately translated into several important European languages.   The book describes the funny experiences of a wandering knight and proves to the reader that the age of chivalry was past, and that the old romances were no longer a proper form of polite literature.   Nevertheless, many of the ideals of the medieval chivalry reappeared in this novel. But Cervantes also drew upon Greek and Italian writers. His prose is indescribably beautiful and he is a master in the use of the dialogue. Even in the English translation you can still feel the power of his able pen.

SPANISH PAINTING. Spain also made notable contributions to the field of the fine arts. About the middle of the seventeenth century two of her painters became famed far and wide for their magnificent works. They were Velasquez and Murillo. The former painted lovely landscapes, portraits of great statesmen, and many of the common people in various walks of life. Murillo was noted for his magnificent coloring. He also was supreme in portraying religious sentiment and lofty idealism.

DUTCH PAINTING. The Dutch school of painting was led by Rembrandt, whose painting, *The Night Watch*, is probably the most valuable in the world today. In this painting he portrays many of the prominent citizens of Amsterdam, and he shows himself a master in depicting life exactly as it was. His skill was such that in this country today many photographers have called their studios after him. He was famous especially for his magnificent landscape paintings and his work in the Biblical field. He painted scenes from Bible history which endeared the characters displayed by him to the masses of the people.

THE ITALIAN SCHOOL DECLINES. The schools of painting in Italy were now declining. They were marked by dullness and poor taste. It was only in Venice that Italian painting retained some of the high qualities of the age of the Renaissance.

LITTLE PROGRESS IS MADE IN ARCHITECTURE. In general it may be said that in the field of architecture even less progress may be noted than in that of painting. During the sixteenth and seventeenth centuries no style was perfected that could possibly compare with the Romanesque or with the Gothic. It was a time of chaos and of intellectual conceit. Refusing to imitate the masters of Gothic architecture, the Italians tried to make a new style of their own, in which they did not succeed. The only imporant style that was produced in the period was called the *Baroque*. It was popular in both the seventeenth and the eighteenth centuries, and it spread rapidly from Italy into all the other important countries. Churches, palaces, museums, opera houses, and almost every kind of public building were constructed after a variety of models, though in almost every instance the design was characterized by unbalanced masses and lines. One of the important examples is the castle at Heidelberg, which was built between 1556 and 1607.

FRENCH ARCHITECTURE. France produced a type of architecture that differed somewhat from the Baroque, and seems to have depended more upon the architecture of the Renaissance. One of the finest buildings was the Louvre in Paris which originally was a palace but is now the national museum of France.

ENGLISH ARCHITECTURE. About the third quarter of the seventeenth century a great architect was kept busy in London. Here he rebuilt many structures that had been destroyed in the so-called Great Fire of London, which occurred in the year 1666. This artist was Christopher Wren, who built St. Paul's Cathedral in London. He followed largely the classical models and styles of the Renaissance, as can clearly be seen in St. Paul's Cathedral.

WONDERFUL WORK IS DONE BY MUSICIANS. Unlike architecture, music was well advanced in the period under discussion. Led originally by the Flemish, the Italians soon made rapid progress. The Madrigal, which was begun in Flanders and perfected in Italy, may be considered the first important development in musical form. It was intended as a song for three or four voices, and its composition demanded the skill of numerous great musicians in Italy and the Netherlands, while afterward England also shared in this process.

THE MASS AND THE OPERA. The Mass was a new form of music which brought out the poetic qualities of the services in the Roman Catholic Church. It was stately and sonorous, and as dignified and inspiring as the nature of the Mass itself. The greatest composer was Palestrina, who lived in the second half of the sixteenth century and wrote nearly one hundred masses. The opera was also developed in the period. It was originally a drama set to music, but different from the sacred music which accompanied the Biblical plays. Unlike the mass, the opera did not come to maturity until the eighteenth century.

SUMMARY OF INTELLECTUAL DEVELOPMENTS FROM 1500 TO 1750. You have learned that Europe was preparing itself for a new age, which may be called the age of reason. Gradually the stage was being set for the unfolding of modern science. At the same time the people became less and less inclined to take the word of authorities for granted.

EUROPEAN SOCIETY IS CLOSE TO GREAT CHANGES. For the first time in thousands of years, the privileged classes began to feel insecure. As the powers along the Atlantic coast were building great colonial empires, as the merchant marines were increased on an enormous scale, and as the industrial revolution was about to be set into operation, the whole structure of European society was placed upon the threshold of a new age. As you will see in the next chapter it now became customary to clamor for reform in the Church, in the State, and in society as well. No longer bound by the decrees of kings, no longer taught by the words of the Bible itself, the philosophers and the statesmen of the second half of the eighteenth century looked about for other sources of information. They exalted human reason to such an extent that they undermined the popular beliefs in religion and in the truth of the Bible. Whether or not this period should be called the Age of Enlightenment, can only be told after we have carefully studied what it did for the people in the western world.

Student Activities

1. With the aid of a dictionary write out the definitions for the following words: *alumnus, elementary, secondary, universal, gymnastics, designed, treatise, utility, maxim, satire, vulgarity.*
2. What did Luther say in his *Sermon on the Duty of Sending Children to School?*
3. Who was Comenius, and what is he noted for?
4. What discoveries did Copernicus and Galileo make?
5. What people were noted for their study of electricity?
6. Who was Hugo Grotius?
7. Who introduced the decimal point in our system of arithmetic?
8. Write an account of the translation of the Bible into English under James I.
9. Name three famous English writers mentioned in this chapter.
10. Have you ever read parts of *Don Quixote?* What is the story about?
11. Who are some of the important musicians mentioned in this chapter?
12. What is an "Opera"?

    Note: The many modern conveniences and aids that we have to make our lives more comfortable, has been the work of many centuries. The Age of Enlightenment of which this chapter speaks was a time when men felt that they could reason everything out themselves. They became so brazen and bold, that they questioned the truths of the Bible. You will read more about it in the next chapter.

CHAPTER 36

The So-called Age of Enlightenment Exalts the Human Reason

WHAT WAS THE NATURE OF THE SO-CALLED ENLIGHTENMENT. The fifty years that preceded the French Revolution are often referred to as the Age of Enlightenment, because in this half century there lived a number of outstanding critics who examined the civilization that flourished in Europe before 1725, and determined that it was full of corruption and abuses. It was held by these "philosophers" that both the State and the Church were badly in need of reform. They began to undermine the authority of the Bible and of the clergy. They openly scoffed at absolute monarchs. They also said that the time had come for the courts of justice to be abolished or to be completely reformed.

SCIENCE BECOMES POPULAR. While the critics of a corrupt State and a supposedly corrupt Church were writing their pamphlets and books, much was also done in the field of the natural sciences. Furthermore, it was during the period between 1720 to 1770 that chemistry and physics were decidedly improved. And in medicine also great progress was made. For the first time since the beginning of modern history, the scientists paid little attention to the authority of the Church and to the customs that nearly everybody followed. They now began to blaze the way for a new system of thought which greatly differed from the ways and beliefs of medieval scientists. Not even public opinion mattered to the scientists of the eighteenth century. These scientists also felt no great respect for the views of Aristotle, or Thomas Aquinas, or any other scientists whose theories could not be proved by experimentation.

WHAT THE UNITARIANS TAUGHT AND STILL TEACH TODAY. The eighteenth century was also characterized by a peculiar condition in religion. It became a widely-spread practice for scholars and their followers to preach toleration and skepticism. Already in the seventeenth century a group of doubters had appeared in England who refused to accept the doctrine of the Trinity, which teaches that God is three persons in one, God the Father, God the Son, and God the Holy Spirit. These scholars said that God the Father was the only member of the Trinity who was divine, and that Jesus of Nazareth was no more than a human being. They founded a separate denomination, called the Unitarian, because they insisted that there was no Triune God. One of the leaders of this denomination was a scientist whose name was John Priestley. He tried to explain to his countrymen that neither Jesus of Nazareth nor the Holy Spirit ranked with God.

In What Respects the Protestants Were Skeptics. In a certain sense all the Protestants were skeptics, for they rejected a number of beliefs which they had come to regard as superstitious. For example, they all believed that human beings who had died could do nothing for those who were still alive, whereas the Roman Catholics firmly held to the opinion that a person could well afford to address his thoughts and fervent wishes to the saints. The Catholics also believed in the power of departed saints to heal the sick upon this earth. For that reason thousands of pilgrims would travel to shrines, which were little structures built upon the graves of saints. Here they prayed, and hoped to be cured through the help of the saints.

Who the Real Skeptics Were. But as a rule the name "skeptic" was applied only to those members of the Christian churches who denied the divinity of Jesus and who refused to accept Him as their personal Savior. Skepticism developed rapidly after the year 1700. First a number of English scientists and philosophers began to attack those doctrines which in our time are called "Fundamentalism." The miracles which are recorded in the Bible, especially the virgin birth of Jesus, His resurrection and ascension, and also many of the events narrated in the book of Genesis, were subjected to serious criticism.

How Modernism Got Started. These scholars argued that the Bible is not a true source of information, and that the theology of the great Christian churches contained many errors. They said that the study of science overthrew the doctrine of sin and atonement, as well as the belief in miraculous deeds performed by the Jewish prophets of the past. In their opinions, Nature alone was trustworthy. God had created the world and had established the laws of Nature, and those laws governed the earth and the planets, as well as all living things.

What Deism Is. The scholars who argued in this manner were called "Deists," and their belief, "Deism." According to the Deists,

God was not interested in human beings any more. The universe was like a watch that was wound up by someone, and after it had been wound up, it would run as a matter of course. God could not be expected to pay attention to all the different human beings that inhabit this earth. They said that it was entirely useless to pray for anything, since you could not expect God to upset the laws He had formulated for nature. Why should farmers pray for rain, when only the laws of nature would produce that rain? And why should a sick person pray for recovery, since only natural causes were at work?

The Deists are Enemies of the Christian Church. The Deists undermined the authority of the Christian Church, for the power of the Church was largely derived from the belief of the people in personal salvation, as it was made possible through the worship in church and through the assistance rendered to the people by the clergy. If prayers were useless, then certainly the sacraments were also of no importance. Then why should one ask the clergy to marry a person, since one might just as well apply to the civil authorities? It was exactly because of Deism that it became customary in almost all the European countries to refuse any longer to be married by clergymen. The United States is one of the few countries left in which it is still fashionable for Protestants to go to a preacher and have him bless the bridegroom and bride as they are about to be married.

The Artists Return to Classical Standards. The fine arts of the eighteenth century are characterized by the principle that the Christian religion is of little value. The artists of that time scoffed at the high ideals which had made possible Gothic architecture and Gothic painting. These artists, led by such able English and French painters as Hogarth, Gainsborough, Reynolds, Watteau, and David, returned to the study of ancient Greece and Rome. Their art was called "Neoclassic."

Classical Features are Seen in the Architecture of the Eighteenth Century. One example of this art is the Royal Exchange in London, while the Bank of England in the same city is another interesting example. The high towers, the slender walls and pillars, the pointed arches, the sculpture and painting that revealed the high religious ideals of the medieval artists, were all despised by many of the leading architects of the eighteenth century. European art reflected the spirit of indifference to supreme devotion in religion, in the home, and in society, so characteristic of the civilized classes which still were the chief patrons of art. The furniture, for example, was very dainty and elegant; paintings and sculpture conformed to the refined tastes of bishops and noblemen, many of whom were too lazy and too vain to inspire artists with a desire for originality. In matters of dress and etiquette France naturally continued to lead all European nations. It is still fashionable today to decorate a home with furniture, drapes, carpets, and tapestry named after Louis XIV, or after Louis XV.

ENGLISH LITERATURE IN THE EIGHTEENTH CENTURY. The literature of the eighteenth century also shows the spirit of the time. Both in prose writings and in poetry the classic models were carefully imitated, and individualism and originality were suppressed to a considerable extent. Some of these authors we have mentioned before, namely, Addison and Steele, whose *Tatler* and *Spectator* contain valuable records of political and social conditions in England during the early decades of the eighteenth century. Another striking figure was Samuel Johnson, commonly known as Dr. Johnson, who was the author of the famous *Dictionary*, and acquired much fame as a literary critic.

WHY THE SCIENTISTS WERE ENCOURAGED BY SO MANY PERSONS. Science, as we observed, was at last coming into its own. It seemed that science could not become important until the Church had lost much of its power. The scientists of the eighteenth century were fortunate to live in an age when their services were really appreciated. Galileo, as we saw, had been compelled by the Roman Inquisition to deny the Copernican theory of the rotation of the earth; he was tried again in 1633 and remained in prison for nine years until his death. But the scientists of the eighteenth century did not have to fear any longer the dreaded Inquisition. On the contrary, they were often subsidized by their respective governments. The kings were so honored by their work that they gladly gave them pensions for life. In England they often secured civil offices which were offered to them by the leaders in Parliament. Several princes in Germany bestowed presents upon their scientists. In various countries great observatories were built at public expense. It became an honor again to be regarded as a leading scientist.

NATIONAL SOCIETIES OF SCIENTISTS ARE FOUNDED. In 1662 the Royal Society of England was founded, while in 1674 the observatory at Greenwich was built. In 1666 the French Academy of Sciences received official recognition from Colbert, and in 1699 the Prussian Royal Academy of Sciences was founded at Berlin.

EXPLORING THE MOON

Enthusiasm for popular science was typical of the period of the Enlightenment. Here amateur astronomers are studying the moon with a primitive telescope.

FREDERICK THE GREAT

The Prussian emperor and warlord is shown here bursting in upon the Austrians at Lissa. His impatient and imperious character is reflected in his pinched, keen face and his hurried step.

THE PILLORY

The pillory was one of the most common of the public punishments which were banished through efforts of the reformers of the Age of Reason. Many of the greatest authors of the time, such as Daniel Defoe, were punished in this way on charges of opposing the government.

The Bettmann Archive

How Popular Science Was. It now became a popular fashion to promote the cause of science. People would buy microscopes and show their friends how queer a fly looked under the lens. They got hold of crude instruments with which they illustrated various elementary laws of physics and chemistry, to the delight and astonishment of the spectators. The observation of nature began to supplant the study of theology. The scientist took the place of the theologian in attracting attention in periodicals and newspapers.

Popular Books on Science Make Their Appearance. Innumerable books were issued for popular consumption, telling about the strange animals that lived in Asia and America, the wonders of the heavens, the mysteries of plant life, the beauties of mountain scenery, the wonderful advancement made in mathematics, the value of chemistry and physics, the progress of medicine, and the joy of living in the present rather than thinking constantly about the life which lay beyond the portals of death.

Why So Few People Had Believed That Human Beings are Born Good. Up to the eighteenth century it had been customary in many Christian countries to think that human society was sinful and corrupt, and that in this world human beings are hopelessly entangled in evil. The idea that progress was possible seldom occurred to the average mind. Poverty, crime, pain, misery, and disease could never be completely removed: so reasoned the preachers, and so believed even well-educated laymen. Most people admitted that the privileged classes no longer deserved their special rights, and that absolutism was not the proper form of government. They also refused to believe that intolerance and cruel torture were the right solution of religious disputes and the violation of law and order. But it did not occur to many scholars to find a way out of corruption and injustice. It was taken for granted that such things were to remain forever.

Optimistic Writers Try to Show That Society Can Be Reformed. However, in the eighteenth century a large number of distinguished writers arose who proceeded to show how society might be reformed, how crime might be lessened, how illness might be checked, how poverty might be decreased, how torture might be abolished, how governments might be improved, and how superstition might be extinguished.

What John Locke Recommended. Just before the opening of the eighteenth century the famous John Locke, whom we have mentioned before, advocated religious toleration, representative government, and popularized education. Locke explained how before the rise of civilization, men were all free and equal, knowing no superiors socially or politically. But when civil society began to displace natural society, the people made a compact or contract with their ruler in order to safeguard their individual rights. In this contract the ruler promised to protect his subjects, while the latter agreed to observe the laws that were passed by the ruler. Locke argued that the legislative branch of the government was much more important than the executive. So he recommended that the power of the king and of the courts should be greatly limited, and that the legislature should be the supreme authority in the state. Locke had many followers in Great Britain, and on the Continent the philosophers taught his political beliefs until the time of the French Revolution.

WHAT MONTESQUIEU SAID IN HIS BOOK CALLED PERSIAN LETTERS. One of Locke's admirers in France was Montesquieu, who wrote a famous work entitled, *Persian Letters*. In this work he satirized social conditions in France. He said: "The king of France is the most powerful prince in Europe. He draws his wealth from the vanity of his subjects, more inexhaustible than mines. He undertakes and carries on great wars with no resources except titles of honor which he has for sale; through human pride his troops are paid, his forts are furnished, and his fleets are equipped." Although Montesquieu lived in a Roman Catholic country, he made bold to say that the Pope was an old idol, to which people burned incense from the force of habit. He admired England, of which he wrote: "England is at present the most free country in the world; I do not except any republic; I call it free because the prince can do no conceivable harm to anybody because his power is controlled and limited by law."

ANOTHER IMPORTANT BOOK BY MONTESQUIEU. In 1748 Montesquieu published his work, *Spirit of the Laws*, which was one of the most important books written in the eighteenth century. The author said that law is generally the same as human reason, "in so far as it governs all the nations of the earth." He recognized four kinds of government: democratic, aristocratic, monarchical, and despotic. He believed that for his own country (France) limited monarchy was more suitable than a republican form of government, though he admitted that in theory the latter was preferable. His great achievement consists in having taught many statesmen of later times to separate three distinct branches of the government, as was done when the American government was established: (1) the executive, (2) the legislative, and (3) the judicial.

THE THEORY OF CHECKS AND BALANCES IN GOVERNMENT. He also was admired for his theory of "checks and balances," by which he meant that any branch of the government should be held in check by the other two. All educated Americans understand fully the immense advantage to be derived from such a practice. It will protect the people against dictatorship of any ruler or any class of people.

VOLTAIRE IS THE GREATEST ENEMY OF THE CHRISTIAN CHURCH IN HIS TIME. Even more influential was Voltaire (1694-1778), who was a Parisian by birth and early training. He gave eloquent expression to the spirit of his age, revealing almost all of its good and bad features. He fully understood the many privileges enjoyed by the upper classes, and the corruption within the French royal court. He also knew the abuses in the Church, and he exposed them all. Besides, he went out of his way to make fun of the clergy as a whole, and made it appear as if every member of the nobility must needs be wicked and unjust. He praised Mohammedans and Buddhists, but attacked the most important doctrines of the leading Christian churches. In many of his plays he had monks and nuns take the part of criminals, and claimed that virtue and justice had to be sought outside the ranks of the clergy and the nobility. He called the Roman Catholic Church the "Infamous," implying that it was responsible for intolerance, persecution, graft, vice, and social injustice.

TWO INFLUENTIAL BOOKS BY VOLTAIRE. In 1733 he published his *Letters on the English,* in which he contrasted the English government and churches with the French government and the Catholic Church. The book was condemned to be burned by the French government, partly because the author had attacked the most sacred things in the Christian faith, denying even the immortality of the soul. He also exposed the abuses in the French government in his work, *The Century of Louis XIV.* In his opinion only feeble-minded persons could still believe that the miracles recorded in the Bible actually occurred, but Thomas Carlyle, the brilliant author of the nineteenth century, wrote of him that he "attacked the Christian religion without understanding it."

WHO THE RATIONALISTS WERE. Voltaire was one of the leading *rationalists,* for he believed that the human reason was the only reliable source of truth. Not the Word of God, not the authority of the clergy, he said, were of any use to a person, but the exercise of his reason. Voltaire did not realize that human beings possess spiritual qualities, and that corruption in State and Church are not the result of civilization or of religion, but of sin. Even reason could be sinful and thus lead to corruption, but that fact was unknown to him, or rather, he refused to acknowledge it.

WHY WE SAY THAT VOLTAIRE'S INFLUENCE WAS NEGATIVE FOR THE MOST PART. Voltaire's influence was largely negative. He could point out what was wrong with society, but he offered very few solutions that went to the heart of the problems. However, he did much good in advocating the reduction of armies, the abolition of feudalism and of serfdom, the enforcement of popularized education, the reform of the criminal code, the introduction of limited monarchy for France and other countries where the people were ruled by autocrats, and a reformation of the Catholic Church. But much of what he said in this direction had been more profoundly stated by honest and humble Christians.

ROUSSEAU'S LIFE AND THEORIES. Rousseau was another French "philosopher" of the eighteenth century. He resembled Voltaire in attacking absolutism in State and Church, and making fun of sacred things in the Church and the Christian religion. In his own life he was even more disgraceful than was Voltaire. He was grossly immoral, dishonest, and finally became partly insane. When a youth he tried his hand at half a dozen occupations but failed in all of them, because he was interested chiefly in his own comfort and liberties, not in his duty to anyone. He talked much about love for your neighbor, but he had not the slightest intention of putting his lovely ideas into operation. Unlike Voltaire, he did not think much of human reason, arguing that emotion must be relied upon to remove injustice and crime. Civilization, he said, had been responsible for the disappearance of human virtues. Man was born free and good, but he has become enchained in social injustice through civilization. People should be willing to return to the habits of savages and give up their system of representative government.

WHAT ROUSSEAU SAID IN HIS BOOK CALLED THE SOCIAL CONTRACT. Rousseau's most famous book is the *Social Contract,* which is often seriously misunderstood by well-meaning liberals who do not happen to know much about Rousseau's own life. He stated that the people are always in the right, and they must be given a chance to express their desires. Originally the people together had delegated their authority to what may be called the State, which is made up of all the male adults assembled together. This was the "social contract" that Rousseau had in mind; it differed very much from that discussed by John Locke and from that which the founders of the American government supported.

WHY ROUSSEAU DID NOT LIKE REPRESENTATIVE GOVERNMENT. Rousseau did not believe in representative government, for in his opinion the people must not surrender any rights to their government. They themselves are the government. Consequently, he reasoned that the British people are free only as long as they are electing the members of their Parliament. But as soon as these men have been elected, so said Rousseau, the stupid British people give all their powers to Parliament. They should surrender nothing and retain everything for themselves. Rousseau's scheme could only be put into practice in very small states, or in federal states made up of self-governing units, where all adult males could assemble many times a year to make laws and operate the government. This idea suited Rousseau perfectly, for he himself had often run away from duty and from work to be done for others.

ROUSSEAU INTRODUCES DANGEROUS IDEAS IN EDUCATION. In the field of education Rousseau also made important contributions. Whether or not they were wholesome, is of course another matter. His novel, *Emile,* tells the story of a boy who was taught to "trust nature," that is, to express himself freely, for human nature is said to be good. Children should not be forced to do things that they are not interested in, nor those that would not be of practical value. And when the children become of age, they should be left free to follow their natural inclinations. Rousseau was a perfect example of this new liberalism. He was an unfaithful husband, a neglectful parent, a vicious, deceitful character, and a false prophet in general. How could his followers in the French Revolution fail to combine excellent reforms with sickening neglect of duty? Popular sovereignty and personal liberty were wonderful ideas to work with, but how could a government carry on when the people refused to pay taxes and refused to make a sacrifice of any kind for their family, or society in general, or the Church?

ADAM SMITH AND OTHERS RECOMMEND LIBERTY FOR BUSINESSMEN. The spirit of "liberty, equality, and fraternity" also entered the field of economics. Here also France produced great leaders, who constantly clamored for "letting business alone." These scholars reasoned correctly that governments should not be permitted to hamper commerce and industry through innumerable regulations. Their ideas were ably set forth by the Scotch writer, Adam Smith, who wrote *The Wealth of Nations*. Like Voltaire and Rousseau, he thought that nature would take care of everything. But what he ignored was the unscrupulous employer who would exploit the poor workman if he were left free to take advantage of his opportunities. In a later age another problem would face the governments of Europe—the labor unions, which, if "left alone," might very well abuse their rights. But in some ways the idea of more liberty for the people was sound, and it bore rich fruit.

WHAT KIND OF RULERS THE "ENLIGHTENED DESPOTS" WERE. Even the autocrats of the eighteenth century, like Frederick the Great and Catherine the Great, were, as we have seen, affected by the desire for reforms. They rank among the "Enlightened Despots," for they sincerely sought to provide the people with an enlightened form of government. Sometimes they are also called "Benevolent Despots," for they were trying to be good to their subjects. In Spain, Sweden, and Austria, as well as in Russia and Prussia, the rulers were obliged to listen to the advice of the philosophers and the reformers.

UNFORTUNATELY FOR THE FRENCH PEOPLE, THEIR NEW KING WAS A POOR ONE. If only the new king of France had taken them a little more seriously than he did, he might easily have prevented the storm that cost him first his throne and then his life. But Louis XVI (1774-1792) and his pretty wife, Marie Antoinette, were so busy with their own affairs that they did not heed the warnings of their intimate friends who saw the dangerous signs of the approaching revolution, though even they did not realize what it would bring to France and to the world.

LOUIS XVI AT FIRST TRIES TO INTRODUCE GOOD REFORMS. In the first two years of the new reign Turgot was the minister of finance. Being a truly enlightened statesman and economist, he insisted that first of all the privileged classes should make some sacrifices for the benefit of the nation as a whole. He also said that commerce should be less restricted by the government than it had been thus far.

THE SELFISH NOBLES PREVENT FURTHER REFORM. But his work was cut short when the nobles persuaded the young king to dismiss Turgot. So the nobles and the higher clergy, which numbered only a quarter of a million out of a population of twenty-five millions, but owned either in their own right or for the Church about forty percent of the real estate in France, continued for a few years to enjoy their unearned privileges. But in the meantime the work of the reformers hastened the day of the final reckoning. Louis XV (1715-1774) had said gayly that after his reign the Deluge might come, but he would be dead then, so why should he care? Louis XVI was less selfish, but he also paid too little attention to the need for reform. Thus the stage was well prepared for the Revolution!

WHY SOME NOBLES SUPPORTED DIDEROT AND HIS ENCYCLOPEDIA. However, it must not be imagined that even the French government was wholly unaffected by the work of the reformers. For example, when Diderot and his associates published their celebrated *Encyclopedia* in 1765—which was a work of seventeen brilliant volumes of text and eleven volumes of plates—a number of influential nobles persuaded the king to support the work, because it was "a step in progress." Diderot had frankly attacked organized Christianity and the autocratic government of the French king, but many of the nobles saw the handwriting on the wall, and wished to be prepared for the worst.

BECCARIA RECOMMENDS THAT TORTURE BE ABOLISHED. The Italian nobleman Beccaria recommended a reform of the criminal codes of the European nations in his book, *Crimes and Punishments*. Many other nobles took pains to clamor with Beccaria for the abolition of public executions and of torture, as well as of the death penalty for insignificant crimes, such as the stealing of one dollar's worth of merchandise from a store! France had its revolution, not because it was the most backward country in Europe, but because there were in that country enough persons of influence who realized what should be done for the masses of the people. Rich and poor were to be found everywhere; crime abounded among all classes of people. But the French were enlightened enough to see what was wrong with their country, and so they began to take action before other nations were ready for social and political reforms.

FORTUNATELY SOME SOUND THINKERS SEE THAT CHRISTIANITY CAN REFORM SOCIETY. While the French philosophers exalted human reason or natural emotions, thinking that outside of religion these reforms could best be introduced, a number of English scholars and clergymen sought a solution of social injustice through a return to the teachings of Jesus of Nazareth. One of these was John Wesley, who happened to be a clergyman in the Church of England, but was not satisfied with conditions in his church. He said that there was too much empty formalism in it and not enough warm religious feeling. He and his brother, Charles, traveled far and wide in order to reach the poor and the sick, who seemed to have been neglected by the Church. Charles wrote the well-known hymn, "Jesus, Lover of my soul."

HOW THE METHODIST EPISCOPAL CHURCH WAS FOUNDED. Their followers in the University of Oxford were nicknamed "Methodists," for they were thought to be too methodical in their religious exercises and charitable work. But the name was not unwelcome; it was adopted as that of a new Protestant denomination which separated near the end of the eighteenth century from the Anglican Church, and has ever since that time devoted itself to the needs of the masses of the people. The Methodists were not interested very much in learned language or many ceremonies, but talked plainly of God's love for sinners.

HOW THE SUNDAY SCHOOLS WERE FOUNDED. The Sunday school system was founded in 1780 by Robert Raikes, who was a humble soul, but he is far more important in the history of western civilization than the famous Hannibal or the brutal Emperor Nero. As soon as the public schools, under the influence of the Era of Enlightenment, began to drop religious instruction, the Sunday schools took over this beneficial task. We should not forget that the founder of the Christian Church was a reformer and preached eloquently against social injustice. He also taught that before God all men are equal, but He was not so foolish as Rousseau and teach the false doctrine that all men have been equipped with the same faculties.

THE CHRISTIAN RELIGION SUPPORTS DEMOCRACY AND FAVORS SOCIAL JUSTICE. Christianity, having been based upon the Hebrew religion, preserved the Ten Commandments of Moses, and added the two of Jesus, which were a summary of the Ten Commandments. The Christians also preached democracy; they also sought to correct abuses in State and Church. Christian reformers have attracted little attention in history thus far, because they were not funny nor criminal. They did not favor revolution nor bloodshed. But a man like Rousseau, who boldly defied the laws of God and man, and taught others to do the same, receives a great deal of attention, just as a person who will kidnap the child of a millionaire will be mentioned in the headlines of nearly every newspaper.

THOUSANDS OF HUMBLE CHRISTIANS QUIETLY HELPED TO REFORM SINFUL SOCIETY. If you want to know just what made modern democracy and religious toleration possible in America and Europe, you must turn to the study of those pious men and women who labored quietly and peacefully among the masses of the people. Their number was enormous at all times, but they were not always able to prevent scoundrels in State and Church from exploiting the poor and the needy folk.

VOLTAIRE AND ROUSSEAU HAVE RECEIVED FAR TOO MUCH CREDIT IN THE PAST. It is indeed a pity that educated scoundrels like Voltaire and Rousseau should have received credit for wholesome reforms for which they at the most were but partly responsible. And as for the Era of the Enlightenment as a whole, we can only say that it has led to much misunderstanding. Like Voltaire and Rousseau, the lesser prophets of the enlightenment failed to distinguish between the Church and the Christian religion. They blamed religion for things done by persons who were not religious, though in some cases they held high offices in the Church. Much of the reform accomplished since 1750 can be ascribed to men like John Wesley and to the founder of the Sunday school movement.

HOW THE HUMBLE PROTESTANTS HELPED THE CAUSE OF DEMOCRACY. As an illustration of what many Christians have done for the promotion of democracy and religious tolerance, we reproduce here the significant words of an English Baptist who lived in the first decade of the seventeenth century: "Our lord the king is but an earthly king and he has no authority as a king but in earthly causes, and if the king's people be obedient and true subjects, obeying all human laws made by the king, our lord the king can require no more. For the religion of men is between God and themselves; the king shall not answer for it, neither may the king be judge between God and man. Let them be heretics, Turks, Jews, or whatsoever, it is not within the power of an earthly ruler to punish them in the least measure."

FOR CENTURIES THE CHRISTIANS SUPPORTED SOCIAL AND POLITICAL REFORM. Furthermore, throughout the fourteenth, fifteenth, sixteenth, and seventeenth centuries, thousands of writers had clamored for a better sharing of wealth. Enlightened scholars had recommended a contract between the ruler and his subjects. In the first half of the seventeenth century there were in the Dutch Republic great historians who argued that all officials in every government should be elected by the people, and that no person should inherit an office or receive an office for his whole life. About the middle of the seventeenth century thousands of Englishmen petitioned their government to establish universal manhood suffrage. And what is still more significant, in the English colonies in North America there were at first no property qualifications for voting. This was especially true of the colonies that made up New England, where rich and poor enjoyed equal political rights. One of the most powerful factors in the establishment of modern democracy was the American frontier, for here there were no such things as servile duties or any remnants of the feudal system.

How the Americans Helped the Cause of Democracy. In the time of President Jefferson many European statesmen used to complain about the simple manners of the Americans, and they even suggested to the President of the American republic that he remind his associates of the importance between the upper classes and the masses of the people. But Jefferson paid little heed to their demands. There is indeed a great difference between the eighteenth century despotism of continental Europe and the democracy that prevailed in North America long before the French Revolution broke out. Whatever there is in the American government that savors of justice, whatever good there is in American political thought, most of it was bequeathed to the nineteenth century by the Puritans, the Pilgrim Fathers, the Quakers, the Baptists, the Lutherans, and other orthodox Christians, who even exerted much influence upon the development of democracy in Europe.

Student Activities

1. With the aid of a dictionary write out the definitions for the following words: *contrasted, exploit, formalism, distinguish, exerted.*
2. What do you understand by the term, "Science?"
3. Who were the Unitarians, and what were their ideas about the Holy Trinity?
4. Modernism is the rejection of all miracles revealed in the Bible. How did "Modernism" get started?
5. Are human beings born good or bad?
6. What measures did John Locke recommend?
7. Why are Voltaire and Rousseau considered great enemies of the Christian religion?
8. Why was Rousseau's idea of education a dangerous one?
9. What were the "Enlightened Despots?"
10. Why was Louis XV a very selfish person?
11. What is Beccaria known for?
12. Write out a short account of how the Sunday School was founded.
13. Why do men like Voltaire and Rousseau receive so much credit for certain good things which they had little or nothing to do with?
14. From which people did the United States receive those things which are good and useful in our system of government?

CHAPTER 37

Economic Progress in the Eighteenth Century

COMPARISON BETWEEN CONDITIONS BEFORE AND AFTER THE YEAR 1700. The eighteenth century compares very favorably with the preceding centuries, when you examine the fields of agriculture, industry, and trade. In early modern times there were to be found many obstacles in the path to economic expansion. In those times roads were poor. Ships were small and often unseaworthy. Since the merchants of the eighteenth century had no such means of communication and transportation as our businessmen enjoy, their achievements were extraordinary. In some of the European countries, especially in France, interior customs barriers, a different set of weights and measures in various parts of the country, and burdensome rules imposed upon the businessmen by the government proved to be obstacles in the way to the expansion of commerce and trade. Even the English government carefully limited the exportation of raw materials, particularly of wool. Several important governments taxed imports to protect home industries, and they restricted all the exports of raw materials to make the country more wealthy. The French government worked out an extremely elaborate tariff system in order to transfer its foreign trade from the hands of the Dutch to those of its own subjects. Frequently high tariffs were the cause of wars.

HOW BUSINESSMEN OVERCAME THE MANY OBSTACLES IN THEIR PATH. However, during the eighteenth century, trade and industry leaped forward on a scale that Europe had not witnessed since the days of the Roman Empire. For example, while England's annual exports amounted to about 320,000 tons, at the opening of the eighteenth century, a hundred years later England exported about 2,000,000 tons a year. There was besides an immense amount of smuggling which naturally was not counted. French trade between 1716 and 1787 increased in value from $42,000,000 to $220,000,000 a year. Between 1701 and 1801 the value of England's foreign trade increased from $60,000,000 to $300,000,000 a year. In the second half of the eighteenth century, England exported woolen goods, linens, iron and steel products, and leather goods. The French produced and sold abroad fine textiles, laces, wines, and leather products. Dutch trade was still considerable, but compared with English and French commerce, it was rapidly declining. Germany had not yet recovered sufficiently from the destruction of the Thirty Years' War to be compared with France, while Spain, Portugal, and Italy were unable to revive their fallen fortunes.

FARMING METHODS ARE GREATLY IMPROVED. It was during the eighteenth century that the so-called Agricultural Revolution occurred in Great Britain. A large number of wealthy landowners combined to improve the methods of cultivation, the breeding of cattle, the draining of swamps, and the use of various fertilizers, artificial and natural. What seems to have been less beneficial, was the "enclosure system," which was a movement started by the same type of landowners to enclose large tracts of land and to turn them over to the sheep for the manufacture of wool. In other words, while the sheep ate the grass, they grew the wool on their hides. It was felt that in this manner the landowners did not have to pay wages to the workmen, and so they could secure a larger return from their investments. The unfortunate result of this enclosure movement was naturally the loss of employment on the part of thousands of workmen in the rural districts. Moreover, it happened in many cases that a farmer who did not have money with which to buy enough land, could no longer compete with those who owned large pieces of land, proper fertilizers, and improved machinery. In this way the Agricultural Revolution indirectly led to the Industrial Revolution.

REASONS WHY THE INDUSTRIAL REVOLUTION STARTED IN GREAT BRITAIN. Great Britain was also the home of the Industrial Revolution; at least during the second half of the eighteenth century, Great Britain led all the world in the progress made in trade and industry. There were several reasons why the Industrial Revolution started in England. In the first place, there was an increased demand for English goods, for the rapid growth of the British colonies helped British industry. After Great Britain had won the great duel for world empire, and its navy had been recognized as the mistress of the seas, British commerce could freely enter immense fields in America, Asia, and Africa which before this time had been closed to it. In the second place, England possessed large deposits of coal and iron which were located very near to each other. In addition to this advantage, it enjoyed a favorable climate for textiles, which need damp weather. The abundant water power in the swift streams of the northwest also aided in the growth of industry. The absence of governmental interference in business, such as was noted in France, also was a distinct advantage to the British.

THE IMPORTANCE OF WOOL AND COTTON. For more than a century, the chief industry in England had been woolen goods. The woolsack, a cushion of wool on which the Lord Chancellor sat, when he presided over the House of Lords, was a symbol of the importance of wool-growing. But the introduction of cotton goods from India at the beginning of modern times had created a demand for cheaper cloth, while the British colonies were amply able to provide the raw material. During the second half of the eighteenth century the English colonies in America exported to Great Britain a large amount of raw cotton. Even after the war of the American Revolution the Americans continued to supply the British with the necessary cotton.

IMPROVEMENTS IN WEAVING AND SPINNING. It was, therefore, in the field of the textile industry that the first inventions were made. As early as 1733 John Kay constructed a simple but extremely useful device called the fly shuttle. This instrument enabled the weaver, by merely pulling a string, to throw the shuttle from side to side, which meant a great saving in time. Formerly the weaver's hand had to be relied upon to a great extent. But now the process of weaving was much improved. However, it did not help to speed up the work of the spinners, who could not supply thread fast enough for the weavers. So, about 1765, James Hargreaves invented the spinning jenny, which all at once spun eight threads in a row. It was installed in hundreds of cottages throughout northwestern England, for it was simple enough to be run by a child. Although these two inventions of Kay and Hargreaves were very valuable to Great Britain, the inventors received slight returns for their work, and still less appreciation. They were attacked by crowds of workmen, who believed that the inventions would cause widespread unemployment.

THE WATER FRAME PROVES VERY USEFUL. In spite of opposition by the workmen, the inventions grew in number. A great improvement resulted from the machine patented in 1775 by Richard Arkwright, whose water frame was run first by horse power and later by water power; it spun harder and firmer thread than the spinning jenny, and it worked more rapidly. As early as 1783 Arkwright made use of steam power in a number of factories which he had himself established. Before 1790 the number of spinning factories in England had grown to 150, and Arkwright is often referred to as "the father of the factory system."

THE INVENTION OF THE COTTON GIN MEANS CHEAPER COTTON. Spinning and weaving were only two branches of the cotton industry which were affected by the new inventions. Before cotton could be spun, it had to go through a variety of processes, and one of these was greatly improved by Eli Whitney's invention in 1792 of the cotton gin, not in England, where cotton was spun, but in North America, where it was grown. You should note that the pressure of increasing demand is one of the chief reasons for inventions. The English inventions called for more cotton; they required cheaper cotton as well. Whitney met the demand with his machine, which picked the seeds out of cotton as rapidly as fifty negroes could do it by hand. Bleaching machines also made their appearance, which, using chemicals, did work in a few hours for which the sun required about six months. Shortly after 1785, machines were perfected to print figures and designs on cotton goods.

STEAM POWER PROVES MORE VALUABLE THAN WATER POWER. Other industries soon followed the lead of the spinning industry, for improvement in one led to demand for inventions in another industry. Although at first water power had been a great advantage, it soon proved to be wholly inadequate. Not only was the amount of water available for the mills subject to changes in the weather, but it was often difficult to obtain enough labor at the places where rivers produced the required power. Once more the pressure for something new and better resulted in an invention; this time it was the steam engine, constructed by James Watt about 1765. Assisted by a wealthy manufacturer who supplied the required capital, James Watt finally succeeded in applying his steam engine to heavy machinery.

THE IMPORTANCE OF IRON IN THE BUSINESS WORLD. The increased demand for iron and steel, which resulted from the rapid production of machinery, led to further inventions. The iron industry had never been carried on extensively in England, because charcoal was the fuel for smelting iron, and wood was scarce. Charcoal is made from wood that burns very slowly, nearly without fire. The lack of timber naturally resulted in the production of coke, which comes from coal that burns very slowly. England had plenty of coal. But even more important was the improvement in the process of smelting and refining iron. If the iron contained more than 2 per cent of carbon, it became cast iron and was then too brittle for most industrial uses. It was necessary first to remove the carbon and the impurities, and then to reintroduce exactly the right amount of carbon in order to produce wrought iron. Before long the inventors turned to the burning of coal. And as soon as iron had thus become much more easy to obtain, iron ships were built, huge bridges were constructed of iron, and all sorts of new machinery were made out of iron. It is not too much to say, therefore, that the development of the iron industry is fully as important as that of the textile industry. The use of iron underlies the whole Industrial Revolution.

IMPROVEMENTS IN TRANSPORTATION. Another important feature of the Industrial Revolution was the growing demand for better transportation. Before the seventeenth century, England had lagged far behind several continental countries in the construction of roads and canals. But the expansion of trade and industry was followed at once by the building of better roads and the construction of canals. One of the most important canals was that which connected Liverpool with Manchester. Liverpool was the great port for the industrial part of England, while Manchester was the industrial center. One of the most useful inventions was that of Mr. Macadam, after whom the Macadam roads were named. He showed how impassable clay roads could be covered with gravel and crushed stone, so that in all kinds of weather carts could be drawn over them. It also became customary to construct roads out of bricks.

RESULTS OF THE INDUSTRIAL REVOLUTION. One result of the Industrial Revolution was that the centers of population in England shifted from the southeast, around London, to the northwest, in the vicinity of Manchester and Liverpool. Another was that it helped to create a new class of capitalists, the manufacturers, who were destined to make their power felt in the nineteenth century. A third result was that it aided in producing the large class of factory workers, which was to become extremely important. The Industrial Revolution also gave rise to great cities, like Manchester, Birmingham, Leeds, and Sheffield. It was indirectly responsible for the expansion of such cities as Liverpool and Glasgow.

SOCIAL CHANGES ALSO OCCUR AS A RESULT. Moreover, the Industrial Revolution caused remarkable changes in the structure of English society. It was responsible for the decline in the rural districts, where for centuries the *gentry* had lived in comparative luxury and ease amidst the tenant farmers. The landowners had exercised enormous political power, which was altogether out of proportion to their limited number. But now the middle class in the cities began to share in the political power. Although it took several decades before the importance of the new cities was finally recognized, we shall see in another chapter that aristocracy finally had to yield to the other classes of people.

THE POOR WORKMEN AT FIRST ARE NOT WELL TREATED. At the same time many thousands of workmen were drawn away from the rural districts to the towns, where they lived together amidst unpleasant and unsanitary conditions. The refuse from factories polluted streams and canals. Volumes of smoke hung over the narrow streets. The hours in the factories were long, and the opportunity to enjoy the fresh air of the country became very limited. Presently labor leaders appeared among the workmen, and explained to them that they were entitled to greater privileges. They insisted that their day of work should be shortened, that their pay should be increased, that they were entitled to better homes, and that neither young people nor women should be permitted to work in the mines. Socialism is indirectly the result of the Industrial Revolution.

THE INDUSTRIAL REVOLUTION ENABLES THE ENGLISH TO OCCUPY VALUABLE COUNTRIES. It is also interesting to note that the population of England increased far more rapidly between 1750 and 1850 than in any previous period of that length, and besides, more rapidly than that of almost any other European country. This remarkable growth made it possible for the English to colonize and occupy exactly those parts of both the Northern and Southern Hemispheres which today seem most important to the peoples of Europe. In the seventeenth century European statesmen had thought tropical colonies the most desirable; but in the nineteenth century the threat of overpopulation made many a government cast covetous eyes upon Canada, Australia, New Zealand, or South Africa, where Europeans have found a suitable climate. At the close of the eighteenth century these regions could be occupied with ease by any nation; but no country was so well fitted to undertake the occupation as was England.

RAPID EXPANSION OF THE INDUSTRIAL REVOLUTION OUTSIDE ENGLAND. During the nineteenth century the Industrial Revolution spread from Great Britain to France, then to Germany, as well as to the United States. As a snowball rolling down a mountain slope increases constantly in weight and volume, so the Industrial

A RURAL HEARTHSTONE

This painting by W. R. Bigg (1783) shows old-fashioned cooking utensils and cooking methods. The scene is one typical of almost all countries in Christendom at this period.

ROADS OF THE OLD REGIME

Until the nineteenth century brought improvements by McAdam and others, the roads of most of the countries of Europe were hardly as good as those in the days of the Romans. Clumsy coaches such as these were the only alternatives to horseback or travel on foot.

LIFE OF THE PRIVILEGED CLASSES

Dinner in a French salon. The life of the upper classes was one of ease and little responsibility. Fine foods, rich wines, and clever conversation were enjoyed amid luxurious surroundings, with little regard for the lot of the poorer classes.

The Bettmann Archive

Revolution, once it had started in Great Britain, continued to grow and spread, until at last it reached every country of the globe. We shall have occasion in another chapter to refer again to this almost unbelievable expansion of modern trade and industry.

Student Activities

1. With the aid of a dictionary write out the definitions for the following words: *Obstacles, unseaworthy, customs, restricted, compete, textiles, simultaneously, covetous.*
2. Make a list of twenty-five machine made goods. Can you name any hand made goods?
3. What is meant by the "Agricultural Revolution?"
4. Why were cotton and wool so important in England?
5. List the inventions enumerated in this chapter.
6. Why did the invention of the Cotton Gin make cotton cheaper?
7. Who was the inventor of the steam engine?
8. How were roads being improved?
9. The Industrial Revolution means a change from making articles by hand to making them by machinery. What were some of the results of this change? Were the results good or bad? Has the Industrial Revolution come to an end?
10. To what other countries did the Industrial Revolution spread?

CHAPTER 38

France Overthrows Its Absolute Monarchy and Its Privileged Classes

WHAT WERE THE CAUSES OF THE FRENCH REVOLUTION. The
French Revolution which broke out in the year 1789, was
the outcome of many different causes. As you have seen, the majority of the people clearly recognized the fact that the king had too
much power altogether. It was clear also that the higher clergy and
the nobility should be taught to give up some of their privileges
and to assume some of the duties that thus far were performed for
the most part by the middle class and by the masses of the people
in the rural districts. Moreover, the recent war with Great Britain, in which France had supported the American colonies, had
been a terrific expense to the French government. Taxes were
numerous and heavy, and they fell largely upon the shoulders of
those who were least able to pay them.

WHICH INDIRECT TAXES CAUSED THE MOST DISSATISFACTION.
Among the indirect taxes was the salt tax. It caused bitter feelings
in many sections of France, because the price of salt varied all the
way from 2 to 60 francs a hundred pounds, or from 2 to 60 cents
a pound in our currency. Everybody was supposed to buy seven
pounds of salt from the government each year, and, because the
people in some provinces had to pay ten times as much as those in
other provinces, smuggling became very extensive. Each person
had to pay for the salt whether he used it or not. There were also
taxes on tobacco, paper, starch, and many other articles, but the
salt tax was hated more than any other. Peasants joined with the
businessmen and professionals in demanding a new system of taxes,
which would do away with inequality, injustice, and wasteful
collection.

THE ESTATES-GENERAL IS CALLED TOGETHER AGAIN. As a
result of all complaints, it became necessary in the year 1788 to
call a meeting of the Estates-General. Although this body had not

met since 1614, it was known very well to the leading thinkers of France that it had once represented the people as a whole. It was made up of the three estates, that is, the clergy, or the first estate, the nobility, or the second estate, and the commons, or the third estate. During the winter of 1788 to 1789, the delegates to the Estates-General were elected, so that in May, 1789, there assembled in Versailles the total of about 1200 men, of whom 300 represented the first estate, 300 the second estate, and about 600 the third estate. Although the third estate comprised more than 95 per cent of the population, they were represented only by as many men as were the first and second estates together. But that did not seem to trouble most of the people at that time. What everybody was interested in, was to save the government from bankruptcy, to provide the poor with proper food and clothing, and to abolish abuses in the State and Church.

How the Members Were To Vote. However, one of the first and most important questions that were brought up was this, Should the 1200 delegates vote by "head" or by "order?" If they voted by head, each of the 1200 would have one vote, and the third estate would equal in power the first and second combined. But if each order had one vote there would be altogether three votes, and only one of the three would go to the third estate. Consequently, the leaders in the group that made up the third estate, led by the outstanding reformers in the country, insisted that the voting should be by head. More than five weeks passed in fruitless discussion, till at last, near the end of June, the members of the third estate declared that they were the popular assembly of France.

The Estates-General Becomes the National Assembly. They were inspired by a great speaker, named Mirabeau, who became one of the most influential orators in France during the early period of the Revolution. His aggressive personality and powerful voice so encouraged the men around him that he decided to defy the king, and during the next three days about fifty nobles and more than half of the clergy joined the deputies of the third estate, who now formed the National Assembly. The king was obliged to recognize the new institution, with the result that on June 27, 1789, the last meeting of the Estates-General in the history of France came to an end. The nobles and the clergy were now commanded to join the deputies in the National Assembly, which therefore contained the same members as had the Estates-General.

A Mob in Paris Seizes and Destroys the Old Prison Called Bastile. But the privileged classes were not yet ready to give up the struggle. They gained the ear of the king, who during the two weeks that followed June 27, permitted a large number of soldiers to be brought from the frontier to Paris and Versailles. When it was seen that the king and his friends were about to take forceful action, mobs collected in the streets of Paris. On July 14 they surged towards the Bastile, which was the symbol of the old order in France. It used to be a prison, hence it was hated by the people of Paris. So the mob stormed the prison, and forced the garrison to surrender the building, which was promptly destroyed. Since that year July 14 was the chief national holiday of the French people, until their country was occupied by the Nazis. The Parisians also set up a city government of their own, and they organized a militia which was called the National Guard.

THE MARCH OF THE WOMEN TO VERSAILLES. Many of the nobles and members of the higher clergy now fled from France and from various foreign countries tried to assist in the restoration of the old social order of France. But the people of Paris were not yet satisfied with the result of their early action. On October 5th a mob of men dressed as women, and accompanied by many real women, marched all the way from Paris to Versailles, a distance of twelve miles. A wild night followed, during which Lafayette, Commander of the National Guard, saved the royal family from the frenzied mob. But the mob did compel the king and queen and their son to return with them to Paris, shouting as they went, "We now have the baker and the baker's wife and the baker's boy," meaning that now they were to be provided at last with food.

AFTER THIS THE ROYAL FAMILY IS OBLIGED TO LIVE IN PARIS. The royal family had also been compelled to recognize the three colors of the Revolution: the white of the Bourbon flag, combined with the red and blue of the arms of Paris — the tricolor of France. A little later the National Assembly was transferred from Versailles to Paris, where it was to hold its sessions in the real capital of France, amidst the radical elements of the French people.

WHAT HAPPENED IN OTHER PARTS OF FRANCE. From Paris the revolutionary movement spread rapidly into the provinces. In the provincial cities the lower classes formed mobs and robbed the homes of the wealthy burghers and the representatives of the king. The middle class thereupon organized armed forces modeled after the National Guard of Paris. They completely changed the city governments, and in many cases they abolished the old corporations that used to control the cities. In the country districts many of the people took up arms and stormed the castles, demanding the records of what the poorer people owed the richer persons. Many of the castles were burned and their noble occupants murdered. Royal representatives were deprived of their authority and taxes were no longer paid. Chaos now reigned in the country.

REFORMS INTRODUCED BY THE NATIONAL ASSEMBLY. In the meantime the National Assembly introduced a number of very important reforms for France. On August 4 the nobles, realizing how much they had already lost, made gestures of generosity by giving up the feudal rights of which the peasants had just deprived them. During the whole night that followed, one reform after the other was put through the Assembly. The clergy joined the nobles by abolishing the tithe, which was a tax on the income of the masses of the people, and had been paid by them to the clergy. The representatives from the cities and from several provinces also surrendered their special rights.

THE DECLARATION OF THE RIGHTS OF MAN AND OF THE CITIZEN. In the same month of August, 1789, the Assembly accepted a charter of liberties, which was entitled *Declaration of the Rights of Man and of the Citizen*. This document contained the following statements: "Men are born and remain free and equal in rights. The rights of man are liberty, property, security, and resistance to oppression. The source of all sovereignty rests essentially in the nation. Liberty consists in being free to do anything that does not injure others. Law is the expression of the general will. The law should establish only such penalties as are strictly and clearly necessary. Every man is considered innocent until found guilty. The free expression of ideas and opinions is one of the most precious rights of man." The document also stated that taxes were to be "equally levied among all citizens according to their means," and every public agent was subject to the will of society, which had the right to require of him "an account of his administration." This charter of liberties was of the utmost importance in practically all the European countries. Its influence is still at work in our own century.

LOCAL GOVERNMENT IS REORGANIZED. Important also were the changes introduced in the government during the same year 1789. All the old divisions in French territory, called the provinces, as well as the offices attached to the administration of these units, were abolished. Since nature alone was to be worshiped, the new divisions were all to be named after mountains, rivers, and seas, that is, natural features, regardless of historical development.

France was divided into eighty-three departments, which were nearly equal in size and population.

THE CHURCH LOSES ITS LANDS. In order to find necessary revenues with which to run the government, it was decided to deprive the Church of all its real estate property. The government issued paper money, called *assignate,* and used as security the property of the Church. From now on the state was to pay the clergy regular salaries and in this way would remedy one of the great evils in the social system of France, namely, the giving of positions in the Church to persons not fit for them at all. Unfortunately, however, the *assignats* soon became worthless, because the government continued to spend money and still did not have the courage to tax the people at large. This was real *inflation.*

A NEW CONSTITUTION IS MADE FOR FRANCE. In 1791 the National Assembly drafted a Constitution for France. It separated the executive, legislative, and judicial branches of the government, in accordance with the theory of checks and balances that had been devised, as you have seen, by Montesquieu. France now became a limited monarchy, somewhat similar to Great Britain. But the legislature was to be made up of only one house, and called the Legislative Assembly. It ruled France from 1791 to 1792. In 1792, the monarchy was abolished altogether, and a Republic set up.

KING LOUIS XVI TRIES TO ESCAPE FROM FRANCE, BUT IS BROUGHT BACK. Louis XVI, when he saw what course of action the members of the Legislative Assembly were taking, decided to leave France, lest he might lose his life. In June, 1791, he tried to reach the eastern border, but before he got that far he was recognized and forced to return to Paris. On two different occasions a mob tried to attack him in his palace, but in each case the royal family escaped their fury. However, early in 1793 the King was executed and soon afterwards the queen was also beheaded. In September, 1792, a large number of persons were massacred in Paris.

WHAT THE "REIGN OF TERROR" WAS. The real "Reign of Terror" lasted from June, 1793, to July, 1794. Various persons were brought from time to time before a committee, which as a rule condemned them to death. But you should note that only three thousand persons were executed in Paris during the "Reign of Terror," while 16,000 were massacred in the various departments. The contemporary sources show clearly that the common people daily went about their business very much as if nothing unusual was happening.

WHAT THE FOOLISH RADICALS DID WHEN THEY WERE IN POWER. For a short time the radicals controlled the French people. "Liberty" was to be the new god. People donned red caps to show their loyalty to the goddess of liberty. Liberty trees were erected in streets and squares, where the rich and poor joined hands and danced around the poles. The tricolor of France, the rights of man, the national holidays, and the constitution became the new ritual of worship. But the services in the churches, with their altars and crucifixes, the sacraments, and the Bible were neglected. Some of the radicals in 1793 entered the famous cathedral of Notre Dame in Paris, and there they instituted the worship of the goddess of Reason, who was represented by an actress. Similar acts were performed in other French cities.

THE NEW CALENDAR OF THE REVOLUTION. The Revolutionists also decided to abolish the old calendar, for they despised especially the system of having six days in which to work and the seventh day reserved for rest. They did not want a calendar which showed the importance of Jesus Christ in the history of the human race, but instead, one which would glorify the Revolution. So their calendar began with September 21, 1792. New names were invented for the days of each month, and as in the case of the departments, natural features provided the new names, such as a harvest month, a snow month, and so forth. There were twelve months in the year, each with thirty days, the remaining five or six days being declared national holidays. Each tenth day was to be devoted to the worship of the Supreme Being, and all pastors who observed the Christian Day of Rest were to be imprisoned.

SOME GOOD REFORMS. However, during the period from 1792 to 1795, some good reforms were actually introduced. In the first place, a system of free public schools was begun. Moreover, the metric system of weights and measures was formulated and used throughout France. Afterwards it was to be adopted by practically all other nations of Europe. The Louvre palace was transformed into a national museum and the royal library became the celebrated National Library. The Government also abolished imprisonment for debt and slavery.

NOT EVEN AFTER THE REIGN OF TERROR DOES FRANCE BECOME DEMOCRATIC. On the other hand, it must not be imagined that France had become a democratic country. It is true that a democratic constitution was drafted on paper, but its application was postponed indefinitely. During the Reign of Terror France was actually ruled by a few hundred men who were not representing the people. It is interesting to note that when in 1795 a new constitution was made for France, the government was made up of a Directory of five men and a legislative body of two houses.

WHAT THE DIRECTORY WAS. The five Directors formed the executive branch of the government. The legislature was dominated by the Directors. Their members could only be elected by those persons of the middle class who owned considerable property and who had lived in one place for at least one year. And after the Revolution had been formally accepted by the French people, and the dictator, Napoleon, was exiled from France, a constitution was drawn up in 1814 which limited the right to vote to about 100,000 persons, out of a population of approximately 30,000,000. It was only in the space of two or three years, when radical leaders of the national and legislative assemblies were in power, that serious attempts had been made to establish a democracy, from which nevertheless nothing came. These facts indicate clearly that democracy in the United States owes much less to the French Revolution than is commonly realized in this country.

FRANCE HAS TO FIGHT AGAINST THE FIRST COALITION (1793-1795). Revolutionary France soon had to face armed resistance on the part of the rulers of Prussia and Austria. In 1792 the first war broke out. In the next year Great Britain and the Dutch Republic also entered the war against France. But in 1795 the Dutch Republic collapsed, and the new republic which followed it, under the name of the Batavian Republic, became an ally of France. Prussia also withdrew from the war, so that only Great Britain, Austria, and an Italian state called Sardinia, continued the war against France in 1795.

NAPOLEON BECOMES FAMOUS IN THE ITALIAN CAMPAIGN. It was during the war against Austria and Sardinia that the brilliant general, named Napoleon Bonaparte, assumed supreme command of the French army. In 1796 he crossed the Alps, defeated the Sardinian forces, and entered the Po valley. He also defeated the Austrians, who had to retreat eastward. In 1797 the Austrian government made peace with France, much to the astonishment of nearly all other European governments. This was the beginning of French expansion under Napoleon. France annexed the Austrian Netherlands, as well as a portion of northern Italy. Now only Great Britain remained at war with France.

Napoleon Goes to Egypt and Syria. After peace had been declared, Napoleon grew restless. He was always exceedingly ambitious, and he could not endure peace at home. So he ventured abroad, crossed the Mediterranean, and entered Egypt with a small army of his own. All went well until one day in August, 1798, the British Admiral Nelson met the French fleet near the mouth of the Nile, and defeated it. Not long after this Napoleon suddenly deserted this army in Egypt and returned to France.

Napoleon Overthrows the Directory. Here he quickly overthrew the government and set up an entirely different one. Making himself the chief of three Consuls, he established a so-called Consulate. Almost immediately he concentrated all executive power in his own hands, and placed France under a military despotism. Thus ended the first period of revolutionary France. The monarchy had fallen, democracy was to have succeeded it, but it never came. Liberty was to have remained supreme, but dictatorship took the place of absolute monarchies. In the midst of the chaos in November, 1799, Napoleon swiftly removed the whole government set up in 1795. What he did to France during his own term of government, we shall learn in the following chapter.

The Object Lesson of the So-called Enlightment and the French Revolution. Now you have seen how little good the French leaders had done for their people. They had weakened the power of the King, it is true, only to find that another man from a foreign race seized greater power in France than the King had ever had. They had abolished the old taxes, but they were too cowardly to introduce new ones. All they could do was to take the property of the Church and print paper money. They destroyed the great privileges of the nobles, but Napoleon restored many of these. They did nothing for the common people except indirectly by taking some privileges away from the rich. They thought that they could reform sinful mankind without the Christian religion. They failed, just as all other attempts have always failed and always will fail. Only the power of Christ can redeem sinful mankind.

Student Activities

1. With the aid of a dictionary write out the definitions for the following words: *smuggling, militia, restoration, frenzied, renouncing, prevalence, established.*
2. Why did the salt tax cause such resentment in the minds of the people of France?

3. What was the Estates-General?
4. Tell about the storming of the Bastile.
5. Why did the "Women" march to Versailles?
6. What were some of the provisions in the *Declaration of the Rights of Man and of the Citizen?*
7. What were the *assignats?*
8. Why did Louis XVI try to escape from France?
9. What was the "Reign of Terror?"
10. What changes did the foolish radicals try to bring about in France?
11. How did Napoleon become famous?
12. Is it possible to reform mankind without the Christian religion?
    Note: The French Revolution is often called one of the great and leading events in history. But you will notice that while it brought about certain changes which were good indirectly, yet it did very little that was good and beneficial.

CHAPTER 39

The Era of Napoleon

WHO NAPOLEON WAS. Napoleon Bonaparte was born in the year 1769, on the island of Corsica, which in the previous year had become French territory. France had bought the island from the republic of Genoa. So Napoleon was of Italian ancestry, and his native language was Italian, although he learned to love France above Italy. He had received military training in a French academy. He was both an extremely successful commander and a statesman of unusual ability. This will explain his brilliant campaign in northern Italy in 1796 and 1797, as well as his success in overthrowing the government of republican France in November 1799. It was in the period from 1799 to 1804 that he showed himself at his best. In 1802 he made himself Consul for life, while in 1804 he became Emperor of France.

HOW NAPOLEON WAS ABLE TO OVERTHROW THE FRENCH GOVERNMENT IN 1799. Napoleon, however, could not have done all these things without the consent of the majority of people in France. When he returned from Egypt in 1799, France was threatened with invasion by the Austrians. No great leader had appeared to save the wholesome elements of the Revolution, and the fervor of international brotherhood that had been preached by the French, had been replaced by intense nationalism. What the French wanted in 1799, was conquest of other lands in Europe. They no longer demanded, as they used to do, liberty and fraternity, but rather hoped to annex some lands in the north, east, and south.

THE NATURE OF NATIONALISM IN EUROPE. Most of the people on the continent of Europe are that way. They do not seem to be greatly interested in the form of government under which they must live, but they are exceedingly interested in national prosperity and national glory. Owing partly to the course of training which they have obtained in school, and partly to other factors, the French, as well as the Germans, and many other peoples of

Europe as well, think more of the glory of their country than of their right to vote. This helps to explain the extraordinary success of men like Hitler and Mussolini in recent times.

WHAT NAPOLEON DID FOR THE FRENCH PEOPLE WHEN HE WAS FIRST CONSUL. During the five years that Napoleon was the First Consul of France, he accomplished a great deal for that country. In 1801 he made peace with the Pope, and agreed that the State retain the property of the Church, and would continue to pay the salaries of the clergy. The bishops were to be nominated by the head of the civil government, but installed by the Pope. Furthermore, he established the Bank of France. He also placed the currency on a stable basis. Still more important was his codification of the laws of France, which resulted in the celebrated Napoleonic Code. He was also responsible for the establishment of a magnificent system of public schools. He standardized local government and placed the various officials in the local units under the control of the central government. Ever since the time of Napoleon, the government of France has been strongly centralized.

MILITARY SUCCESSES OF NAPOLEON IN THE SAME FIVE YEARS (1799-1804). In these same five years Napoleon was also supreme on the battlefield. From 1799 until 1802 he fought against Great Britain, Russia, and Austria. These three countries formed the Second Coalition. He defeated Austria in 1800 and again in 1801, so that in 1801 Austria had to sign a very humiliating peace agreement. In 1802 the British also ended hostilities. If at this point Napoleon had been able to hold his ambitions in check, he might have created a French empire which might still be in existence today.

THE WARS OF THE THIRD AND FOURTH COALITIONS. But this was not to be. When he observed that he would face again the combined forces of Great Britain, Russia, and Austria, he sold Louisiana to the United States in 1803, so that he could concentrate his attention upon European affairs. The War of the Third Coalition was fought in 1805. Once more he defeated the Austrians, and once more he made them sign a disastrous peace treaty (1805). In 1806 he dissolved the Holy Roman Empire, keeping the land west of the Rhine under France. Then he set up a federal state which was called the Confederation of the Rhine. Austria was not included in this state and now became the Austrian Empire. In 1806 Prussia once more joined the other powers against Napoleon. This was the fourth coalition. But in a short time Prussia was forced to surrender and to yield a large portion of her territory to Napoleon. Finally he turned against Russia, and inside of one year disposed of that power also.

NAPOLEON AND THE CZAR OF RUSSIA DIVIDE EUROPE BETWEEN THEM. In 1807 Russia signed the Treaty of Tilsit with Napoleon, on which occasion the Russian czar proudly said to him that Europe was little more than his country and that of Napoleon's. Now Napoleon had only one enemy left, which was Great Britain. Would he now be able to do with Great Britain what he had done with Sardinia, Austria, and Prussia? This question could not be easily answered, because Great Britain was primarily a sea power and Napoleon did not possess a great fleet.

GREAT BRITAIN STILL DEFIES NAPOLEON. He decided first of all to engage in a tariff war with Great Britain. He declared in three successive decrees that products of Great Britain and her colonies were not to be sold in his dominions. Since he ruled over northern Italy, France, Switzerland, western Germany, all of the Netherlands, and a corner of northwestern Germany, his decrees affected a large part of Europe's population. It was partly because of this tariff war with Great Britain that he got his downfall. Great Britain replied with the so-called Orders in Council, and declared that all of Napoleon's countries were to be blockaded. When this became known, the government of the United States declared the Embargo Act in 1807, and the War of 1812 was the direct result of the career of Napoleon. The American government decided to fight against Great Britain, instead of against France, although both countries had offended our government.

NAPOLEON MAKES SOME BAD MISTAKES. From 1804 to 1814 Napoleon made some serious mistakes, which partly caused his overthrow as the Emperor of France. In the first place, as you saw, he annoyed the majority of his subjects with the tariff war against Great Britain. In the second place he humiliated important nations which were certain to rise against him at the right moment. This was especially true of the Austrians and the Prussians, who were at one time completely at his mercy but who disliked his pride and his impudence. Thirdly, he invaded Spain, and placed the government under the rule of his brother, Joseph. This action angered the Spaniards, and matters became worse when his army of occupation cruelly repressed local insurrections. The Portuguese, being allied with England, assisted the Duke of Wellington, who in 1812 engaged in the so-called Peninsular Campaign.

THE INVASION OF RUSSIA IS THE BEGINNING OF NAPOLEON'S DOWNFALL. Perhaps his greatest error was the invasion of Russia in 1812, where several hundred thousand of his soldiers perished on the battlefield, or from exposure to the cold weather. Just as Napoleon was ready to spend the winter in Moscow, a fire destroyed nearly all its buildings, and his return march was terrible. like Schiller and Herder, and by able statesmen, the Germans planned the destruction of Napoleon. Led by patriotic writers like Schiller and Herder, and by able statesmen, the Germans secretly prepared an army. In 1813 they were assisted by the Austrians and the Swedes, and in the Battle of Leipzig, or the Battle of the Nations, Napoleon was defeated. His empire collapsed within half a year. He had to surrender to the enemies, who exiled him to the little island of Elba, situated near his native Corsica.

NAPOLEON ESCAPES FROM ELBA, BUT LOSES THE BATTLE OF WATERLOO. But Napoleon did not long remain on this little island. In March, 1815, he escaped to France, and quickly raised an army there. Many of his former companions were delighted to see him come back. His march to Paris was like a triumphal parade, and before long he had a large army ready once more. However, the English under the Duke of Wellington, and the Prussians under Blucher, converged upon him at the little town of Waterloo, near Brussels. There he suffered his final defeat in the month of June, 1815, much to the relief of the peoples whom he had previously oppressed. The British decided to remove him sufficiently far away in the midst of the Atlantic Ocean to make sure that he would never trouble Europe again. He lived on the little island of Saint Helena during the remaining six years of his life.

THE FRENCH CANNOT FORGET HIM. During these six years, the harm done by his foolish ambitions was once more forgotten by his admirers in France. In the eyes of the French people, he became a martyr and his cause was identified with that of the Revolution. It was believed that Napoleon had devoted his best energies to the welfare and glory of France. A legend grew up which idealized the character of the great emperor, and as the years went by, this "Napoleonic Legend" credited all the blessings of the French Revolution to Napoleon and the humiliation and misfortune which attended the fall of his empire to the king who succeeded him. But in the countries surrounding France, no illusions were entertained regarding the character of Napoleon.

THE RESULTS OF THE FRENCH REVOLUTION CONTINUE TO
SPREAD. Nevertheless, the reforms started by the revolutionary
leaders in France could not all be undone. Wherever serfdom and
feudalism had been abolished, they did not return. Much of the
old social inequality had been removed, while worn-out administrative and judicial machinery likewise were given up. From France
and its immediate vicinity, the reforms introduced by the Revolution in this region slowly spread to the north, east, and south,
while even in Great Britain they had some influence. Napoleon,
in a certain sense, had inherited the French Revolution, and he had
appeared at the right moment to save France from chaos and
disorder, and so prevented the restoration of an old social order
which the people had gladly abolished.

THE GREAT EUROPEAN POWERS PREPARE AND SIGN THE
TREATY OF VIENNA. The great powers who had several times
combined against Napoleon now decided to change the map of
Europe and to restore much of the map as it had been before 1789:
(1) The ruling houses deprived of their lands by Napoleon were
restored in Spain, Naples, Sicily, Sardinia, the Netherlands, and
some of the smaller Italian states. (2) Austria received Lombardy
and Venetia in northern Italy. (3) Napoleon's puppet state, the
Federation of the Rhine, was replaced by the German Federation,
made up of 38 and sometimes of 39 units. The ruler of Austria
was the presiding official of the delegates of these states that made
up the national government. Prussia retained West Prussia, which
it had received in the First Partition of Poland in 1772. It also
annexed almost half of Saxony and several important territories
in western Germany. The Austrian empire continued its existence
almost unchanged until 1867, and ruled over Hungary, Bohemia,
and several other regions. (4) Sweden received Norway from
Denmark, as a reward for having opposed Napoleon, but it gave
Finland to Russia. (5) The new Kingdom of the Netherlands
comprised the former Dutch Republic and the former Austrian
Netherlands. This region was ruled by King William I, of the
House of Orange. (6) Great Britain received Cape Colony, half
of Guiana, and Ceylon from Holland; she also obtained Malta,
Trinidad, and Tobago. (7) Russia received more than half of
what was formerly the kingdom of Poland.

THE TREATY OF VIENNA IS UPON THE WHOLE A FAIRLY GOOD
ONE. The Treaty of Vienna, which in 1815 was concluded by the
so-called Congress of Vienna, was on the whole a fairly good
piece of work. It certainly compares favorably with that which

was drafted in 1919, at the conclusion of the World War. But, although the spirit of nationalism was very powerful at the time, in the teritorial changes almost no attention was paid to it. For example, the Norwegians became subjects of Sweden, which was not at all to their liking. Moreover, the French-speaking people of southern Belgium became a part of the kingdom of the Netherlands, much against their will.

France Is Very Well Treated by Her Victors. In November, 1815, the four great powers signed a treaty with France. The French were not punished severely for the bad behavior of Napoleon. They merely had to pay an indemnity of 700,000,000 francs, which at that time was equivalent to $140,000,000. They also lost a few small pieces of territory on the eastern frontier, but aside from those losses, France emerged from the upheavals caused by Napoleon practically unharmed. Most of the fighting had been done on foreign soil, and the expenses of the war of Napoleon had been borne largely by other peoples. Now that most of the ruling houses had been restored to their own respective states, and conservative statesmen were back in the saddle, it seemed in 1815 as if the French Revolution had spent its force outside of France by battling in vain against the principles of restoration and reaction. We shall see in the next chapter what was done by the various rulers to prevent the forces of political and social reform from repeating the work of the revolutionary leaders in France.

Student Activities

1. With the aid of a dictionary write out the definitions for the following words: *Intense, currency, standardized, converged, puppet state, indemnity.*
2. Who was Napoleon?
3. What do you understand by the term, *nationalism?*
4. List the nations which Napoleon defeated.
5. How did Napoleon try to destroy Great Britain?
6. How did the United States become involved in a war with Great Britain?
7. In what battle was Napoleon finally defeated? Where was he placed?
8. Why did the French continue to remember Napoleon?
9. How did the Congress of Vienna settle affairs in Europe after the Napoleonic Wars?
10. How was France treated by the Congress of Vienna?
    Note: The Napoleonic Wars lasted about fifteen years. They placed all of Europe in a turmoil during those years. But after those wars there was comparative peace in Europe for about thirty years. The peace which was made at Versailles in 1919 after the First World War barely lasted twenty years.

CHAPTER 40

Fifteen Years of Revolution and Reaction

THE QUADRUPLE ALLIANCE IS FOUNDED. In the same year that the Treaty of Vienna was signed, the reactionary forces who were led by an Austrian statesman by the name of Metternich, agreed to form the so-called Quadruple Alliance. This was a combination of the four great powers that had defeated Napoleon, namely, Great Britain, Russia, Austria, and Prussia. The statesmen of these four countries agreed to prevent further revolution, and to stifle all forces that were intended to undermine the respect of the people for their government.

CZAR ALEXANDER I PREPARES THE DOCUMENT CALLED THE HOLY ALLIANCE. In November of the same year Czar Alexander I of Russia had a document drawn up, which was called the Holy Alliance. Most of the rulers of the European countries signed this document, in which they agreed to support the principles of the Christian religion, to give to the people a just government, and to suppress radical forces. Since this was a mere document, and in no way an alliance, it should be carefully distinguished from the Quadruple Alliance.

WHAT IS THE ERA OF METTERNICH? Many historians have called the period from 1815 to 1830 the era of Metternich, because of his enormous influence upon the rulers of Russia, Prussia, Austria, and France. For example, when the Greeks revolted against the Sultan of the Ottoman Turks, he persuaded Czar Alexander I not to help the Greeks. In Italy he enabled several princes to abolish reforms which had been previously undertaken. In Spain the reactionary forces also received his support. It was owing to his influence that in the Germanic Confederation both students and professors were prevented from freely expressing their ideas. In 1819 the Diet of the Germanic Confederation passed the Carlsbad Decrees, which were intended to curb the reformers.

PRUSSIA PREPARES FOR THE TASK OF GERMAN UNIFICATION. In the meantime Prussia forged ahead in many directions. In 1818

Prussia adopted a uniform tariff system for her scattered territories, and in 1834 she and sixteen other states formed the general customs union, which was the first concrete beginning of German unification in the nineteenth century. It is true that the Germanic Confederation, which was set up by the Congress of Vienna in 1815, was in a sense a union of Germanic states. But it must not be forgotten that in this union Austria played a leading role, while in the unification of Germany it was the constant aim of the Germans to exclude Austria from the newly formed state.

FRANCE REMAINS CONSERVATIVE. The statesmen in France who sought to restore much of the former conditions, were led by King Louis XVIII (1815-1824), in whose reign only those who owned extensive properties were permitted to vote. As we have observed in the preceding chapter, only 100,000 prsons could vote. Charles X (1824-1830) was even more conservative and reactionary than Louis XVIII. He was the youngest brother of Louis XVIII, and both were brothers of the former king of France, Louis XVI. Charles X in 1830 felt strong enough to limit the freedom of the press and the right to vote. But now the conservatives had gone too far, and you will see soon that the revolution of 1830 ended much of the work accomplished under Charles X.

THE BRITISH CONSERVATIVES REMAIN POWERFUL. The conservatives were also powerful in Great Britain during the period from 1815 to 1830. Many of the British statesmen had been frightened by the radicals of the French Revolution. Led by the eloquent Edmund Burke, they had pointed out that the leaders in France in the period from 1798 to 1799 were for the most part inexperienced. These Frenchmen had no idea of what a government should be like, nor were they familiar with the history of the French people. As a result, the Tories were able for a long time to prevent important reforms from being carried through in Parliament. They were ably led by William Pitt the Younger, the son of William Pitt the Elder.

IRELAND IS UNITED WITH GREAT BRITAIN. In 1800 Ireland was united with Great Britain in the United Kingdom of Great Britain and Ireland. Now Pitt proposed that the Roman Catholics receive equal political rights with the Protestants. But King George III refused to grant this concession. He was even more reactionary than the Tories. The Duke of Wellington was also one of the Tories. So it is not surprising that the Tories remained in power until 1830.

A Few Reforms Are Introduced Before 1830. However, certain reforms were actually introduced, such as that in the tariff system and another in the criminal code. In 1828 the Protestants who did not belong to the Church of England were permitted at last to hold public office, while in 1829 the Catholics received this same right.

France Joins the Quadruple Alliance. Under the influence of the British statesmen, France was permitted to join the Quadruple Alliance, which now became the Quintuple Alliance; it was also called the Concert of the Powers. Although Britain was thus allied with some exceedingly conservative nations on the Continent, her statesmen as a rule were liberal in this respect that they favored the attempts made by small nations in trying to become independent. The British reasoned that these small nations would open their ports to British goods.

The British Do Not Like to See Small Nations Suppressed by the Big Ones. This is the reason, for example, that, when in 1820 a number of Spanish colonies and Brazil rose against Spain and Portugal, the British heartily favored the cause of independence, and they combined with the United States in formulating the Monroe Doctrine of 1823.

The Revolution of 1820 in Spain Leads to the Monroe Doctrine. In 1820 a revolution had broken out in Spain. But this had been nipped in the bud by the Quintuple Alliance, whose representatives ordered that France should send an army and put down the revolt. The result was that in 1823 absolutism triumphed again in Spain. In the meantime the Spanish and Portuguese colonies in America rose against the mother countries as we have just observed. The British told their friends on the Continent that they would not permit the Spanish and the Portuguese to put down the revolt in South America. Canning was their spokesman and found ready support from Monroe in the United States.

The Greeks Win Their Independence from the Turks. While the Spanish revolt was put down, the Greeks were successful in their revolt against the Ottoman Turks. Beginning their fight for independence in 1821, they continued to rebel until they were assisted by Great Britain, Russia, and France, who defeated the Turks in the naval battle of Navarino (1827). In 1829 Greece, Serbia, and the two provinces which later made up Rumania, received local independence.

A New Revolution Breaks out in France. In 1830 there followed two other successful revolutions, the first in July, and for that reason called the July Revolution. It broke out in Paris, where Charles X was overthrown and was succeeded by Louis Philippe, the Duke of Orleans. Now the flag of the Bourbons had to give place to the tricolor of France, that is, the red, white, and blue of the Revolution. Thus the people of France had shown that they no longer wished to be ruled by members of the house of Bourbon. At the same time the right to vote was extended somewhat, but real democracy was by no means introduced as yet. The wealthy members of the middle class had taken the place of the clergy and the nobility. They now proceeded to control the policies of the French government for their own benefit.

Belgium Becomes an Independent Nation. In the same year the Belgians revolted against their Dutch king, partly because he was a Protestant, and partly because he tried to impose the Dutch language upon the inhabitants in the south who spoke a French dialect. An important cause of the revolution was the objection of the Belgians to the very small representation that they had received in the national government. Supported by the French and the British, they won their independence, which was formally guaranteed in 1839 by Great Britain, France, and Prussia.

Why the Belgian Treaty of Independence Was Called a "Scrap of Paper." It was this agreement of 1839 that in 1914 was considered a "mere scrap of paper" by a leading German statesman, when the Germans proceeded to violate Belgium's neutrality. But this sort of thing has happened many times in the past. Governments will solemnly swear to uphold the principles of justice, and to protect small nations. Undoubtedly in many cases the officials who have made such statements intend sincerely to keep them. But whenever a time arises when it does not seem profitable for a certain government to maintain its promises, it often happens that this government will find some way of evading its duties.

The Revolutions in Poland and Italy Result in Failure. In 1830 there also occurred a revolution in Poland, which was a dismal failure, so that Poland became a mere province of Russia, having lost its constitution. It used to be an important state in Russia, because Czar Alexander I in 1815 had been liberal in granting a constitution. But when the next czar observed the course of the revolution, he turned more reactionary than he had been before, so that he proceeded to deal very harshly with the unhappy and unfortunate Poles. Similarly, several attempted revolutions in Italian states met with failure. The time had not yet arrived for the forces of liberalism and political progress to help lighten the burden of the masses of the people. For a few more years the men and women who formed the aristocracy continued to enjoy privileges out of proportion to their number.

Student Activities

1. With the aid of a dictionary write out the definitions for the following words: *reactionary, eloquent, neutrality, dialect.*
2. What was the "Holy Alliance?"
3. Who was Metternich?
4. Why did Great Britain favor the independence of small nations?
5. Who was Canning? Monroe?
6. How did Belgium become an independent state?
7. Where did the phrase, "Scrap of Paper," originate?
8. Which revolutions mentioned in this chapter resulted in complete failure. which ones were more or less successful?
9. Who were the "Tories" in England?
10. Who was the last Bourbon to rule France?

CHAPTER 41

Liberalism, Nationalism, and Socialism

THE IMPORTANCE OF LIBERALISM, NATIONALISM, AND SOCIAL-
ISM. In the forty years between 1830 and 1870 three powerful
forces were at work, establishing an important change in European
society. These forces were liberalism, nationalism, and socialism.
They often assisted each other, although there were important
differences among them. No one can hope to understand the civilization of the twentieth century without studying with the utmost
care the character and the history of these three very important
movements.

WHAT EUROPEAN LIBERALISM IS. European Liberalism was a
system of thought that was supported largely by members of the
middle class, or *bourgeoisie,* who favored increased liberty for
their own class and indirectly for the masses of the people. As long
as the latter did not in their turn ask for so much freedom that
they would endanger the security of the middle class, Liberalism
heartily supported their desires for a larger share in the government of the nation as a whole. Among the reforms that were
recommended by the Liberals were the freedom of the press, religious tolerance, extension of the right to vote, a more humane
criminal code, a more extensive system of education, and less interference by the government in business.

THE WORLD STILL NEEDS THESE REFORMS. These issues are
still attracting the attention of all the important statesmen of the
western world. Almost every time we pick up a newspaper or a
magazine, we see a reference to these questions. It used to be
thought that there was continued progress in politics, economics,
and in the social order; but now it appears that several important
states in Europe have actually gone backward. Today there is no
longer freedom of the press in Germany, no longer religious
toleration, no longer liberty for the businessman. The same is
true of Russia and to a lesser extent of Italy. Although the

Liberal Party in most of the European states has ceased to be an important political party, the forces of Liberalism as they were at work in the period under discussion, are still very busy, both in Europe and in the United States.

THE GOOD POINTS IN EUROPEAN LIBERALISM. On the whole we may say that European Liberalism has had many bright sides. It accomplished a great deal for the masses of the people, although it was directed by the higher classes and by the more wealthy element in the middle class. But European Liberalism has also had its dark side. Whenever it allied itself with socialism against orthodox Christianity and the organized denominations, such as the Roman Catholic and the other important churches we have mentioned thus far, Liberalism often became intolerant.

LIBERALISM BECAME INTOLERANT TO THE CHRISTIAN CHURCH. It may seem strange that the movement that stood for religious toleration, could itself ever become intolerant. But such was unfortunately the case. In several countries the Liberal Party tried to restrict the power of the Church in the field of education and charity. The Liberals often attempted to make private schools subject to control by the civil government. Their idea was to abolish all private schools, as well as religious instruction. They argued that education should be entirely controlled by the State. In some instances they did not even permit the Roman Catholics to maintain private schools for the education of their priests. They also objected to private charity, suggesting that the poor could well be taken care of by the civil government. But it was only natural that Liberalism should turn itself against the Church, for originally men like Voltaire and Rousseau had prepared the way for Liberalism. They had pointed out the abuses in the Church, for which reason the Liberals continued to attack the Church, even after it had been reformed and had lost both political and economic power.

TO WHAT EXTENT COMMUNISM AND FASCISM ARE THE OFFSPRING OF LIBERALISM. In some respects, European Liberalism laid the foundations of Communism and Fascism, and it is for this reason that the Communists and Fascists proudly call themselves the Liberals. They, as well as the Liberals, exalt the State far above the Church.

HOW THE CHURCH HAS LOST MUCH OF ITS POWER. Before the nineteenth century, vast numbers of poor persons used to depend upon the Church or private charity for their means of living. But since 1830 charity has had to give place to public welfare and relief. Private schools have also yielded to state control, or else they have been closed in several countries. Finally, politics has become more and more removed from the influence of the clergy.

WHAT NATIONALISM HAS DONE IN THE WORLD. Nationalism, as you saw, was often allied with Liberalism, because both were the opponents of the reactionary forces. Wherever oppressed peoples sought independence, they were moved by the spirit of nationalism, for they wished to establish a nation of their own. The liberals supported them against the governments that refused to grant the desire independence, as happened at the time the Greeks arose against the Turks and received aid from many Liberals, including the British writer, Lord Byron.

IMPORTANT LEADERS IN THE FIELD OF NATIONALISM. In Italy the torch of nationalism was lit by Mazzini, who founded the society called "Young Italy." He urged his countrymen to overthrow the rule of the Austrians in Italy. Hungarian nationalism was inspired by Deak and Kossuth, who urged the Hungarians to revolt against the Austrians. Likewise, the Slavic peoples in Austria began to dream of national independence for their own peoples. Moreover, the Poles hoped to revive their former state. Chopin, the Polish musician, spent much of his time in Paris trying to win support for his cause.

LIBERALISM TRIUMPHS IN BRITAIN. THE REFORM BILL OF 1832. In Great Britain the cause of Liberalism was fostered by the Whigs, who in 1830 returned to power under Earl Grey. In 1831 they introduced the Reform Bill, which passed Parliament in 1832. This bill extended the voting power to fewer than 350,000 voters, making the total 650,000 out of 25 millions. But at least a beginning in the right direction had been made. It also abolished the "rotten boroughs," which had very few inhabitants and in a few cases none at all. This happened because in certain regions the people had moved away, while in one instance the town (borough) had been buried under the waves of the sea. Moreover, this bill established a uniform qualification for voting in the towns (the ownership of a home that was worth ten pounds a year in rent). Finally, the larger towns got new seats or else more than before.

THE HOUSE OF LORDS IS WEAKENED. What is significant about the Reform Bill besides, is the fact that the Tories tried in vain to prevent its passage in the conservative House of Lords. **Popular** pressure for reform was so strong that the House of Lords had to yield to it against the wishes of the majority of its members. Hereafter the House of Lords lost most of its former power to veto bills that had passed the House of Commons, until in 1911 it was deprived entirely of it by the Parliamentary Act. Now it can no longer do anything about financial bills, while it can merely delay the passage of other bills for a maximum of two years. In this respect it differs greatly from our Senate in Wasington. But remember that in the House of Lords the members sit for life.

MORE AND MORE PERSONS IN GREAT BRITAIN ARE PERMITTED TO VOTE. When once the way was paved for reform, it became a simple matter to extend the voting power gradually to all adult males; a moderate extension was made through the second reform bill (1867), and a more comprehensive one through the third reform bill (1884), while in 1918 women also received the *franchise (suffrage)*.

OTHER REFORMS PUT THROUGH BY THE LIBERAL PARTY. Under the leadership of the Liberal Party, which was formerly called the Whig Party (while the Tories came to be called the Conservatives), other reforms were introduced during the reign of Queen Victoria (1837-1901). For example, in 1846 the duty on edible grain (called "corn" in England) was removed as a result of the agitation by the Anti-Corn-Law League. As long as the rural districts had been more important than the cities, the government had protected the farmers against importation of cheap grains. But this meant high prices for bread in the cities, and so the change in 1846 revealed the rising power of the cities.

SLAVERY IS ABOLISHED IN THE BRITISH EMPIRE. In one respect the British surpassed the Americans in the movement for social reform. In 1833 their government passed a bill which required all the owners of slaves in the British colonies to set them free. The said owners received from the government the total sum of about $100,000,000 in our currency at that time. Furthermore, about the middle of the nineteenth century the British government granted home rule to the dominions, such as Canada, Australia, and New Zealand.

THE BRITISH GOVERNMENT DOES MUCH FOR THE WORKMEN. Much also was done for the workman. The British government appointed a committee that was instructed to investigate conditions in the factories and the mines. The work was honestly done. The report issued by the committee revealed shocking conditions, which later were done away with as a result of the Factory Act of 1833 and the Mining Act of 1842. The former restricted the working hours for young people; the latter prohibited the working of women and girls in the mines, where they had formerly labored under positively degrading conditions. Other laws followed in due course of time, requiring the owners of factories to keep the buildings clean and well ventilated.

ANOTHER REVOLUTION BREAKS OUT IN FRANCE. Liberalism in France was also influential at this time. Since King Louis Philippe (1830-1848) was a mediocre person, he pleased very few members of the political parties. Besides, only about 200,000 men could vote, wages of workmen were very low, and their hours long. Consequently, the Liberals under the guidance of Thiers recommended numerous reforms, and when these were not forthcoming, they roused the populace of Paris to swift and concrete action. In February 1848 Paris started the third French revolution, and once more other countries were greatly affected by it. Louis Philippe had to flee to England, but this time no other king succeeded him as ruler of France.

THE FRENCH GET THEIR SECOND REPUBLIC, AND THEIR SECOND EMPIRE. The Second French Republic was set up, which in the course of four years was followed by the Second French Empire. Both were ruled by Louis Napoleon, the son of one of Napoleon's brothers. From 1848 he was president, and from 1852 to 1870, emperor of France. But what was more important to the French people, was the fact that now for the first time they had a democratic government, for at last the voting power was given to the workmen.

THE REVOLUTION SPREADS TO OTHER COUNTRIES. The revolution of 1848 rapidly spread to Germany, Austria, and Italy, where the Liberals overthrew Metternich and forced two monarchs to abdicate in favor of younger and more liberal rulers: In Austria, Francis Joseph (1848-1916) ascended the imperial throne, while in Sardinia Victor Emmanuel II succeeded his father as king. There was also considerable fighting and bloodshed in the various dominions ruled by the Austrians, such as Hungary, and northern Italy. But little was accomplished by the Liberals there. The same may be said of the situation in Germany, where an attempt was made to reorganize the government.

THE RESULTS OF THE REVOLUTION IN GERMANY. The time had come at last for the Germans to express a powerful nationalism of their own. They were also ready for important reforms. Large numbers of Liberals got together and arranged for an election of 568 members to represent the German people in the so-called Frankfurt Parliament. These men had been chosen by universal male suffrage, but nearly all of them belonged to that middle class group which stood for Liberalism. Their first meeting was held in May, 1848, but for some ten months they could not agree on who was to rule the country, and which states should be in it. Finally, in 1849 they decided to have Austria excluded, and to have the King of Prussia become the German Emperor. But King Frederick William IV refused the offer, partly because he wanted Austria to be in the empire, and partly because he had little respect for the Liberals. He said that they had no power to make anybody an emperor. Moreover, the Austrian government still had the upper hand, and saved the existence of the Germanic Confederation. In 1850 Prussia, however, did get a constitution. Liberalism in Germany also weakened the power of the Church. On the one hand many Germans left the country when Liberalism did not succeed well enough to suit them, and on the other hand many devout Lutherans came to the United States, in order to enjoy more freedom of religion. In this way the Missouri Synod of the Lutheran Church was started in the United States.

OTHER RESULTS OF THE REVOLUTION OF 1848. The Revolution of 1848 was by no means lacking in permanent results. Both Prussia and Sardinia received a constitution, while the governments of the Netherlands (Holland) and Switzerland were changed for the benefit of the masses of the people. In Austria and Hungary the remnants of feudalism and serfdom disappeared. In France, as you saw, the king had to leave. He was the last king France has had since 1848. Most important of all, democracy finally triumphed in France, before it could emerge completely victorious in Great Britain, though long after the United States had become democratic. Liberalism, it must be remembered, was not the same as democracy. It favored the rule of the middle class, while democracy supports the rule of all classes acting together, each receiving a share in proportion to the number of its members, not in proportion to the wealth of its members.

THE UNITED STATES WAS A GREAT LEADER IN THE MARCH TOWARD DEMOCRACY. Before the end of the eighteenth century the United States was already a democratic country, while both Great Britain and France were controlled by representatives of the middle class and the higher classes. It is the widespread mis-understanding of the nature of the French Revolution in this country that has generally prevented the public from receiving the truth about the rise of democracy. The French Revolution did by no means help establish democracy in the United States; it could not even do this in France itself. It merely abolished practices that have never existed in the United States. You could say with a considerable degree of assurance that democracy was partly begun in France about the middle of the nineteenth century under the influence of the United States. France became democratic in 1848, and Great Britain in 1884; but the United States in 1787.

How Socialism and Communism Began. If Europe had followed the lead of the United States more readily than it chose to do, such movements as Socialism and Communism would have been unnecessary. Socialism, unlike Liberalism, devoted itself primarily to the task of promoting the welfare of the masses of the people. One of the first Socialists was the Frenchman Louis Blanc, who during the revolution of 1848 persuaded the government to institute "national workshops," like our W.P.A. Here workmen were employed in the pay of the national government. But the idea did not become popular at this time.

The Communist Manifesto. In the same year appeared the well-known pamphlet entitled, *The Communist Manifesto,* by Karl Marx and his associate, Engels; Marx was a Jew, but Engels was not. In this pamphlet they advocated the sharing of wealth in such manner that the private ownership of the means of production be abolished. Land, factories, utilities, mines, and railroads were to be owned and operated entirely by the national government; business in general was also to be under the supervision of the government. Marx also wrote a book called *Capital,* in which he attacked the capitalistic form of society, such as we still enjoy in the United States today, though it has recently been modified somewhat under the Roosevelt administration.

Karl Marx and the Communists Attack Decent Family Life. Not only did Marx wish to deprive the middle class of their corporations and factories and stocks, but he also prepared the way for Communism in his attack upon the family life of the middle class. He stupidly argued that men and women in the middle class exploited their children and held their wives in common; since that was the case, he reasoned, why not openly recognize and permit such a system of holding wives in common? But in the nineteenth century no European people wished to follow his advice. Not until Russia was completely demoralized as the result of defeat by Germany in the World War, that is, in 1917-1918, could a country be found that would favor the destruction of family life and the robbery of persons who happened to own extensive property.

THE SOCIAL DEMOCRATIC PARTY IS FOUNDED. Since 1848 many kinds of Socialists have abounded in Europe, some of them favoring the radical ideas of Marx, others more moderate principles. In 1875 the Social Democratic Party was founded in Germany, when the Marxians combined with a party established by Ferdinand Lassaile, a German Jew. Some of the radical parties favored the idea of having *syndicates,* that is, unions of workmen who were to seize factories and operate them.

TRADE UNIONS ARE ESTABLISHED. Trade unions followed the rise of Socialism, for it was believed by many that only through the force of numbers organized to fight against selfish employers, could anything be done for labor. As a rule the Socialists worked with the labor unions and the labor leaders, while the Liberals held aloof from them, though agreeing with them that the State must have more influence than the Church and religion.

WHAT THE COOPERATIVE MOVEMENT IS. During the second half of the nineteenth century the *cooperative* movement originated. It was based upon the principle of doing away with the middleman. Farmers would unite to market their crops for higher prices, while in the cities people would start stores which were owned collectively by the customers of these stores. The movement gained much headway in Scandinavia, though it never spread so far as to undermine the old-fashioned means of trading. After all, even the man who works for his own friends and associates has to have something for his labor, and he is more likely to loaf on the job than when he owns his store himself.

THE CHRISTIAN CHURCHES DO MUCH FOR THE CAUSE OF SOCIAL JUSTICE. In the meantime, the great denominations of Christendom did not lag behind in the popular movements for social reform. They were only putting into practice what Christ had urged upon all of His followers. One of the most remarkable illustrations of excellent work done by the clergy in this direction is the encyclical, or official pronouncement, by Pope Leo XIII in 1891, called the *Rerum Novarum.* The Pope showed himself to be as much in favor of social justice as many a radical labor leader.

KIND-HEARTED WRITERS URGE THE PUBLIC TO HELP THE POOR. Influential writers also contributed their share to these problems, such as Charles Dickens, Victor Hugo, Thomas Carlyle, John Ruskin, Zola, and Tolstoy. Among the important writers of the twentieth century rank Bernard Shaw and H. G. Wells. Altogether the forces at work in behalf of the masses of the people were powerful and very effective. Europe has caught up with the United States in this respect, but its various peoples need not have taken up many practices and theories which in themselves were not required in order to bring about social justice. And so it has come about that the United States still leads Europe in sane living and thinking.

RECENTLY EUROPE HAS RETURNED TO AUTOCRACY, RELIGIOUS INTOLERANCE, PAGAN TEACHING, AND MILITARISM. You are now in a position to understand how inferior are Socialism, Fascism, Naziism, and Communism to the Christian religion. After all the talk about liberty and fraternity, what have all these people done for the human race? Is there anything good in their work that Christianity could not have done better? The big nations swallow the smaller ones. The Jews are brutally persecuted. Labor unions and political parties are suppressed. There is no more voting, no liberty of the press. People are told that they may not listen to their radios. The Christian churches have lost their schools, not because they taught evil doctrines there, but simply because the Liberals and their offspring hated Christianity. The State must rule over everything, and it must own all mines, railroads, factories, telephone and telegraph companies, electric and gas companies, farms, stores, and offices. Boys must be produced in greater numbers, so that the State can feed them to the cannon as fodder for the glory of the pagan government. Workmen may not have collective bargaining any more. They also may not strike any more. Religion is made fun of, and the clergy are told what to say and what not to say. That is what has come to Europe because its leaders would not listen to the teachings of Christ.

Student Activities

1. With the aid of a dictionary write out the definitions for the following words: *intolerant, qualifications, maximum, urban, degrading, exploited, demoralized, associates, resorted.*
2. What three forces were at work in Europe between 1830-1870?
3. What are some of the things that the Liberals favored?

4. How did Liberalism show that it was opposed to the Christian churches?
5. What is Nationalism?
6. What was the good point about the Reform Bill in 1832 in England?
7. How did England set all the slaves free throughout her empire?
8. How were the slaves freed in the United States?
9. When did the Germans attempt to unite into one nation?
10. What is communism?
11. Who was Karl Marx? How did he show that he cared nothing for Divine commands and ordinances?
12. Which country has adopted communism? Why?
13. What is a "Trade Union?"
14. What is the general condition of Europe at the present time? Godlessness and wickedness always brings severe punishment. Remember the story of the Flood, Sodom and Gomorrah, and others. Europe and in many respects the United States also has been in a terrible condition since 1914 when the First World War began.

CHAPTER 42

The Unification of Germany and Italy

Germany and Italy Badly Need Unification. While Great Britain, France, Russia, Spain, and other nations were continuing on the road to national unity and expansion beyond their original borders, both Germany and Italy failed to share in the race of European imperialism. They remained weak politically, because they were still divided into a large number of states that were almost independent powers in themselves. It is this backwardness in the political field that kept Germany and Italy so poor in colonies. No wonder that in recent years they have demanded more land and have been drawn together because of their common needs!

The Italians Are First Aided by France. Italian unification received its first great start in 1859, when the kingdom of Sardinia allied with France in a war against Austria. The Austrian armies were promptly defeated in a brief campaign. As they began their retreat from Lombardy, which had been an Austrian province, together with Venetia, the spirit of nationalism suddenly seized upon the people in all parts of Italy. Inspired by the brilliant military commander, Garibaldi, both Naples and Sicily freed themselves from the rule of their Bourbon king.

Italian Unification Continues. Moreover, in Parma, Modena, Tuscany, and part of the Papal States, the inhabitants revolted and wanted to be joined to the new state to be formed under Sardinian leadership. Napoleon III agreed to this on condition that France obtain Nice and Savoy, which was done. Thus the Kingdom of Italy was founded. Its king was Victor Emmanuel II, who was ably assisted by his great minister, Cavour.

Further Gains in 1866 and 1870. The new kingdom was enlarged when in 1866 Italy supported Prussia in a war against Austria, and obtained Venetia. Furthermore, in 1870 a war was fought between France and Prussia, which encouraged the Italians to seize the rest of the Papal States, including the city of

332

Rome. Thus far the French had supported the Pope. But after 1870 he retained but a small plot of ground in Rome and a little castle near Rome.

WHO LED THE GERMANS IN THEIR UNIFICATION. Meanwhile, a strong king (William I) and a great minister (Bismarck) did for Germany what Victor Emmanuel II and Cavour did for Italy. Prussia was the leading state in German unification, as Sardinia was in Italy. King William I set about to strengthen the Prussian army, in which task he was assisted by Von Moltke, the general, and Von Roon, the minister of war. Bismarck favored the use of military force, for he had disapproved of the speech-making of the Liberals in 1848 and 1849, which had brought nothing but humiliation for Germany. He said that "blood and iron" was needed. It was through war that Germany was finally united.

THE GERMANS ANNEX SCHLESWIG AND HOLSTEIN. First of all came the Danish War of 1864—the result of Bismarck's desire to annex Schleswig and Holstein. He persuaded Austria to assist him, so that the king of Denmark was quickly defeated and lost both duchies. Austria received the right to administer Holstein, and Prussia the same right for Schleswig, as provided in the Convention of Gastein (1865).

THE WAR OF 1866 FORCES AUSTRIA OUT OF THE GERMANIC CONFEDERATION. The Austro-Prussian War of 1866 was also the work of Bismarck for the most part. He wanted a break with Austria, so as to force this country out of the German Confederation and strengthen the position of Prussia. The war lasted only seven weeks. The decisive battle was fought at Sadowa in Bohemia. Italy, as you saw, aided Prussia, and though defeated by Austria, received Venetia. Since a number of German states supported Austria, Bismarck could use this fact as an excuse in annexing them at the end of the war. He naturally took also Schleswig and Holstein.

WHAT THE NORTH GERMAN CONFEDERATION WAS. The German Confederation was now dissolved and the North German Confederation set up. This included only the states north of the river Main. The King of Prussia was to be the president of the new state (the *Bund,* or Confederation). He was to be assisted by the *Bundesrat,* or Federal Council, which was made up of diplomats who directly represented the rulers of the states; and by the *Reichstag,* or National Diet, the members of which were to be elected by universal manhood suffrage.

WHAT NAPOLEON III OF FRANCE WANTED TO DO. Napoleon III, the emperor of France, now became thoroughly alarmed by this continued aggression by Prussia. He had sought to gain power for France and for himself by sending a French army to Mexico to help set up an empire under an Austrian prince, but he had met with resistance from the government of the United States as soon as the Civil War was ended in 1865. He also entertained plans of annexing Belgium or Luxemburg, which plans Bismarck promptly made known to various German princes, in order to arouse their suspicion of the French ruler. Thus Bismarck prepared for the Franco-Prussian War. He was aided by the following events:

THE SPANISH THRONE IS OFFERED TO A GERMAN PRINCE. In 1868 the Spanish people were without a satisfactory ruler, and after some hesitation finally offered the throne to a member of the German house of Hohenzollern. The French loudly protested, and the prince declined the offer, much to the displeasure and humiliation of Bismarck. But new trouble was started in July, 1870, when the French ambassador to Prussia insisted that King William I of Prussia should definitely promise never to permit a member of the Hohenzollern family to become a candidate for the Spanish throne. William refused to do this, as he stated in a telegram he sent to Bismarck (the "Ems Dispatch," for William was at Ems, a summer resort). Bismarck shortened the message, in order to make it appear that William had insulted the French. So Napoleon III at once declared war.

REASONS WHY FRANCE LOST THE WAR OF 1870. Napoleon was surprised to learn that no nation would support him, but Bismarck was not surprised, for he was a great diplomat. The French were also wholly unprepared for the war, while the Prussians were quite ready. The Prussians invaded Alsace-Lorraine, where they defeated the French at Sedan and Metz. Napoleon was taken prisoner at Sedan with his whole army, and also lost his position as emperor.

PARIS FALLS IN JANUARY, 1871. Now the Third Republic was declared by the French, and the new government decided to prolong the war. But resistance was useless, though the city of Paris withstood a German siege for four months. In January, 1871, Paris fell, and France had to accept humiliating terms.

FRANCE LOSES ALSACE-LORRAINE. In May, 1871, the official treaty was signed at Frankfort. France lost Alsace and eastern

Lorraine, and had to pay an indemnity of five billion francs, equal at that time to one billion dollars.

THE GERMAN EMPIRE IS FOUNDED. In the meantime the process of German unification was completed. In the Hall of Mirrors at Versailles, where 48 years later the Germans would be forced to sign suicidal terms for their country at the end of the World War, the King of Prussia became the "German Emperor." The south German states were joined to those in the former North German Confederation. They all became now a part of the German Empire.

THE GOVERNMENT OF THE GERMAN EMPIRE. The government was almost the same as that of the North German Confederation, except that the number of states was larger. The people were not truly represented in the legislature, for the Bundesrat was responsible only to the princes and the governments of the three city-states (Hamburg, Bremen, and Lubeck). Moreover, the Emperor (*Kaiser*) appointed a Chancellor who was responsible only to him and could not be dislodged even if all the members of the Reichstag voted for his dismissal.

THE EMPIRE WAS A FEDERAL UNION. Within the Empire there were four kingdoms, six grand duchies, five duchies, and ten other states. Alsace-Lorraine was considered merely as imperial territory until 1911. Bavaria had its own postal system, and some of the other large states also enjoyed special privileges.

PRUSSIA EXERTS A REACTIONARY INFLUENCE. Prussia, which was more important than all the other states together, had only 17 votes in the Bundesrat out of 58 (61 after 1911), but only 14 were required to veto. Prussia had a very old-fashioned form of government of its own, with the Emperor at the head as the King of Prussia, and a legislature of two houses. The more wealthy a person was in Prussia, the more votes he controlled in the election of members of the House of Representatives.

CIVIL SERVICE IS EXCELLENT. However, civil service was excellent, and especially the city governments were admirably conducted. The average German was more interested in efficient government than in his own share in it as a voter. The reason why he liked the civil service is that under this system a person receives a position only if fit for it, after an examination. This means that family connections or any form of favoritism, such as party membership, will not count in the appointment to office in the civil government.

BISMARCK WAS A VERY GREAT STATESMAN. The Germans had good reason for being satisfied with their government, for in the period from 1871 to 1890 Bismarck dominated European politics. This was the result partly of his own ability, partly of the absence of powerful rivals, and partly of the political and economic strength of the German Empire, which by 1914 had a population of nearly seventy million. Moreover, Germany had the strongest army in the world, a marvelous industrial system, unsurpassed schools, many of the world's foremost scientists, and great economic resources in the presence of rich deposits of coal and iron.

BISMARCK ESTABLISHES SOCIAL SECURITY FOR THE POOR. To forestall the influence of the Social Democratic Party and partly also for other reasons, Bismarck adopted advanced measures of the nature of state socialism. He introduced insurance for old age, sickness, and accidents. So admirable did this work seem that many nations have since that time copied him. It is only in the last few years that the American government has taken such action.

Student Activities

1. With the aid of a dictionary write out the definitions for the following words: *imperialism, disapproved, pretext, prolong, dislodged, favoritism.*
2. Which two countries were still disunited while other countries were becoming larger and larger?
3. Which nation wished to prevent the formation of the Italian nation?
4. Who was Garibaldi?
5. Why is Bismarck considered such a great leader in German history?
6. How did Bismarck bring about a war between Germany and France?
7. Why did France lose the war of 1870-1871?
8. How many states made up the German Empire when it was formed in 1871?
   Note: Bismarck is considered one of the greatest if not the greatest German statesman. A good statesman is a leader who makes his country great and its people happy. How did Bismarck try to make the German people happy and satisfied?

CHAPTER 43

Russia, Austria-Hungary, and the Near East

THE REIGN OF CZAR ALEXANDER II. In the first half of the nineteenth century, as you saw, Russia was ruled by two autocratic czars in succession. But in 1855 followed Czar Alexander II (1855-1881), under whom a small measure of liberalism was introduced. In 1861 he abolished serfdom up to a considerable extent by enabling the peasants to buy some of the lands which they were cultivating. After a rebellion broke out in Poland in 1863, however, he turned conservative. He was assassinated in 1881 by a revolutionist.

MILLIONS OF SUBJECTS OF THE CZAR ARE GREATLY DISSATISFIED. Gradually a vast number of dissatisfied subjects rose against the Czar. In the first place, many subject races, such as Jews, Poles, Finns, Lithuanians, and Ukrainians, wanted independence for their people. In the second place, millions of peasants were extremely poor and owned no land, since in most cases the land around each village was owned collectively by the so-called *mir,* or community. They found a voice in the writings of influential Liberals.

HOW BAD CONDITIONS WERE IN RUSSIA, AND HOW SOME OF THE LIBERALS AND SOCIALISTS WERE PUNISHED. Shortly after the Revolution of 1848 the pastors in the Russian churches had to read a message to their congregations in which it was stated that the evil influences of western civilization were entering Russia. One day the police officers in St. Petersburg, which was then the capital of Russia, found some young men, some army officers, and some professors in a certain room reading socialistic writings. Thirty-three men were arrested and brought to a trial, which lasted six months. Twenty-one of them were condemned to death. A special commission was set up for the purpose of stopping books at the Russian frontier, and of examining books and papers in the libraries. Of the seventy million inhabitants in Russia, only 2900 were students in the universities. Only official newspapers were published, that is, papers controlled by the government. But even these had only a circulation of 12,000. Between 1832 and 1852 some 150,000 persons were sent in exile to Siberia, where the climate was horribly cold.

TERRORISTS AND ANARCHISTS MAKE CONDITIONS STILL WORSE. You understand that if the government of a country does not want to give the people the liberties they should have, many of them will become stubborn and want to take the law into their own hands. They feel that one injustice must be met by another one. For example, we had such a case recently in our own country. Labor leaders said that the General Motors Corp. and the Chrysler Corp. were not giving their workmen proper wages, and they were also not giving them a decent treatment. The men had to work too fast, and they were not permitted to bring their complaints collectively to their employers. In other words, they could not bargain with the employers in large numbers, and thus force the employers to give them better terms. So some leaders suggested to the men that they seize the factories and occupy them. They were not to let the owners and the representatives of the owners, such as presidents and superintendents, come into the factories. This was our notorious "sitdown strike." Many well-known writers thought that this step was a good thing, but our Constitution plainly says that it protects private property. Finally our Supreme Court declared that the sitdown strike was illegal. In Russia, of course, still worse things were done. Owners of factories were attacked and killed, and also officials in the government, including Czar Alexander II (1881). You will be interested to know that our worst labor leaders have taken over many radical ideas from the Russians. Among them there have been also some *anarchists,* whose aim is to overthrow the regular government.

THE ORTHODOX CHURCH MIGHT HAVE HELPED IMPROVE SOCIETY. The state church of Russia was called the Orthodox Church. The word "orthodox" means that a person or a doctrine is true to the teachings of the past. Orthodox Christians, for example, believe that the Christian Church as founded by Christ is the only true church; its teachings are correct. Modernists on the other hand say that there are many errors in the Bible and in the teachings of the earlier churches. The Orthodox Church in Russia was introduced by missionaries from Constantinople. It may also be called the Greek Catholic Church, for its founders brought into Russia the teachings of the Greek Church. Since the Christian Church was Greek in the beginning, as far as its language was concerned, and since the first Church Councils were all held in the eastern half of the Roman Empire, the Greek pastors and their pupils in Russia concluded that the eastern church was much better than the western church. The Russian clergymen were very slow to change their opinions, even when they were in the wrong. They did not condemn the wicked rulers when the poor were oppressed, and when Jews and foreign races were persecuted. That is why in the first two decades of the twentieth century so many Jews helped the Communists in attacking the leaders in the Church.

AT LAST THE RUSSIANS GET A LEGISLATIVE BODY CALLED THE DUMA. Czar Nicholas II for years refused to reform his government. But it so happened that in the years 1904-1905 Russia was involved in a war with Japan which is called the Russo-Japanese War. Russia lost this war, and now the government of this unhappy country naturally was blamed for the misfortunes that followed when peace was signed and Russia had to surrender to the Japanese a valuable region in Asia called Southern Manchuria, and a very important harbor called Port Arthur. The Liberals became much bolder now than they had been before. The Czar was afraid of being assassinated or of losing his throne. A revolution did break out in the year 1905, and so the ruler had to yield to the demands of the Liberals. The Czar granted the Russian people a constitution and a legislative body called the Duma. But as soon as conditions in Russia became more quiet, the ruler took much of the power away from this body. About ten years later, Russia was to be defeated again, and you will see that this time a very real change was made. The Communists overthrew the government entirely.

AUSTRIA AND HUNGARY MAKE AN AGREEMENT TO HAVE A COMMON GOVERNMENT. The situation in Austria-Hungary closely resembled that in Russia. Subject races and down-trodden peasants began to demand a voice in the government, to say the least. From 1849 to 1867 Hungary was dominated by Austria, but in 1867 a compromise was made between those leaders who wanted a unified country under German control and those who favored a federal state with local self-government for Hungarians, Slavs, etc. The compromise is known as the *Ausgleich,* the German word for compromise. Austria and Hungary each received a constitution and parliament, but they were jointly ruled by an emperor and had a common army and foreign policy, and they formed the Dual Monarchy. Each country ruled over many races (see map).

THE WAR FOUGHT BETWEEN RUSSIA AND TURKEY CAUSES MANY CHANGES. The foreign policies of both Russia and Austria-

Hungary were strongly affected by events in the Near East. Russia in 1877 declared war on Turkey, partly because the Turks nearly had devastated the country of the Bulgars who had rebelled against the Turks in 1876. Russia defeated Turkey, and in March 1878 the treaty of San Stefano was signed, giving Russia so much power in the Balkan Peninsula that Great Britain and Austria-Hungary took action to change the terms inposed by Russia.

ONE RESULT OF THE WAR IS THE CONGRESS OF BERLIN (1878). In 1878 the Congress of Berlin settled the frontiers in the Balkan Peninsula for 30 years. Here was present Disraeli, Prime Minister of Great Britain and a bitter foe of Russia. The statesmen assembled in Berlin decided to (1) reduce the size of Bulgaria and restore part of it to Turkey, (2) place the rest of Bulgaria under Turkish supervision, (3) declare Rumania, Serbia, and Montenegro independent of both Russia and Turkey, and (4) name Austria-Hungary as the protector of Bosnia and Herzegovina (they were annexed by Austria-Hungary in 1908).

WHY TURKEY IS CALLED THE "SICK MAN OF EUROPE." However, in 1885 Bulgaria seized part of the lands taken away from her in 1878, and in 1909 she became entirely independent of Turkey. Meanwhile, the former Ottoman Empire had become so greatly weakened that it was simply called Turkey. In cartoons it was often referred to as the "sick man" of Europe, because of its decadence. Moreover, a Mohammedan power in Europe seemed altogether out of place. The Mohammedans had long ago been driven out of Spain and Sicily. Why should they not leave the Balkan Peninsula as well? The only reason why they kept Constantinople was the jealousy among the great European powers, who did not wish Constantinople controlled by a state that would be likely to close the straits between the Black Sea and the Aegean Sea. The "sick man" remained ill, but did not die.

Student Activities

1. With the aid of a dictionary write out the definitions for the following words: *autocratic, abounded, exiles, compromise, decadence.*
2. Who were the *Nihilists?*
3. Describe conditions in Russia as depicted in this chapter.
4. What is meant by the term "Terrorists"?
5. What was the "sitdown" strike?
6. Explain the "Duma."
7. What is meant by the word "Ausgleich"?
8. Who was the "Sick Man of Europe"?
9. Why didn't the "Sick Man of Europe" die?
10. What were some of the faults of the Orthodox Church of Russia?

CHAPTER 44

Great Britain and France Finally Become Democratic

THE REIGN OF QUEEN VICTORIA. It was during the reign of Queen Victoria (1837-1901) that the British people at last got a truly democratic form of government. Her reign was one of the longest in European history. During those 74 years the British were exceedingly prosperous and powerful. Their ships covered all the great seas and oceans; their colonies were scattered in many parts of the world. Much progress was also made in the field of education, while the masses of the people received more attention from the government than ever before. Little did the average Englishmen then know what was in store for the island of Great Britain. It seemed indeed as if the British, together with many other western peoples, would continue for centuries to come on the road to more wealth, more enlightenment, and more happiness. Many were the teachers who told their pupils in those days that the human race had risen from misery and barbarism. No wonder that in their opinion the people could expect even more advancement in the twentieth century. All of this seemed to come without the permission or the power of God. That is exactly the reason why both Great Britain and France were so severely punished afterwards when they felt it was no longer necesary to rely upon God for peace and happiness.

LIBERALS AND CONSERVATIVES. Public opinion was divided between the ideas of the Liberals and of the Conservatives, who were led for decades by Gladstone and Disraeli. Gladstone was Prime Minister for the first time from 1868 to 1874. Being an ardent Liberal, he did much for the masses of the people. Unlike many Liberals on the Continent, he was deeply religious, and for many reasons he afterward received the title of the "Grand Old Man." First of all, he was responsible for the law of 1870 which established the public elementary school system of Great Britain. This country had lagged far behind Prussia and other continental nations in having sadly neglected to provide for universal elementary education, so that before 1870 fewer than half the children of school age received any education in school at all.

THE VALUE OF CIVIL SERVICE IS EXPLAINED.   Another reform of the utmost importance was that in the civil service. It was passed also in 1870, enabling anyone who had the required ability to pass public examination for offices in the civil government. Once more we must reflect on the importance of such a custom, for even in our own enlightened country there is still a need for more of it. It does not matter at all in the good performance of public duties whether a purchasing agent of a certain state happens to be a Republican or a Democrat; why should a person who is to forecast the weather be asked to serve above all his own party? Many a good citizen wonders sometimes whether the wholesale turnover of public officials in certain states every two years (or at least whenever a certain political party in power loses in the state elections) is necessary or desirable.

THE UNIVERSITIES ARE OPENED TO CATHOLICS AND PROTESTANTS ALIKE. Gladstone also was instrumental in opening the universities of Oxford and Cambridge to Roman Catholic students and to those Protestants who did not belong to the Church of England. This happened in 1871, and goes to show that in the growth of religious toleration Great Britain did not play a prominent part. Again we must recall the remarkable position of the United States.

THE CONSERVATIVES DEFEAT GLADSTONE AND STOP FURTHER REFORMS. Since millions of Englishmen were offended by Gladstone's reforms, his party was defeated in the elections of 1874 by the Conservatives under Disraeli, who was Prime Minister from 1874 to 1880. Disraeli favored a strong foreign policy, while Gladstone had followed a weak policy abroad, which was another reason for his defeat in 1874. One important step taken by Disraeli was the purchase of a block of shares in the Suez Canal (1875), which had been dug in 1869 by a French company to connect the Mediterranean Sea with the Red Sea and India beyond. Disraeli also did much for British interests when he attended the Conference of Berlin, as you saw (1878).

TWO IMPORTANT POLITICAL REFORMS IN 1884 AND 1885. But the Liberals soon returned to power under Gladstone, whose reform bill of 1884 extended the voting power to about two million men. In 1885 there was a third redistribution of the seats in the House of Commons, giving England 495, Scotland 72, and Ireland 103, making a total of 670.

The Irish Question Comes Up When Gladstone Returns to Power. Gladstone also wished to relieve the Irish people of some of their burdens. As you saw, many English landlords owned much land in Ireland. They usually spent the income from these lands in England. Certain unfair laws weighed heavily upon the Irish tenants, and until 1868 the Catholics in Ireland were compelled to pay taxes for the support of the Church of England. Gladstone *disestablished* the Church of England in Ireland in 1868, while in 1870 he also improved the land laws of Ireland for the benefit of the Irish tenants. Several times in succession Gladstone tried to give the Irish Home Rule, but not until 1910 was a Home Rule Bill passed; it was not yet in operation when the World War broke out in 1914. After the War other demands were made, so that the Home Rule Bill never went into effect.

Why Millions of Irishmen Leave For the United States. In the meantime, several million Irishmen left for America. Especially about 1845 Irish emigration was heavy, owing in part to the so-called potato famine, for the dampness of the weather for several years in a row caused the main crop of the Irish to rot in the fields. But there were also the factors mentioned above which forced numerous Irishmen to seek better conditions in the United States. They settled in especially large numbers around Boston.

In How Far the Governments of Great Britain and Our Country Are Alike. Since 1911 there have been no important changes made in the British government, so that we are now in a position to compare the workings of that government with our own. Among the points of similarity we note: (1) the democratic feature is present, for all adult males (and later the females as well) able to be about in public may vote; (2) there is the division of the legislature into two houses; (3) the executive, be he called king or president, has only limited power, the people exercising its sovereign power mainly through the operation of the legislature; (4) the government is regularly elected in accordance with each constitution, though the members of the House of Lords and the king in Great Britain are not elected but retain their offices for life — we have in mind here the main power in the government; (5) political parties may be freely formed without interference from the government in any capacity, except that anarchists and unruly radicals will be somewhat restricted in their activities. These five features compare very favorably with those of any other major government in the world today, or at any time in the past.

IMPORTANT DIFFERENCES BETWEEN THE TWO TYPES OF GOVERNMENT. There are also important differences between the two governments under discussion: (1) Our president is elected for a period of four years, but the king of Great Britain inherits his title for life; we must repeat here the fact, which is often overlooked, that Parliament has no power to decide who shall be the next king when one dies or has been deposed; only God can tell who the heirs of any king shall be. (2) The American cabinet comes and goes with each president, and it can be seen in advance how long it will assist the president, though the president may remove some members; but the British cabinet holds office only as long as the Prime Minister retains his post, which is decided by the members in the House of Commons. These ministers in the cabinet, including the Prime Minister, may not remain for more than five years, for at least once in five years there has to be a new election for seats in the House of Commons. If the Prime Minister fails to please the majority in the House of Commons, he will at once lose his office, and then the whole cabinet will go with him. Sometimes there will be a new election on such an occasion, and sometimes not, the issue being determined by the gravity of the situation. (3) In this country the executive and the legislative branches of the government often engage in a conflict, but in Great Britain the two branches are controlled by members of the same party and work in the same direction. (4) In our Senate the members sit for six years and are elected for that term; in the House of Lords the members sit for life and either inherit their seats or are appointed to them by the king. (5) In our House of Representatives the members have seats for two years; in the House of Commons they sit for a maximum of five years and sometimes may not remain more than a few days, their term of office depending entirely on how soon there will be another election. (6) In Congress the division of power is balanced between the two houses; in Parliament the House of Lords has lost nearly all its former powers.

How MUCH POWER THE BRITISH KING HAS. It is difficult to estimate the power of the British king. One might say that he "reigns but does not rule," but that statement is often misunderstood. The king wields invisible power. We have nothing in this country to compare with this office. But we must be careful to refrain from thinking that the king has nothing to do with the functions of the government. He weathers all storms, unless he is a most undesirable person. He belongs to no political party, but stands above them all. He is the permanent mast on the British ship of state.

THE THIRD FRENCH REPUBLIC IS ESTABLISHED. We must now turn to the political history of France after 1870. It will seem peculiar to you. The French people, as we saw, in 1870 overthrew their Second Empire, and set up the Third Republic. In 1871 a civil war threatened to ruin France, but it passed. The tactful Thiers persuaded various political leaders to bury their differences until the huge war debt was paid. In 1875 the Third Republic was fully established under the "Organic Laws." Three such laws were passed, and formed the constitution.

HOW FRANCE WAS TO BE GOVERNED. The new constitution provided that the system of departments established in 1789 remain the same, and also the government of the smaller units. The executive power was to be wielded by a president, assisted by ministers who were responsible to the legislature. The latter was made up of two houses, namely, the Senate, whose members were elected by indirect election for nine years, and the Chamber of Deputies, chosen for a term of four years by manhood suffrage, which was no longer limited by property qualification but was universal and also direct. The president was elected by a joint meeting of the two houses; his term of office was seven years.

THE POLITICAL PARTIES AND THE PRIME MINISTER. Political parties in France have been numerous, and as a rule the position of a Prime Minister has been rather short in duration, often less than a year. But when he lost his office, there was no great need of a new election, as often happens in Great Britain.

THE POLITICIANS WEAKEN THE CHURCH AND THE CLERGY. From 1875 to 1914 French politics were marked by anti-clerical agitation. The Liberals weakened the power of the clergy and of the church in general. In 1905 the Concordant of 1801 was dropped and the Church and State were separated. As a result, the pastors no longer receive a salary from the government, but the Church has not recovered its lost property.

IN FOREIGN AFFAIRS FRANCE REMAINS WEAK. French foreign policy before the World War was far from brilliant or impressive. But, after having been isolated for twenty years by Bismarck, France found a strong friend in Russia. In 1894 she signed with that country the Dual Alliance, which strengthened her against an attack by Germany. You will hear more about this friendship with Russia in another chapter.

Student Activities

1. With the aid of a dictionary write out the definitions for the following words: *allegiance, prominent, policy, disestablished, similarity, refrain, tactful, wielded, isolated.*
2. Why is the reign of Queen Victoria so important in British history?
3. Who was Gladstone?
4. Who was Disraeli?
5. What is meant by the term, "Civil Service"?
6. Why were the Irish opposed to the English?
7. Where did most of the Irish locate when they came to the United States to settle?
8. In what ways are the governments of the United States and Great Britain alike, and in what ways are they unlike?
9. How much power does the British king have?
10. Who is the prime minister of England?
11. In what nation did France find a friend before the World War?

CHAPTER 45

Trade and Industry Continue to Expand

CAPITALISTIC SOCIETY HAS MADE IT POSSIBLE FOR BUSINESS TO EXPAND. The rise of capitalistic society in the western world since the middle of the eighteenth century has been accompanied by an enormous expansion of commerce and industry. This in turn has resulted in a demand for swifter means of transportation, cheaper and more rapid ways of production, and numerous inventions.

AT FIRST GREAT BRITAIN WAS AHEAD OF THE UNITED STATES AND GERMANY. Great Britain, as we saw, was the first to experience the Industrial Revolution. Only two other countries — the United States and Germany — have enjoyed advantages that can be compared with those possessed by the British. They both have had excellent deposits of coal and iron, and they both have been blessed with an industrious population. Moreover, in both countries certain areas at least enjoyed excellent natural means of transportation, which have resulted in the rapid growth of large cities.

WHY THE OTHER COUNTRIES COULD NOT KEEP UP WITH THESE THREE. France did not possess enough coal for her needs, Italy had still less, Austria lacked both coal and fertile soil that could be cultivated, Spain was backward for the same reasons, and Russia had been very slow to develop its natural resources, because for a long time it was far removed from the western countries.

FULTON INVENTS THE STEAMSHIP. As we have seen, rapid means of transportation were a decided advantage in the development of commerce and industry. In 1807, Robert Fulton acquired fame with his paddlewheel ship called the *Clermont,* which under its own steam power navigated the Hudson River. You can easily understand how much this invention helped to increase trade and traveling.

Stephenson Invents the Steam Locomotive. Steamships Cross the Seas. About 1825 the British inventor, George Stephenson, made a usable steam locomotive, with the result that in 1825 the first commercial steam railroad was opened between Stockton and Darlington. In 1830 the passenger line between Manchester and Liverpool was completed. At the same time steam power was applied to ocean shipping. In 1819 the first ship using steam power crossed the Atlantic Ocean, but about twenty years passed before ships propelled by steam power only could successfully cover the three thousand miles that separate Europe from America.

What the Telegraph, the Telephone, and the Postage Stamp Have Done for Us. Means of communication were aided also by new inventions. In 1844 Samuel Morse, an American inventor, perfected the electric telegraph; and in 1875 Alexander Bell, another American inventor, completed the telephone. In the meantime, a cable was laid in the English Channel to connect England and France by 1851, and in 1866 the cable between England and the United States was finished. The adoption of the postage stamp by the British government in 1840 was another aid to rapid communication.

Chemists Show How to Make Iron and Steel. Electric Power Comes into Use. Of great importance in the industrial world has been the development of chemical processes which have made it possible to extract iron from its ore. The production of steel has also been accompanied by important inventions. Besides, the development of electric power has been of great value to mountainous countries which possessed an abundance of water power but almost no coal, such as Italy, Switzerland, and Norway. The petroleum industry has likewise become a rival of coal, but a distinct asset to many nations.

Edison Invents the Electric Light Bulb. One of the greatest inventions was perfected by Edison, who developed the electric light bulb. But the use of gas has also had considerable historical importance. Today it is used more for heating purposes than for lighting.

Other Useful Inventions. The art of photography and reproduction of sound through the phonograph form two other fascinating fields of human enterprises. Scientific agriculture has been vastly assisted by the harvester machinery, such as that first developed by Cyrus McCormick in 1831. Needless to say, the automobile, the typewriter, the dictaphone, the sewing machine,

THE FIRST
AUTOMOBILE

This steam omni-
bus ran between
London and Bir-
mingham in 1833.

LAYING THE
ATLANTIC
CABLE

Among the diffi-
culties encountered
were whales which
fouled the line as
it was being low-
ered into place.

THE COTTON
PRINT
MACHINE

This was the meth-
od employed in
printing cotton
goods in 1840.

A MODERN
COTTON MILL

Endless rows of
twisters show the
complex machinery
of a modern tex-
tile factory.

the printing presses, the production of rubber tires, and artificial refrigeration have brought endless comforts to the human race.

How Capitalism Works. The rapidly growing commerce and industry in the period between 1750 and 1900 was accompanied by an enormous expansion in banking facilities. Moreover, numerous corporations sprung up, and shares of stock were sold by the millions in the great cities of the western world. In this way modern capitalism reached its greatest extent and power. The building of factories and the installation of heavy machinery required a vast amount of capital, which as a rule was supplied by the men who did not perform the mechanical labor, while the workmen who did supply the labor seldom acquired a share in the ownership of the means of production.

Population Increases Rapidly. At the same time the increase in population was remarkable. For example, the population of England and Wales between 1801 and 1901 grew from less than nine million to thirty-two million; today it is over forty-five million. At the same time the cities grew with still greater speed while the rural population remained stationary, and in some cases decreased considerably. Emigration was another phenomenon of the nineteenth century. It was caused partly by unfavorable economic conditions in various European countries and partly by unpleasant political developments.

The Bad Features of the Factory System as First Used. We may repeat here that in the early stages of the Industrial Revolution many evils accompanied the rapid expansion in commerce and industry. The workmen and their families in most cases had moved from healthful rural districts to crowded cities. The clouds of smoke hung above the town all day and all night. Streams and canals were polluted with dirt from the factories. Not only did the workmen have to work from ten to fourteen hours a day in stuffy factories, but mere children and young women were employed in both factories and in mines. They had left their homes and now were working for strangers who often cruelly exploited them.

General Results of the Factory System. A sad feature of the early factory system was the inability of skilled and ambitious young artisans to compete with men who owned large buildings and working capital. Moreover, mass production has led to a deplorable loss of individualism and personal independence. Lack of social security resulted in much unrest and misery, and these conditions in turn produced such movements as Socialism and Syndicalism, as you have observed in an earlier chapter.

Student Activities

1. With the aid of a dictionary write out the definitions for the following words: *accompanied, perfected, petroleum, artisans, deplorable.*
2. Which country went ahead first in the building up of factories?
3. Why are Fulton and Stephenson important persons in the story of transportation?
4. In what way has the introduction of the postage stamp helped to increase communication?
5. Make a list of important inventions and inventors mentioned in this chapter.
6. What effect did the Industrial Revolution have on populations?
7. What were some of the bad features in the factory system?
   Note: The word, "Capital," generally means the money that is necessary to build and run factories. This capital is usually loaned by banks to men who direct the building and running of factories. These men are called "industrials"; in the United States they were called "Captains of Industry."

CHAPTER 46

Western Civilization in the Nineteenth Century

EUROPEAN CIVILIZATION BECOMES WORLD-WIDE. During the nineteenth century European civilization followed European commerce, so that it spread into all the countries of the world. In this manner European civilization, or western civilization, became world-wide. At the same time, however, European civilization itself was affected by constant contact with various other countries, as in Asia, America, and the islands in the Pacific Ocean. The world will never again be what it once was, for now it will be impossible for a civilization to develop entirely apart from those that were before it. You will see that in many respects the civilization of the nineteenth century was highly advanced, while in other directions it did not compare favorably with the culture of earlier periods.

SCIENTIFIC PROGRESS. Since nineteenth century civilization was dominated by scientific progress, we shall begin our survey with a brief description of this remarkable progress. We are struck first of all by the admirable work done by the experts in physics. Lavoissier had indicated in the eighteenth century that matter is indestructible, and about 1850 it was shown that energy remains constant and is conserved. Since 1850 much attention was paid to the atom, which was a part of a molecule. Later it was proved that the atom is a very small solar system comprising electrons which rotate.

ADVANCEMENT IN CHEMISTRY. In the field of chemistry equally fine work was accomplished. After 1850, when the Germans became very active in the field of the physical sciences, analytical chemistry was combined with the newer science, that is, creative chemistry. For example, the scientists learned to produce over 300,000 compounds of carbon with other elements, only a few of which had been made by nature itself. Moreover, over 5000 artificial dyes have been produced.

CHEMISTRY HAS HELPED THE FARMER AND THE BUSINESSMAN. Chemistry has also become a great asset to modern industry and agriculture, in that it has assisted various scientists in the manufacture of rubber, rayon, synthetic minerals, and fertilizers.

ELECTRICAL ENGINEERING. Electrical engineering developed into a new science of great importance. Volta (after whom the "volt" was named) and Galvani (whose name is given to the *Galvanic* battery) made valuable experiments with electric currents. Marconi did much for the perfection of wireless telegraphy.

THE STUDY OF PLANTS AND ANIMALS LEADS TO THE THEORY OF EVOLUTION. Under the leadership of Charles Darwin, who wrote *The Origin of Species,* many scientists came to the conclusion that mankind has existed upon this earth for more than 300,000 years. Man, they said, has been developed out of a type of creature that was partly animal and partly human. They said that this type of ape-man no longer exists. They believed with Darwin that species are not fixed and unalterable but change in the course of many centuries, and thus new species are started.

MISTAKES MADE BY DARWIN AND HIS FOLLOWERS. These Darwinian scientists did much useful work, but they failed to recognize many spiritual factors which their instruments could not show. They paid too little attention to the element of planning in creative work, and too much attention to the work done by the creatures. They thought so seldom about God and Christ that they became blind in a certain way, for they could not see the power of God. It is true that some of these scientists were able to produce new kinds of flowers and fruits, but even so their work did not get very important results. For example, much was said about the new plants, the new flowers, and the new animals. But what did this all mean? Merely a different sort of tulip, for example, or a new kind of a cabbage, or an improved kind of a cow or dog. How poor were those "creations" when compared with God's creation of plants and animals!

EXCELLENT WORK IS DONE IN THE FIELD OF MEDICINE. Especially in the field of medicine, science proved itself to be of the utmost benefit to the human race. The inventions and the discoveries of the medical experts have been more beneficial to the human race than any others. The death rate has been cut in half, the birth rate has gone up, young mothers have received much better care in childbirth, pain has been removed during operations through the use of anesthetics, and the nature of germs in the course of disease has been made known by Pasteur and others.

Moreover, the work of insects in the spread of disease has also been noted: The mosquito carries yellow fever, and the rat and the flea transmit the Bubonic (Black) Plague.

The Social Sciences. In a certain sense, history, political science, economics, geography, sociology, and anthropology belong also to the sciences, for they are now called the social sciences. In this enormous field new knowledge and new methods are constantly added to the knowledge of former centuries. Archeologists have discovered traces of human life and work in ancient Egypt and Mesopotamia that prove how true is the old Bible history. Their labors seem to indicate clearly that mankind was highly civilized almost from the very beginning, but that in regions far removed from ancient Egypt and Mesopotamia the high level of culture was not originally maintained, so that afterward it had to be restored through renewed contact with these first centers of civilized life.

We Live in an Age of Specialists. We now have so many experts in so many fields that it is entirely impossible for one person to obtain more than an elementary knowledge of several subjects. Nevertheless, it is most necessary for the student of history to try to follow progress in all the sciences, as well as in literature, the fine arts, and education in general.

What Realism and Romanticism in Literature Are. It may be said for the literature of the nineteenth century that it certainly is as interesting as that of any other century. We note in particular two remarkable movements called respectively Romanticism and Realism. Romanticism was a literary movement that was intended to glorify the "romantic" qualities in human nature and in the world about us, that is, mysterious, wonderful, impressive, and stirring themes. Romantic literature revived interest in medieval civilization, when "knighthood was in flower," and it paid less attention to classical culture than the writers of the eighteenth century had done. For that reason it was more nationalistic than the earlier school. It also was colored by revived interest in religion and medieval philosophy.

Examples of Romantic Literature. Among the notable examples of Romantic literature may be mentioned the German poetry of the Storm and Stress Movement (*Sturm und Drang*), written by Heine and Schiller (Goethe's *Faust* also partakes of elements of Romanticism). Other authors were Walter Scott, who wrote admirable historical novels; the American poet Longfellow; Thomas Gray, the author of *Elegy Written in a Country*

Churchyard; Oliver Goldsmith, who composed *The Deserted Village;* Wordsworth and Coleridge, the poets of the Lake District in England; and the landscape poets in the United States, such as Lowell, Bryant, and Whittier. Among the writers of fanciful verse rank Keats and Shelley.

SOME WRITERS PRODUCED BOTH TYPES OF LITERATURE. Writers who belonged to both the Romantic and the Classical movements abounded in many countries. Goethe (the author of *Faust*) was perhaps the greatest of these. Schiller's *William Tell* is classical in structure but romantic in content. Victor Hugo wrote romantic drama. Great writers of novels were Dickens, Jane Austen (who came much earlier), Balzac, Freytag, Manzoni, and Sienkiewicz.

NATURE OF REALISTIC LITERATURE. Realism is usually distinguished from Romanticism in that it tends to frown upon the products of the imagination, and devotes itself very largely to a description of things as they actually are. Moreover, it shows a greater interest in the more common and vulgar aspects of human life than does Romanticism.

EXAMPLES OF REALISTIC LITERATURE. Among the important writers of realistic literature are Victor Hugo, the author of the famous work entitled *Les Miserables;* De Maupassant, who wrote admirable short stories; Thomas Hardy and George Meredith, who represent the Victorian school in England; Zola, Hauptmann, and Sudermann, who were noted for their radical political views; the same is true of the two great Russian writers, Tolstoy and Turgeniev. Excellent poetic dramas were produced by the two poets, Tennyson and Browning. One of the greatest of all the realistic writers was Ibsen, the author of the famous dramas, *Brand* and *Peer Gynt.* Kipling acquired a great reputation with his popular stories and poems.

THE GERMANS LEAD IN THE FIELD OF MUSIC. Music in the nineteenth century was enriched by the Germans, notably by the labors of Von Beethoven, who is regarded by many critics as the greatest expert in the history of music. Moreover, Wagner was the outstanding composer of grand opera. Other German composers were Schubert, Schumann, and Mendelssohn. Strauss, a native of Vienna, composed admirable waltzes, of which the *Blue Danube* is the most popular.

OTHER COMPOSERS OF FINE MUSIC. Other great composers of the nineteenth century are Chopin, a Pole; Tchaikovsky, a Russian; and Verdi, an Italian.

THE MODERNISTS ATTACK THE BIBLE AND THE CHRISTIAN RELIGION. Religion and philosophy in the nineteenth century were greatly affected by biblical criticism and modernism. Under the leadership of Voltaire, a school of philosophers and critics developed which taught that a large part of the Bible is inaccurate. The most famous of these critics was Ernest Renan, who stated in his biographies of Christ that He was but a mere man, and that both the New Testament and the Old Testament contained numerous myths and legends.

WHY FEWER PEOPLE WENT TO CHURCH. Both modernism and Socialism resulted in much skepticism among the masses of the people. Consequently, they began to desert church services and they lost interest in religion. Besides, the rapid means of transportation tempted many weary workmen to spend the Sunday somewhere in the country. Finally, the introduction of the radio into millions of homes afterward added to the numerous distractions.

RELIGIOUS DEVELOPMENTS. Nevertheless, it was in the nineteenth century (1870) that the higher clergy in the Roman Catholic Church decreed the doctrine of papal infallibility. According to this doctrine, the Pope never errs in matters of faith. Moreover, in the same century occurred a great religious revival within the Church of England, which is called the Oxford Movement.

THREE FAMOUS GERMAN PHILOSOPHERS. Among the outstanding philosophers of the nineteenth century we may note Kant and Hegel. Kant was of the opinion that the knowledge gained through the senses is the only reliable information, but that religious experience and doctrines are of the greatest value. Hegel was an idealist. Nietzsche had much to say about the super-man, and he thought that the Germans would become the foremost race of super-men.

EDUCATION BECOMES MORE WIDESPREAD THAN EVER BEFORE. The nineteenth century was characterized by the greatest increase in popular culture that the world has ever known. The universal franchise and popular education inevitably led to a high level of popular culture. Moreover, even the humblest laborer began to participate in the increased demand for more comforts and more knowledge and more amusements. Class distinctions gradually tended to become more vague, but did not entirely disappear. In the matter of clothing and housing we observe the same tendency. Even in the field of architecture, as well as in the industrial arts, the tendency of mass production removed to an increased degree the distinction between superior qualities and mediocre work.

COMPARISON BETWEEN NINETEENTH CENTURY CIVILIZATION AND THE SITUATION IN OUR OWN TIME. When we compare the culture of the western world in the second half of the nineteenth century with that in the first third of the twentieth century, we are struck by the loss of political liberty and the increase in international hostility that had come about since the end of the nineteenth century.

Student Activities

1. With the aid of a dictionary write out the definitions for the following words: *dominated, admirable, solar, rotate, synthetic, anesthetics, expert, animosity.*
2. What do you understand by the term, "Science"?
3. Who was Darwin?
4. What good work was done in the field of medicine during the nineteenth century?
5. Why is it impossible to learn everything that is to be known? What are "Specialists"?
6. Make a list of five important authors named in this chapter.
7. In what way did the "Modernists" attack the Bible?
8. Why did fewer people go to church?

CHAPTER 47

A Century of European Imperialism

THE BRITISH ACQUIRE AUSTRALIA AND NEW ZEALAND. During
the nineteenth century Great Britain continued to lead all
European powers in the expansion of her fleet, her merchant
marine, and her colonial empire. Owing in part to the immense
successes achieved during the Industrial Revolution of the second
half of the eighteenth century, the British proceeded to occupy
valuable territories in those parts of the world where the climate
was temperate, so that it was suitable for European settlers. In
Australia the British organized a penal settlement for convicts.
The country was excellent for the cultivation of wheat and for
sheep ranching; gold was mined in moderate quantities. In 1840
the British annexed New Zealand. In 1842 they took the important
port of Hong Kong near the coast of China. In the next year they
began their occupation of Natal in Africa.

BRITISH RULE EXPANDS IN INDIA. On the mainland of India,
Great Britain consolidated its various settlements along the coast,
and gradually occupied large portions of the interior. The native
princes, however, were not bothered after 1857, in which year
the British officials learned, as a result of a rebellion, that it was
unwise to remove the native princes. Today there are still several
hundred of them. Impressed by the enormous size and the possi-
bilities of colonization in India, Queen Victoria in 1876 assumed
the title of "Empress of India."

BRITISH AND BOERS IN SOUTH AFRICA. We have seen in an
earlier chapter that in 1815 Great Britain received from the
Dutch the valuable territory in south Africa called Cape Colony.
Between 1830 and 1850 the settlers of Dutch descent, who were
called the Boers, were not entirely satisfied with British rule.
For that reason a large number of them moved to the north, where
they founded two republics, called the Transvaal and the Orange
Free State. About 1880 the British made an attempt to annex the
Transvaal, but the Boers defeated the British troops at this time.

However, the British were more successful in Egypt, which country they occupied in 1882.

THE SUEZ CANAL PROVIDES THE BRITISH WITH SEVERAL AD-VANTAGES. You have already seen that Disraeli bought a large block of stock in the Suez Canal Company. This block of stock belonged to the ruler of Egypt, who was in financial difficulties in 1875, and for that reason sold his stock to the British government. On an average the British have secured one hundred percent return from that investment each year. The sum that the British paid for it originally was about twenty million dollars, which no doubt was one of the best investments ever made by them.

THE FRENCH AND THE BRITISH IN THE SUDAN. HOW THE BRITISH GOT EGYPT. South of Egypt was located the valuable region called the Sudan. It used to belong to Egypt, but about 1885 Egypt lost control of it. For about ten years no European power occupied it. But in 1898 the French took steps to annex it, much to the displeasure of the British. It seemed for a time as if war was to break out as a result of the rivalry of the French and the British in this territory, but in 1904 the French agreed to let the British occupy it, but on condition that they themselves would receive a free hand in Morocco. In 1914 Egypt became a British protectorate, owing to the fact that the Turks, who had possessed Egypt ever since 1517, were now at war with Great Britain. So now, for the first time in about four hundred years, Egypt was independent of Turkey.

THE BOERS ARE DEFEATED AND THE UNION OF SOUTH AFRICA IS SET UP. At the end of the nineteenth century, Great Britain decided to take steps to annex the whole of South Africa, largely because of the fact that gold and diamonds had been discovered there, and much money had been invested in the mines by the British. Friction with the Boers resulted in the so-called Boer War, which lasted for three years (1899-1902), and in which the Boers were defeated, and lost their independence. In 1909 the federal union of South Africa was set up as a British Dominion. The British wisely gave the Boers a fairly reasonable treatment, so that about half of them have remained loyal subjects of the British government.

FURTHER ANNEXATIONS OF TERRITORY BY GREAT BRITAIN. The British also occupied other parts of Africa, especially in the region between Egypt and South Africa. They wanted to have enough land in various regions so that they could construct a railroad later reaching all the way from the Mediterranean coast to

South Africa. They also annexed certain regions in northwest Africa, as a study of the map will show you.

THE FRENCH COLONIES IN AFRICA. Although Great Britain finally secured a larger part of Africa than any other European power, it should be noted here that France was the first to annex a large section of Africa. As early as 1830 France led the revival of European imperialism by seizing Algeria. In 1881 she began her occupation of Tunis in northern Africa. A little later the French extended their colonial empire in the Sahara Desert, and they also annexed the large island near the east coast of Africa called Madagascar. In the Far East the French still held a valuable region called Indo-China.

GERMANY AND FRANCE GET NEW COLONIES AFTER THE WAR OF 1870. At the conclusion of the Franco-Prussian War in 1871, both France and Germany suddenly felt a strong desire for obtaining colonies, in order that they might find markets for their manufactured products and raw materials for their industries. Furthermore, the extraordinary inventions that had resulted in more rapid transportation brought the world beyond the oceans into closer contact with Europe. As you have seen, a French company dug the Suez Canal. The Germans established the colonies called German Southwest Africa, German East Africa, and the Kamerun.

PORTUGUESE AND ITALIAN COLONIES IN AFRICA. The Portuguese still held two valuable colonies in Africa, namely, Angola on the west coast and Mozambique on the east coast. Italy seized two strips of land to the east of Ethiopia (Abyssinia). In 1911 she took Tripoli (Libya), shortly after having failed to conquer Ethiopia. This region she wrested from the Ottoman Turks, after having declared war on them.

THE BELGIAN CONGO. Even little Belgium participated in the scramble to secure a part of Africa. King Leopold II of Belgium took a personal interest in the exploration of a vast territory in central Africa, which came to be known as the Congo Free State. Unfortunately, the king did not keep this region free at all, and in 1908 he sold his claims to this territory to the Belgian government.

EUROPEAN EXPANSION IN THE FAR EAST. European imperialism was also felt in the Far East. China had for centuries refused to open her frontiers to the merchants and settlers of Europe. This country was the oldest in the world in that it had retained its own culture for more than two thousand years. Behind their Great Wall, which was the largest structure ever put together in the history of the world, the Chinese had preserved their ancient civilization. Before the year 1000 A.D. they had invented printing, the manufacture of gun powder, the production of porcelain, and the mariner's compass. You will remember that about 550 A.D. the Chinese secret of silk manufacture was discovered by some Christian monks who carried it to the Byzantine Empire. The Chinese had learned the Buddhist religion from the peoples of India, but they had also added a religion of their own, which had been established by Confucius. Their civilization was marked by great respect for authority, which was noted especially in the obedience of children to their parents.

THE CHINESE BECOME INDEPENDENT OF THE MONGOL RULERS. In the Middle Ages the Chinese had been subject to a Mongolian people that was closely related to them, that is, the Manchus, after whom Manchuria was named. But in early modern times the Chinese had absorbed most of the Manchus, so that in the nineteenth century only the rule of a foreign dynasty remained as a proof of the conquest of ages ago. The Chinese were now ruled by a despotism. Their Emperor was assisted by a bureaucracy, which was inefficient and corrupt. For that reason the foreigners in China usually insisted on the enjoyment of extraterritoriality, which means that they would be subject to the laws of their own country. In 1911 the Manchu government was overthrown at last.

THE GREAT EUROPEAN NATIONS SEIZE CHINESE TERRITORIES. The Chinese government had tried to end the use of opium, which was imported from India. Opium is a very harmful drug, but the British traders made big profits in selling it to the Chinese. In the friction with the British government that followed this action, the British had taken Hong Kong. After 1860 France, Russia, and Germany all tried to obtain slices of Chinese territory, but they were all surpassed by the Japanese.

JAPAN BEGINS TO TRADE WITH EUROPEAN COUNTRIES. Originally Japan had received nearly all the elements of her civilization from China. The country was ruled by an absolute monarch, the *mikado*. From 1600 to 1641 the Dutch had made the Japanese acquainted with western civilization, and for the next two hundred years they continued to trade regularly with Japan. They took the place of the Portuguese by 1641 because they had not made a strong effort to convert the Japanese to Christianity, and because they were now more powerful in the Far East than any other European nation.

OUR COMMODORE PERRY FORCES THE JAPANESE TO ADMIT FOREIGN TRADERS IN LARGER NUMBERS THAN BEFORE. In 1853

Commodore Perry brought Japan into a more active contact with the western world, and from this date the Japanese rapidly reorganized their government, their army, and their navy. Also in the field of commerce, industry, agriculture, and education Japan successfully imitated the Europeans and Americans.

JAPAN SEIZES THE ISLAND OF FORMOSA. The war that was fought between Japan and China in 1894-1895 showed clearly the advantages that Japan had derived from its adoption of European civilization. China was quickly defeated and surrendered to Japan the island of Formosa and some territory on the mainland of Asia.

RUSSIA GETS SOUTHERN MANCHURIA AND PORT ARTHUR. But part of this land was occupied by Russia, which took Port Arthur. The important country of Korea remained independent. Germany, France, and Great Britain each obtained a lease of some other coastal territories.

JAPAN ANNEXES PORT ARTHUR AND KOREA. Friction between Russia and Japan resulted in the Russo-Japanese War (1904-1905), in which Japan decisively defeated Russia. In 1905 Russia lost Port Arthur to Japan, and Korea became a province of the Japanese, although they did not annex Korea until 1910.

THE JAPANESE ENTER SOUTHERN MANCHURIA. In the meantime the Japanese encroached on Manchuria. In 1932 they seized the whole country from China and renamed it Manchukuo. The war between Japan and China which began in 1937 may be considered a continuation of Japan's efforts to occupy China, as you will see soon.

Student Activities

1. With the aid of a dictionary write out the definitions for the following words: *penal, consolidated, protectorate, annex, absorbed, superceded.*
2. Make a list of those parts of the world which Great Britain annexed.
3. What was the chief cause of the war between the Boers and the British?
4. Which parts of Africa did the French take over?
5. Draw a map of Africa showing the parts which belong to European nations.
6. Which parts of China were seized by European nations?
7. Who were the Manchus?
8. Who opened Japan up to the western nations?
9. What has Japan been trying to do since about 1895?
10. When did the Japanese take over Korea?
    Note: You have noticed how each nation is trying to grab as much territory as possible in the so-called backward parts of the world. Much of this was pure robbery, and all nations were guilty of it. Man as well as a nation is very greedy by nature.

CHAPTER 48

The World Is Plunged Into War

THE FIRST WORLD WAR IS CAUSED BY MANY FACTORS. Like the Reformation of the sixteenth century, and the French Revolution of the eighteenth century, the World War, which broke out in 1914, was caused by a variety of factors. Some of these were of long duration, and they could scarcely be noticed. Others were what you might call immediate causes of the war, and these could be more easily detected by journalists and historians. In this chapter we shall analyze the most important causes that started the World War, and at the same time we shall also consider the question as to which power was more guilty than some of the others.

TWO ALLIANCES PREPARE FOR WAR. Among the underlying causes of the World War which will be considered here are first of all the two sets of alliances which divided almost the whole of Europe into two armed camps. The older of the two alliances is the so-called Triple Alliance. It was the work of Bismarck, who was no doubt the outstanding diplomat of the nineteenth century. Even before Bismarck had begun to form this alliance, he had been successful in cementing friendship among the three European emperors of Russia, Austria-Hungary, and Germany; and thus he had established the Three Emperors' League in 1872. This league was renewed in 1875, but at the Congress of Berlin, Bismarck was sorry to observe the hostility between the Russians and the Austrians.

RUSSIA WANTS TO EXPAND INTO THE BALKAN PENINSULA. Russia, as we have seen, had just concluded a successful war against the Turks, and she had proceeded to enlarge her power in the Balkan Peninsula, much to the displeasure of the Austrians, who had persuaded Bismarck to call in Disraeli and so the Congress of Berlin had resulted in 1878. Here Russia had been told in no uncertain terms by the rulers of Great Britain, Germany, and Austria-Hungary, that she must not extend her power any farther to the south in the Balkan Peninsula. Little

362

wonder that at this time Bismarck was no longer able to continue with his Three Emperors' League. For this reason he began to rely more and more on a closer friendship with Austria-Hungary.

How the Triple Alliance Was Formed. In 1879 followed the alliance between Germany and Austria-Hungary, which was intended to protect Austria against Russia, and Germany against France when supported by Russia. It was as a result of this "Dual Alliance" of 1879 that Germany and Austria-Hungary were allies in the World War. In 1882 the Triple Alliance grew out of the "Dual Alliance," when Italy joined the other two powers. Italy at this time was angry at France, for in 1881 France had annexed Tunis, which Italy had expected to take herself. Italy promised to aid Germany if Germany were attacked by France, and both Germany and Austria-Hungary promised Italy that they would support her if she were attacked by France. But Italy did not agree to help Austria-Hungary if she were attacked. The Triple Alliance was renewed every five years, but it lapsed in 1915.

After Bismarck Is Gone the German Government Is Unable to Keep the Friendship of Russia. When in 1890 William II became emperor of Germany (the *Kaiser*), he dismissed the powerful Bismarck, and now Russia drew away from Germany, and became ever more friendly with France. Between 1870 and 1890 France had been isolated by Bismarck, but after 1890 Germany was gradually being isolated by France, Russia, and Great Britain.

From 1878 to 1900 the British Show Little Interest in the European Continent. In the nineteenth century Great Britain had developed a policy that was officially called the "splendid isolation." The British were so concerned with their colonies and their commercial pursuits, that they followed with little interest the course of European diplomacy.

The Boer War Makes the British Unpopular on the Continent. But during the Boer War (1899-1902) the British saw with alarm how much adverse criticism their actions in South Africa had produced in the great nations on the Continent. Moreover, it was just at this time that Germany began to build a huge navy and to demand a larger share in world markets.

The British Try to Win German Friendspip. Consequently, some of the leading British statesmen were anxious to foster friendship with Germany. But the Germans did not seem to appreciate this cordiality. They knew that England needed an ally on the Continent, but they had no idea that the English would turn to France, for in 1898 rivalry between the British and the French in Africa had nearly caused a war between these two countries.

THE FRENCH AND BRITISH ESTABLISH THE ENTENTE CORDIALE. But this so-called Fashoda incident of 1898 had been smoothed over by the great colonial expert of France, the tactful Delcassé. As we saw, the French agreed to let the British occupy Sudan, and the British promised the French a free hand in Morocco. This agreement is called Entente Cordiale (friendly understanding), and was made in 1904. In this connection it is well to note that Queen Victoria had been succeeded in 1901 by King Edward VII (1901-1910), who was more friendly to France than the Queen had been.

THE BRITISH AND THE RUSSIANS ALSO BECOME FRIENDS. What was still worse for Germany, the British and the Russians were at last becoming kindly to each other. Although Great Britain and Russia had been rivals in western Asia, the defeat of Russia in the Russo-Japanese War made Russia seem less powerful than she had been before. Moreover, in 1902 the British had made an alliance with Japan, and for that reason felt secure in the Far East.

RUSSIA AND GREAT BRITAIN EACH TAKE A LARGE SLICE OF PERSIA. In 1907 the rivalry between Russia and Great Britain in the region between Russia and India was ended by the agreement to partition Persia in such manner that the northern third became a Russian sphere of influence, the center a neutral territory, and the southern portion a British sphere of influence. Moreover, Afghanistan was to remain independent, and thus would constitute a buffer state between Russia and the British possessions.

THE TRIPLE ENTENTE IS BEGUN. ITALY MAKES AN AGREEMENT WITH FRANCE. In this manner the Dual Entente of 1904 became the Triple Entente in 1907, and now Europe was for the most part divided into two hostile camps. Italy was no longer a reliable member of the Triple Alliance, for in 1902 she had signed an agreement with France, in which Italy promised France that she would remain neutral in case France were attacked by another power.

GERMANY STARTS BUILDING THE BERLIN TO BAGDAD RAILWAY. In the meantime the Near East contributed to the dangers that faced Europe before 1914. Germany was now the protector of Turkey, and was engaged in the plan of building the "Berlin to Bagdad" railroad, which was to extend from Berlin across Austria-Hungary, the Balkan Peninsula, and Asia Minor to Mesopotamia. This naturally alarmed the British.

THE "YOUNG TURKS" MAKE TURKEY MORE POWERFUL. In 1908 a group of liberal leaders, called the "Young Turks," compelled their ruler, Sultan Abdul-Hamid II, to westernize his country and to grant a constitution. Encouraged by this seeming weakness in the Turkish government, Bulgaria declared its independence, and Austria-Hungary annexed Bosnia and Herzegovina.

ITALY GETS LIBYA. In 1909 the Turks deposed their ruler and remodeled their army under the supervision of German experts. Before the Turks could complete this reorganization, Italy declared war on them and seized Tripoli (1911), which they now called Libya.

THE FIRST BALKAN WAR IS FOUGHT IN 1912. Now followed the two Balkan wars. In 1912 Bulgaria, Greece, Serbia, and Montenegro attacked the Turks together and decisively defeated them in the winter of 1912-1913. In the Treaty of London of 1913 the Turks were obliged to surrender to these four little states nearly all the territory they still retained in Europe, but keeping for themselves Constantinople and immediate vicinity.

THE SECOND BALKAN WAR FOLLOWS IN 1913. But the victors soon began to quarrel over their spoils, and so the second Balkan war began. This time it was Bulgaria that was attacked by all the others, including even Rumania, so that naturally the Bulgarians were promptly defeated. The war was marked by unspeakable atrocities on both sides. In August 1913 the Treaty of Bucharest ended this war. Once more the map of the Balkan Peninsula was altered, but once again another war was to break out and cause further changes in the frontiers.

FRANCE GETS MOROCCO. Moreover, the Morocco Question kept all Europe in turmoil from 1909 to 1912, when France formally established a protectorate over Morocco, while Spain received a portion near the Strait of Gibraltar. In order to please the Germans, France agreed to cede to Germany about 100,000 square miles of French Congo.

WHAT THE GREAT UNDERLYING CAUSES OF THE WAR WERE. Among the general causes of the World War we may specify the intense nationalism of the time, the division of the major European powers into two hostile camps, the colonial rivalry between Germany and Great Britain, and the disturbing question of racial minorities. This last factor means that many races living among more powerful ones were not well treated and tried to start revolutions.

THE GREAT STATESMEN TRY TO PREVENT THE COMING OF THE WAR. In vain did the leading statesmen of Europe try to stave off the war. Twice a great conference was held at the Hague, the capital of the Netherlands (1899 and 1907). But nothing of practical value was accomplished there. It was also hoped that a satisfactory naval code could be formulated, in order that the great powers could be restricted by human justice and equity. In 1909 such a code was actually drawn up by naval experts, but Great Britain refused to ratify it, and so it was never enforced.

PREPARATIONS FOR THE WAR CONTINUE. In 1912 and 1913 the British and the French held numerous meetings as to what should be done in case of war with Germany, and thus the public was becoming prepared for that which was dreaded but fully expected. France was nearly allied with Great Britain. Terrific was the race for the most powerful armaments; it undoubtedly hastened the coming of the war. Although both Great Britain and Russia withdrew most of their objections to the completion of the Berlin to Bagdad railroad, this was but a forced recognition of what was actually taking place. Every new mile added to the road increased the tension. Russia was getting ready to pounce upon Constantinople whenever a favorable opportunity should present itself.

WHAT THE IMMEDIATE CAUSE OF THE WAR WAS. The immediate cause of the war was the assassination of Archduke Ferdinand and his wife, which occurred on June 28, 1914, in the town of Sarajevo in Bosnia, the newly annexed province of Austria-Hungary.

THE ASSASSINATION OF THE AUSTRIAN ARCHDUKE LEADS TO A WAR BETWEEN AUSTRIA AND SERBIA. It was the work of certain Serbians who were plotting to end the Austrian rule in Bosnia, and it appears that some Serbian officials were involved in the plot. On July 5th the German emperor assured the leading Austrian minister that he would support Austria under any circumstances, and so Austria obtained the "blank check" to go ahead. On July 23rd Austria sent an ultimatum to Serbia which comprised six points, of which Serbia accepted five, but could do no more without surrendering much of its independence to Austria. The Kaiser thought that now all causes for war had disappeared, but the Austrians were not certain how much the Serbians were willing to concede in fact rather than merely on paper. Consequently, Austria-Hungary declared war on Serbia.

GERMANY DECLARES WAR AGAINST RUSSIA AND FRANCE. Russia hesitated for a few days but on July 30th began to mobilize her army. Now Germany had to take swift action for fear that both Russia and France would be fully prepared to engage Germany's armies on both fronts. Only quick strokes on Germany's part could prevent such a calamity. Two ultimatums to Russia and France were followed by declarations of war, and within two days after Russia's mobilization Germany began to invade France by way of Belgium.

WHICH OTHER NATIONS ENTER THE WAR. Great Britain also did not hesitate long and on August 4th declared war on Germany. The violation of Belgium's neutrality had much to do with this action. Other powers followed suit in their own order, Japan aiding Great Britain, its ally; Portugal doing the same, being also an ally of Great Britain; Turkey joining Germany for obvious reasons; Italy hesitating till 1915, when she joined the British against Germany; Bulgaria coming in on the side of Germany in 1915; and Rumania siding with the Allies in 1916.

Student Activities

1. With the aid of a dictionary write out the definitions for the following words: *analyze, adverse, atrocities, specify, ultimatum, obvious.*
2. What is meant by a "System of Alliances?"
3. Why were Austria and Russia unfriendly towards one another?
4. What nations comprised the "Triple Alliance?"
5. Why did the British try to win German friendship?
6. What nations comprised the "Triple Entente?"
7. What nations took part in the First Balkan War?
8. What caused the Second Balkan War?
9. What was the immediate cause of the First World War?
10. Give as many of the steps as you can to show how almost all of Europe became involved in the First World War.
11. Why did Turkey join Germany in the First World War?

CHAPTER 49

Four Years of World War

How the World War Differed from All Earlier Wars. The World War differed from all preceding wars in its enormous scope. Formerly only small professional armies used to fight, and after the French Revolution broke out in 1789, a person would be merely a civilian until he was drafted for war service. But in the countries that were in the World War, every able-bodied man and woman was liable for some service either at the front or in a camp or at home.

The Germans Are Well Prepared and Seize Northern France. The Germans were better prepared for war than any other nation in Europe. They were very efficient in almost every respect. They hoped to strike at the heart of France before the Russians could get ready to engage the Germans on the eastern front. In the first month the Germans swept through Belgium and northern France, and finally they were stopped on the Marne river by Joffre. The Germans failed to push as far as Paris, for the French had found a weak spot in the center of the German line and had made a bad dent in it. So on September 10th the Germans began to entrench themselves, and now fighting ceased to move back and forth over a wide area.

The Russians Invade Eastern Germany, but Are Beaten Back. At the same time the Russians were invading eastern Germany, which made necessary a withdrawal of German troops from France, and thus the German plan of a quick thrust at Paris had failed. The Russians successfully pushed westward into East Prussia and the eastern section of Austria-Hungary, but in both regions had to withdraw with heavy losses, owing to the work of Hindenburg and Von Mackensen. After this first year the Russians gradually became weakened, but they saved France in the course of 1914-1915.

The Italians Have to Withdraw Southward. In the second year of the war Italy joined the Allies, or Allied Powers, as the great powers who fought against Germany in the World War were called. Italy at first met with considerable success, as had Russia in her first year; but Italy also had to withdraw and then retreat. In 1917 the Italians lost some valuable lands in the northeastern part of their country. But after they dug in on a new front, they were able to hold their lines intact.

Serbia and Rumania Are Quickly Defeated. In the Balkan Peninsula the central powers also gained much. In 1915 Bulgaria joined them, and now Serbia was quickly overrun. When in 1916 Rumania decided to enter the war on the side of the Allies, she also was forced to surrender to the Germans and their allies. Moreover, the Turks controlled the straits leading from the Mediterranean to the Black Sea, thus preventing the Entente powers from sending troops to Russia.

Turkey Is a Poor Ally for Germany. The year 1916 was indeed most favorable to the central powers. But in the next year the situation in the Near East changed for the worse. Not only did Greece enter the war now on the side of the Allies, but Turkey began to weaken, so that the British were able to take Jerusalem and Bagdad, and to stir up a revolt among the Arabs against the Turks. Meanwhile British sea power deprived Germany of her colonies in Africa, and Japan and Australia (together with New Zealand) occupied the German colonies in the Far East. It really was the sea power of Great Britain that defeated the Germans.

Russia Collapses and Makes Peace with Germany. However, in 1917 it seemed that Germany might yet be successful. The Russians could no longer keep up the war, and the revolution in 1917 overthrew the government of the czar, with the result that the Russians withdrew from the World War, surrendering to Germany large regions in western Russia and in the Ukraine, where Germany was able to obtain vast stores of grain. Moreover, Germany obtained the oil fields of Rumania, from which she drew very valuable supplies of gasoline. You might well ask at this point what the Allies would have done without the United States.

Reasons Why Our Government Decides to Declare War on Germany. There were several reasons why the American government in April 1917 declared war on Germany. But it is certain that the ruthless submarine campaign carried on by the Germans in 1917 was chiefly responsible for the American declaration of war. In the closing months of 1916 the Germans had been willing to give ships on the seas warning before they sank them, and now the American government appeared to be satisfied with the attitude of the German government. The Americans had grievances against both the Allied Powers and the Central Powers, for Great Britain had often interfered with American mails and American shipping, while the Germans sank American ships. The situation in 1916 was similar to that in 1812, when the American government was greatly annoyed by both Napoleon and his British enemies. But while in 1812 the Americans had decided to fight the British, in 1917 they determined to support the British.

THE SUBMARINE CAMPAIGN LEADS TO WAR WITH OUR COUNTRY. In the first month of 1917 the Germans suddenly decided to stake almost everything on their submarine campaign. A submarine can attack a vessel without itself being subject to attack, except for a brief moment. Only when the submarine is visible on the surface can it be destroyed by the vessel about to be attacked, or by airplanes. It is true that there are other ways in which submarines were finally removed, such as huge nets and mines. But the main difficulty experienced by the British in 1916 and in the first month of 1917 was the terrific toll of her shipping taken by the Germans through their submarine campaign. In this manner the Germans hoped to starve the British into submission, and if they had succeeded, they would no doubt have won the war. But where they made their supreme error, was in underestimating the power of the United States. Many of their military leaders and statesmen were not certain that the United States would enter as early as it did. At any rate, beginning with January 31, 1917, the German government issued a warning to all nations that in a certain area surrounding the British Isles all ships would be sunk without warning. This was no doubt the chief reason why President Wilson a few months later recommended to Congress that our government declare war against Germany.

A FULLER DISCUSSION OF THE REASONS WHY OUR COUNTRY ENTERED THE WAR. Of course we all remember that Wilson said much about "making the world safe for democracy," but he implied by that statement that the submarine campaign was only a symptom of the barbarous manner in which the German government threatened to overthrow the democracies of the western world, especially the British Empire. The violation of Belgium neutrality had also turned the minds of millions of Americans against the Germans. Much was said in this country about the cruel Huns, implying that the Germans, like the Huns, were exceedingly brutal. That our newspapers and magazines exaggerated the evils committed by the Germans, is undoubtedly true, since much of the war news came through British channels, and the American people had no way to find out the exact truth in the situation. Much has also been written about the loans granted by American bankers to the Allied Powers. This was also a factor in the decision by the American government to declare war against Germany. But when all details of the situation are carefully examined, it will be seen by the honest observer that the submarine campaign of Germany, caused by the overwhelming sea power of the British, was the determining factor in the American declaration of war.

THE AMERICANS GIVE ENORMOUS AID TO THE ALLIES. Early in 1918 the Germans tried desperately to break the lines of the allied forces on the western front. Foch was now placed in supreme command of the allied forces, thus adding much efficiency in that quarter. The Americans under Pershing nobly performed their duty also. As a matter of fact, the entrance of the United States in the war more than overcame the advantage that the Germans had derived from the defeat of the Russians and the occupation by the Germans of Rumania. The Americans and the British were now able to build ships faster than the Germans could destroy them. Moreover, the American troops did more than fight for the allies. They gave the Allies what they most sorely needed in the closing months of 1917, namely, new hope and new courage.

THE GERMANS REALIZE THAT THEY CANNOT WIN THE WAR. It soon became apparent to the officials in control of the German government that victory was extremely difficult to attain; so they at last became willing to listen to moderate terms of peace. As their troops in the West finally began a rather disorderly retreat, and the Turks, the Austrians, and the Bulgarians capitulated to the Entente Allies, the Kaiser fled to the Netherlands, the princes in Germany gave up their titles, and Germany became a republic.

Our President Wilson Offers a Fair Peace Plan. It was with this new government that Wilson was now ready to establish an armistice on November 11, 1918, and a peace treaty. In January, 1918, Wilson had issued his famous Fourteen Points, which offered a reasonable platform for the discussion of a treaty. He recommended that diplomacy should be public rather than secret, as it had been in the past; that the seas should be free; that armaments be reduced; that France acquire Alsace-Lorraine; that various subjugated peoples and territories be set free; and that a league of nations be established.

The Allied Statesmen Reject Wilson's Moderate Terms. The Allied powers objected to some of Wilson's points. The British did not favor the idea of the freedom of the sea, and the Allies were not satisfied with a mere restoration of conquered territories by the Germans; they wanted a huge indemnity. Moreover, they had promised Italy and Japan certain regions that were to be taken from the central powers. Wilson refused to accept these secret treaties, but he was to discover that his attitude would be politely ignored.

Some Important Results of the War. The results of the World War were numerous and far-reaching. As we have seen, the Emperor of Austria-Hungary, like the Kaiser, lost his throne. But, unlike the situation of Germany, the whole nation was dismembered. Besides, a large number of monarchical governments were overthrown in cental Europe, and for a time it seemed as if soon there would be no more monarchs left in Europe.

Europe Is Not Made Safe for Democracy. In Russia the government of the czar was overthrown, the upper classes were deprived of their property and their social privileges, and Communism was established. Soon the newly formed democratic governments in central Europe were to be removed in turn, because the countries in question were not ready for democracy. In this way dictatorships were to arise. Instead of having made Europe safe for democracy, the Americans as well as the European Liberals learned to their sorrow that Liberalism and democracy could not so easily be forced upon peoples that did not understand such political philosophy.

Evil Results of the War. A terrible disorder was the aftermath of international hatred and bloodshed. More than nine million soldiers had been killed in the war, and many more millions were maimed and crippled for life. The periodicals and newspapers of many nations belched forth their harmful poison of hatred and revenge. Friendly cooperation among nations was now for the most part a thing of the past. Tariff walls, increased nationalism, and bitter trade rivalries spoke an eloquent testimony of the folly of war and bloodshed. In addition to these economic evils, currency inflation in Russia, Germany, Italy, France, and Belgium wiped away the savings of millions of innocent people. Finally, Communist outbreaks in Hungary, Italy, and Bavaria were accompanied by strikes and bloodshed. It took years before Europe was able to return to the ordinary channels of respectable society, and it is to be doubted that some of the European countries had fully recovered when another world war got started in 1939.

Student Activities

1. With the aid of a dictionary write out the definitions for the following words: *scope, entrench, access, ruthless, underestimating, capitulated, armaments, indemnity, dismembered.*
2. In what way did the First World War differ from all other wars before?
3. How did the Russians save France in 1914?
4. Why did the United States enter the war in 1917?
5. What did President Wilson try to do after the First World War ended?
6. Why did Wilson fail in his plan?
7. What were some of the results of the First World War?
8. Did the war help democracy?
9. Does a war as a rule improve any situation?
10. How many lives were lost in the First World War?
    Note: The First World War, which lasted over four years, killed off an enormous number of people and destroyed countless wealth in the form of ships, houses, food supplies, etc. Furthermore, the longer a war lasts, the deeper become the hatreds of those that take part in it. Luther calls war a most terrible punishment of God.

CHAPTER 50

The Peace and Its Aftermath

THE ALLIED STATESMEN ARE CERTAIN TO MAKE A BAD PEACE. The Treaty of Versailles, which officially ended the World War, clearly revealed the hatreds the war had aroused. Unfortunately, the Allied and Associated Powers refused to negotiate directly with Germany, and practically dictated their terms of peace to that country. Wilson's reasonable terms were scorned by his European friends, notably Lloyd George, Clemenceau, and Orlando, who represented in turn Great Britain, France, and Italy.

WHAT GERMANY LOST IN EUROPE. The terms of the treaty with Germany were signed at Versailles on January 28, 1919. Germany lost the following territory in Europe: Alsace-Lorraine to France; Eupen and Malmédy to Belgium; Northern Schleswig to Denmark: Posen and West Prussia to Poland; a portion of upper Silesia to Poland, but after a plebiscite; Danzig to the League of Nations; the Saar Valley for fifteen years to France, after which a plebiscite would determine whether or not it would remain French; and the city and districts of Memel to Lithuania (but not immediately).

GERMANY LOSES ALSO ALL ITS COLONIES. Germany also lost all its colonies: Southwest Africa to the Union of South Africa, East Africa to Great Britain, Kamerun and Togoland to Great Britain and France, and the Pacific Islands to Japan, Australia, and New Zealand.

WHAT IS DONE TO AUSTRIA-HUNGRY? The treaty with Austria-Hungary included the following terms: (1) Italy received Tirol to the Brenner Pass, including a district in the north where about a quarter of a million Germans lived; and the peninsula of Istria, where was located the important port of Trieste. Some years later Italy also got Fiume. (2) On the east coast of the Adriatic Sea a new state was founded called Yugoslavia, which included all the lands formerly belonging to Austria between Serbia and the German-speaking part of Austria proper. (3) Hungary lost to Rumania the district called Transylvania. To Yugoslavia she also lost an important region directly to the north of Belgrade. (4) To the north of little Hungary the new state of Czechoslovakia was carved out of Bohemia and a long strip of land to the southeast.

BULGARIA AND TURKEY ALSO LOSE MUCH TERRITORY. The treaties with Turkey and Bulgaria stated that Turkey must surrender Syria to France, Mesopotamia and Palestine to Great Britain (having lost Egypt in 1914 besides), and Arabia to its inhabitants, who formed an independent state. But Greece, which had hoped to gain a portion of Asia Minor and some lands near Constantinople, had to be content with some annexations at the expense of Bulgaria. Syria, Mesopotamia, and Palestine became "mandates," or states held in trust for the inhabitants. (In recent years Mesopotamia has become an independent state under the name of Iraq.) The lost colonies of Germany were likewise called mandates.

GERMANY MUST DISARM. The Treaty of Versailles also called for disarmament measures: (1) Germany and its former allies were severely punished in having to give up their fleets and military forces. Germany kept only 100,000 armed men. It could no longer use submarines, and the island of Helgoland in the North Sea was dismantled. (2) The east bank of the Rhine was not permitted to be fortified, and allied troops were to occupy the lands to the west of the Rhine for a maximum of 15 years. (3) Turkey had to dismantle the shores of the straits between the Aegean Sea and the Black Sea.

GERMANY MUST PAY REPARATION BILLS. Reparations demanded from Germany were suicidal. The treaty of 1919 did not specify how much Germany should pay the Allied Powers. In 1921 the sum was fixed at 132 billion gold marks (about 80 billion dollars in our present currency). France was to receive more than half of this amount, and the balance was to go to Italy, Belgium, Great Britain, and a few other states. But Germany was unable to pay such an enormous sum, though she did cede an immense amount of raw materials, especially coal, and also several billion dollars.

THE KAISER IS TO BE TRIED FOR HIS CRIME. Finally, the Kaiser was to have been brought before an international court, but the Dutch refused to surrender him to the Allies, and the matter was quietly dropped. At one time Lloyd George had been elected prime minister partly because he had promised to have the Kaiser hanged!

THE LEAGUE OF NATIONS IS SET UP. The League of Nations was a creation of the Treaty of Versailles, and partly for this reason the United States has not seen fit to join in. (Our Congress refused to accept the Treaty of Versailles.) The city selected for the seat of the League of Nations was Geneva, because it was situated in the neutral country of Switzerland, but in the French-speaking part of the country, near France, which fact was bound to please the French, who had wanted to select Brussels instead. Most of the officials at the peace conference did not favor Brussels for the simple reason that Belgium was likely to be too closely attached to France and consequently not a suitable country for the purpose they had in mind.

WHY THE LEAGUE OF NATIONS WAS SO WEAK. The League has had no armies or navies of its own, which is the chief reason why it has failed to perform the task it had been expected to do. Since 1914 only force has made governments in Europe come to terms. The League was to apply "sanctions" (Pressure) to states that did not abide by its decisions, such as boycotts; and in extreme cases the League could call upon its members to furnish armies and navies with which to punish disobedient powers.

THE GOVERNMENT OF THE LEAGUE OF NATIONS. Two councils were to be set up: (1) the Assembly, in which every member nation would have equal representation, exactly as do our states in the Senate at Washington; and (2) the Council, on which every member of the Great Powers had a permanent seat, and four members of the smaller nations were to have non-permanent seats, which number was later increased to ten. A secretariat took care of routine matters. Since the Council and the Assembly were to settle disputes of a diplomatic nature, the Covenant of the League of Nations set up the Permanent Court of International Justice in The Hague. The Treaty of Versailles also provided for an International Labor Office, which the United States joined in 1934, though refusing still to join the other bodies.

THE MEMBERS OF THE LEAGUE. Among the first members were Great Britain, France, and Italy. Germany belonged to it from 1926 to 1934; Italy left in 1937. Japan was an original member, but left when the League disapproved of its occupation of Manchuria. Russia joined as late as 1934, but was ousted by the League in 1940. The smaller nations have been its best supporters.

Useful Work Done by the League. The League of Nations has performed much useful work, notwithstanding its serious shortcomings: (1) It helped combat disease and saved the lives of many refugees. (2) It enabled 400,000 prisoners of war to return to their homes. (3) It reduced the trade in opium and other drugs. (4) In some cases it reorganized the finances of small powers on the verge of bankruptcy, as was done for Austria. (5) It administered the Saar Valley until it was returned to Germany. It also administered the city of Danzig. It had supervision over mandates, and was of help to oppressed minorities. (6) It aided nations who were not large enough to defy its decisions, such as Finland and Sweden, Poland and Lithuania, Greece and Bulgaria.

Important Work That the League Failed to Do. But it sadly failed to prevent the Japanese occupation of Manchuria and of a large part of China. It did very little to halt fighting in Spain, and it seemed unable to do anything for Czechoslovakia in 1938, nor did it protect Ethiopia in 1935.

Disarmament Conferences After the War Are a Part of the Peace. The disarmament conferences after the World War also are a part of the peace and its aftermath. Suspicion and hatred among the powers resulted naturally in a general feeling of insecurity; consequently, the need of conferences in order to establish security. In 1925 the Locarno Pact was signed at Locarno in Switzerland, where delegates from Great Britain, Germany, France, Italy, and Belgium pledged not to resort to war with any of these powers but rather to solve disputes through arbitration. However, in 1936 Germany repudiated the pact, for the so-called "spirit of Locarno" had vanished before that year!

The Kellogg-Briand Peace Pact. In 1928 a more extensive pact was signed in Paris, called the Kellogg-Briand Pact, named after Briand, the French minister of foreign affairs, and Kellogg, the American Secretary of State. (It is also called the Pact of Paris.) Nearly all nations agreed hereby to give up war, but little did they know then what the future would bring in a few years. Their own promises were worthless.

The Washington Conference. The integrity of the Chinese Republic was guaranteed by the leading naval powers in the

Washington Conference of 1921-1922. The ratio of the tonnage of the respective navies was set as 5:5:3 for the United States, Great Britain, and Japan. France and Italy were each permitted to have a navy a little larger than half of the Japanese. Japan eventually broke this agreement.

GERMANY IS UNABLE TO PAY THE REPARATION BILLS. Since 1921 the war debts and reparations have constantly reminded statesmen of the problem left by the peace of 1919. When Germany failed to make the annual payments forced upon her, the French impatiently occupied the rich Ruhr district in western Germany (1923), but gained little by that method. Now followed the Dawes plan, named after the American financier C. C. Dawes, which permitted payments in accordance with German ability to pay. Owen D. Young, another American financier, was the sponsor of the next plan (1929), and to encourage Germany still further, in 1930 the allied troops were withdrawn from the Rhineland five years before they were obliged to go. The American government similarly extended more generous terms to the Allies, who owed it over ten billion dollars. But the great depression of 1930-1932 resulted in a general moratorium, and it is now impossible to say what should have been done about the war debts.

Student Activities

1. With the aid of a dictionary write out the definitions for the following words: *negotiate, plebiscite, disarmament, dismantled, reparations, cede, insecurity, arbitration, repudiated, moratorium.*
2. List those regions which Germany lost after the First World War.
3. Draw a map of Europe as it was set up after the Peace Treaty of Versailles.
4. In what other ways aside from losing certain territories was Germany punished after the war?
5. How much was Germany supposed to pay in reparations?
6. What was the purpose behind the League of Nations?
7. Did the United States join the League of Nations?
8. What useful work did the League perform?
9. What are disarmament conferences?
10. What did the nations of Europe try to do at Locarno?
11. What was done to make Germany able to pay the large bill for damages?
  Note: Many attempts have been made in the past to abolish war, but it has been impossible to accomplish such a thing. Naturally, as long as there is hatred and greed there will also be wars. Jesus said that "whosoever hateth his brother is a murderer." Wars originate in the evil hearts of man, and are caused largely by greed and a desire for revenge.

CHAPTER 51

Eastern and East Central Europe Between World War I and World War II

THE LIBERALS IN RUSSIA ARE DEFEATED BY THE BOLSHEVISTS. As we have seen, it was in 1917 that the Russian government collapsed, owing to the terrific strain of the war which was too much for the weak government to bear. Czar Nicholas II had been unable to maintain an efficient army and government, partly because he himself was not an efficient person. A number of liberal politicians now tried to save the situation for Russia. Among those was Alexander Kerenski, who, however, failed to observe that what the people and the soldiers wanted was peace, not victory. The Liberals were opposed by the majority party among the Socialists, called the Bolsheviki, who dominated the Soviets, or Councils of Workmen's, Soldiers' and Peasants' Delegates.

THE BOLSHEVISTS SET UP A NEW FORM OF GOVERNMENT. In November, 1917, the Bolsheviki overthrew the provisional government of the Liberals. They now established the dictatorship of their own party, that is, of the radical Socialists. The Soviets became the national government, at the head of which was the Council of Peoples' Commissars. These in turn were led by a Marxian Socialist called Lenin. His aim was the same as that of his master, Karl Marx, who had recommended the establishment of the "dictatorship of the proletariat." Next to Lenin ranked the Jew Leon Trotsky, the Commissar for Foreign Affairs. Because these men favored the abolition of privately owned means of production, they have become known as the Communists.

WHY RUSSIA GOT UNFAVORABLE TERMS OF PEACE. Since Russia had failed the Allied Powers in the closing year of the World War, and since the Russians would not cooperate with Kerenski, who had intended to assist the Allied forces in

Russia, she was deserted by the Allies in the peace settlement. Russia lost Poland, which became an independent republic; and also all territory along the eastern shore of the Baltic Sea. Here were set up the following independent countries: Finland, Estonia, Latvia, and Lithuania.

RUSSIA BECOMES A FEDERAL STATE IN WHICH THE COMMUNISTS CONTROL EVERYTHING. Russia itself was reorganized on an entirely new basis; it now became a federal state, whose official title was the Union of Socialist Soviet Republics, or, U.S.S.R. Among the more important states within the union may be mentioned Russia proper, Ukraine, White Russia, and the Federation of the Caucasus. The various races within the country as a whole were all considered equal before the government. Each was permitted to retain its own language, and to send delegates to the central government. These delegates were indirectly elected by voters who formed the proletariat. In this manner the government was indeed a "dictatorship of the proletariat." Clergymen, members of the former nobility, and members of the middle class were not permitted to vote; moreover, the peasants as a whole received a more limited franchise than the workmen in the cities. Although the population of Russia was about 160 million, only two million were members of the Communist Party.

HOW THE COMMUNISTS KEEP THEIR POWER. Actually the government of Soviet Russia was in the hands of a small council which was called the Council of People's Commissars. The real ruler of Russia was the leader of the Communist party, for no other person was permitted near the top of the great Communist party. It was not an easy matter to become a member of this party, for the members were carefully selected from among those who had really supported the Communists. In order to prevent conspiracy and rebellion, tribunals were set up which exercised great powers. In the years 1917 to 1924 several thousand political prisoners were executed every year.

STALIN SUCCEEDS LENIN. When in 1924 Lenin passed away, he was not immediately succeeded by another dictator. However, there rose from the ranks a powerful personality who received from his comrades the name of "Stalin," or *man of steel*. He was indeed a man of steel, and he ruthlessly removed from his path all rivals whom he disliked. Among these was Trotsky, who was banished from Russia.

Communism Is Put Into Practice. The first period in the economic history of Soviet Russia was marked by the confiscation of the privately owned means of production, that is the cultivated lands, the factories, the mines, and the utilities. The public debt was cancelled and the old currency was permitted to inflate until it became worthless. When Lenin observed that the sudden change from capitalism to Communism was too swift for the comfort of the people as a whole, he was willing to make a compromise with the capitalists. However, state socialism was retained in its fundamental essence.

The First Five-Year Plan Has Some Good Results. The first Five-Year Plan (1928-1933), which was formulated by Stalin, was upon the whole successful. Large factories were built, many railroads were constructed, and a large number of peasants stopped working on the individual farms and began to cooperate with their neighbors in working on collective farms. Unfortunately, though many factories turned out huge quantities of articles, they were often of poor quality. Or they would have to stand at some railroad station, where they began to rust before they were removed; or they might have to remain a long time in the fields, because the peasants did not know how to use them. It was not unusual for engineers and superintendents to be sent to a prison camp or to be shot for their supposed mistakes when the articles were not turned out properly or were not used properly.

The Communists Neglect Higher Education and Turn Against Religion. The Communists deserve much credit for having greatly enlarged the elementary school system. But in the field of higher education, as well as in that of creative art and literature, they have made no progress whatsoever as compared with what was accomplished in Russia before 1914. The attitude of the Communists toward religion, especially the Christian religion, was one of hatred. Those who went too often to worship in a church, or a synagogue (a Jewish church), or a mosque (a Mohammedan church), were deprived of membership in the Communist Party. Moreover, religious organizations were not permitted to teach children or to aid the poor and the sick.

The Communists Are Intolerant and Immoral. The censorship of the press, the use of spies, the maintenance of the secret police, and the exile to penal colonies were like the intolerant order of the Czars. In the matter of morality the

Communists were even worse than the rulers before 1917 had been. Children were regarded as the property of the state, and family life was no longer considered so sacred and private as it had been regarded by the Orthodox Christians. Moreover, divorce was frightfully easy to obtain.

THE LITTLE BALKAN STATES ARE INDEPENDENT FOR ABOUT TWENTY YEARS. We have just noted that Finland, Estonia, Latvia, and Lithuania were separated from Russia at the conclusion of the World War. The population of each of these states ranged from a little over a million to three million. Poland is a much more important nation than the other four states; it has a population of more than thirty million. All of these five states at first were democratic republics, but just before 1939 there was a tendency in Poland and Lithuania toward dictatorships. In 1940, all these states lost their independence, except Finland.

AUSTRIA-HUNGARY IS BROKEN UP. In east central Europe also a number of new states were constructed at the conclusion of World War I. This was done at the expense of both Austria and Hungary. Austria suffered much in this arrangement, for it had formerly been a leading state in an empire with fifty million inhabitants, and Vienna, its capital, had drawn upon the resources of the whole nation. Now Austria had only six million left, but still possessed the same huge capital of Vienna, with its population of nearly two million. It is no wonder that in the early years after the war Austria wanted to be united with Germany, especially so since almost all its inhabitants were Germans in race and language. But when in 1938 Hitler came to annex Austria to Germany, the situation was somewhat altered, because now Germany was ruled by a dictator and his National Socialist Party.

WHAT WAS LEFT OF HUNGARY. Hungary, like Austria, was a republic; and, again like Austria, it had shrunk from a large state that had ruled over many dependencies to a little republic that was smaller than some of the newly created states.

THE NEW REPUBLIC OF CZECHOSLOVAKIA. Czechoslovakia, which had been hastily put together out of several units with at least three different Slavic races, had a population of about fifteen millions, and was as important as Austria and Hungary put together. Along its western, northern, and eastern borders lived more than three million Germans, who would have been united with Germany in 1919 if only the Allied Powers had permitted this. As soon as Hitler had sufficient power, he took matters into his own hands, and annexed this region (1938). It was a great shock for the friends of democracy to observe how Great Britain and France deserted the little republic, which stood as an oasis in the midst of nations that were tending to become the pawns of dictators or absolute monarchs. However, something had to be done for the region inhabited by the Sudeten Germans.

THE NEW KINGDOM OF YUGOSLAVIA. Yugoslavia was even larger than Czechoslovakia, and was more highly favored in that it possessed a coast line. It was established as a kingdom, and remained a kingdom until 1940. Compared with the turbulent times just before the World War, this region was much improved.

RUMANIA IS ENLARGED. Rumania, unlike Yugoslavia, was one of the older states and had been a kingdom before the war. But now it was much larger than ever before, and had a population of about eighteen million. Today it still is a prosperous country, blessed with much fertile soil, an excellent climate for the production of corn, and valuable deposits of oil.

THE STATES IN THE NEAR EAST. In the Near East we note the following states; Bulgaria, Albania, Greece, and Turkey. Bulgaria, having supported Germany in World War I, was deprived of western Thrace, with its valuable coast line along the Aegean Sea. It was still a kingdom. Albania emerged from World War I as an independent kingdom, practically the same as she had been constituted just before World War I broke out.

WHAT HAPPENS TO GREECE. Greece, having supported the Allied Powers, received western Thrace, but that was only a portion of the lands that she had been promised by the Allied Powers. So the Greeks started a war with Turkey, but were promptly defeated. For some years after this defeat Greece was a republic, but in 1935 the kingdom was restored. The outstanding Greek statesman of the twentieth century was the brilliant minister Venizelos, who died in 1936.

THE TURKS ADOPT WESTERN CIVILIZATION. One reason why Turkey had been able to defend itself so ably against the Greeks, was that it had in its leader Mustafa Kemal a powerful force for national union. When the new Sultan was prepared to surrender Constantinople and the western portion of Asia

Minor, which was exactly what Greece was promised by the Allied Powers, his subjects rallied under a new party, organized a new army, and drove the Greeks out of their country. In 1923 the Sultan was deposed and a republic set up. The Turks now adopted western codes of law, the western calendar, the Latin alphabet, and western fashions in dress and social customs. The Turks even granted equality to all religions in their country, and they gave up the practice of polygamy. At last European civilization had conquered the Near East from the shore of the Aegean Sea to the Syrian desert. Turkey became a stable country, but very small, compared with what it was before 1914.

NATIONALISM STIRS IN ASIA. In recent years the Arabs in Syria, Palestine, and Iraq, encouraged by newly fomented nationalism of both Europe and Asia, have begun to clamor for independence. Even in distant India, in Persia, and in northern Africa the Mohammedans joined together to find a way to complete independence. The first region to secure independence was Iraq. Arabia is also an independent state, having been liberated by the British in 1917. Palestine has such a large Arab population that it will be difficult, even with the aid of the British, who have governed the land under a mandate, to set up here a Jewish state. The Zionist movement aims to accomplish this feat nevertheless. It certainly is remarkable to observe how many changes have recently occurred in the Near East, in former Austria-Hungary, and in Russia!

Student Activities

1. With the aid of a dictionary write out the definitions for the following words: *provisional, arbitrary, banished, confiscation, censorship, savored, resources, pawns, turbulent, rallied, liberated.*
2. Who was Alexander Kerenski?
3. Why was Russia forgotten in the peace settlement at the end of the First World War?
4. Who is Stalin?
5. What is the greatest fault of communism?
6. What happened to Austria-Hungary after the war?
7. Write a short essay on Czechoslovakia.
8. What happened to Greece after the World War?
9. What changes took place in Turkey after the First World War?
10. What is the "Zionist Movement?"
    Note: Communism is a line of thought and ideas which wants to destroy Christianity. Remember how the Roman emperors tried to destroy Christianity and failed most miserably. Christianity is still with us, but the Roman Empire has disappeared long ago.

CHAPTER 52

Germany and Italy Under Dictatorships

ITALY IS DISTURBED BY COMMUNISTS. The peace of 1919 came as a disappointment to Italy, for she received much less territory than the Allied Powers had promised. Communism raised its head in many cities, and in 1920 a huge sit-down strike resulted in the operation of factories in northern Italy by more than 500,000 men. The owners of private property hoped to escape the fate that had befallen the Russian people, but they were beset by fears, for Communism thrived wherever chaos had reigned. Fortunately for the owner of property, in 1921 a new political party originated in Italy, which was led by Mussolini.

THE FASCISTS RISE TO POWER. Small groups of war veterans had organized into units called *fasci*, wearing black shirts, and seeking everywhere the supporters of the Communists, many of whom they killed in street fights. In 1922 the Fascists seized Rome, expecting to set up a republican form of government, but King Victor Emmanuel III was much more friendly than they had believed possible, so that the Fascists decided to retain the limited monorchy. The national government was now reorganized under Mussolini, who received the title of *Il Duce*, the "Leader." He abolished local self-government, and placed a governor over every city.

WHAT WAS DONE BY THE FASCISTS IN ITALY. The Fascists were very successful in improving economic conditions in Italy. But the liberty of the individual practically disappeared. Both employers and employees were organized into groups controlled by the government. In 1936 Mussolini abolished the chamber of deputies, which had formerly represented the people. State socialism had conquered Italy, though private property was not completely abolished.

MUSSOLINI MAKES AN IMPORTANT AGREEMENT WITH THE POPE. Mussolini signed the Lateran Accord with the Pope, which provided that the Pope receive financial compensation for having lost the Papal States and Rome. The Pope kept a small plot in Rome where stood the Vatican Palace and the adjoining Church of St. Peter; he was permitted to rule it as a sovereign state. Fascism differs from Communism in that it has made the study of the Christian religion compulsory in all elementary and secondary schools.

Good Things Accomplished by the Fascists. Italy has benefited in many directions from the Fascist rule. Her roads have been improved, her beggars have disappeared, the hotels and public buildings have been renovated and enlarged. Hygiene has replaced dirt and insects that used to abound almost everywhere.

Fascism Has Destroyed Political Liberty. But the Italian people lost their political rights which they enjoyed before 1914. Freedom of speech and of the press largely disappeared, together with the right to form political parties and to be represented in a legislative body which really rules the nation, as does our Congress and the British Parliament. Business was also fearfully hampered by government control and government exploitation.

The Foreign Policy of the Fascists. In foreign affairs the Fascists continued the policy begun by the statesmen who unified Italy from 1859 to 1870. You have seen in a previous chapter, dealing with European imperialism, that Italy obtained Tripoli in 1911, while she occupied Ethiopia in 1935. No doubt Mussolini entertained additional plans of expansion, partly in Africa and partly in Europe.

The Nazis Rise to Power in Germany. Since 1933 Germany has resembled Fascist Italy in many ways. As we have seen, Germany became a republic at the close of the World War, but failed to get much benefit from republicanism and democracy. Hindenburg was elected under the new constitution as president (1925), and he was able to keep the quarreling political parties from undermining the efficiency of the central government. But the economic depression hit Germany so hard that the people blamed the conservative elements in the government, and the majority voted for Socialist candidates, especially for those who supported the party now rising to national power under Hitler, the National Socialist German Workers' Party (abbreviated as "Nazi" Party).

HITLER AND HIS FRIENDS DESTROY THE DEMOCRATIC GOVERN-
MENT. Although in 1932 Hitler was not yet able to have himself
elected president, his party was now the strongest in Germany,
so that in January, 1933, Hindenburg appointed him as chancellor. But Hitler was by no means satisfied, and had a law
passed in the Reichstag which suspended the constitution and
gave the government then in power dictatorial rights for four
years. Gradually all other political parties were dissolved,
and the Nazis ruled Germany with an iron hand. Even so
popular an idol as Hindenburg had been for years, was
stripped of real power.

LOCAL SELF-GOVERNMENT IS ABOLISHED IN GERMANY. As in
Italy, the new government abolished local self-government,
and the great states of the past, even Prussia, became mere
provinces. Private property was not directly molested, but
the state became absolute in power over human lives and
property. Liberty of the press, of speech, of race and religion,
disappeared. The Nazis, like the Communists, were far from
kind to the Christian religion; but the Nazis, unlike the Communists, persecuted the Jews with extraordinary fury. The
Nazis were noted especially for insisting on racial purity,
which the Communists could not very well do in Russia. You
know that in Russia many races lived side by side. In general
it may be said that the Nazis and the Communists are much
the same.

THE NAZIS ARE IMPERIALISTIC. Hitler's official title was that
of the Führer, or, the "Leader." The national emblem was the
swastika. Nationalism, as in Italy, is the corner-stone of the
policies of the government. Imperialism likewise characterized both Italian and German policies. You probably know
already what Germany and Italy had done thus far in trying
to gain more territory abroad and more power at home.

WHAT GERMANY OBTAINED IN THE MUNICH PACT OF SEP-
TEMBER, 1938. Many commentators have recently observed that
Hitler surpassed Napoleon as a statesman. In the closing
months of 1938 he succeeded in having Chamberlain, the Prime
Minister of Great Britain; Mussolini, representing Italy; Dala-
dier, the Prime Minister of France, agree with him on the
Munich Pact, enabling him to annex the German sections of
Czechoslovakia. Thus, without any bloodshed, he had obtained
more valuable concessions from Great Britain, France, and
Italy than Napoleon secured for France.

THE NAZIS PLEASED THE GERMAN PEOPLE TO A CONSIDERABLE EXTENT. In this connection you might well speculate on what Germany might have gained if she had remained a republic. Would democratic government have brought Germany more power in Europe? Or if not, have the German people perhaps lost more at home than they have obtained beyond its former frontiers? Hitler seemed to the Germans a political and economic savior, for when the shadows of the great economic depression darkened over Germany in 1932 and 1933, Hitler did relieve unemployment and he did restore the confidence of powerful business men. He was careful to emphasize the "national" side of his National Socialist Party, rather than the "socialistic" side, which is exactly what Mussolini also has done.

MANY GERMANS REASON THAT DEMOCRACY ALONE IS NOT GOOD ENOUGH. In addition to having brought to Germany much economic gain, the new party in power also made possible the annexation of Austria, the occupation of the Sudeten region in Czechoslovakia, the fortification of the Rhine Valley, the return of the Saar Valley to Germany, and the rebuilding of the German fleet and army. Democratic statesmen, like dictators, may make serious errors, which are bound to result in punishment for the democratic peoples. Germany, under a dictatorship, rectified some injustices committed by men like Lloyd George, Clemenceau, and Orlando, who in 1919 represented democratic powers, but not just and fair policies. Perhaps we should conclude from our study of these important developments that democracy cannot be relied upon to convert unjust diplomats and unfair governments. Even the people as a whole, unlike those men and women imagined by Rousseau and other founders of European Liberalism, are likely to make bad mistakes if they have only democracy and have not added to democracy the guiding principles of the Chritian religion.

BUT YOU MUST NOT CONCLUDE THAT HITLER HAS BEEN A BENEFACTOR. On the other hand, the events of 1938 show Hitler in an unfavorable light. He deprived all Jews in Germany of civil and professional rights; from Roman Catholic and Protestant pastors he took the right of free speech and the press; he subjected business and society to a rigid government control. Perhaps this is what the majority of the Germans wanted him to do, and perhaps this form of government—a dictatorship with a weak legislature and the absence of political parties—did suit Germany better than democracy. But you cannot help feeling that Germany might have obtained all the advantages which Hitler made possible, through the guidance of a man who combined effective government with justice and democratic principles.

Student Activities

1. With the aid of a dictionary write out the definitions for the following words: *thrived, compensation, compulsory, renovated, hampered, rectified, rigid.*
2. Why was the peace of 1919 a disappointment to Italy?
3. Who is Mussolini?
4. What did the Nazis of Germany, the Fascists of Italy, and the Communists of Russia have in common?
5. What did Germany get in the Munich Pact of September, 1938?
6. In what ways did the Nazis please the German people?
7. How did the Nazis treat the Jews?
   Note: No policy or party based on hatred can continue to exist. Ask your teacher to explain that statement. Hatred is like a consuming fire which destroys the one who is carrying it around. Communism, Nazism, and Fascism are based on hatreds, and therefore they will disappear because in time the Lord will throw them in the corner as one throws useless and filthy rags.

CHAPTER 53

Great Britain Weathers Many Storms

GREAT BRITAIN COMPARED WITH THE TOTALITARIAN STATES. Great Britain and the dominions of Canada, Australia, South Africa, and New Zealand form a marked contrast to the totalitarian (or collectivist) states we have just discussed, namely, Russia, Germany, and Italy. In the latter nations the state was the supreme power over all aspects of human life and property; hence the word "totalitarian." It compelled individuals to give up many of their former personal liberties, so that henceforth they should collectively work for the nation as a whole. Their dictator united them in the domestic and foreign policies of the "collectivist" estate. Great Britain, on the other hand, together with the dominions just mentioned, who have adopted political institutions like those of Great Britain, have kept democracy, that is, the rule by the people through their representatives in the legislature, who are freely chosen by them. Political parties in these nations continue to function as they used to do before the World War.

THE LABOR PARTY COMES INTO POWER. At the conclusion of the war, Lloyd George, chief of the Liberals, was still Prime Minister. But the Conservatives in 1922 came back to power. However, in 1923 the Conservatives were defeated by a combination of Liberals and the members of a new party, the Labor Party. J. Ramsey MacDonald became Prime Minister, and now the old system of having two political parties was gone. For a time there were three parties, the Liberals, the Conservatives, and the Labor Party. Gradually the Liberals lost members to the Labor Party, until finally they disappeared as a great party.

THE IRISH FREE STATE IS ESTABLISHED. In the meantime, the Irish Question returned to plague the leaders in Parliament. As you saw, Ireland was given a Home Rule Bill, but before this bill went into effect, the World War broke out. After

390

the war Ireland was divided into two very different parts, the Protestant north called Ulster, which wanted to remain united with Great Britain, and the rest, which was much larger and became the Irish Free State. For a few years civil war spread over the unfortunate island, but finally the new state was set up under the leadership of De Valera. He tried to separate Ireland completely from Great Britain, but before he was able to accomplish this work, the British replied with a tariff on imported goods from Ireland.

EGYPT ALSO RECEIVES A LARGE DEGREE OF INDEPENDENCE. A similar situation developed in Egypt, which was eventually recognized as an independent kingdom, but Great Britain still controlled the Suez Canal, the Sudan, and the foreign policy of the Egyptian government.

IN INDIA THE PEOPLE ARE LED BY GANDHI. THE NATIVE RULERS GET MORE POWER. India was torn between a group of leaders who wanted complete independence from Great Britain and those who desired home rule only. Gandhi was an influential Hindu leader, who advocated a boycott of all British activities in India. By way of compromise the British granted much power to native princes and local governments, but retaining, as in Egypt, control of the foreign affairs. In addition to that, the British also were able to maintain a general supervision and control over the military forces and the means of transporation.

GREAT BRITAIN AND THE DOMINIONS FORM THE BRITISH COMMONWEALTH OF NATIONS. The self-governing dominions were Canada, Australia, New Zealand, and the Union of South Africa. Newfoundland temporarily became a Crown Colony, in order to receive from the home government some financial assistance, which was badly needed as a result of the economic depression of 1930-1932. In 1931 the Statute of Westminster decreed that the dominions were exempt from the regulations of the British parliament and had complete control over their own legislation. The term "British Empire" has gradually been replaced by that of the "British Commonwealth of Nations." The British king remained, however, as the tie that bound all the dominions together.

WHO THE THREE LATEST KINGS HAVE BEEN. King George V (1910-1936) was highly respected. In 1936 King Edward VIII ruled but a short time, for his marriage with a divorced wife displeased so many of his subjects that he felt obliged to abdicate. He was succeeded by his brother, George VI.

WHY THE CONSERVATIVES BECAME SO STRONG. Returning now to some important domestic happenings, you recall that the Labor Party remained powerful for a few years, but after that the Conservatives returned with a great majority of seats in the House of Commons. MacDonald acted as Prime Minister less than one year (1924). But Baldwin was Prime Minister three times, and in 1937 he was followed by Neville Chamberlain, another Conservative. The general strike of 1926 was a detriment to the cause of the Labor Party, while the Liberals also lost many seats after this strike, though they themselves had not favored it.

RADICAL LABOR LEADERS HARM THE CAUSE OF LABOR. The situation in Great Britain from 1923 to 1926 was similar to that in the United States from 1933 to 1937. In both cases the national government was so anxious to have justice done to the cause of labor that it did not seem to pay sufficient attention to radical labor leaders who harmed labor through their unwise tactics. The general strike of 1926 in Great Britain was a stupendous affair. First the workmen in the coal mines began to strike, because the government had refused to grant their request for action to make all coal mines government property. Coal mining was a depressed industry in Great Britain, for several European nations had begun to mine coal themselves (such as the Netherlands), or had found a substitute for coal in the use of oil or electric power. So the workmen reasoned that if the government bought or seized the mines, they would be working for the government, and hence would be certain to receive adequate wages. Moreover, the government also refused to continue paying a subsidy on the mines that were absolutely unprofitable, arguing that such mines should be closed.

HOW THE GENERAL STRIKE OF 1926 HURT THE CAUSE OF LABOR. What made the strike of 1926 notorious is that workmen in other industries started strikes in support of the miners, which is called a "sympathy strike." About three million men tried to tie up transportation and printing industries. But hundreds of thousands of voluntary strike breakers prevented the strike from succeeding, and it collapsed in nine days. Even the coal miners had to give up their strike after six months of painful waiting for help from any unforeseen quarter. The general public, annoyed by the "sympathy strike," exerted pressure upon Parliament, which in 1927 passed the important Trades Disputes Act. It prohibited "sympathy strikes." It also forbade "political strikes," which were intended to force the government into action in support of the strikers; besides, it declared that no one was permitted to intimidate strike-breakers. But the labor unions remained extremely powerful, having a membership of about six million out of a total population of about forty-five million. What we term "collective bargaining" between organized labor and employers, was deemed useful. In recent years American government officials have studied with great care the history of the strike of 1926 and the provisions of the act of 1927. The British appear to have led the way in the process of collective bargaining.

THE CONSERVATIVES GAIN ON THE LABOR PARTY. In 1929 MacDonald once more was elected Prime Minister, but not because the Labor Party controlled a majority of seats in the House of Commons. Nevertheless, for the moment the Labor Party was doing very well: It obtained 289 seats in the House of Commons, while the Conservatives got 259, and the Liberals only 58. But it was only a fleeting victory, for in 1931 new elections were held, in which the Labor Party got only 52 seats, and the old Liberal Party of Lloyd George but 4. It was a time of gloom for Great Britain, which in 1931 was forced off the gold standard, and saw its shipping greatly diminished. However, under the Conservatives protective tariffs appear to have increased British industries, and the cheapening of the English pound was a distinct aid in recovering some of the lost markets for British goods.

EXTENT AND POPULATION OF THE BRITISH COUNTRIES. Although it can no longer be said that Canada, Australia, South Africa, and New Zealand belong to the British Empire or are British colonies, since they have the right to send ambassadors (or rather, ministers, for the latter represent the smaller powers) to foreign capitals, they are still tied to the British crown; they accept the rule of the British king above that of their own legislatures and prime ministers. India, with its 350,000,-000 inhabitants, is no longer a British colony. But vast areas in Africa and numerous islands are still British colonies, so that we may conclude that Great Britain as the center of the British Empire, remains the greatest colonial power in the world.

We know that in 1914 the area of the British Empire was 12,000,000 square miles. But that included the four dominions just mentioned, which in 1914 were still considered colonies of Great Britain. On the other hand, in 1919, Great Britain received some control over a part of Germany's former colonies and over a part of the former Ottoman Empire of the Turks.

Student Activities

1. With the aid of a dictionary write out the definitions for the following words: *dominions, decreed, abdicate, detriment, intimidate, ambassador.*
2. What is a "Totalitarian" nation?
3. Who was J. Ramsey MacDonald?
4. In what manner do the British rule and control India?
5. What is the difference between a "colony" and a "dominion?"
6. List the British dominions.
7. Why did Edward VIII give up the British Crown?
8. How did the General Strike of 1926 hurt the cause of labor?
9. What is a "strike-breaker?"
10. How large is the British Empire?
    Note: "Collectivism" is a form of government where almost every person is assigned a particular job. There is little freedom of choice, and the individual person counts for very little. To give you an example from ancient times, think of the huge pyramids of Egypt. They are grand and glorious monuments which glorify the kings who built them thousands of years after. But the kings which had those pyramids built cared probably very little about the fact that it cost many lives and brought much misery to thousands and thousands of people who did the actual building of those huge structures. It was not a question of bringing happiness to the individual person, but of glorifying the king.

CHAPTER 54

France Is Torn Between the Friends and Foes of Democracy

THE FRENCH GOVERNMENT REBUILDS THE DEVASTATED AREAS.
France came out of World War I in a decidedly weakened condition. First of all, the ruined regions in the north had to be rebuilt, the budget had to be balanced, and the franc had to be stabilized. But, although progress was not always maintained and years of gloom and political upheaval followed some of the better years, the franc was saved from complete inflation. Its value was reduced to about one-fifth. But compared with the complete destruction of the German and Russian currencies, the French franc did very well indeed. The same may be said, by the way, of the currencies of Italy and Belgium. One reason why the French franc lost a large part of its value was because of the immense expense incurred by the French government in rebuilding the destroyed towns and villages in the north. This work of reconstruction cost the French government about seven billion dollars, of which Germany contributed less than half. Since the French government had to finance this work, it was obliged to borrow with the result of currency inflation.

FRANCE TRIES TO KEEP GERMANY WEAK. The foreign policy of France was at first directed toward the attempted weakening of Germany, not only politically, but also economically. France allied itself with Poland and with some of the states that had profited from the destruction of Austria-Hungary, notably Czechoslovakia, Rumania, and Yugoslavia. The latter three powers comprised the so-called "Little Entente," for they had benefited by the policies of the big powers which had made up the Entente Powers. France, as we have seen, was the original member of the Entente, for in 1904 she had persuaded Great Britain to join her in the Entente Cordiale.

FRANCE AND ITALY DO NOT GET ALONG VERY WELL. French relations with Italy, on the other hand, were sometimes strained, because a rivalry for naval and colonial power in the Mediterranean caused bitter feelings. For example, many Italians believed that the island of Corsica, which France in 1768 had purchased from the republic of Genoa, should be restored to Italy. Corsica, like Sardinia and Sicily, was inhabited by Italian-speaking peoples when the nineteenth century opened. Sardinia and Sicily had remained with Italy, but Corsica had become French in many respects. This naturally grieved many patriotic Italians, who were also of the opinion that Tunis should be ceded by France to Italy.

ITALY WANTS TUNIS AS WELL AS CORSICA. We recall that in 1881 France had taken possession of Tunis, much to the displeasure of the Italians, who at that time were not yet in a position to expand beyond the sea. It was because of French occupation of Tunis that Italy in 1882 had joined Germany and Austria-Hungary in the Triple Alliance. When in 1915 Italy decided to withdraw from the Triple Alliance and support the Allies against Germany, she hoped to obtain more colonies in Africa. At the conclusion of World War I the Italians were sorely disappointed, because they received very little as compared with Great Britain and France, who already held huge colonial territories before the World War.

RUSSIAN COMMUNISM HAS GREAT INFLUENCE IN FRANCE. We also recall that before the World War France had been allied with Russia. But because the Russians had left the Allies in the lurch during the critical years 1917 and 1918, and because the Russian government had refused to pay the debts contracted with the French before the World War, the French for more than fifteen years were slow to renew the old ties with Russia. However, in 1936 radical Socialism and Communism had increased to such extent in France that the French government became once more strongly interested in Russia. It was in 1936 that the so-called "People's Front" was formed out of the left-wing parties, that is, the radical Socialists and the Communists. They acquired a majority of the seats in the Chamber of Deputies, so that one of their members, a Socialist, became Prime Minister. This was Mr. Blum, who in 1937 was forced to resign, although the People's Front, or Popular Front, still retained much power in the legislature.

It Seems Strange That the Popular Front Could Have Gained So Much Power in France. It is rather remarkable that the Popular Front should have won so many followers, for the French domestic policies have for many generations been ruled by the numerous peasants, who love their little plot of ground and their humble homes with utmost devotion. The average French peasant does not like Communism, nor can he be easily won over to Socialism, which promises much to the workmen in the cities but can do little for the peasants who own their land. At any rate, in 1936 the Popular Front controlled the foreign policies of the French government and agreed to a pact with Russia. You might call this pact a defensive alliance, if it were not for the fact that from 1931 to 1941 many agreements were broken with the utmost ease.

The French Government Between 1930 and 1940 Was Shaky. Ever since the establishment of the Third French Republic, the central government of France has been marked by lack of stability. Although, as we have seen, the term of office for the president is seven years, his power is extremely small when compared with that of the Prime Minister, or Premier. His position is somewhat like that of the king of Great Britain, who also weathers many political storms, while prime ministers and cabinets come and go. But where the French government differs from that of Great Britain, is in the fact that France has about a dozen ephemeral parties which combine into various groups and may at any time overthrow a Prime Minister with his cabinet. However, the French have grown accustomed to these many changes, for the Republic is always maintained, no matter how much turbulence there is in the Chamber of Deputies.

The Great Sit-Down Strike of 1936 Reveals the Influence of the Communists. In 1936 a huge sit-down strike occurred in France, owing largely to the favorable attitude of the Popular Front government toward the labor leaders. About a million and a half workmen participated in it throughout various departments. They literally "sat down" at their jobs, whereas the Italian movement of a similar kind in 1920 had ended with the attempt to seize the factories and also operate them. The French strikers held them as a ransom, in order to get more favorable terms for the workmen. However, the general public, resembling that in Great Britain during the general strike of 1926, resented the forceful occupation by workmen of property belonging to others, so that the Popular Front government had to take steps to evacuate the factories. This was done peacefully, showing that men can be made to obey the laws of the land without recourse being had to bloodshed.

As a Result the Popular Front Parties Are Weakened. Gradually during the course of 1937 the Popular Front parties lost much of their power, and in 1938 they were defeated by the more conservative elements under the new Prime Minister Daladier. The latter adopted the policy of cooperation with Germany, rather than the attitude adopted formerly by such leaders as Clemenceau, who had not yet been able to overcome their original hatred of Germany and the German people. At the same time, the French government showed less anxiety to please the Russian Communists, while the alliance with Czechoslovakia was largely ignored.

Why France Let Czechoslovakia Be Reduced in Size. Thus it happened that at the end of 1938 the Germans were permitted to annex the fringe of Czechoslovakia where the Sudeten Germans live. This act was naturally discussed in a variety of ways by commentators who were moved by hatred or sympathy for Germany or its enemies. You might ask how France could have permitted the amputation of a small state that was a democratic oasis in the desert of totalitarian states? Well, there have been many surprises in Europe since 1914. Perhaps the French and the British were not yet prepared for war against Germany and Italy. The latter two countries have formed the so-called Rome-Berlin axis, and they seem to be allied in some respects with Japan.

The Treaty of Versailles of 1919 Was Not Satisfactory. There is also, as we saw, much unrest among the Mohammedan subjects of Great Britain and France. Many prominent British writers claimed that the borders between Germany and Czechoslovakia should have been drawn in 1919 so as to give Germany the region with the large German population. Others pointed out that in 1921 over 90 percent of the people in western Austria voted to be annexed to Germany, but that the Allied Powers forcefully prevented this union at the time.

Chamberlain and Daladier are Willing to Admit That Mistakes Have Been Made. Was it then not advisable for France to admit that the peace settlement of 1919 had not been entirely fair to Germany? So at least it seemed in 1938 to Daladier and Chamberlain. They also had other motives for their apparently weak attitude over against the two dictators in Germany and Italy. They were not certain what Russia might do for them in a conflict with Germany. Russia had refused to pay its debts; it had failed the Allies in 1917 and 1918; would it also fail France in 1938? And would not Communism be a terrible thing if allowed to spread in France? It seemed that the more privileges the government granted to the workmen, the more they wanted, and apparently the spread of Communist doctrines resulted in the loss of patriotism. Perhaps the same thing was going on in Russia, which had its purges and its unreliable diplomats. All these thoughts were in the minds of the two prime ministers from Great Britain and France when they agreed to the Munich Pact of 1938. They prevented for the time being the outbreak of a great war, they checked the spread of Communism, and they could now prepare themselves for a possible war against Germany, Japan and Italy. In the meantime the American government was informed of the whole situation in Europe and the Far East. You will see soon how the United States was being affected by the work of the European diplomats.

Student Activities

1. With the aid of a dictionary write out the definitions for the following words: *budget, stabilized, ephemeral, evacuate, amputation, motives, purges.*
2. Why was France in such a bad condition after the First World War?
3. How did France attempt to keep Germany in a weakened condition after the War?
4. What was the "Little Entente"?
5. Why did France and Italy quarrel?
6. What was the "Popular Front" in France? In what way did this "Popular Front" do great harm to France?
7. Describe the great "sit-down" strike in France.
8. How did France show her great weakness in 1938 and 1939?
   Note: It is a terrible thing when people lose patriotism, and are only bent on personal gain without any regard for anybody else including the nation. That is just exactly what has happened in France. Now the French are bitterly lamenting their fate. France has completely disappeared as a great nation.

CHAPTER 55

Spain and the Smaller Powers of Western and West Central Europe

$\mathcal{S}$PAIN HAS A LITTLE DICTATOR WHO IS UNABLE TO RETAIN MUCH POWER. Although Spain had not taken part in the World War I, this country could not fully escape the unfortunate results of the war. The disturbance of international trade and the moral decline everywhere were shown in the behavior of the leading Spanish officials. The Mohammedans in Spanish Morocco also caused added difficulties by revolting against their European masters. As a result of the general discontent, a dictatorship was tried in 1923 under General de Rivera, who ruled by military force rather than parliamentary government. King Alfonso XIII, however, was permitted to retain the throne, just as did the king of Italy when the Fascists took control of the Italian government in 1922. De Rivera successfully put down the revolt in Morocco, and attempted to do for Spain what Mussolini was doing for Italy. However, he was a much less able person than the Italian dictator, so that in 1930 he had to resign, while in 1931 the king was forced to abdicate.

SPAIN UNDER THE REPUBLICAN GOVERNMENT. Now followed a republican form of government under a legislature made up of one house, and called the *Cortes*. There were regular elections and political parties, such as was the case in France and Great Britain. Could Spain perhaps enjoy the fruits of democracy, now that universal suffrage was established? It seemed quite possible until 1936, when the radical Socialists and Communists formed a combination like that of the Popular Front in France. They were about to set up a dictatorship of the proletariat, but suddenly the conservative elements in the population asserted themselves under General Franco.

A CIVIL WAR BREAKS OUT, AND FRANCO WINS AGAINST THE RADICALS. They started a civil war and received valuable aid from Italy and Germany, because of their opposition to Communism and radical Socialism. They were called the "rebels" or "insurgents," for they had risen against the party in power. Perhaps Spain was not yet ready for democracy, for in democratic countries it is customary to attack one's opponents in Parliament or Congress, not with the sword upon the battle field. However this may be, the insurgents fought real battles against the "loyalists." The latter were supported by the Russian Communists.

After Two Years of Civil War Franco Becomes the Real Dictator. To the British and the French the situation looked ominous, since it might easily lead to another World War. Was this new war to be one between Fascism and Communism, or what might one now expect? It was suggested that the neutral powers establish a patrol force along the coast of Spain and so check the influx of men and munitions. But the war continued through 1937 and 1938, with little indication of what the million men sacrificed in it had died for. Finally, during the opening months of 1939 the "loyalists" were defeated.

What Happened in Belgium From 1919 to 1940. Belgium, like Portugal, gained little from her participation in the World War. She did, however, receive three bits of territory from Germany on her eastern frontier. Her currency was permitted to seek a lower level, but from time to time it was stabilized. However, in recent years it has sunk so low that it has retained only about one-tenth of its former value, when Belgium was still on the gold standard, and its franc had the same value as the French franc, that is, about one-fifth of our gold dollar. Belgium was disturbed by a bitter rivalry between its two different races. But a compromise was reached by permitting the Germanic people in the north to have a university (Ghent) in which instruction was given exclusively in the Flemish language, while in the elementary schools the language of instruction was also Flemish. In the University of Louvain instruction is given in both Flemish and French, while in the other two universities of Belgium French only was used until the German occupation. For nearly twenty years after the World War the foreign policy of Belgium was largely dominated by that of France, but in 1937 the Belgian government determined to break with this subservient attitude, and it asserted its complete independence. The tiny state of Luxemburg had since 1922 a common customs union and currency with Belgium, though it retained its political independence. It is located in the southeast of Belgium.

POLITICAL DEVELOPMENTS IN BELGIUM. Belgium has been a kingdom since 1839, but it has been governed by a democratic legislature. Three great political parties fought with each other, namely, the Catholic, the Liberal, and the Socialist parties. Belgium is a much more conservative country than France. Even its Socialists are exceptionally moderate in their policies. The Communists and the Fascists have tried very hard in recent years to gain seats in the Belgium parliament, but they have failed to achieve any considerable amount of success. Belgium is a very thickly populated country; it possesses very valuable deposits of coal; it still owns the great Congo region in central Africa. Consequently it does not offer a fertile field for either Communism or Fascism, which originally thrive on political or social chaos.

THE KINGDOM OF THE NETHERLANDS. Much of the same may be said about the Netherlands, which is also a kingdom with a monarch who enjoys relatively little power. Its population in Europe is now over nine million, or just a little more than that of Belgium. This country built up one of the most valuable colonial empires in the world, namely, the Malay, or East Indian Archipelago. Here the Dutch ruled over more than sixty-five million subjects, most of whom are Mohammedan in religion. The form of colonial government that has been maintained here by the Dutch for more than three hundred years ranks with that of the British in its unusually enlightened features. The rich islands possess immense deposits of oil and coal, while the tropical climate and the enormous expanse of fertile land promises for the future enough production of rubber, sugar, coffee, tea, spices, quinine, rice, tobacco, and fruits to provide a living for two hundred million inhabitants.

THE DRAINING OF THE ZUYDER ZEE. One remarkable feature of the Netherlands is its low-lying lands in the western portion of the country. Dikes have been erected to prevent the sea and the great rivers from flooding these low lands. But along a large part of the western coast nature has thrown up a formidable barrier in the nature of sand dunes. It is back of these dunes that the muck has been covered with just enough sand from the dunes to provide perfect soil for the production of tulip and hyacinth bulbs, for which this country has become famous all over the world. Another economic development that has attracted much attention among foreigners is the draining of the Zuyder Zee, which is a large salt water body. Part of this work has already been completed, and now thriving villages and fertile fields abound where once the waves of the sea rolled over the bottom of the Zuyder Zee.

WHAT SORT OF A COUNTRY SWITZERLAND IS. Switzerland, like the Netherlands, succeeded during World War I in remaining a neutral power, although she continued to be a republic in the form of a federal state, which is made up of little *cantons*. The Swiss government recognizes four official languages, though nearly two-thirds of the inhabitants are German in race and language. The country is blessed with superb scenery and an industrious population, but practically no mineral deposits are to be found here. However, the tourist business used to make up for the absence of mineral resources.

WHAT ARE THE THREE SCANDINAVIAN COUNTRIES. Three other powers in Europe still remain for brief discussion. They are the three Scandinavian countries of Denmark, Norway, and Sweden. Although they are not so small as Belgium and the Netherlands, they have never been able to support a large population, partly because they are located so far to the north, and partly because both Norway and Sweden possess very little fertile soil suitable for cultivation. The inhabitants are all of Germanic stock, and they are noted for their peaceful nature and their industry. Moreover, they are also clean people, as well as most efficient in practically everything that they undertake to do. Those who have emigrated to the United States have become desirable citizens over here.

POLITICAL AND SOCIAL CONDITIONS. Each of the three countries had until 1940 a government patterned after the British model; each had a king and a legislative body resembling the British parliament. Illiteracy has practically disappeared in these countries, and at the same time social justice and democracy in its most desirable form have made Scandinavia an object of much respect in many other countries, especially the United States. For this reason in 1938 the American government sent a commission to Sweden to study its enlightened labor laws.

COLONIES BELONGING TO THE SCANDINAVIAN COUNTRIES. It is now centuries ago since the Scandinavian peoples established colonies beyond the seas and controlled the commerce of certain other European countries. Iceland in theory belonged to Denmark, though in 1918 the Danish government granted local self-government to the people in this island. It is now fully independent. Norway in 1919 received Spitsbergen and some adjacent islands, which the Norwegians value highly because of their rich deposits of coal. Sweden in the seventeenth century colonized a small region near the mouth of the Delaware River. But after a few years this Swedish colony was seized by the Dutch, who in 1664 surrendered it to the English. Denmark used to own a few small islands in the West Indies, namely, the Virgin Islands, but these she sold in 1917 to the United States.

Student Activities

1. With the aid of a dictionary write out the definitions for the following words: *ominous, subservient, illiteracy.*
2. Who was De Rivera?
3. Who were the "insurgents" and the "loyalists?"
4. Write a fifty word account on Belgium from 1919 to 1940.
5. What outstanding thing could be said about the Netherlands?
6. Which are the Scandinavian countries?
7. Where are the Virgin Islands?
   Note: The Civil War in Spain was a prelude to the Second World War which broke out in September, 1939.

CHAPTER 56

Turmoil in the Orient

THE WEAKENING OF CHINA BY THE WESTERN POWERS RESULTS IN CIVIL WAR. Just before the beginning of World War I, China was torn by a civil war which broke out early in 1912. Nationalism had found expression in China, just as it had asserted itself in Austria-Hungary and in Russia even before the World War. For a long time the Chinese had been angered by the aggression of the western powers, which had gradually occupied important regions along the coast. China had also lost its economic independence. A large proportion of her mines, banks, railways, steamship lines, factories, and ship yards were controlled at least in part by foreign powers. Moreover, the practice of extraterritoriality enabled the foreigners to be tried in their own courts under their own laws, so that they could not be punished by the Chinese government for misdemeanors and crimes that they had committed upon Chinese soil. As in Persia, so in China, certain western powers had established spheres of influence where each respective European nation enjoyed special rights.

MANY WELL-EDUCATED YOUNG CHINESE WANT TO STRENGTHEN THEIR COUNTRY. A large number of Chinese students had studied abroad, particularly in the United States, and upon their return they were shocked by the weakness of their government. They blamed the officials in the government for all the misfortunes that had befallen China during the past fifty years. As a result a number of young Chinese leaders took quiet action to instill into the weak government new blood and new efficiency. But they were resisted by the older generation of statesmen, so that civil war seemed the only way out of the difficulty.

THE JAPANESE PRESENT THE FAMOUS ULTIMATUM OF 1915. While the Chinese were thus engaged in civil war, the Japanese took advantage of China's weakness and seized the colonies and concessions that had been previously occupied or received by the Germans. Although the Chinese opposed this action on the ground that such land could not be transferred from a European power to Japan, the Japanese went ahead nevertheless. In 1915 the Japanese presented a demand to the Chinese government in which they formally annexed the various grants belonging to Germany before the World War. They also asked for exclusive use of Japanese capital in the important industrial and commercial development in China; besides, preferential rights for the Japanese in railways, industrial establishments, mines, and loans; also the exclusive right for the Japanese to supply China with military, financial, and political advisers; and finally, Japanese control of arms and munitions factories and free trade for the Japanese in China.

JAPAN HAS TO CANCEL SOME DEMANDS. This demand caused terrific opposition among the Great Powers in Europe, so that the Japanese were forced to withdraw some of its terms, but the mere fact that they presented them as early as 1915 is an indication of their plans to establish a protectorate over China. All the recent actions of the Japanese government are, therefore, a mere continuation of what had been tried as early as 1915.

REASONS WHY THE JAPANESE HAVE BECOME SO IMPERIALISTIC. All the world knows that the Japanese are a prolific people living on small islands, relatively speaking, which are not able to support the population of about seventy-five million inhabitants. For that reason the Japanese for a long time have sought to find an outlet for this *surplus* population. At one time many of them settled in California, but the state of California quickly took measures to stop Japanese immigration. Furthermore, their success in finding settlements in various South and Central American countries also did not result in a satisfactory solution to their problem. Their most suitable outlet would of course be China.

THE JAPANESE BEGIN TO OCCUPY LARGE AREAS IN CHINA. Although China has already a population of more than four hundred million, Japan could at least obtain a control of the commerce and industry of China, and through exploitation of the coal mines and other natural resources, Japan might increase her own industries, and so her own people need not emigrate. The Japanese are by nature a clever people, and they have taken full advantage of all the benefits that can be derived from western civilization. They reorganized their army and navy, they reformed their government, they built beautiful roads, and they cleverly devaluated their currency, the Yen, so that in competition with Great Britain and other European powers, they were extremely successful in getting a controlling interest in the import trade of India and the Dutch East Indies. Both the British and the Dutch saw with alarm how the Japanese took away from them the lucrative trade of their own dominions. The textile mills in both Great Britain and the Netherlands suffered terrifically from the aggression of the Japanese trading interests.

FURTHER JAPANESE EXPANSION ON THE MAINLAND OF ASIA. Similar steps were taken by Japan in China and Manchuria. As we have seen in an earlier chapter, the Japanese in 1931 took possession of Manchuria and declared it separate from China. When the Chinese replied with a boycott of all Japanese goods, the Japanese in turn resorted to further measures of aggression, occupying eastern Mongolia and the northern provinces of China itself. They also landed troops in the great port of Shanghai. Manchuria now became Manchukuo, a protectorate of Japan.

THE JAPANESE SUBJUGATE ONE-HALF OF THE CHINESE. Although for a time Japan withdrew her troops from Shanghai and other parts of China, in 1937 the Japanese returned in greater numbers. They did not officially declare war upon the Chinese, and yet they acted very much as if they were at war with China. They seized enormous pieces of land, much to the surprise of certain western powers, who had reasoned from the beginning that in this occupation Japan would shatter her resources and man power. On the contrary, Japan with her swift means of communication and transportation, was able to defeat the Chinese everywhere. The latter, torn so long by civil strife, and not yet able to establish an efficient government, had to withdraw everywhere into the interior, so that not only Shanghai but Canton and many other ports became bases for operation of the Japanese troops. By the end of 1938 more than half of China's four hundred million inhabitants were subjects of the great Japanese empire.

RUSSIA IS UNABLE TO STOP THE JAPANESE. It can easily be understood what must have been in the minds of the British, the French, the American, and the Dutch statesmen who watched with concern the amazing progress made by the Japanese in China and Manchuria. The question was often asked whether Russia would do something before it was too late. But Russia seemed to be busy with her own difficulties. Lack of efficiency and of patriotism apparently hampered the Russian government in fortifying itself and in preparing for a major conflict with Japan. Since Japan was allied with Germany, it seemed that some of the great western powers would eventually be drawn into a war against Germany, assisted by both Japan and Italy. These are the three totalitarian states against which President Roosevelt in his opening message to Congress on January 4, 1939, made repeated allusions. We shall refer to this message again in the next chapter.

THE EUROPEANS ARE BEATEN BY THE JAPANESE IN THE ORIENT. It would seem that the western powers have not been nearly so clever as the Japanese have been. In the past they could seize lands and colonize them without interference from other powers. But now the tables have been turned, and Japan seems able to beat the Europeans in their own field. It must not be so readily assumed that the Chinese naturally love the Europeans. Nor are they especially favorable to the Christian religion. Many times in the past the Chinese have turned against Christian missionaries and have murdered them. Long before Japan began to encroach upon Chinese territory, certain European powers, notably Russia and Great Britain, offended the Chinese by their aggression.

WHAT KIND OF TACTICS THE JAPANESE USED IN CHINA. The tactics that were followed by Japan in the closing months of 1938 were intended to make the Chinese population so tired of continued warfare that the people would gladly submit themselves to Japanese rule. The Japanese were able to tell these people that their government would be far superior to that established by various generals who happened to be fighting among themselves all the time. China had been torn by warfare before the Japanese invaded China in the course of 1937. The question for the Chinese was then whether they preferred civil war of their own or Japanese rule.

MANY CHINESE BELIEVE THE JAPANESE. The Japanese could easily persuade many of the Chinese into believing that their government would be far superior, their taxes much lower, and their whole system of management much more to the liking of the peaceful peasants and traders. What the commentators in the western countries were always harping on was plain enough, that is, the unspeakable atrocities committed by the Japanese soldiers in China. It was very harmful to Japan. On the other hand, the question still remained for the Chinese, as to whether they were to have bad rule of Chinese statesmen or efficient government by the Japanese. Would they rather have peace under the Japanese or war under their own leaders? Furthermore, it was obvious to anyone who could read the newspapers that while the Americans were buying from Japan raw silk in great quantities, they thereby enabled Japan to buy raw materials from the United States out of which they could make their ammunition for invading China. Although the attitude of the American government was absolutely fair to both parties, it just happened to seem to be helpful to the Japanese.

The British Fortify Singapore, After Withdrawing From China. We must conclude, therefore, that the situation in the opening months of 1939 was very serious for the western powers. Japan was building an enormous empire that would have a total population of about five hundred million. If Germany and Italy were added to that empire in a close alliance, these three powers, being favorably located both in the Far East and in the Mediterranean area, could certainly break the British empire. Then there were the rich colonies of the Netherlands, which were entirely unprepared for a defensive war against a country like Japan. If Japan should seize those rich islands belonging to the Dutch and exploit their tremendous natural resources, especially the oil and the rubber, what would Great Britain and France be able to do in fighting such a power in the Orient? It was for this reason that Great Britain hurriedly built huge fortifications at the port of Singapore, which was located almost in the center of the Dutch East Indies. Great Britain spent almost a billion dollars in this work of fortification. It was significant that the American government sent a warship to participate officially in the dedication of this great base of Great Britain in the Orient. We must now turn to the question of what is the status of the American government in the Far East, as well as in other parts of the Pacific area.

Student Activities

1. With the aid of a dictionary write out the definitions for the following words : *preferential, surplus, prolific, reorganized, encroach, fortifications.*
2. What were some of the troubles in China before the outbreak of the First World War?
3. Draw a map of China.
4. Why did the Japanese try to conquer China?
5. How did the Chinese attempt to protect themselves against the Japanese?
6. How much of China have the Japanese conquered?
7. Why did England build those huge and expensive fortifications at Singapore?
8. Why were the Japanese able to get many Chinese on their side?
9. Where did Japan get most of her supplies from in her war against China?
10. Draw a map of Dutch East Indian Possessions.

CHAPTER 57

The United States Faces New Problems

WHERE THE UNITED STATES DIFFERS FROM ALL EUROPEAN COUNTRIES. The United States of America still remains the most powerful nation on the face of the earth. Born in a struggle against autocracy, raised under the colors of Christianity, democracy, and personal liberties, it established a government such as Europe had never seen. Not once in the history of the world was a nation founded by men who could so firmly build upon orthodox Christianity and religious freedom and best features of democracy such as were present when the United States was born.

THE VERY FAVORABLE BEGINNINGS OF OUR COUNTRY NEED MORE EMPHASIS. It is unfortunate that many educators and writers in the last few years have forgotten how this country first made its appearance and in what sort of a world it first showed its infant head. When our constitution was framed in 1787, when new states were joined one by one to the original thirteen colonies, Europe still lay under the cloud of autocracy and despotism. Even France during the whole course of the French Revolution, and particularly during the thirty-three years which followed the downfall of Napoleon, was far from being a democratic nation. Only for a few months, when inexperienced radicals were trying to shape a constitution, was any serious attention paid in France to the basic principles of democratic government.

WHERE EVEN THE FRENCH REVOLUTION FAILED TO DO WHAT OUR PEOPLE DID. It was all very well to remove the privileges of the clergy and the nobility, but such things had never been known on this side of the Atlantic Ocean. France by overthrowing the remnants of feudalism and serfdom did not set up itself to be a leader among democratic nations. How well did Thomas Carlyle express this deep truth in his famous work on the French Revolution; he was speaking of conditions in

France at the time King Louis XV lay upon his death-bed. This was the king who had cared not at all how he ruined the French people. He had said, as you will recall, that after him and his friends there would be the Deluge. Now the king was near the point of death, and Carlyle says about this scene: "Alas, much more lies sick than poor Louis: not the French king only, but the French kingship; this too, after long rough tear and wear, is breaking down. The world is all so changed. Borne over the Atlantic, to the closing ear of Louis, king by the grace of God, what sounds are these; muffled, ominous, new in our centuries? Boston harbor is black with unexpected tea: behold a Pennsylvanian congress gather; and ere long, on Bunker Hill, Democracy announcing, in rifle-volleys death-winged, under her star banner, to the tune of Yankee-doodle-doo, that she is born, and, whirlwind-like will envelope the whole world!"

How the Americans Led the World in the Fight for Liberty. Thomas Carlyle, the outstanding British historian and literary figure during the nineteenth century, fully realized what that spirit of American liberty was and how it differed from the spirit that prevailed in France during the last quarter of the eighteenth century. Even Great Britain at that time knew little about liberty. When tens of thousands of witches were burned at the stake in various European countries, and even for a short time in our own New England a little reverberation was felt here; and when state churches condemned all persons who refused to conform to them, religious toleration and political democracy were developed in the new republic in North America. What this republic has done for modern Europe is seldom revealed in our own public schools. Since that is the case, how could Europe be expected to know the truth?

The Three Pillars Upon Which Our Government Was Built. Now the great problem which confronts the American people is this: How can our nation maintain the three pillars upon which the structure of our government was built more than 150 years ago? These three pillars are orthodox Christianity, democracy, and international good-will. If we know how to retain these sacred possessions, no other power on earth will ever be able to overthrow our system of government, or to invade our shores, or to subject our people to their rule. But if these three should be deserted by our statesmen, if radical labor leaders and diplomats and students from the totalitarian states are permitted to circulate their views freely, and to have them instilled in the minds of the teachers of our public schools, then the United States will surely follow the path which leads to national destruction. Upon that path all other great nations were led to their own doom. Let us note the inspiring words of President Roosevelt as he addressed the opening session of our sixty-seventh Congress on January 4, 1939:

PRESIDENT F. D. ROOSEVELT TOLD THE TRUTH IN 1939. "All about us rage undeclared wars—military and economic. All about us grow more deadly armaments—military and economic. All about us are threats of new aggression—military and economic.

"Storms from abroad directly challenge three institutions indispensable to Americans, now as always. The first is religion. It is the source of the other two—democracy and international good will. Religion, by teaching man his relationship to God, gives the individual a sense of his own dignity and teaches him to respect himself by respecting his neighbors.

"Democracy, the practice of self-government, is a covenant among free men to respect the rights and liberties of their fellows.

"International good faith, a sister of democracy, springs from the will of civilized nations of men to respect the rights and liberties of other nations of men.

"In a modern civilization, all three—religion, democracy, and international good faith—complement each other. Where freedom of religion has been attacked, the attack has come from sources opposed to democracy. Where democracy has been overthrown, the spirit of free worship has disappeared. And where religion and democracy have vanished, good faith and reason in international affairs have given way to strident emotions and brute force.

"An ordering of society which relegates religion, democracy, and good faith among nations to the background can find no place within it for the ideals of the Prince of Peace. The United States rejects such an ordering, and retains its ancient faith.

"There comes a time in the affairs of men when they must prepare to defend not their homes alone but the tenets of faith and humanity on which their churches, their governments, and their very civilization are founded. The defense of religion, of democracy, and of good faith among nations is all the same fight. To save one we must now make up our minds to save all."

SOME DIFFICULT PROBLEMS WHICH NEED A SOLUTION. President Roosevelt also indicated to Congress what were some of the other problems that are still awaiting solutions. He referred to the fact that our soil must be conserved, agriculture must be improved, and means must be provided to find food, shelter, and medical supplies and care for all people in this country. Moreover, youth must be given more opportunities for work and education, the morale of all the population must be dignified and sustained, so that the aged, the helpless, and the needy will be certain of proper care. Patriotism also must not be neglected. Every citizen must realize fully that we are all a part of a whole, and in neglecting our duties to the whole, we become undesirable citizens.

CAPITAL AND LABOR MUST COOPERATE. Perhaps the most urgent problem before the American people is to establish the proper relationship between capital and labor. President Roosevelt pointed out that dictators find a solution through the use of force. In this way they succeed for the moment at least. But democratic peoples abhor the methods employed by dictators. How can the American people relieve unemployment, find a way to balance the budget, and at the same time encourage the free enterprise of businessmen? The object of our government still is to put private capital to work. In a democracy property and capital must be protected, while at the same time labor must receive proper consideration.

OUR PEOPLE CONTINUE TO FIGHT AGAINST ALL EVIL FORCES. The American people once more have a sacred duty to perform. They must show the great countries now ruled by dictatorships (including Japan, which is controlled by a very small number of military dictators) that the American Revolution still carries on. We are still fighting battles against autocracy, despotism, and dictatorship. We still abhor despotism of employers, despotism of labor leaders, and despotism of autocrats in the civil government. We still abhor religious persecution. We still believe that all religions, all denominations, can live peacefully side by side. We trust that Jews, Mohammedans, Christians, and infidels can learn to be good citizens in a democratic nation. We still retain our faith in a capitalistic order of society. That order has been maintained in this country for more than two hundred years, and whatever is wrong with society today is not because of capitalistic enterprise but because of the sinful nature of mankind.

Could anyone possibly prove that Russia is better off than the American people today? How could anyone convince the red-blooded American that persecution of businessmen and of minorities is preferable to what this country has achieved during the past fifty years? Never in the history of the world was a people so blessed with a proper knowledge of how to use their own resources and to establish friendly relations with foreign powers. Never before did the masses of the people enjoy so many privileges under so enlightened a form of government as the United States still possesses today. When you consider the size of our country and the terrific problems that assail our government on every hand, you should think a thousand times before asserting that the principles that guided our president and Congressional leaders in the past must now be thrown overboard.

OUR YOUNG PEOPLE SHOULD BE TAUGHT WHAT OUR COUNTRY NEEDS MOST. Far better it would be to ask all pupils in the schools to memorize from year to year the opening paragraphs of the excellent message delivered by President Roosevelt to Congress on January 4, 1939. Let all our pupils in the elementary and secondary schools and all the students in our institutions of higher learning remember that we cannot possibly do without the three pillars that have accompanied the establishment of our capitalistic order of society. Even that order, like all other orders, will fall and will be replaced by another one if these three pillars will be forsaken and broken down. But as long as they remain, capitalistic society will also remain and will insure prosperity for as many people as could possibly be supported under any other order of society.

THE CHRISTIAN RELIGION AND DEMOCRACY WILL SAVE US FROM DISASTER. Whether the Republicans or Democrats are in power, it matters little as long as religion, democracy, and international good will are preserved by our government and our people. Then labor and capital will know how to solve their problems, and then husbands and wives, government and subjects, parents and children, and teachers and pupils will understand how they must learn to cooperate and how to

combine liberty with duty. Then the United States will continue on the road to world leadership.

OUR GOVERNMENT IN 1919 WAS MORE UNSELFISH THAN ALL
OTHER GREAT POWERS. Speaking of international good will, we
may truthfully say that no nation which engaged in the
World War was so unselfish as the United States. This
country asked for no territorial or financial gain, not even
any mandated lands. Since the end of the war our government
has continued this enlightened and unselfish policy. Once
there was a time when the United States followed an imperialistic course of action. Our government annexed some land
taken from Mexico, and in 1898 it obtained from Spain the
Philippine Islands and Puerto Rico. In the same year the
Hawaiian Islands were also occupied by the Americans. In
1917, as we saw, the Virgin Islands became American. Moreover, in order to construct the Panama Canal (1904-1914),
a strip of land was acquired in Central America. Now the
United States faces both westward and eastward. It cannot
possibly close her eyes to important developments in Europe
or Asia. Let us hope that only a desire to help other peoples
will guide the actions of our government in the future!

Student Activities

1. With the aid of a dictionary write out the definitions for the following
   words: *prevailed, indispensable, morale, sustained, abhor, imperialistic.*
2. In what ways is the United States different from all other nations?
3. What according to the words of President Roosevelt are the three
   pillars on which our American Way of Life rests?
4. What are some of the dangers which threaten the United States?
5. What did the United States obtain from the First World War?
   Note: Unbelief and the resultant lack of Christianity destroy a nation.
6. Write a brief essay on what you understand by the "American Way
   of Life."

CHAPTER 58

The Second World War

GERMANY WANTS TO BECOME "GREATER GERMANY." One of the chief causes of the Second World War was the desire on the part of Hitler to recover every piece of land that Germany had lost in the treaty settlement of 1919. Furthermore, so reasoned Hitler, Germany ought to annex other areas also, as subsequent events plainly revealed. From 1934 to 1938 a great military machine was built up by the Nazis, in preparation for the aggression they had deliberately planned. In 1938 Hitler invaded and annexed Austria, and during the month of September he received, as we saw, permission from the British and French governments to take those outlying districts in Czechoslovakia called the Sudetenland. Still not content, he seized all the rest of that country in 1939. The same thing happened in Memel.

RUSSIA AND GERMANY FORM THE PACT OF 1939. The Germans and the Russians were now being drawn closely together. They both wanted to annex a large part of Poland, and they both felt that thus far Great Britain and France had kept them in check, which they naturally did not like. The Russians still remembered how in 1919 they had been deprived of Finland, eastern Poland, the little Baltic states, and the eastern portion of Rumania; they knew that the British and the French had been largely responsible for this action. So they gladly signed a pact with the Germans, aimed at mutual assistance in their attempts to enlarge their respective countries.

THE CONQUEST OF POLAND. As soon as the Nazis entered western Poland, Great Britain and France declared war against them (September, 1939). There was nothing, however, they could do to stop the conquest of Poland. The Germans took the western half in such a short time that their war was termed the *Blitzkrieg,* or "lightning war." While Germany took western Poland, Russia seized eastern Poland, and the central portion was set aside for the "real Poles," as a protectorate of Germany. In one month Poland had disappeared.

RUSSIA CONQUERS PARTS OF FINLAND AND RUMANIA, BESIDES ESTONIA, LATVIA, AND LITHUANIA. During the winter of 1939-1940 the Russians occupied the ports of the three small Baltic states, but they failed to conquer more than a restricted corner of Finland. They annexed Bessarabia once more, while the Hungarians seized a large part of Transylvania. Finally, the Russians formally annexed the three Baltic states mentioned.

FRANCE AND THE LOW COUNTRIES SURRENDER. In the first half of 1940 the Nazis not only occupied Denmark, which offered no opposition, but they also conquered Norway. Next they invaded Holland and Belgium, which fought in vain for a very short time, and then surrendered. Northern France fell in June and July, and the British had to evacuate their army at Dunkirk, sustaining huge losses. Paris had to open its gates to the Nazis, and the seat of the French government was moved to Vichy, where the Germans supervised to some extent the government of southern France which they did not at once occupy themselves.

THE BATTLE OF GREAT BRITAIN. During the invasion of central France the Italians declared war against France, expecting the downfall of Great Britain and a favorable peace within one year. But, although tremendous damage was done in Great Britain by German airplanes, the British held fast. In northern Africa the Italians, supported by the Germans, moved into western Egypt. But in 1941 the British recovered much territory in that vicinity, and they also conquered Ethiopia. In the meantime the Nazis took Rumania, and a little later all the rest of the Balkan Peninsula. They even seized the island of Crete.

WAR IN THE FAR EAST. Meanwhile, the Japanese suddenly announced that they were going to establish a "New Order" in the Far East, meaning that they would do in Asia what the Germans had done in Europe. From 1937 to 1940 they had occupied vast areas in eastern and southern China. In 1940 they signed a formal alliance with Germany and Italy. Now they proceeded to invade parts of Indo-China.

THE FOREIGN POLICY OF THE UNITED STATES. The American government placed an embargo on all exports of strategic minerals to the belligerent powers, notably Germany, Japan, and

Russia. American citizens were prohibited from going abroad on foreign ships, while American ships were forbidden to call at the ports of the warring nations. Peace time conscription was passed by Congress and a huge armament program was begun. "Lend lease" goods were sent to Great Britain, including airplanes and ammunition, thus making the United States a real ally of Great Britain. Much concern was felt by President Roosevelt about the colonies of Great Britain and The Netherlands in the Far East.

GERMANY ATTACKS RUSSIA. In the summer of 1941 the Germans suddenly invaded Russia, breaking their pact without warning, and placing the Russians at a great disadvantage. Within one year they reached the suburbs of Moscow and Leningrad, the southern tip of the Crimean Peninsula, the Caucasus mountains, and the river Volga. They crippled Russia to a great extent, and we may conclude that if the United States had not been drawn into the war on Russia's side, that country could not have survived the struggle.

JAPAN ATTACKS THE UNITED STATES. On December 7, 1941 the Japanese attacked Pearl Harbor in the Hawaiian Islands, damaging and sinking all of the eight battleships in that great harbor. The United States immediately declared war against Japan, as well as against Germany and Italy. The production of arms was swiftly ordered at home, so that the Japanese would soon feel the mighty power of the world's richest nation.

JAPANESE CONQUESTS. In December of 1941 the Japanese invaded the north shore of Luzon in the Philippines and occupied the island of Guam. Early in 1942 they took Wake Island. They also drove through Siam (Thailand), the Malay Peninsula, and the strait to Singapore. They soon took that port, which had not been fortified for an attack by land. The Dutch East Indies fell almost at once. In the Philippines the conquest was slower, but Bataan Peninsula was well fortified, and the island fortress of Corregidor held out a long time. But it was all in vain. The Japanese also overran Burma and invaded India. The year 1942 ended with an outburst of German and Japanese power, but the Allies had prepared at last for the reversal of the tide of conquest.

ALLIED VICTORIES IN THE FALL OF 1942 AND THE YEAR 1943. In December the Russians threw the Germans out of Stalingrad on the Volga. The British drove the Nazis from Egypt into

Libya. Next the Americans suddenly invaded Morocco and Algeria. From east and west the Allies advanced upon Tunisia. At the same time the Japanese lost heavily in British New Guinea, the battle of the Coral Sea, and at Guadalcanal in the Solomon Islands. At Midway they also suffered a smashing defeat. Just before the end of 1942 the French lost the rest of their country to Germany, but the Germans were now on the defensive. In 1943 they lost the Caucasus province to the Russians, next the great city of Rostov on the lower Don, then Kiev, the capital of the Ukraine, and much territory west of Moscow. The American commander MacArthur in the meantime seized the Gilbert Islands and won the battle of the Bismarck Sea, destroying the whole force of 22 Japanese vessels. In Africa the Allied armies advanced rapidly, taking Tunisia. In June they landed in Sicily, and in the same month Mussolini resigned his position. Finally, in September the Italian government signed an armistice with the Allied forces. But soon after this the Germans marched in from the north to block the Allied armies.

ALLIED VICTORIES IN 1944. The Americans moved into the Marshall Islands and next into the Carolinas, taking the great fortified base of Truk. On July 4 they took two towns on the island of Saipan in the Mariana Islands, as well as the island of Guam. Now they moved carefully along the north shore of Dutch New Guinea, then turned northward and seized the island of Morotai, and on October 19 American forces landed on the east shore of Leyte in the Philippines. The desperate Japanese foolishly moved a huge fleet into the straits near Leyte to stop the Americans, who promptly inflicted upon them the greatest naval disaster in Japan's history. The battle lasted three days. By the end of December MacArthur was within 100 miles of Manila. The Chinese were being somewhat neglected at this time, but they were to learn soon that their delivery was near. The Russians in 1943 drove the Germans westward to the frontier, forcing Rumania to surrender and Finland to sign an armistice. In Italy the Germans were pushed to the Po Valley.

THE ALLIED INVASION OF FRANCE. On June 6, 1944, the long-awaited D-Day arrived on the beaches of Normandy. American, British, and Canadian troops performed bravely and pushed ever farther into France. Before the end of the first day five divisions had been landed. The great port of Cherbourg fell on June 27, and Paris was taken on August 25. On August 15 another invasion had taken place in southeastern France near Cannes, which made the Germans retreat in central France and thus hastened the fall of Paris. The Allied armies now marched into Belgium, taking Antwerp in September. They crossed the Dutch frontier in the same month, but at least six months were to pass before they could liberate the Dutch people. They did, however, occupy the southern territory up to the great rivers. In October the famous German city of Aachen was taken, and in the next month Alsace-Lorraine was freed from the Nazis.

THE WAR IS BROUGHT TO AN END. In the Far East the Americans won tremendous victories, seizing Manila in February, 1945, besides Bataan Peninsula and Corregidor. In the same month the island of Iwo Jima was invaded, and in April the Americans landed on Okinawa in the Ryukyu Islands. In April and May the British occupied Burma. Australian and Dutch forces took the rich oil island of Tarakan on the east shore of Borneo; they then went southward and seized the oil port of Balikpapan. Huge American aircraft pounded all of the leading cities in Japan, just as they were doing in Germany. The Russians now moved across Poland into Germany, while in the west the Allies marched into the Rhine Valley, crossed the Rhine, and swept up to the Elbe. Under General Dwight S. Eisenhower the Americans moved rapidly forward into southern Germany, and from the south other forces crossed the Po and marched into Austria. On April 25, 1945, the armies of Russia and the United States first made contact with each other in central Germany. A little later Hitler died somewhere in Berlin, and on May 7, 1945, the German government capitulated.

SURRENDER OF JAPAN. When the United States had acquired a fleet of 55,000,000 tons it was becoming clear to all nations that Japan was fully doomed. Moreover, some 100,000 airplanes moved forward to smash the Japanese into submission. Finally, the atomic bombs dropped on the cities of Hiroshima and Nagasaki in August spelled total disaster for Japan, which notified the Allied nations on August 10, 1945, that she would surrender at once. At this time General George G. Marshall, who was our Chief of Staff, revealed that in the fall of 1945 Japan would have been invaded by a huge American force.

Student Activities

1. What did the Nazis want to do in the period from 1938 to 1941?
2. What was the nature of the Russo-German Pact of 1939?
3. Why did Poland's plight cause Great Britain and France to declare war against Germany?
4. How did the Second World War begin?
5. What is a *Blitzkrieg*?
6. Did Russia gain from the pact of 1939?
7. What happened in 1940 to Denmark, Norway, Holland, and Belgium?
8. Explain how France fell in 1940.
9. How was Great Britain saved in the fall of 1940?
10. What happened at Pearl Harbor on December 7, 1941?
11. Outline the conquest by Germany and Japan in 1942.
12. Discuss the Allied victories in 1943 and 1944.
13. What was the significance of the atomic bomb?
14. Did Russia help defeat Japan and Germany enough to entitle her to make the claims for annexation she has recently advanced?
15. How great a share in the defeat of Germany and Japan did the United States have?

CHAPTER 59

Transition From War to Peace

THE CONFERENCE AT BRETTON WOODS, N.H., JULY, 1944. Long before the end of hostilities the Allied nations made preparations for reconversion from war to peace. The meetings in July, 1944, dealt with economic questions. It was decided that an International Monetary Fund was to be appropriated by the United Nations, each of which was to contribute its proper share. The International Bank for Reconstruction and Development was to be organized.

THE DUMBARTON OAKS CONFERENCE. At the estate in Washington, D.C., called Dumbarton Oaks, the representatives of the United States, Russia, China, and Great Britain met from August 27 to October 7, 1944, and agreed upon proposals for setting up a second League of Nations under the title of United Nations. On October 7th they issued a draft for the machinery to be used for this purpose. It provided that this new league would maintain international peace and security, as well as sovereign equality for all peace-loving nations, each of which was entitled to membership. The four main organs of government were to be: (1) the General Assembly, in which all members would have representation and which would be the seat of final authority; (2) the Security Council, in which eleven members would be represented, five of them receiving permanent seats, namely, the United States, Russia, China, Great Britain, and later on, France; (3) the International Court of Justice; and (4) the Secretariat.

THE YALTA CONFERENCE. On February 11, 1945, President Roosevelt, Premier Stalin, and Prime Minister Churchill of Great Britain issued at the town of Yalta in the Crimean Peninsula the statement known as the Yalta Declaration. Among the terms are the following: (1) Germany after the war was to be occupied by the three powers mentioned as the chief victors, namely, the United States, Russia, and Great Britain, each state receiving its own zone; (2) a commission would hold meetings in Moscow to determine the damage inflicted by the Germans upon the Allies; (3) the liberated countries were to receive political and economic assistance in the process of reconversion; (4) Poland's eastern frontier was to be the Curzon Line, giving Russia the eastern part of Poland; (5) the first United Nations Conference was to be held in San Francisco.

THE UNITED NATIONS CONFERENCE IN SAN FRANCISCO. The meetings lasted from April 25 to June 26, 1945. It was decided that the United Nations, unlike the League of Nations, would in case of necessity employ armed forces to maintain peace and punish offending nations. Russia received three votes in the General Assembly, but the United States remained content with its one vote. The draft for the government adopted at Dumbarton Oaks was accepted with a few slight modifications.

THE POTSDAM CONFERENCE. The representatives of the United States, Russia, China, and Great Britain met here; and on July 26, 1945, they issued the Potsdam Declaration. It contained the following provisions: (1) the authority and influence of those who had led Japan into war must be eliminated "for all time;" (2) Japanese territory must be occupied by Allied forces until the peace of the world is assured; (3) Japan was to be stripped of all recent conquests, including Manchuria, Korea, Formosa, and the islands to the north and south of Japan proper.

THE SURRENDER OF JAPAN. On September 2, 1945, the Japanese representatives finally signed the formal document of surrender. This happened in Tokyo Bay on the USS *Missouri,* in honor of President Truman, whose home state was Missouri. On the same day the Japanese government issued instructions to all of its armed forces in occupied territory, such as the Dutch East Indies, to lay down their arms and cease hostilities.

THE RUSSO-CHINESE PACT OF AUGUST, 1945. This was completed on August 14, 1945, in Moscow where Stalin announced the following terms: (1) Outer Mongolia was separated from China and would be an independent country under Russian influence; (2) Port Arthur would be a naval base under joint control of Russia and China; (3) the port of Dairen in southern Manchuria would be jointly owned by Russia and China, but the harbor would be Russian; (4) the two main railroads in Manchuria would be jointly controlled and owned by Russia and China; (5) Russia would recognize the supreme executive power of Chiang Kai-shek and Chinese sovereignty in Manchuria.

RECONVERSION IN CHINA. Eight years of war (1937-1945) had left China in a sad condition, and civil war still continued far into the year 1946. Twenty-five million Chinese had to be moved back to their native towns and homes. Industrial activity had been increased by the war, and now the Chinese could count on the production of many articles formerly imported. They also began to operate mines to a greater extent than before. The democratic government recommended by Sun Yat-sen could be put into operation.

A NEW DEAL IN THE EAST INDIES (INDONESIA). On December 7, 1942, one year after the Pearl Harbor incident, Queen Wilhelmina of the Netherlands announced that the inhabitants of the East Indies would receive local self-government and constitute one or more commonwealths united with Holland, but on a basis of full partnership and equality. In 1946 this promise was fulfilled. Under President Sukarno the Indonesian Republic was set up, comprising Java, Sumatra and a smaller island near Java. The British took over from the Japanese the military rule of the huge archipelago, and at the end of 1946 the Dutch in turn took charge of all the territory outside of the Republic of Indonesia, and also of the two largest cities in Java with some land in their vicinity, besides the largest cities in Sumatra. This action was taken to protect the property of foreigners and to resume commercial and industrial reconversion. Early in 1947 the United States of Indonesia was formally recognized by the Dutch government, and Sukarno took swift action to make the extremists sign a compromise agreement. However, in the summer of 1947 fighting broke out between the Dutch and Indonesian forces, and the situation became so serious it called for the attention of the United Nations Organization.

THE PHILIPPINES SET FREE. In 1935 the Philippines had been promised complete political independence by the government of the United States, which would occur on July 4, 1946. Such did also take place, in spite of the recent war and the terrible destruction wrought in the archipelago. But American businessmen received valuable economic concessions, and the United States demanded the retention of important military bases, to insure peaceful developments in the region.

JAPAN UNDER ALLIED OCCUPATION. During the last four months of 1945 MacArthur had complete control over the occupation of Japan, although the Russians, Chinese, and British did have some officials stationed there also. On September 2, 1945, some 35,000 American troops were landed in the Tokyo area, and during the next three months about half a million more. The number was somewhat reduced in 1946. Emperor Hirohito politely cooperated with the Americans to restore order in devastated regions. His power, however, was greatly reduced, and the Japanese received instruction in the art of establishing democratic government. In December, 1945, the Conference of the Three Foreign Ministers met in Moscow and issued a declaration to the effect that henceforth Russia, China, and Great Britain would have a share in the occupation of Japan. The Allied Council in Japan was set up to give advice to MacArthur. But only a few military and civil advisers arrived from those three countries to assist in the military occupation. The Americans continued with their own work, very much as before this time. A small number of troops from the British Dominions came to augment the American forces.

INDONESIA BECOMES INDEPENDENT. The events of 1946 and 1947 did not satisfy the nationalist leaders in Indonesia, and in 1949 they finally signed with the Dutch an important agreement which made the whole of Indonesia a federal republic. But in 1950 and 1951 the nationalists changed this agreement in their own favor by turning Indonesia into a state ruled by themselves in the capital called Jakarta (the former Batavia). According to the written agreement made with the Dutch, the new nation formed a union with the Kingdom of the Netherlands under the crown which Queen Juliana had recently taken over from her mother, Queen Wilhelmina. The Dutch government in 1953 declared that the western half of the huge island of New Guinea did not belong to Asia but to Oceania, together with Australia and New Zealand. The Indonesian nationalists claimed that western New Guinea was a part of Indonesia. The governments of Australia and the United States have in recent years favored the claims of the Dutch, and as the result western New Guinea is a Dutch possession, with Hollandia as the capital. Here large deposits of oil and nickel have been found. There are also huge forests, while millions of acres of fertile clay soil, favored by a tropical climate with an abundance of rainfall, may some day be cultivated by a large population. Here rice could be grown in vast quantities.

INDIA AND PAKISTAN BECOME INDEPENDENT NATIONS. In August 1947 the Union of India and the new nation called Pakistan were separated from each other. They both became independent of Great Britain. After two and a half years of bitter strife among Hindus and Mohammedans in the two new nations, causing tremendous massacres and migrations, the governments of the two powers drafted a peace treaty (April, 1950), establishing more friendly relations. Immediately large numbers of Mohammedans moved from India into Pakistan and other masses of Hindus from Pakistan into India.

THE JEWS ESTABLISH A NEW NATION IN PALESTINE. In the year 1948 the Jews set up a new nation called the Republic of Israel. The year before the General Assembly of the United Nations had partitioned Palestine between Arabs and Jews. In January 1949 Great Britain and France gave official recognition to the new republic, while Russia and the United States in May 1948 had given partial recognition. In the same month of May 1948 Israel was elected as the 59th member of the United Nations. About 800,000 Arabs lost their homes in Palestine. They had to move eastward into Arab territory, where they lived a wretched existence until in 1954 a slight improvement was made for them through American help.

CHINA IS CONQUERED BY THE COMMUNISTS. In 1948 the Communists conquered Manchuria, in 1949 nearly the whole of China proper, and in 1950 the extreme south up to Indo-China and the island of Hainan. The Nationalists retreated to the island of Formosa, near the east coast of China. In December 1949 Chiang Kai-Shek assumed the title of President of China, which he had given up in January 1949, when the Communists were about to conquer the Chinese capital named Peiping or Peking. Early in 1950 Mao Tze-Tung, the leader of the Chinese Communists, signed a treaty with the Russian government, confirming for the most part the pact of 1945, but giving China a few more powers in Manchuria than had been the case in 1945.

THE MARSHALL PLAN. In June 1947 George C. Marshall, our Secretary of State, announced his plan to render financial assistance to a number of states in western and southern Europe. In April 1948 Congress passed the Foreign Assistance Act, which authorized a little over six billion dollars for Europe and China. In September 1949 Congress voted a total of about $5,800,000 for the nations of western Europe, and besides about $1,314,000 for military assistance to Greece, Turkey, South Korea, and the Philippines. During the following five years further grants were voted, with the result that in the countries of western and southern Europe which had suffered the most in the Second World War swift recovery was made possible.

THE NORTH ATLANTIC PACT. In October 1948 the following nations drew up the North Atlantic Pact (Treaty): Great Britain, France, the Netherlands, Belgium, and Luxembourg. Their representatives met in Paris and invited the United States and Canada to join, which was done by those two countries on April 4, 1949. At the same time the five following countries also joined: Denmark, Iceland, Italy, Norway, and Portugal. All these powers promised to assist each other in case any of them was attacked by an outside nation.

THE EUROPEAN DEFENSE COMMUNITY. Soon after the formation of the North Atlantic Pact and the North Atlantic Treaty Organization (NATO), another defensive alliance came into being. This is often confused with NATO, but the EDC and NATO are not the same. For example, the first country to join was the Netherlands, and France did not do so after years of debating. Western Germany, which was not a member of the NATO, voted to join the EDC in 1954, while France was still outside. The British promised to aid this group, while the United States did most of the pushing. Since the Russian government was very strongly opposed to the formation of the EDC, the French and the British both were very much afraid to become real allies of the U.S.A. Italy agreed to join with great reluctance, but in the summer of 1954 various events occurred that made the founding of a complete EDC impossible. The French were not willing to let the Germans fully rearm, and the other countries of western Europe were wondering what would happen to them if Russia should suddenly decide to attack them with atom and hydrogen bombs. The following six countries were to form the EDC: France, Western Germany, Italy, the Netherlands, Belgium, and Luxembourg.

THE KOREAN WAR. In June 1950 the southern section of Korea was suddenly invaded by the armed forces of the North Korean Republic. The United Nations took prompt action to repel the invaders. General Douglas MacArthur was commander of the U.N. forces and attempted to drive the North Koreans back to their northern borders. But the Chinese Communists joined the invaders, so that MacArthur was repulsed, and his soldiers retreated far to the south. After two years of bitter contest the Americans enabled the U.N. forces to advance to a line just north of the 38th parallel. Here in July 1953 a truce was signed and the line was left about the same. The Americans, who had done most of the fighting and spending of money, counted about 140,000 casualties, mostly wounded.

THE WAR IN INDO-CHINA. While the Dutch gave up their political powers in Indonesia and the British granted India full independence, the French were not willing to do the same in their colony called Indo-China. In the year 1946 the nationalists started their war for independence. Gradually they received help from the Chinese Communists. In the year 1954 the situation became very serious for the French. In May of that year an international conference met in the Swiss city of Geneva for the double purpose of ending the uneasy truce in Korea and establishing a peace settlement in Indo-China. Nothing was accomplished for the Koreans, while the same thing would have happened in the other direction if suddenly the French government had not decided to make peace with the Communists at almost any price. This move greatly disturbed George F. Dulles, the American Secretary of State, who urged the British and the French to help form an Oriental alliance similar to the NATO. But the latter did not wish to offend the Chinese Communists more than they thought they could afford to do. The French began to negotiate directly with the Chinese Communists. The British and the Dutch had previously recognized the Communist government of China, believing that this move would be of great advantage to them. For example, the Indonesian government also recognized the Chinese government in Peiping, and since the Dutch still enjoyed enormous economic benefits in Indonesia, they did not wish to sacrifice these. Finally the situation became so critical that Sir Winston Churchill, the Prime Minister of Great Britain, and his colleague, the Foreign Minister, flew to Washington near the end of June to mend the breach in the Angli-American relations. They were cordially received by President Eisenhower, but little was accomplished.

THE UNITED STATES IS THREATENED WITH THE DESTRUCTION OF MANY CITIES. The British and the French in the summer of 1954 became so fearful of Russian hostility that they wanted to do everything possible to avert further warfare. No matter how angry the American Secretary of State might become, they did not mind that as long as they could show the Russians that they themselves were neutral. Suppose that a few hydrogen bombs were thrown at London and Paris, what good would American friendship do? And suppose that the Chinese Communists would permit the French and the Dutch to salvage much of their business in the Far East, how could they afford to offend these Communists? There were about two million Chinese in Indonesia alone, while in British Malaya there were also a great number of them. It was suddenly made clear to the American people that before long they might have no important allies left in Europe at all. With Russia and China gaining repeated advantages all over Asia, and with Great Britain and France clamoring for a "deal" with the Communists, the government of the United States was faced with the very real threat of warfare on a large scale, as soon as the Communists thought the time had come to take a chance, just as the Japanese on December 7, 1941, decided to take their chance at Pearl Harbor. If suddenly a large number of planes arrived from Russian bases, prepared to drop hundreds of atom and hydrogen bombs, this would mean the destruction of perhaps more than fifty large cities in the U.S.A. The future looked very somber, and the Christians remembered the words of Jesus: "If it had not been for the elect, no flesh would have been saved."

Student Activities

1. What was done at the Bretton Woods Conference?
2. Describe the work of the Dumbarton Oaks Conference.
3. Compare the decisions made at the Yalta Conference with those made at the Potsdam Conference.
4. What was done at the San Francisco Conference of the United Nations?
5. Describe the formal surrender of the Japanese government.
6. Mention some of the terms of the Russo-Chinese Pact of 1945.
7. What did the Dutch agree to grant to the people in Indonesia?
8. How were the Philippines finally set free?
9. Describe Japan under American occupation.

CHAPTER 60

Twentieth Century Civilization

SCIENTIFIC PROGRESS CONTINUES. During the first four decades of the twentieth century science has continued to dominate industry, commerce, agriculture, and culture in general. The perfection of the X-ray and the use of radium have been great aids to the medical experts and other scientists. It has also been demonstrated that a person can change one metal into another, by rearranging the atoms with their electrons.

In the fields of biology and medicine great triumphs have been achieved, so that a multitude of diseases have become more properly analyzed and placed under control of those who care to use it. But unfortunately, insanity has continued to increase.

OUR CENTURY IS INDEED AN AGE OF MECHANICAL ADVANCEMENT. At the same time, in the field of mechanical devices, progress has also been stupendous. The improvement in the means of transportation, of heating, refrigeration, and lighting, and of labor-saving methods has been such that no other century can possibly be compared with the twentieth. The airplane industry is now only in its infancy, and the reproduction of sound and pictures has just begun to reveal to the human race what is actually going on in the world which was once entirely beyond understanding. But it would seem that science cannot do much more for the relieving of human misery and mental disorders. Science in many respects has taken the place of the Church, which has lost much of its former power, so that the clergy can no longer hope to impress laymen with the exalted authority of those who wield the "keys of the kingdom of heaven."

SOCIAL CHANGES ARE ALSO OCCURRING ALL THE TIME. At the same time the former nobility has almost completely disappeared in the western world. Class distinctions have become ever more vague. The ownership of large estates, of great parks and forests has become a sign of selfish disregard for the well-being of the masses of the people. Moreover, the distinction between the two sexes has also been largely removed in the political and the social order. In many countries women have received the suffrage and may enter public office, while in factories and many of the professions they have found new occupations. Changes in dress and in the management of homes have also accompanied this process.

How the Human Race Should Examine the Evil Forces Which Are More Important Than Mechanical Progress. It would now be well for the human race if less emphasis were laid on mechanical improvements and more on the unspeakable atrocities which have recently been permitted in such countries as China and Spain. The continued habit of keeping national budgets unbalanced, the loss of political liberty in important European nations, the sanitariums which have been overflowing with patients suffering from mental disorders, the persecution of certain classes of people in a manner that was almost unknown everywhere in the nineteenth century, the lack of respect for parents, and the appalling unemployment and relief problems indicate clearly that the human race is making no real progress until it can learn to practice the *precepts* preached long ago by prophets and reformers who emphasized the importance of spiritual health and spiritual knowledge.

Developments in Architecture, Painting, and Sculpture. Interesting changes have been introduced in architecture, and the skyscraper has become an object of beauty in many localities. The use of the steel frame has been a great boon to the builders of tall structures. Moreover, the introduction of glass in the building of walls and roofs has been very beneficial. Although architecture has done fairly well, painting and sculpture have not been marked by much improvement in accuracy or idealism. On the contrary, a vast number of horrid paintings and statues have been produced in recent years, which are a disgrace to the artistic profession. Many modernistic paintings and figures plainly reveal the unbalanced mind of artists and thinkers in general. But this does not imply that good painting and sculpture has disappeared. Much good work is still going on, but it can hardly be said that there is anyone now who can be compared with such men as Michelangelo or Rembrandt.

CHANGING STANDARD IN MUSIC. Much the same can be said about music, which has been marked by many sad tendencies toward intellectual conceit and atrocities. The jazz music has been a symptom of the disorder in western civilization since the World War. Again we must bear in mind, however, that good art is produced every year, and that excellent musicians continue to delight audiences with their mastery in voice or in instrumental music.

GOOD AND BAD PRACTICES IN THE FIELD OF EDUCATION. In the field of education there has also been a great variety of views and accomplishments. Likewise, there has also been a notorious lack of achievement. Universal elementary education has been accompanied by a wholesome desire to aid the child in every possible respect. The art of self-expression has been encouraged, but in many schools it has been pushed to such a degree that now some educators are of the opinion that a little more discipline would be most helpful. It cannot be denied that pupils graduating from our high schools today do not show a desire for knowledge that equals their opportunities. It seems that when pupils have gone a a bit too far in expressing themselves they lose the ability to concentrate and to continue with any task that taxes their nervous energy. Many of the young people today cannot understand the great books of former ages, and in many cases books of profound significance are permitted to go unnoticed by reviewers and readers alike.

QUEER AND SENSATIONAL THINGS ATTRACT MUCH ATTENTION. However, such symptoms have been the characteristics of many another age in the past. It is not a new experience for the general public to ignore superb works performed by writers, artists, educators, or businessmen. On the one hand queer and silly actions and words receive undue attention in newspapers and in periodicals, while saints and inventors often go entirely unheeded. When sinners are converted, nothing as a rule is said about it in our newspapers. But when unspeakable crimes are committed, they receive immediate attention in the headlines or on the front pages of our greatest newspapers. When enlightened businessmen seek to do all they possibly can for their workmen, they sometimes receive no praise for their efforts at all, but when radical labor leaders try to achieve the same ends through ruthless methods and the illegal seizure of private property, they occupy space that should have been reserved for saints and reformers.

Our Country Has a Great Duty to Perform in the World Today. As our rising generation now faces a world threatened by chaos in politics, economics, and sociology, it would seem that the United States holds a decided advantage over both European and Asiatic nations. Whether we turn to the field of international diplomacy, or to the development of the arts and the sciences, or to the question of the proper relation between the employer and workman, everywhere the human race needs the application of religion, democracy, and international good will. True religion must be based on the personal faith of the individual person in Jesus Christ as his saviour from sin, death, and the power of the devil.

Student Activities

1. With the aid of a dictionary write out the definitions for the following words: *suffrage, sanitariums, precepts, conceit, elementary, enlightened, diplomacy.*
2. What is meant by "mechanical advancement"?
3. What social changes have taken place during this century?
4. What do you understand by "unbalanced national budgets"?
5. What do the modernistic paintings show?
6. What are some of the bad practices in education at the present time?
7. What type of news seems to attract attention? Why?
8. What is the basis of true religion?
9. What in your opinion is the hope of the world?

INDEX